HINDOOSTAN
By J. Rennell F.R.S. 1782.

Cultural Atlas of
INDIA

Senior Editor and Project Manager
 Susan Kennedy
Art Editor Chris Munday
Design Adrian Hodgkins
Picture Editor Linda Proud
Picture Manager Jo Rapley
Cartographic Manager Richard Watts
Senior Cartographic Editors Sarah Phibbs,
 Polly Senior
Cartographic Editor Tim Williams
Editorial Assistant Marian Dreier
Index Ann Barrett
Production Clive Sparling
Typesetting Brian Blackmore

AN ANDROMEDA BOOK

Planned and produced by
Andromeda Oxford Limited
11–15 The Vineyard, Abingdon
Oxfordshire, England OX14 3PX

Copyright © 1996 by Andromeda
Oxford Limited

For information contact:

Facts On File, Inc.,
11 Penn Plaza,
New York, NY 10001

Library of Congress Cataloging-in-Publication Data

Johnson, Gordon, Ph. D.
    Cultural atlas of India / Gordon Johnson,
        p.   cm.
    Includes bibliographical references and index.
    ISBN 0–8160–3013–8
    1. India--Civilization.   2. India--Civilization--Maps.   I. Title.
DS421.J6 1996
954--dc20   94-31213
                                                                      CIP

Facts On File books are available at
special discounts when purchased in bulk
quantities for businesses, associations,
institutions or sales promotions. Please
call our Special Sales Department in New
York at 212/967–8800 or 800/322–8755.

Origination by Eray Scan, Singapore

Printed in Spain by Fournier Artes
Gráficas, S.A., Vitoria

10 9 8 7 6 5 4 3 2 1

Cultural Atlas of
INDIA

India, Pakistan, Nepal, Bhutan, Bangladesh & Sri Lanka

Gordon Johnson

Facts On File, Inc.

AN INFOBASE HOLDINGS COMPANY

CONTENTS

Special Features

List of Maps

Regional Maps

CHRONOLOGICAL TABLE

POLITICAL

From c.4000 major settlements in Indus Valley
c.2300–c.1700 Indus valley civilization at height
c.1750 movement into India of Vedic Aryans via Afghanistan and Iran

From 900 state formation in Gangetic plain
c.540 rise of Magadha
364 Nanda dynasty
327–325 Alexander the Great in northwestern India
321 Chandragupta Maurya seizes Magadha
268/7–233 rule of Ashoka
c.166–150 Menander rules Bactria
141 BC Sakas seize Punjab

Between 78 and 144 accession of Kanishka; Kushan state at height
2nd century rise of Pallava dynasty in south India
c.250 Chandragupta I establishes Gupta dynasty in north India
375–413/15 rule of Chandragupta II
from 500 incursions of the Huns
606–647 rule of Harsha
711 Arab rule in Sind
c.850 emergence of Chola power in Tamil Nadu

1001 Mahmud of Ghazni begins raids on India; destroys Somnath 1024–25; occupies Punjab 1031
From 11th century establishment of Rajput dynasties
1192 Mahmud of Ghur defeats Rajput confederacy; expansion of Muslim rule in north and eastern India
1206 foundation of Delhi sultanate
1210–36 Iltutmish sultan of Delhi
1290–1320 Khalji dynasty rules Delhi
13th century Pandyas of Madurai replace Cholas as the dominant power in south India
1320–88 Tughluq dynasty at Delhi
1327 Muhammad Tughluq moves capital temporarily to Daulatabad
1336 Vijayanagara state founded in Karnataka
1347 Bahmani sultanate founded in central India
1398 Timur sacks Delhi
1450 Lodi dynasty at Delhi

ECONOMIC

Before 10,000 extensive Stone-Age settlements throughout the subcontinent
c.7000 agriculture and animal husbandry, Baluchistan, northwestern Pakistan, eastern Afghanistan
c.4000 management of rivers and flood plains in Indus basins; use of bronze and copper
From c.1200 pastoral nomadism gives way to new agricultural settlements in western Gangetic plain
c.1000 use of iron

c.800–c.400 spread of gray ware pottery
By 600 agricultural settlements throughout the Gangetic plain to the Bay of Bengal; Phoenician traders handling Indian goods
c.500 Sinhalese settlement of Sri Lanka

1st century trade with Rome from south India at its height
from 1st century development of sophisticated irrigation systems in northeastern Sri Lanka and in the deltas of south India
By 9th century major commercial links between India and peninsular and island Southeast Asia

Late 15th century Portuguese pioneer a new sea route from western Europe to the Indian Ocean
1498 Vasco da Gama at Calicut

CULTURAL

c.10,000 cave paintings along Vindhyan mountain ranges
After 1500 primitive forms of brahminic Hinduism; composition of *Rig Veda*

Hinduism established in western Gangetic plain; early theories of caste hierarchies
From c.800 composition of *Mahabharata*; Vedic Hinduism under criticism
c.527 death of Mahavira, founder of Jainism
c.528–c.461 Siddharta Gautama, founder of Buddhism
c.500 composition of *Upanishads*
c.350 composition of Kautilya's *Arthashastra* and Panini's *Grammar*
Mid 3rd century major Buddhist missionary activity; buildings at Sanchi and Amaravati; earliest Tamil inscriptions; anti-brahminical *bhakti* movement within Hinduism
From 3rd century rock-cut temples, sculpture and art

1st–5th centuries Gandharan Buddhist art
1st century Christianity in southwest India
1st century final composition of *Ramayana*
2nd century *Laws* of Manu take final shape; schism between Majayana and Hinayan Buddhism
Mid 3rd century major rebuilding of Buddhist stupa at Amaravati
4th century revival of Hinduism under Gupta patronage; flowering of classical Sanskrit literature in all its forms
405–411 Chinese Buddhist scholar, Fa-hsien visits India
5th century paintings at Ajanta caves
7th century temple complex at Mamallapuram
c.788–820 Shankara, founder of Advaita Vedanta
10th–11th centuries temple complex at Khajuraho

12th century Vaishnava reform movement
1142–1235 Mu'in ud-Din Chishti, who brings *sufi* order to India
1193 Qutb-ud-Din Aybak begins Quwwat-ul-Islam mosque at Delhi
1199 builds the Qutb Minar (Tower of Victory) at Delhi
13th century temple complex at Konarak
c.1440–1518 Kabir, mystic poet
1469–1538 Guru Nanak, founder of Sikhism
1485 birth of Chaitanya, Bengali mystic and founder of sect devoted to Krishna

Figure of Mother Goddess, c.2nd century BC

Kanishka reliquary, Gandhara, c.100 AD

Boar incarnation of Vishnu, late 5th century

Jain statue of the 23rd Tirthankara, 12th century

1510 Portuguese seize Goa
1526 Babur defeats Ibrahim Lodi at Panipat to found the Mughal empire
1556–1603 reign of Akbar, Mughal emperor
1656 defeat of Vijayanagara by the Muslim sultanates of the Deccan
1603–27 reign of Jahangir, Mughal emperor
1627–58 reign of Shah Jahan, Mughal emperor
From 1640s rise of the Marathas
1675 coronation of Shivaji as Hindu king
1658–1707 reign of Aurangzeb, Mughal emperor
1681 Aurangzeb establishes Aurangabad in the Deccan as a center of Mughal power

Breakdown of central Mughal authority, emergence of successor states – Bengal, Hyderabad, Oudh
1720s onward expansion of Maratha power under the *peshwas*
1740s English and French embroiled in politics of south India
1756 Siraj ud-daula sacks Calcutta
1757 battle of Plassey re-establishes the English East India Company as a force in Bengal politics
1761 battle of Panipat checks Maratha expansion in the north
1761 Haidar Ali seizes Mysore
1765 English East India Company *de facto* rulers of Bengal
From 1770s British territorial expansion around coast and up Gangetic plain
1782 Tipu Sultan succeeds in Mysore
From 1780s Ranjit Singh establishes a Sikh state in Punjab
1799 British defeat Tipu Sultan

First half of 19th century British consolidate their political position in India
1818 final defeat of Marathas
1828–35 Bentinck as Governor-General attempts major reform in British Indian territories
1840s annexations of Sind and Punjab
1856 annexation of Oudh
1857 mutiny of the Indian army accompanied by widespread rural revolt in north India
1858 assumption of direct responsibility for India by the British crown
1861 and **1892** constitutional reform acts for India passed by the British Parliament
1885 first meeting in Bombay of the Indian National Congress

1906 All-India Muslim League
1909, 1919, 1935 major constitutional reforms passed by the British Parliament
1920 Mohandas Karamchand Gandhi takes effective control of the Indian National Congress
1920–22 non-cooperation movement
1930–33 civil disobedience
1936–7 elections: Indian National Congress wins control of 7 provincial governments
1940 Muslim League passes resolution demanding Pakistan
1942 "Quit India" movement
1947 British transfer power; partition of the subcontinent into India and Pakistan
1948 end of colonial rule in Sri Lanka
1950 India adopts a republican constitution but stays within the Commonwealth
1950s re-organization of state boundaries within India
1964 death of Nehru
1966–77 and 1980–84 Indira Gandhi prime minister of India
1971 breakaway of East Pakistan to form Bangladesh
1984–89 Rajiv Gandhi prime minster of India

Rise of European commercial interests in India. Portuguese establish a presence in Asian trade from Goa
from 1610s rise of Dutch commercial presence in Indian Ocean
1612 English trading in Surat; **1641** at Madras; **1691** at Calcutta
1687 French at Pondicherry

Relative rise of the economic importance of the coastal regions
1750 onwards Lancashire cotton industry drives Indian textiles out of western markets
1770s famine in Bengal
From c.1775 prolonged agricultural depression in northwestern India; expansion of Indian trade with China, including export of textiles and opium to finance tea trade from China to Britain

Improvement of internal communications
1850 first railway in India
From 1850s slow population growth and substantial expansion of peasant cultivation; economic re-alignment with faster development of Punjab, Gujarat, the Andhra deltas, and part of Gangetic plain and southern India; substantial growth of Calcutta, Madras and Bombay
1869 opening of Suez canal makes Bombay the first port of call in India for shipping from Europe; rise of economic importance of Bombay

From c.1920 unprecedented and sustained population growth
1930s primary producers hit by the Depression
From 1950s state planning of the economy
Late 1960s "Green Revolution" achieves self-sufficiency in food
1985 onward liberalization of the Indian economy

1532–1623 Tulsidas, mystic and composer of *Ramcharitmanas*, popular Hindi version of *Ramayana*
1542–45 St Francis Xavier in India
From mid 16th century flowering of Mughal culture – Indian, Iranian and Central Asian influences brought to bear on art, architecture, literature and music
1569 Humayan's tomb built
1571–85 Fatehpur Sikri built
1574 Harimandir (Golden Temple) of Sikhs built
1589 Babur's *Memoirs* translated into Persian
First half 17th century Mughal miniature painting at height; Akbar's tomb built at Sikandra, the Red Fort and the Taj Mahal at Agra
1520s onward new building at Minakshi temple at Madurai
1650s Prince Dara Shikoh attempts reconciliation of Hinduism and Islam in *Majma 'al-Bahrain*

Kangra Pahari painting flourishes in minor courts in Punjab; artists thrive at Bundi and Kota in Rajasthan; major temple building at Varanasi
1727 Maharaja Jai Singh II founds new capital at Jaipur; builds the Jantar Mantar observatory
1784 Sir William Jones and others found the Asiatic Society of Bengal

Renaissance of Hindu and Bengali learning
1828 Rammohan Roy founds Brahmo Samaj
1835 Government of India decides to promote Indian education in English
1836 English becomes the official language of government in India
1850–85 Harischandra, Hindi essayist and journalist
1855 Bombay Photographic Society
1857 Universities founded at Calcutta, Madras and Bombay
1862 Archaeological Survey of India
1875 Dayanada Saraswati founds the Arya Samaj
1875 Syed Ahmed Khan founds the Muhammadan Anglo-Oriental College

1901 Rabindranath Tagore founds Shantinekitan; 1913, Nobel Prize for literature
From 1905 the *swadeshi* movement encourages use of indigenous products
1910 Gandhi publishes *Hind Swaraj*
1913–31 Edwin Lutyens and Herbert Baker design New Delhi
1932 Indian State Broadcasting Service started
1936 *Godan* by Prem Chand, novelist and short story writer in Hindi
1940 *Twilight in Delhi*, Ahmed Ali
1955 Satyajit Ray directs *Pather Panchali*
1968 H. G. Khorana, Nobel Prize for Medicine
1979 Abdus Salam, Nobel Prize for Physics
1980s Indian television reaches over 70% population; production of *Mahabharata*
1981 *Midnight's Children*, Salman Rushdie
1983 S. Chandrashekar, Nobel Prize for Physics

Qutb Shahi tomb, Golconda, 16th century

Base of a hookah, Mughal style, late 17th century

Rabindranath Tagore, from a drawing by A. Bose, c. 1920

PREFACE

It has proved an almost insurmountable challenge to write this book, for the subject matter, which records the human experience and achievements of the fifth of mankind who have inhabited the Indian subcontinent, is so rich and diverse. Moreover, it covers such a long period of time and is set in so vast a landscape that is is almost beyond one man's comprehension. Only a tiny part of the subject matter can be grasped, let alone fully understood. Inevitably, much has been simplified and even that is highly selected. Others would have judged differently what should or should not be included, and many will contest the baldness of some of the arguments presented here. Yet the task has been worth the labor, for no one can deny that India has been the setting for great human endeavors. India is important in itself but even more for what it tells of the whole human condition. Any book that will entice its reader to go further and add to knowledge and understanding is therefore justified.

In this *Atlas* I have attempted to provide an introduction to India and its cultural history. In the opening chapter I have tried to make explicit some of my own assumptions, amazements and limitations. Then follow introductory accounts of the land and its peoples, their societies and their histories. The book ends with brief surveys of the main regions today. On each page, in word, picture and map, the reader is reminded that what is being seen is but the briefest glimpse of the subject, and that this is only the beginning of the story.

Throughout the book a number of themes recur that I believe to be important: India is a wonderful place and many will find strange and exotic its social and political organization, its religions, its arts, literature and sciences. But it is also in the mainstream of human experience – indeed it could not be otherwise given the large number of peoples involved. India is distinct, but it has never been disconnected from its neighbors nor immune from forces acting upon it from the outside. In its turn, India has influenced other societies and reached out to countries distant from it. Over thousands of years, great diversity has flourished in the subcontinent; peoples have refused to conform or to restrain their creativity. Sometimes this has meant conflict, oppression and exploitation; but different peoples and different cultures have in fact lived alongside each other over long periods of time: they have mingled and separated but have woven a rich tapestry that is the envy of others. The Indian experience also reveals that traditions worth the name are not dead ones, but are vital, alive, and newly made for each generation: this book is not about a stagnant society bound by the past, but one that moves and constantly reshapes and rediscovers itself.

A book like this could not be written without relying on other scholars. In what I have written here I have been particularly influenced by the work of Bridget and Raymond Allchin, Catherine Asher, Christopher Baker, Christopher Bayly, Milo Beach, Paul Brass, Randolf Cooper, Christopher Fuller, John Gallagher, Stewart Gordon, J. S. Grewal, Irfan Habib, Ayesha Jalal, Hermann Kulke, Edmund Leach, Anthony Low, Peter Marshall, John Richards, Francis Robinson, Burton Stein, Eric Stokes, Romila Thapar, B. R. Tomlinson, and David Washbrook. An immense debt is acknowledged to Joseph E. Schwartzberg and his colleagues whose *Historical Atlas of South Asia* is a truly remarkable academic achievement, and also to Ainslee T. Embree and his colleagues, whose *Encyclopedia of Asian History* has proved invaluable. Without Anil Seal I would never have become interested in Indian history, while Rajnarayan Chandavarkar has consistently kept me to the mark. I have received very considerable help with Part III from Margaret Shepherd, while Michael Jansen, George Michell, Norbert Peabody, Linda Proud, John D. Smith, Simon C. Smith, Deborah Swallow and Andrew Topsfield are the authors of some of the special features. In so far as this book has merit, it is because it exists as an anthology of the learning and research of these scholars and of countless other.

The production team at Andromeda have produced superb maps and pictures; but Susan Kennedy has borne the greatest burden. I owe her tremendous thanks for being so fair and generous an editor, and also for being so demanding and for ensuring that this *Atlas* lives up to the high standards of its predecessors.

Lionel Carter at the Centre of South Asian Studies in Cambridge, colleagues at the University Library, the Faculty of Oriental Studies and at Selwyn College and Wolfson College, Cambridge have given me tremendous help and support. Much writing was done during the summers of 1993 and 1994 in the congenial environment of North Haven, Maine, a place and a society I hold particularly dear. Faith, my wife, has lived with this book and its heavy demands from a very distant beginning. I particularly value the kindness of my sons, and so this book is for Timothy, Nathaniel and Orlando Johnson.

Gordon Johnson

PART ONE
THE PHYSICAL AND CULTURAL BACKGROUND

HINDU KUSH

KARAKORAM RANGE

K2
8611

CHINA

Kabul

Khyber Pass

AFGHANISTAN

Islamabad

Line of control

Indus

SULAIMAN RANGE

Plateau of Tibet

Gumal Pass

HIMALAYAS

Amritsar

Faisalabad

Lahore

Quetta

Ludhiana

Brahmaputra

Bolan
Pass

IRAN

KIRTHAR RANGE

PAKISTAN

Sutlej

Dhaulagiri
8172

Indus

NEPAL

Mt Everest
8848

New Delhi Delhi

Kathmandu

Thimphu

BHUTAN

Thar Desert

Jaipur

Yamuna

Lucknow

Kanpur

KHASI HILL

Karachi

ARAVALLI RANGE

Ganges

Allahabad

Varanasi

Patna

BANGLADESH

Rann of Kutch

INDIA

Dhaka

Gulf
of
Kutch

Ahmadabad

VINDHYA RANGE

Narmada

Calcutta

Chittagong

Indore

Vadodara

Khulna

Kathiawar

SATPURA RANGE

Gulf
of
Khambhat

Surat

Tapti

Nagpur

Bombay

Godavari

ARABIAN
SEA

Pune

Deccan

Bay of Bengal

Hyderabad

WESTERN GHATS

Krishna

EASTERN GHATS

Bangalore

Madras

Laccadive Islands
(India)

NILGIRI HILLS

Kaveri

Anai Mudi
2695

Palk Strait

■ capital city

□ other important city

▲ mountain summit
(height in meters)

international boundary

disputed boundary

SRI LANKA

Gulf of
Mannar

Colombo

meters
5000
4000
2000
1000
500
200
0 sea level
1000

Dondra Head

scale 1: 15 000 000

0   400km

0   300mi

MALDIVES

INDIAN OCEAN

70°   75°   80°   85°   90°

INTRODUCTION TO THE SUBCONTINENT

The outsider's view of India

The Indian subcontinent is huge and populous. Perhaps for as long as people have inhabited the world as many as one in every five of them have lived somewhere in the subcontinent. While not approaching the size of Africa, its area exceeds that of Europe without Russia and is roughly five-sevenths that of the United States of America. Moreover, the peoples of the subcontinent exhibit a great range of human achievement and social organization. The story of their civilization is, therefore, particularly rich and complex.

"India has in all ages excited the attention of the curious, in almost every walk of life," wrote the British cartographer James Rennell (1742–1830) at the end of the 18th century. "Its rare products and manufactures engaged that of the merchants; while the mild and inoffensive religion of Brahma, and the manners inculcated by it, attracted the notice of philosophers. The structure of its language too, is remarkable; and has a claim to originality." But, Rennell continued, "the softness and effeminacy induced by the climate, and the yielding nature of the soil, which produces almost spontaneously" had laid the peoples of India open to the attacks of their more hardy neighbors and had rendered them "an easy prey to every foreign invader". The result was that India has been subject to wave after wave of conquest and settlement. Indeed, Rennell even thought it possible that the Indians "have seldom had a dynasty of kings, from among their own countrymen".

This, of course, makes the contrast between what is Indian and what is foreign much too sharp, for from the dawn of history it has been almost impossible to determine what, if anything, is wholly indigenous. Nonetheless, those coming new to the subcontinent and whose curiosity was excited by India usually found the country and its inhabitants very different from any others they may have known about already. Babur (1483–1530), the founder of the Mughal empire in northern India, recorded in his diary that he was drawn to India by the prospect of ruling a large country "full of men, and full of produce" with "masses of gold and silver". He was awestruck by the fact that India was "a different world; its mountains, rivers, jungles and deserts, its towns, its cultivated lands, its animals and plants, its peoples and their tongues, its rains, and its winds, are all different." Though some of the districts he traveled through had similarities with the provinces he ruled from Kabul in Afghanistan, mostly they were different. "Once the water of Sind [the Indus] is crossed, everything is in the Hindustan way; land, water, tree, rock, people and horde, opinion and custom."

It is, however, one thing to note that a country is different from one's own, quite another to go beyond simply identifying the exotic in another civilization to discover what it is that makes it truly distinct. Moreover, it is often the case that the foreign observer is at first most impressed by those things that differ strongly from the conditions of his own country and the customs of his own people. He consequently finds in another civilization a coherence and unity that, on closer scrutiny, is difficult to define or to justify, and ignores the things humanity shares in common the world over.

Most people tend to think of India as one place, which has supported from very ancient times a coherent and unified culture. True, it has to be admitted that politically the subcontinent has had a very checkered history: India has witnessed many conquests and its peoples have been ruled often by foreigners. Further, the subcontinent has only rarely, and even then most incompletely, come under the control of a single government. But this, it would be argued, is only politics. Beneath the superficial lay of government, the traditional civilization, secure in countless villages and bound together by unique social institutions and moral values, has remained intact: "Dynasty after dynasty tumbles down," wrote the British administrator and sometime Director of the East India Company Charles Metcalfe (1785–1846) in a compelling early 19th-century formulation of the argument, "revolution succeeds to revolution; Hindoo, Patan, Mogul, Mahratta, Sikh, English, are all masters in turn; but the village community remains the same." From here, in less discerning minds, it is a very short step to argue the case for a changeless society held fast by tradition through all the whirligig of time.

But such a conclusion would be unreasonable, for it ignores the vast size and diversity of the Indian subcontinent. Moreover, throughout history it has been subject to recurring interaction with the peoples of Central Asia, Afghanistan, Iran, and the eastern Mediterranean. Some of the earliest human settlements were to be found in India, and the highly developed societies of the Indus valley, which flourished at the same time as the earliest towns of Mesopotamia, can lay claim to greater antiquity than those of Egypt.

Though much of the early history of India is unknown, and most of it is probably lost forever, it is reasonable to suppose that its great expanses of potentially productive alluvial land, especially in parts of the Indo-Gangetic plains, made colonization easy and attractive. South Asia was one of the most important places for the development of human society, its land-surface capable not only of supporting large numbers of people but also of accommodating, over the centuries, the settlement of many different populations. As the 20th-century anthropologist J.H. Hutton so graphically put it, "The subcontinent of India has been likened to a deep net into which various races and peoples of India have drifted and been caught." So the observer who has first noticed the distinctiveness of India when compared with other parts of the world next goes on to marvel at the internal diversity of Indian culture, the immense variety and richness of South Asia's traditions, and the truly remarkable range of its peoples' organizations and achievements. A distant view of India thus gives way to a closer prospect of not one but many Indias.

A common Indian identity?

Now begin the difficulties of studying the place and its peoples. In order to move away from the most superficial understanding of the subcontinent, we are now able to see that Indian civilization has a complex and various ancestry, and that, far from being a fixed tradition, it has modified its form as new people or new ideas have made their home there. And particular historical circumstances have allowed people to make their own mark, that has outlasted their own time or carried their influence beyond their own place. Inevitably, in the process of identifying such historical developments, many of the certainties about what is characteristically and uniquely Indian begin to dissolve and disappear.

What are the ties that hold the civilization together? They cannot be bonds of race, for the variety of ethnic types represented in the population is immense. Moreover, the domestic arrangements of the people – what they eat, what they wear, what social practices they follow, and what ceremonies they observe at different seasons of the year and at birth, marriage and death – vary greatly from region to region, town to town and village to village. Nor does religion provide much cohesion: Hinduism, the faith most commonly and specifically associated with South Asia, includes within its scope numerous theologies and philosophies, while its rites and customs differ enormously from sect to sect and from place to place. Nor is the subcontinent exclusively Hindu: apart from numerous local animist traditions and magical practices, several other major religions, such as Buddhism and Jainism, have their roots in India, while Zoroastrianism has found refuge there and Sikhism has developed in a special Indian context. Christianity, in very ancient as well as more modern forms, has grown into as Indian a religion as any other. Finally, the subcontinent is home to the largest number of Muslims in the world: Islam, in all its theological and evangelical variety, has been truly resident here for over 1,200 years, revealing in the subcontinent some of its finest philosophical, literary and artistic manifestations.

Unity cannot come from language, for dozens of major languages and countless dialects are spoken by the peoples of India; nor is there a single classical literary heritage, for the indigenous Prakrit, Pali, Sanskrit and Dravidian languages, as well as forms of Old Iranian, Persian, Arabic and English, have all contributed in varying degrees to the development of South Asia's languages and literatures. While it might seem easy, therefore, to sense that India is different from other major civilizations, it becomes all too apparent that it is very hard to define conclusively what is essentially Indian, or to see how such a diversity of peoples and cultures can be related to one another.

Confronted by the massive physical scale of the subcontinent, the huge size of the population, and the long reach of its traditions, arguments that stress the diversity of the Indian experience become more attractive, for they make the problem of understanding the civilization of India more manageable. The student can perhaps best catch a glimpse of the whole by pursuing the specific and studying the particular. South Asian social institutions, so baffling in their continental multiplicity, become clearer observed on one village; political or economic history, misleading or sometimes just banal if approached at an all-India level, becomes intelligible once the country is broken

down into its regional or local components; religion, so often by its very nature difficult of comprehension, comes more easily within reach when studied through a definably related group of texts, or looked at in the context of one temple or from the point of view of one particular persuasion.

The danger of this approach, however, is that some special authority will be claimed for what is, by the nature of things, only a special case; and arguments will be brought forward that begrudge other examples an equal place in the Indian tradition. The regional or the local points of view all too often encourage parochialism and a passionate, but narrow, cultural chauvinism. The temptation is to deny that India exists at all except as a geographical expression, and that what is taken for a coherent civilization is nothing but a motley of local cultures, often in conflict with one another.

The influence of geography and climate

For all its size, the Indian subcontinent displays a very straightforward set of physiographical features that have shaped the movement of people both into and within it. Great mountain ranges separate the subcontinent from Eurasia to the north; to their south is the Indo-Gangetic plain, of exceptional extent and flatness. Farther south again a series of hilly uplands containing pockets of plains and river basins, difficult to penetrate, divide off peninsular India – a plateau of ancient bedrock tipped from west to east. Around the coast are constricted and discontinuous plains; in some places hills and deserts run right to the shore, in others the mouths of great rivers continually reshape the coastline, depositing and shifting silt carried from far inland. All affect ease of access by sea.

Climate and vegetation also determine patterns of

Above Though one of the most densely populated regions of the world, there are areas of desert, forest, mountain and rocky terrain that are not hospitable to human settlement. The temperate cloud forest that grows at heights of more than 1,000 meters in Himachal Pradesh is among the region's few remaining areas of natural wilderness.

Cultural zones of the subcontinent Physical geography has played a major part in determining the movement and settlement of peoples. Few areas are immune from neighboring influences, but there are a number of zones where particular cultures are dominant. The Dravidian languages and distinctive forms of Hinduism are found in the south; Hindi and its related languages predominate in the north. Western India is influenced by both, while in a few areas of isolated terrain local populations have kept their own cultures. The northern mountains have links with Tibet and China, the northeast with Burma and Southeast Asia. In the northwest, constant interaction with Iran, the Middle East and Central Asia has resulted in a complex interplay of cultures; Islam predominates. In the east Bangladesh combines Islam with Bengali (Hindu) influences.

Right India is a place of profound religious traditions. Every year more than a million Hindu pilgrims travel to the city of Varanasi to bathe in the waters of the holy river Ganges. At dawn the riverbank is crowded with pilgrims washing themselves.

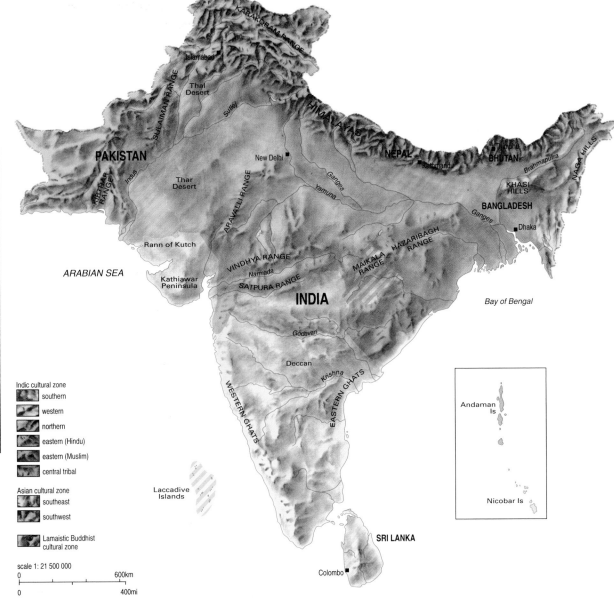

Indic cultural zone
southern
western
northern
eastern (Hindu)
eastern (Muslim)
central tribal

Asian cultural zone
southeast
southwest

Lamaistic Buddhist
cultural zone

scale 1: 21 500 000
0   600km
0   400mi

human movement and settlement. Some parts of the plains are too dry to sustain life easily and, despite their flatness, make travel as difficult as the most arduous mountain terrain. The mountains themselves are not necessarily a bar to passage, where the presence of sheltered and well-watered valleys have facilitated the development of routes through their fastnesses. In very wet places, the dense forests shelter wild animals and are a haven for disease, making them inhospitable to human travelers and settlers. Even the seas around the coasts may be easy or difficult to cross dependent upon their depth, the force of their currents, and their exposure to the prevailing winds.

The cultural zones of the subcontinent

Within India the boundaries between distinct cultural entities, whether they are defined by language, religion, politics, economy, or social organization, are far from being clear cut or immutable. But, in order to come to terms with the problems posed by its scale and variety, the subcontinent – following the scheme formulated by the German historian Hermann Kulke – can conveniently be divided into four major cultural regions or zones: the northern plains, the hills to the south, the peninsula, and the southeastern coastal plain. Each of these zones can be further subdivided.

The alluvial lands of the Indo-Gangetic plain, some 300 kilometers wide from north to south and over 3,000 kilometers in length from west to east, includes the Indus valley, the Delhi-Agra country, the mid-Gangetic plain (the lands between the Ganges and Jamuna rivers), and the territory running eastwards from Bihar to embrace Bengal and Bangladesh. This was the part of the country that, from the end of the 2nd millennium BC onward, was claimed, cleared and settled by numerous warrior bands, who moved away from a life of nomadic pastoralism to form the agricultural villages that are so typically associated with Indian culture.

The hilly country to the south covers an area some 450 to 650 kilometers from north to south and running for 1,600 kilometers from west to east. Consisting mostly of difficult terrain, it is much more sparsely populated than the other cultural zones. North of Gujarat in the west lies desert; in the east Orissa is surrounded by complex mountainous and river zones, but both provinces are open to influences from the sea. Within this important intermediate zone lie four isolated enclaves – the relatively fertile plains of Chattisgarh in the east (the Daksina Kosala of ancient texts); Vidarbha, the area around Nagpur, noted for its cotton fields and oranges; the Malwa plateau centered on Ujjain, called Avanti in earlier times; and Rajasthan, the country of the Rajputs, with its main centers at Jaipur and Udaipur.

The peninsula also supports four key sub-regions with long histories of settlement and distinctive cultures. The lava ranges of the northwest were the original lands of the Maratha farmer-warriors, with their centers at Aurangabad, Daulatabad, Paithan and Ahmadnagar; Hyderabad was and is the focus of the central region; the territories to the south and west were ruled at various times from Badami, Vijayanagara, and Bidar; and the Mysore plateau supported dynasties such as the Haysalas and, famously in the 18th century, Haidar Ali and his son Tipu Sultan.

The southeast coast can also be divided into four sub-regions, each the home of an ancient kingdom. The flourishing lands of the Krishna-Godavari deltas are separated by difficult hill country from the area around Madras, the seat of the Pallava dynasty of the 4th to 9th centuries. Farther south come the Kaveri river and its delta, where evidence of human activity stretches back to the earliest stone age, where the Cholas had their base and where the great temple complexes of Thanjavur (Tanjore) are located. At the very tip of the subcontinent lies the country of the Pandyas with its center at Madurai. Then, as a pendant to the main landmass, hangs the island of Sri Lanka – sufficiently cut off from the subcontinent by the sea to have its own history, but sufficiently close for its destiny to have been influenced by developments in the Tamil district to the north.

The history of the subcontinent may thus be regarded as one where cultures have taken root in particular core regions and have met, fought and coalesced with each other in shifting patterns over the centuries. Particular economic or political circumstances may, from time to time, have allowed one well-endowed area to become pre-eminent and to adjust its relative standing with its neighbors, perhaps forming a hub from which imperial influence radiated, but rarely have such centers established a permanent dominance. Within each core region there has been a long history of rivalry between its sub-regions for control of the lands and peoples belonging to each other. The quarrels in the 18th century between the kingdom of the Marathas, Mysore, Hyderabad and Madras for domination of the land and trade of south India confirm this as much as the confused tribal and dynastic history of the Indo-Gangetic plain in the early period.

Though there is a case for regarding Delhi as a strategic center of some importance, great states based either in the north or in the south have always found it difficult to overcome the problems of communications and control posed by the middle region. Until recently it has been rare for a single government to settle successfully in both the northern plains and the peninsula. Even then it has had to be pragmatic in its politics and recognize that its survival depends on the accommodation of powerful local interests.

A blurring of distinctions

Nevertheless, no rigid boundaries separate one cultural zone from another, and the frontiers between them have tended to be continually modified and blurred. Within the same locality, or even within the same person, historical and cultural traditions are confused, and the search for identity may not always be a comfortable one. Early in the 20th century, the ethnographer H.H. Risley observed that the "Vaidu herbalists of Poona [Pune, southeast of Bombay], who speak Marathi to their neighbors, explain the fact that they use Kanarese among themselves by the tradition that they were brought from the Kanara country by one of the Peshwas and settled in Kirki. The Kasar coppersmiths of Nasik speak Gujarati at home and Marathi out of doors. The men dress like Marathas but the women still wear the characteristic petticoat of Gujarat instead of the Maratha *sari*."

Lala Lajpat Rai (1865–1928), one of India's early nationalist leaders who was very active in the Arya Samaj, an influential and evangelical Hindu revivalist movement, recorded in an autobiographical fragment that his family were Hindu Aggarwals by caste. His grandfather had been a shopkeeper. He also served as a village accountant, "made friends with people very quickly and was ever ready to start on journeys". A very strict Jain by religion, he "belonged to that sect of Jains whose Sadhus [holy men] keep a piece of cloth tied round their mouths. He used to perform religious duties twice a day regularly. He was fond of the company of Sadhus of this sect and was very hospitable to them." By contrast, his son, Lajpat Rai's father, went to a school where the headmaster was a Muslim *maulvi* (*malwa*, or religious teacher) and the language of instruction was Persian. The master's "lofty character" influenced all his pupils; many become converts to Islam and "even those who did not formally accept Islam, remained Muslims by conviction much the greater part of their lives."

Lajpat Rai goes on to say that for the first 25 or 30 years of his life his father "was a believer in Islam according to the Suni School. He used to recite *namaz* and to observe the *ramzan* fast; and he cultivated acquaintance among the Ulema [Muslim scholars] and Maulvis. When Sir Syed Ahmad [Sir Sayyid Ahmad Khan (1817–98), a prominent Muslim educational reformer] started his socio-religious mission, he read Sir Syed's works and became a follower of his. Up to his fortieth year he was a Muslim of the Sayyid Ahmad school that was popularly known as the 'natural religion' school. During this period he was antagonistic to Hinduism and the Arya Samaj, and used to criticize

the teachings of both in the Brahmo press. But when I joined the Arya Samaj and he studied the best of Hindu literature, his outlook underwent a radical change so much so that in old age he has become a Vedantin, and is now a believer in the Vedanta [a school of Hindu philosophy]." Lajpat Raj's account of his father's life promotes a striking example of the way traditions mix but do not necessarily merge together. The historian needs to separate and relate the various strands if he is to understand of what India consists and how it is composed.

India and the outside world
What is equally remarkable is the extent to which India, throughout recorded history, has influenced and has in turn been influenced by contact with its neighbors. Despite the high mountain barricade that divides it from Asia, and the vast expanses of ocean around its coasts, the subcontinent remains an integral part of the great Eurasian landmass. Much of the Middle East, Central Asia, China and mainland southeast Asia lies less than 2,000 kilometers from Delhi. Substantial parts of Europe and Africa, nearly the whole of the Southeast Asian archipelagoes, the rest of China and all of Japan are within 4,000 kilometers of Delhi. Only the Americas and the southern polar regions are truly remote.

Of course, simple distances, as the crow flies, do not in themselves mean that there is easy intercourse between India and the rest of the world. The configuration of the earth's surface determines where people can go; the ease with which journeys are made depends both on the lie of the land and the method of transportation used. Some journeys can be made with relatively simple technological knowledge – a map or verbal description – but others, even over short distances, may require highly sophisticated navigational knowledge to be successfully accomplished. Others may not be attempted at all without transportation other than human muscle and pack-animal. Moreover, even if movement is possible, it may require the stimulus of economic, political, or ideological necessity to drive people from where they are comfortably settled. Travel as cultural curiosity is, after all, a fairly contemporary phenomenon.

That being said, it is important to note that, however formidable the natural frontiers of the subcontinent, they seem never to have inhibited the movements of peoples into it or the progress of their populations, goods and ideas out of it. The mountain chain that rises in the northeast out of wet and densely forested land has certainly proved an obstacle to large-scale migration, but has not prevented a steady trickle of peoples from the east from making their way into the Assam valley and present-day Bangladesh. By contrast, in the northwest, where the mountains form complex knots that tie together the Iranian plateau, Central Asia, and the Indian subcontinent, a series of passes have, since time began, allowed the easy flow of people in to India – as traders, conquerors, settlers and pilgrims. It was along these routes that the Aryan people of the Iranian plateau entered India in ancient times, to be followed by countless numbers, of great ethnic and cultural diversity, in the centuries since – part of the ebb and flow of peoples across the great spaces of Central Asia and Iran. Nor has this been a simple one-way traffic: the mountain passes of the northeast are one of the great trading and cultural crossroads of the world. Through them luxurious

Indian textiles and precious goods found their way to the trade routes that linked the heart of Asia with the lands of the Middle East and the Mediterranean. By the same route Buddhism traveled from India to the high plateau of Tibet and on to China.

By sea, the subcontinent has long-established connections with the countries of the Persian Gulf, the Red Sea and the east coast of Africa. It was Arab merchants, trading in Indian goods, who first brought Islam to the subcontinent by this coastal route. From the trading cities of the peninsular coast, and from Sri Lanka, the peoples, products, and religions of the subcontinent spread into mainland Southeast Asia and the Indonesian archipelago. Europeans – first the Portuguese and the Dutch, then the French and the British – also came by sea. From the 16th century onward they pioneered the seaways around Africa and into the Arabian Sea and the Bay of Bengal in search of cheaper and more plentiful supplies of spices, and soon developed a taste for the magnificent fabrics and other articles of trade manufactured in India. In the 19th century, the steam ship and the opening of the Suez Canal brought the subcontinent within three weeks' travel of the rapidly growing and expansive economies of western Europe. The shrinking of the world since then has propelled peoples from the subcontinent to spread abroad – at first mainly within the confines of Britain's 19th-century empire, as labor to Africa, the Caribbean and Southeast Asia. Subsequently an even more significant migration of entrepreneurs has carried the talents, ideas, religions and customs of the subcontinent to all the major countries of the world.

The history of the Indian subcontinent has thus been marked by continual interaction with territories and peoples beyond its natural geographical frontiers. This intercourse has not always been without strain or violence, and its legacies have been both creative and destructive. But in trying to discern what is unique and interesting about the cultures of the subcontinent, it is important to recognize that the peoples of India are, and for thousands of generations have been, part of a larger human enterprise; and that as such, they have been influenced from beyond their frontiers even as they have changed from within.

Agrarian societies

The peoples of South Asia have always been predominantly rural, their settlements widely dispersed throughout the habitable countryside. While India has supported great cities from the most ancient times, their general influence has often been weak or transitory, and few of them, before the 20th century, can be reckoned to have exerted a powerful hold over society at large. The social functions of most towns are far from being clearly distinguishable from the surrounding countryside, and nearly all of them have proved remarkably subordinate to the interests and values of rural society.

The strength and resilience of Indian society is founded in its countless villages and hamlets. The countryside has consistently resisted the press of the city upon it, and the state too – as ruler after ruler has learnt to his cost – has depended for its successful functioning upon reaching a political accommodation

Above The subcontinent's huge rural heartland has always played an important role in shaping its character. To this day almost three-quarters of the population live in its numerous scattered villages. Here, in the Punjab state of Pakistan, the flat roofs of the village houses are used as additional living and working areas. Beds are arranged there in the hot weather, and food is prepared and cooked in ovens on the roofs.

Previous page A man reads the Qu'ran in a mosque in Lahore, Pakistan. Islam has been one of the most enduring influences to enter the subcontinent from outside. Most of the region has seen centuries of government by Muslim rulers. In Pakistan and Bangladesh, both created as Islamic states, the Qu'ran touches upon all areas of life from law to banking. India possesses some of the architectural masterpieces of the Islamic world, including the Taj Mahal. It also has an important Muslim minority – more than 10 percent of the population. Several cabinet ministers and two of the country's presidents have been Muslims.

with the rural societies it could not hope independently to control. The main feature of almost all South Asian political and administrative systems has been the extraordinary diffusion of power exercised through them, hindering the centralizing tendencies of ancient despotisms and the interfering urges of the modern state alike. Until quite recently, it must have been fairly easy to avoid an over-intrusive overlord or unwelcome conqueror by moving away and re-establishing a local society, virtually self-sufficient in its basic needs and beyond the reach of his authority. Moreover, the loss of wealth, or decline in political fortune, has not always meant that the dispossessed have been obliterated or absorbed by new conquerors. Those who achieved power quickly realized that to hold what they had won by force meant respecting the traditions they found and following to some degree the customs already established in the country.

In this way, different peoples lay alongside each other, and culture added to culture. With the attendant stresses and strains, the subcontinent can boast a particular form of a genuinely plural society, and one of considerable antiquity. The most striking unities within the subcontinent are those thrown up by social institutions and cultural practices that, at the same time, allow people to live together and permit them to remain apart. Not surprisingly, conflict plays a large part in the historical development of the subcontinent; but even this is not straightforward to read. While much of the political narrative tends to highlight the movements of invaders from the outside, it reveals also divisions within the intricate interactions between internal disputes and the opportunities offered for resolving them by the appearance of an external force. Politics, after all, begin around the domestic hearth, and violence is ever most acute within the family. It requires, therefore, a real effort to understand the particular influences at work in any given situation and then to comprehend its place within the wider whole.

The problem of material evidence

A practical difficulty faces the historian of India. Though the Indian civilization is reckoned to be very ancient, its material remains are very scanty, the literary and artistic evidence fragmentary, and the source materials generally tainted. Very little of what is really old has survived to inform later generations; that which has, has most ingeniously to be worked upon to yield its secrets. Lack of evidence, or lack of scholarly endeavor to handle ancient artifacts or to interpret difficult texts, prevent us from knowing as much about India as we would like.

The problem begins with the archaeological evidence. Unlike the temperate zones of Europe, where much of archaeological science, in both theory and practice, was developed, the land surface of the subcontinent has experienced major movements within historical time, and its climate has acted much more harshly upon it. The very rapid rate at which soil erosion and deposition takes place means that the archaeological record is all too easily confused and obscured so that, in the words of the British archaeologists Raymond and Bridget Allchin, "a Stone Age site in use several hundred thousand years ago may be exposed on a low hill, while a few hundred yards away another of the same period may be buried under more than a hundred feet of silt in a river valley."

Two centuries ago James Rennell noticed the discrepancy between what was claimed for ancient India and what remained of the visible proof of her attainments: "The accounts of 22 centuries ago, represent the Indians as a people who stood very high in point of civilization: but to judge from their ancient monuments, they had not carried the imitative arts to anything like the degree of perfection attained by the Greeks and Romans; or even by the Egyptians." His explanation for this was, that like the Chinese, Indians had only "carried the arts just to the point requisite for useful purposes; but never to have approached the summit of perfection, as it represents taste, or boldness of design."

But there is a simpler and more obvious explanation. India, at once rich and fertile, is no lover of immortality. Allowing man to survive from year to year, and usually providing enough for the present, the climate preserves nothing. In 1836, while serving in Calcutta as the Law Member of the Government of India before he had achieved fame as an historian, Thomas Babington Macaulay (1800–59) wrote, "One execrable effect this climate produces – it destroys all the works of man with scarcely one exception. Steel rusts; – pins become quite useless; – razors lose their edge; – thread decays; – clothes fall to pieces;

Below The sacred status of the cow in India stretches back hundreds of centuries. Cows roam cities and villages freely, usefully devoring garbage, and are decorated with sprigs of jasmine, bells and painted patterns. Traffic circulates around them as they lie in the road, and a motorist who accidentally strikes one can find himself surrounded by an angry crowd.

– books moulder away and drop out of their bindings; – plaister cracks; – timber rots; – matting is in shreds. The sun, the steam of this vast alluvial tract, the infinite armies of white ants, make such havoc with buildings that every house requires a complete repair every three years."

So take away the active hand of man, and nature regains possession of the land. Cities disappear from the face of the earth; huge temples are lost in the jungle; sites that once witnessed the daily bustle of thousands of men and women are effortlessly reclaimed by plants, insects and other animals. In a very short time, the weather reduces what man has made to rubble, just as the great plains themselves are formed out of the debris of the mountains.

The impermanent character of life's material trappings astonished the Mughal invader Babur: "In Hindustan", he wrote, "hamlets and villages, towns indeed, are depopulated and set up in a moment! If the people of a large town, one inhabited for years even, flee from it, they do it in such a way that not a sign or trace of them remains in a day or day and a half. On the other hand, if they fix their eyes on a place in which to settle they need not dig watercourses or construct dams because their crops are all rain-grown . . . They make a tank or dig a well; they need not build houses or set up walls – *khas* grass abounds, wood is unlimited, huts are made, and straightaway there is a village or a town!"

It is hard to follow the progress of such a shifting society through the centuries. Once deserted, Harappa and Mohenjo-Daro, the great cities of the Indus Valley civilization, were lost to human knowledge for nearly 3,000 years. The initial impact of many foreign invasions, or the forceful shifting of the balance of power among the core regions of the subcontinent, must have destroyed much of what might well until then have been guarded against the depredations of ants and the monsoon rains. Huge Buddhist monasteries and old capital cities disappeared in the wake of early Muslim invasions, and Hindu temples were razed and their property despoiled as the power of Islam moved down the Gangetic plain. Shifts in the economy have reduced once thriving centers of manufacturing and commerce to insignificant villages.

For so long a settled country, permanent material remains more than a few hundred years old in age are remarkably few. Archaeologists have only just begun to appreciate the enormity of the task that lies before them in identifying and excavating sites in the subcontinent; and at every stage arise methodological and theoretical problems of interpretation of the remains. The oldest extant Indian manuscripts do not date back beyond the 11th or 12th centuries, though some important history can be reconstructed from works carried out of India by travelers and pilgrims, and preserved in caves and religious houses in the dry, cold climates of Central Asia, or in libraries and museums in more temperate countries. There is a mass of religious literature, but scholars have barely begun to mine it for historical purposes. Such sources are in any case very difficult to handle, since they were passed down over generations as oral tradition and, when they were written down in one form or another, were subject to translation, interpolation and interpretation. An account of affairs in the distant past, therefore, may actually say more about the time when it was recorded than about the events it purports to describe.

Public records are few and often equivocal in their character. Coins, seals, inscriptions on metal and stone, reveal the existence of sophisticated administrations, but give little clue as to how they worked and what they did. With all the resources of modern scholarship it has still not been possible, for example, to date the accession of the Kushan king Kanishka – and he was no mere local lordling – more closely than at some time between AD 78 and 244. In fact, the historian has to wait until relatively recent times – say the 15th or 16th centuries – before being able to draw upon a reasonable range of evidence or utilize a fair variety of documents.

British interpretations of India

Even in more recent times there are limits to what can be discovered from some of the most accessible source materials. From the mid 18th until the mid 20th century the ascendant political power in India was British. While there can be no complaints about the amount of information available for this period, it was collected and worked upon to allow an alien power to manage the complex societies of the subcontinent for its own specific economic and political purposes, and the record therefore tells us primarily about the nature of British interests in India. Further, foreign observers inevitably view a different culture through attitudes formed at home, and it requires a tremendous effort of creative will and imagination to see the simple facts of another's society, to understand its workings, and so to experience the force of its culture, though some will make the effort. Warren Hastings (1732–88), governor general of India from 1774 to 1786, commissioned the translation of Indian manuscripts; Sir William Jones (1746–94) promoted the study of Sanskrit and of Persian while serving as judge of the supreme court in Calcutta; and many lesser men read papers to each other at the learned societies founded in Calcutta and Bombay. Slowly aspects of India's past were brought to light again: archaeology, philology, theology and history all played their part.

It was not just the recovery of the past that concerned the rulers; they wanted, too, to understand the present and create a contemporary record of the subcontinent. In his preface to the 1881 Census Report on the Punjab, Denzil Ibbetson ranged far and wide over questions of caste, religion, social organization and economic life. He did so deliberately to make his readers aware of what could be discovered. He wrote "Our ignorance of the customs and beliefs of the people among whom we dwell is surely in some respects a reproach to us; for not only does that ignorance deprive European science of material that it greatly needs, but it also involves a distinct loss of administrative power to ourselves."

So India would be studied, but from a European perspective, and, in part, for rather specific purposes: knowledge would bring with it the power to control and to force changes in direction. From this, it is only a short step to current cultural controversies about the nature of knowledge and whether understandings of the past can ever be neutrally deployed in contemporary concerns. Thus, in the opening chapter of Salman Rushdie's *Midnight's Children* (1981), arose the disquieting absurdities and resentments that intruded upon Aadam Aziz's prayers one Kashmiri morning that "India – like radium – had been 'discovered' by the Europeans" and that what separated him from his friends in Heidelberg was "this belief of theirs that he was somehow the invention of their ancestors".

Above The landscape of India often seems to be without change. In Khajuraho, Madhya Pradesh, temples stand as they have done for nearly 1,000 years, and fields are plowed by bullocks just as they would have been when the first temple stones were laid. But the powerful Chandella dynasty that ruled this part of central India when the temples were built have vanished virtually without trace, and little is known of their society and history.

Contemporary concerns

In the world of today, the exotic has become commonplace and knowledge of foreign places, foreign societies, foreign languages and foreign cultures is easy to come by. New influences are brought to bear directly upon the lives of South Asians, coloring the way in which contemporaries view their own society and its past. At the end of the 20th century, the subcontinent no longer stands in quite the same relationship to the rest of the world as once perhaps it did. The relative isolation of human societies has been broken down more completely than at any other time in history: India's connections with the world outside the subcontinent are more numerous, more intrusive, and more imperative than ever before, and Indian influences play more powerfully on distant continents.

Changes within India have meant that its peoples have become more aware of each other and that they impinge more upon each other. Inevitably, new tensions have arisen. Schemes for political and social reform are proposed in the light of a foreign ethic and morality; religious orthodoxies are revivified and redefined, and newly created traditions acquire great potency, by utilizing new methods of communication. Peoples have become more self-conscious, keen to find their identities and to assert them. Even the most conservative and chauvinistic enter the debates about the future shape of their society and its cultural origins in response to arguments and opinions they most dislike. The problem has become one of how to give indigenous content to a modern form. The process is deeply disturbing and India, as the novelist V. S. Naipaul has so keenly observed, is shaken by a million mutinies now. South Asia is important, its history fascinating, its cultures complex. The following pages cannot pretend to be a comprehensive account of such great societies as have flourished there over millennia. But it is to be hoped that they will provide at least a first sight of the extraordinary variety of this vast continent and its store of human richness.

LAND, CLIMATE, AGRICULTURE

Ancient cosmologies

For those who lived in India in ancient times, the subcontinent was a special place. Descriptions of India's geography, history, religion, and culture, that may have originated over 2,500 years ago, were set down in literary form between 400 and 600 AD in the encyclopedic collections of old narratives and lore known as the *Puranas*. In one of these we read "The country that lies north of the ocean, and south of the snowy mountains, is called Bharata: for there dwelt the descendants of Bharata. It is nine thousand leagues in extent, and is the land of works, in consequence of which men go to heaven, or obtain emancipation."

From the very earliest times, the inhabitants of India had exceedingly complex ideas about the creation of the world and the universe. And every time a new theory was advanced it rarely replaced an older one, but took its place alongside all the others, even if it was inconsistent with them. Many attempts were made to reconcile the various versions of how the world began, but almost invariably the stories were aggregated together, or enfolded one within another. The different accounts were accommodated by making them occur successively rather than interpreting one story as an allegorical alternative to another.

Even in the most primitive cosmogonies there are inconsistencies and complications. The earliest known body of literature – the *Rig Veda*, a collection of sacred writings, the earliest parts of which perhaps go back nearly four millennia – has five different words to refer to the earth. In some accounts, the universe consisted simply of two parts – the earth and the sky – but others distinguished between the earth, the air, and the

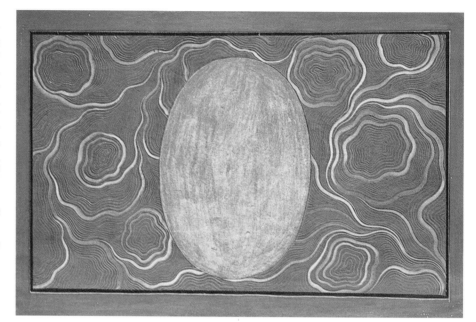

Above This depiction of the cosmic or golden egg, the *hiranya garbha*, was painted in the Punjab in the early 18th century; it illustrates a creation myth in the *Bhagavata Purana*. The egg, representing the origins of life, is surrounded by swirling clouds of matter.

sky. Each of these parts had three layers, and so already creation was composed of six or nine parts. Before long a hemispheric world of light – a vault for the heavens – was added to the picture, and then a matching vault for an underworld. So the earth came to be seen as a disk suspended between two great bowls turned toward each other, and thus was born the idea of the cosmic egg, or golden womb, of Brahma, the primeval being.

Expanding universes

No one could agree on the size of creation, except that it was very large. For some, the distance between the earth and the sky was the distance a horse could cover in a thousand days; for others, it could be measured by the height of a thousand cows standing one on top of the other. By the time the great Indian epics (the *Mahabharata* and the *Ramayana)* and the *Puranas* came to be set down, not only was the earth and its universe seen as a system made up of increasingly differentiated segments, but other universes, almost infinite in number, were being added. Moreover, all three of the subcontinent's major religious traditions – Hinduism, Buddhism and Jainism – were preoccupied with a doctrine of last things and judgements, whereby souls were subjected to a potentially endless round of rebirths. This led to the notion of an expanded and stratified universe with numerous heavens and nether worlds to provide an appropriate niche for the soul at any stage of its long journey toward or away from ultimate release. In general, in this system, the good went up and the bad went down.

Just as the individual soul moved through a cycle of rebirth, so did the whole universe. As with space, so time was perceived as staggeringly large and complex. Brahma's life might be calculated as 311,040,000 million years, but a year was not measured by the short natural span of the earth's seasons. And time was

Subdivisions of a MAHAYUGA

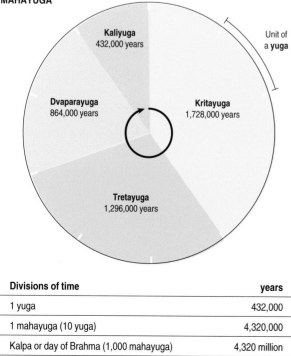

Kaliyuga
432,000 years

Unit of a **yuga**

Dvaparayuga
864,000 years

Kritayuga
1,728,000 years

Tretayuga
1,296,000 years

Divisions of time	years
1 yuga	432,000
1 mahayuga (10 yuga)	4,320,000
Kalpa or day of Brahma (1,000 mahayuga)	4,320 million

Left The diagram shows a *mahayuga*, or great age, which is divided into four *yugas*. One thousand *mahayugas* constitute a single day (a *kalpa*, of 4,320 million years) in the life of Brahma. At the end of each *kalpa* the world is annihilated and a new one created. The length of each *yuga* is calculated in multiples of 432,000. We are now part way into the shortest and darkest of the *yugas*, the *kaliyuga*. According to the *Mahabharata*, Brahma has a life of one hundred years. Fifty Brahma years are supposed to have elapsed since the incarnation of the current god. At the end of the cycle, Brahma will be replaced by a new incarnation. These astonishing computations have no comparison in any other major world culture. Only modern science, with the aid of computers, can speak in terms of such massive figures. In the Vedic tradition, however, there has always been an understanding of the staggering immensity of time.

arranged in cycles, with cycles within cycles postulated. Most of the early commentators agreed that since the great war in India – the subject of the *Mahabharata*, reckoned to have taken place around 3120 BC – the earth was now in the *kaliyuga* – the fourth and most imperfect age of the world, an age of strife. But this dark age was but one of a thousand *kaliyugas* in the present cycle of time, and that in turn was but one of 720 cycles of time in a single year of Brahma.

The expansion and growth of complexity of the cosmos was accompanied by a multiplication and evolution of those who dwelt within it. Thus a primordial first being, Brahma, soon gave way to the existence of numerous gods, demi-gods and miscellaneous spirits of varying status and power, and a great variety of terrestrial creatures came into being. In some texts, the continent where India was located was known as *Jambudvipa* – the Rose-apple island – after the *Jambu* tree that grew at its center. This tree had a trunk of enormous girth, 15 *yoganas* around, (a *yogana* can be anything between 3 and 14 kilometers long). Its branches extended for 50 *yoganas*, and it was twice that high.

A common feature of ancient Indian cosmology was to see the earth in its universe centered on an axis, specified as Mount Meru or Mount Sumeru. This mythical mountain was actually identified as being in the Pamir mountains in central Asia, or as being Mount Kailas in Tibet. Even in Vedic times, the earliest period of Hindu culture and history, this axis was thought to join the celestial vault and the underworld,

the mountain soaring 84,000 *yoganas* above the earth. Meru's shape was unlike that of ordinary mountains because it was composed of several distinct layers, each the domain of some particular supernatural being. Some authorities believed that it had a peak; but others saw the summit as broadening out to a great plateau. All agreed that there was space enough for its divine occupants.

Around the mountain were arranged in systematic and concentric fashion a number of continents. According to some accounts there were four, lying to the north, south, east and west: often the continents were depicted as the petals of a lotus, with Meru forming the carpel. Other versions saw the earth as consisting of seven concentric rings, separated by oceans. The continent containing India lay at the center, and as they moved away from the center, each was twice the size of its predecessor. Some cosmologies expanded this arrangement to contain as many as 9, 13, 18 or 32 continents. But as far back as the 7th century BC it was acceptable to combine these two visions. As one of the *Puranas* put it: "it is useless for men to offer to prove or disprove anything in the description of the earth . . ., that [such] conceptions ... are beyond the scope of human thinking . . . and that such matters . . . should be taken for granted."

Another way of explaining the world saw it as a huge tortoise, the arched shell being the heaven and its flat underside the world. This concept, which provided a ready guide to divinations, went back to the

Below In Hindu architecture, the tapering towers of temples are representations of the mythical Mount Meru, as here at Konarak, Orissa. Constructed in the mid 13th century, the Konarak temple was also built in the likeness of a vast chariot with 24 stone wheels, pulled by seven horses. It was designed so that the morning sun would shine into each chamber in turn, before reaching the statue of the sun god and, as it was believed, replenishing him with energy.

Astronomy

The astral sciences in India are interesting in that their practice was so intimately tied to statecraft. Given Hindu notions of the universe in which the social and the natural (not to mention the celestial) partook in a single unified analytic field, in which divine kings enjoyed a crucial ordinating role, astronomy developed as a branch of government. As such, Indian astronomy possessed a tremendous capacity to combine close and "objective" observation of heavenly phenomena with rather "unscientific" beliefs about how the universe was organized – including such ideas as the center of the universe being on Mount Meru. (This capacity appears less striking as we begin to appreciate how the development of western science has also been informed by social and political considerations.) The most famous of India's rulers to have an interest in science was Maharaja Sawai Jai Singh of Jaipur (1699–1743) who built five spectacularly large observatories in Delhi, Jaipur, Varanasi, Mathura and Ujjain. But Jai Singh was not alone. Muslim, as well as other Hindu, rulers took a keen interest in propagating astronomical knowledge. Indeed, so closely was the strength of the polity tied to the quality of its astral science, that the Rajput ruler of Kota had his astronomical instruments built into the battlements of his capital city. Interestingly, early British officials in India also saw the need to patronize the Indian astral sciences if they were to establish their position on the subcontinent, to judge by an early 19th-century British resident of Delhi who had an observatory built near Kashmiri Gate.

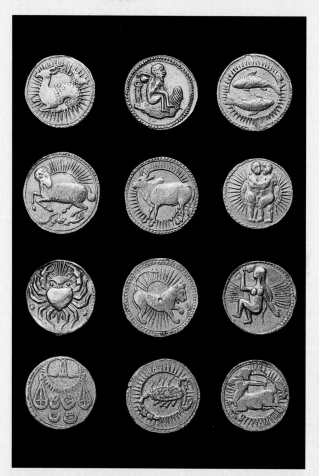

Left Hindu notions of kingship in which the monarch regulated both the mundane and the divine gradually informed the way the Mughals legitimized their rule. These coins, minted during the reign of Jahangir (1605–27), depict the signs of the zodiac. Though the zodiac, as a system of organizing astral observation, may initially have been of Middle Eastern origin, its use on Mughal coins refers both to the emperor's divine sanction as well as to his competence in governing the movements of the heavens (something strict Islamic law would not recognize).

Left Jaipur's Samrat Yantra, built by Maharaja Jai Singh, is an enormous sundial that determines the time to an accuracy of two seconds. Being a solar instrument, the time given is Jaipur standard time, which was used in almanacs distributed throughout the maharaja's dominions. By defining the calendar, the maharaja powerfully influenced how his subjects ordered their lives.

mid 1st millennium BC but continued to be elaborated for many centuries following. It commonly depicted the tortoise as resting on Vishnu, one of the two major gods of India, its head pointing toward the east and its shell divided into 9 parts. Each of these was assigned to a triad of lunar mansions or constellations, and from this astrologers could in part determine which countries or districts were vulnerable to suffering and disaster in accordance with the movement of malignant planets through the sky.

In all these various accounts, the earth comprised only a small part of the universe. It was commonly held that there might be an infinite number of universes, each with its own worlds, heavens and underworlds. In our own system, the gross elements had been thrown together in a compact mass – the world egg – which rested on the oceans and which was surrounded by realms of water, wind, fire, air and other substances. These views of creation saw no need to exclude whatever was apparently inconsistent or incompatible, and were prepared to concede the existence of the unknowable. This did not necessarily mean that there was tolerance of other views – people who are good at aggregating information tend also to be adept at sorting it and establishing hierarchies, arguing with passion for particular interpretations of the mass of ideas at their disposal. Generosity of accommodation does not preclude sectarian strife.

Though fantastic in form and elaboration, these ancient Indian cosmologies often began with the known and the local. Stories about creation, maps and pictures of the universe, combined the largest general theories of time and space with detailed and localized geographical data: the geographical sections of the *Puranas* work outward from the village and nearby towns to more distant but correctly located cities and provinces before slipping almost without notice into arrangements of continents, oceans, heavens and hells beyond the ken of the conventional map-maker. In these ancient Indian stories of creation it is hard to separate speculative fancy from empirical description.

Modern scientific explanations

In many respects, the contemporary scientific explanation for the particular existence of India is just as wonderful and amazing as those propounded in the ancient myths. Since the 1960s, studies of the earth's crust have transformed our understanding of the earth's physical structure. Of particular significance to the geology of the Indian subcontinent is the science of plate tectonics – the study of the massive movements over time of the rocky plates of the earth's outer shell on which the continents are adrift.

For all its size and varied local detail, looked at through the eyes of a late 20th-century geologist, the Indian subcontinent is divided into three major geological regions: the great mountain ranges of the north, a series of great plains, and a large southern plateau. This configuration owes much to the dramatic movements within the earth's crust about 40 million years ago when the southerly plateau, the Deccan – the part of India that forms an inverted triangle hanging from the Eurasian landmass into the Arabian Sea and the Bay or Bengal, and is part of the Indo-Australian plate – collided with the Eurasian plate. This compressed and buckled the sedimentary layers of the ocean floor, forcing them upward to form the Himalayas; as the ocean between the two plates disappeared, the great plains were formed.

Left This celestial diagram, from the eastern Deccan or Tamil Nadu (c.1750) represents the limits of the universe including the paths of the sun and the planets, the zodiac, and two eclipse cycles. Because, according to Hindu notions of divine rulership, the king's authority rested in part on his ability to predict (and hence control) heavenly phenomena, knowledge of celestial movements and eclipses was a central element of statecraft, and the science of astronomy received lavish royal patronage and consequently became highly developed.

Above An inscription on this brass celestial sphere shows it to be the work of Ziya al-Din Muhammad and is dated 1067 AH/1656–7. Forms of astronomical knowledge (including knowledge of how to make instruments needed to make the necessary calculations) were often monopolized by particular lineages over the course of several generations. Ziya al-Din Muhammad's family started its service to the Mughal court in the 16th century when Shaikh Elahad was employed by Humayan. The family continued making instruments for the court during the reigns of Akbar, Shah Jahan and Aurangzeb.

Below The introduction of western forms of astronomical knowledge and instruments of observation by the British did not immediately condemn either Indian astronomy or astrology to obscurity. This painting of a star-map according to the Hindu system was executed in the mid 19th century by an Indian artist and bound in a manuscript with European astronomical representations by the same artist. As both astronomical systems were connected to social life in different ways, they did not necessarily constitute competing and incompatible forms of knowledge. Rather, they were treated by Indians as parallel orders of reality.

The ancient rocks

Peninsular India, including Sri Lanka, is one of the oldest and least disturbed landmasses in the world. Once part of the ancient continent of Gondwanaland, which included Australia, Antarctica, Africa and South America, it was formed over 3,000 million years ago in the pre-Cambrian period, and though it seems never to have been covered by sea for long periods, it contains sedimentary rocks deposited by rivers and glaciers. Underlying all are the highly crystalline, contorted and faulted Archaeon rocks that go back before there was any kind of organic life on the planet. These include the charnockites and khondalites that form the Nilgiri and Palani Hills in the Western Ghats. The Eastern Ghats and the highlands of Sri Lanka, which may be more than 3,100 million years old, are similarly composed, and farther north major belts are found in Rajasthan in the west and in Bihar and Orissa in the east.

Then there are the Archaeon greenstones, less metamorphosed (compacted by the effects of pressure and heat) than the older rocks and originating from the recrystallization of volcanic sedimentary basins. They were formed around 2,300 to 2,700 million years ago and are prominent around Dharwar and Mysore in the west, in the Jabalpur and Nagpur districts in the center, in the Aravalli Range in the northwest and in the Chota Nagpur in the northeast. These rocks are rich in minerals, including gold (for which Bangalore is particularly famous), silver and copper. In the Aravalli Range are extensive supplies of manganese ore and great marble quarries; Chota Nagpur is rich in iron ores. Superimposed on this Archaeon base are a series of sedimentary rocks, the oldest of which (still pre-Cambrian) are the sandstones, shales and limestones that constitute the Vindhyan series. They run from the Aravalli Range eastward to southwest Bihar, and in some places are more than 4,000 meters thick. The lowest layers are marine in origin, the higher ones laid down by river action. Diamonds are found in these beds, especially at Golconda and Panna.

Younger than these, and dating back to the post-Cambrian period that began some 250 million years ago, are further layers of sedimentary rock, the Gondwana series. In places 6,000 meters deep, the oldest of these layers were deposited under glacial conditions and the latter deposited by rivers. The geological record testifies to massive processes of erosion, of the filling in of faults and depressions, of the land being subject to periods of enormous climatic change. The Gondwana sedimentaries are most prominent in the Damodar valley in Bengal, along the Mahanadi river valley in Madhya Pradesh, and in the Godavari valley from Nagpur to its delta on the Bay of Bengal. In these rocks are rich seams of coal and iron ore.

Clash of continents

The ancient rocks of the peninsula are related to those of the other landmasses that once formed part of Gondwanaland. Over millions of years, tremendous forces of heat and pressure within the earth caused the plates that form the earth's crust to move. In a process that started about 180 million years ago, the ocean floor ruptured and spread, Gondwanaland broke apart and the Indo-Australian plate, separated from the rest, was spun away to the northeast. During this process of rupturing, about 100 million years ago, lava bubbled up from within the earth and spilled out over an area of 500,000 square kilometers in the

northwestern part of the peninsula. Parts of the Archaeon basement and the Vindhyan strata were completely covered, around Bombay to depths of up to 3,000 meters. The molten rock forced its way between the layers and along the faults and fissures of the earlier formations, creating the distinctive landscapes of northwestern Maharashtra.

The widening of the Indian Ocean, caused by the raising of the Maldive Ridge, divided the Indian plate from Africa, propelling it on a northern course away from Australia. As recently as 50 million years ago, the land that now makes up peninsular India and straddles the Tropic of Cancer still lay within the southern hemisphere. Moving only a few centimeters a year, it was headed for collision with the Eurasian landmass. As the leading edge of the small Indian plate met that of the larger continent to the north, it was, and continues to be, forced beneath it. The edges crumpled and folded and the ocean sediments and parts of the oceanic crust were forced upward to form, about 30 million years ago, the Himalayan and associated mountain ranges.

This mountain wall runs east–west for more than 2,500 kilometers in the north of the subcontinent.

Above The Himalayas, highest mountain chain on earth, are the violent consequence of the collision between India – then a drifting continent – and Asia, some 30 million years ago. The mountain range contains no few than 92 of the world's 94 highest peaks. The mountains are still rising, especially in the Karakoram region of northern Pakistan, where earthquakes and landslides are common, and roadbuilding is a constant struggle against the elements.

Top right The broad, flat Indo-Gangetic plain (seen here outside Calcutta in West Bengal) was originally a long trough of ocean left as the Indian continental plate buckled and was forced beneath that of Asia. Gradually it became filled with sediment brought down from the Himalayan range newly formed to the north. Now its fertile soils serve as the agricultural powerhouse of the subcontinent.

Above right The south of the subcontinent, in contrast to the north, is a tropical land, with warm temperatures throughout the year. Along the western coast, as here in Goa, monsoon rainfall keeps the land lush and green. Palm trees grow in great numbers and are an important economic resource. Sap from the palmyra palm provides sugar, while the coconut palm has at least a dozen uses. The fiber of the coconut is processed into coir, which is made into ropes and mats, while the milk offers a refreshing drink and the white flesh is a source of food, oil and soap. Even the leaves are used for making baskets and for roofing.

Made up of the largest and most massive ranges in the world, with an average height of about 6,000 meters, it contains the world's highest mountain, Mount Everest (8,848 meters); more than 90 peaks are over 7,300 meters. The geology and geophysics of the whole area are very complex. The granites, gneisses, schists and sedimentary rocks that compose the bulk of the central Himalayan ranges are of much more recent origin than those of the peninsula, but rocks of all the major geological ages are to be found in the mountains – an indication of the scale and severity of the impact between the two plates.

Some ocean remained in the trough formed between the two plates as the smaller was forced under the larger. But the landmasses moved ever closer, and as the rising mountains were eroded by wind and water and their dust and rocks deposited farther downhill by fast-flowing rivers, the trough began to fill. Gradually the Indo-Gangetic plain – consisting of the floodplains and deltas of the Indus, Ganges and Brahmaputra river systems – came into being. The clays, sands and limestones carried from the mountains lie in a layer that varies in depth from less than 100 meters to more than 5,000 meters, and is at its deepest around Delhi

and the Rajmahal Hills. After the passage of millions of years, this fertile alluvial plain provides as extensive an area for dense human settlement as is to be found anywhere on earth.

An unstable environment

The boundaries between the plates, and between the plains and the mountains remain very unstable. The Siwalik Range, the most southerly of the northern hills, consists of sandstone deposits laid down as a result of erosion of the main Himalayan system. As India continues to push into Asia, mountain-building continues; there is violent movement deep under the earth's crust and earthquakes occur regularly. In 1897, an earthquake in Assam – the shockwaves of which were felt across 3 million square kilometers – altered the arrangement and height of hills within an area of nearly 26,000 square kilometers.

Such violent action can throw up obstacles that force rivers exiting from the mountains to change their course, cutting new gorges in the highlands. Sometimes they thwart their own progress to the sea by silting up their channels, and have to find a new way through the plains. In recent historic times the course

Weather

With very few exceptions, the Indian subcontinent is a harsh and unyielding environment in which to live. As agriculture still dominates the economy of the sub-continent, the vagaries of temperature and rainfall have a direct, sometimes devastating effect on the patterns of life. By far the most significant climatic consideration is rainfall. In areas of dense population, failure of the monsoon rains can have far-reaching and tragic consequences – famines on a massive scale have occurred throughout history. It is the landless laborers who suffer greatest deprivation, but in a prolonged drought even land-owning farmers can find their resources stretched to breaking point. In recent times the effects of drought have been offset by improved irrigation and concerted action by central government to provide emergency supplies in affected areas. However, lack of rainfall can still have disastrous repercussions. During the Bihar famine of 1967, the almost total failure of the monsoon decimated yields from winter rice, as well as severely reducing wheat production. Drought is, nevertheless, only one of the hazards facing the inhabitants of the subcontinent. Heavy monsoon rainfall brings flooding to many regions. Bangladesh, where nearly 90 percent of the land is low-lying, is especially vulnerable. Houses are built on mud platforms to keep them above the level of the floodwaters, but even so whole villages may be swept away overnight: 500,000 people drowned in floods in 1970 and upwards of 150,000 in 1991. In the Gangetic plain a scorching wind known as the *loo* sears the landscape during the hot, dry season, or *garam*, and during prolonged periods of high temperatures deaths from heatstroke are frequent.

Above Cyclone damage in Bangladesh. In April-May, and again in October-November, cyclones sweep in from the Bay of Bengal. They sometimes produce wind velocities in excess of 160 k.p.h. and can cause enormous devastation and loss of life in the densely populated delta regions. Those whose homes are destroyed are forced to flee to the squatter encampments of the major cities, especially the capital Dhaka, which provide their only refuge and source of livelihood.

Left Monsoon floods, Porbandar, Gujarat. Heavy rainfall during the wet season, or *kharif*, often results in severe flooding. The stoicism and resourcefulness that characterize the local response to natural disasters is exemplified by this tailor as he struggles to save his precious antique sewing machine.

Right A group of women huddle together for safety as strong winds sweep the arid landscape of Rajasthan, one of the driest regions in India.

of the Kosi river that rises in eastern Nepal to join the Ganges in Bihar has shifted appreciably to the west, and the confluence of the Ganges with the south-flowing Ghaghara and the north-flowing Son, west of Patna, has also moved considerably. In Pakistan, the raising of a limestone sill across the Indus at Sukkur, perhaps as a result of an earthquake, has had important consequences for the history of the southern reaches of the Indus valley.

Change is evident in the coastal regions also. Towns that once were ports, like Tamluk in West Bengal and Kayal in Tamil Nadu in the south, now lie well inland. An earthquake of 1810 altered the configuration of the Rann of Kutch, on the India-Pakistan border, and the Makran coastal region in western Pakistan. Most of present-day Bangladesh, with the exception of the Chittagong Hill Tracts, is deltaic in origin, formed from the silts deposited by the Ganges-Padma and the Brahmaputra-Meghna river systems. Over time, the delta mouths have steadily extended farther and farther eastward into the Bay of Bengal. The delta is the world's largest, covering about 60,000 square kilometers, but the rate at which new land has been formed, and its extent, has varied enormously over time. Moreover, the region – surrounded by warm oceans and overlying one of the earth's major plate junctions – is subject to periodic violent natural events. A cyclone or shock wave racing across the Bay of Bengal can sweep away in hours the alluvium deposited over decades.

Perhaps it is not entirely fanciful to see in the geology and geophysics of the subcontinent some of the elements that the early Indian cosmologists sought to explain, and to discern in them also some of the underlying complexities of the civilizations of the subcontinent. Here is a land created of the very ancient and the very new; a terrain rich in mineral resources that includes within its boundaries a vast alluvial plain continually renewed by the deposits from great river systems. The subcontinent is perilously sited over a part of the planet's surface that is subject to great forces from movements deep within the earth. That these are barely understood, and indeed even now hardly knowable, make these modern cosmologies as fascinating as their ancient counterparts.

Land of the monsoon

As might be expected of so vast a region, and one that shows such extremes of altitude, there is enormous climatic variation. The glacial slopes of the high Himalayan ranges are among the coldest places on earth; the southern peninsula enjoys a tropical climate. On the whole, temperature in India does not limit plant and animal life; it is precipitation that affects what can be grown where, and what crop yields will be. When the seasonal rain-bearing monsoon winds meet the mountains of the west and east coasts, they are among the wettest places on earth; elsewhere, rainfall may be very sparse – the Thar desert, lying between the Aravalli Range in northwest India and the Indus valley of southeast Pakistan, receives almost none at all.

Over much of the subcontinent there are, in effect, three rather than four seasons of the year – a cool, dry season (*rabi* – October to late February); a hot, dry season (*garam* – late February to May); and a less hot, wet season (*kharif* – late May to September). It is the monsoon – the wind that blows fairly consistently from the northeast in winter, and between late May

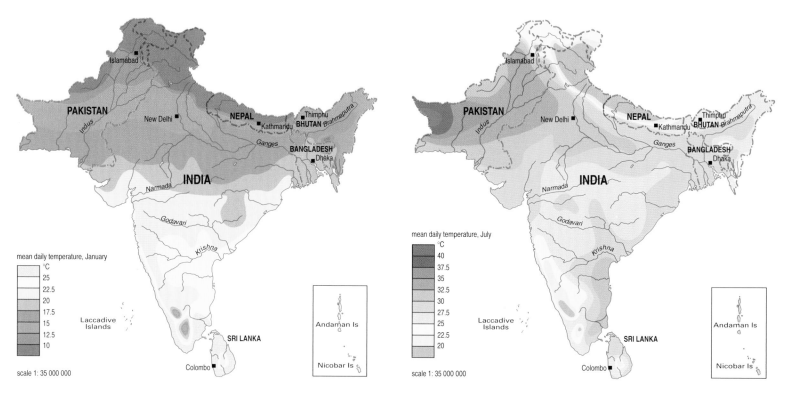

mean daily temperature, January
°C
25
22.5
20
17.5
15
12.5
10

Laccadive
Islands

SRI LANKA

Colombo

scale 1: 35 000 000

Andaman Is

Nicobar Is

mean daily temperature, July
°C
40
37.5
35
32.5
30
27.5
25
22.5
20

Laccadive
Islands

SRI LANKA

Colombo

scale 1: 35 000 000

Andaman Is

Nicobar Is

and mid September comes from the opposite direction – that dominates the climate. The dynamics of the monsoon system are exceedingly complex, but the chief cause of the wind's dramatic shift lies in the increase in solar radiation reaching the surface of the earth as the overhead sun travels northward from the Equator to the Tropic of Cancer between March and June. The sea absorbs the heat of the sun and disperses it, both through vertical conduction and by the flow of the currents in the ocean, but the land does not disperse heat so easily and, as a result, warms up more quickly than the surrounding ocean, rapidly heating the air above it.

Temperatures climb rapidly in the subcontinent as the sun moves north. April is the hottest month along the west coast as it swelters beneath the deepening cloud cover that precedes the onset of the rains; by May temperatures in southern Pakistan exceed 45°C and sometimes rise to above 50°C; they fall rapidly in the mountains of Baluchistan and the North-West Frontier Province. In the far east, Bangladesh has its hottest month in April, with a mean maximum temperature around 35°C. The barrier of the Himalayas prevents cooler air from being drawn down from the north, and so the central and northern plains of India become very hot, with temperatures of more than 40°C being recorded in May from Nagpur on the northern edge of the Deccan up to Punjab in the Himalayan foothills. Though the mountains are appreciably cooler, even in sheltered valleys of the Himalayas temperatures can climb quite high: Kathmandu in Nepal, at 300 meters above sea level, achieves a mean summer maximum of 25°C.

The summer monsoon develops as moist southwesterly winds are drawn in from the Arabian Sea to replace the rising air over the subcontinent. At the same time, there are complex shifts in the prevailing airstreams in the upper atmosphere. Toward the end of May, the westerly jet stream that in winter flows over the Indo-Gangetic plain migrates north of the Himalayas. An upper air trough, then over the Bay of Bengal, shifts westward. This change in the upper

atmosphere causes the humid southwesterly winds, which are sweeping up through the southern part of the peninsula, to double back and carry the rain-bearing monsoon winds northwestward from the Bay of Bengal across the Indo-Gangetic plain to Pakistan.

Altitude markedly affects the amount of rainfall brought by the summer monsoon. Annual precipitation in the southwest peninsula can exceed 4,000 mm, most of it falling between May and September as the winds from the Arabian Sea hit the Western Ghats, the line of hills along the coast. These cast a rainshadow to the east, and annual precipitation inland rarely exceeds 800 mm. The winds pick up moisture over the Bay of Bengal before they turn westward, and so the volume of rainfall increases in the northeast; annual figures reach 1,600 mm in West Bengal and over 2,000

Mean daily temperature (*above*)
The subcontinent shows wide variation in temperature. The greatest extremes are found in the northwest, where temperatures can reach between 30° and 40°C in July and fall well below 15°C in January: the highest temperatures across the Indo-Gangetic plain are recorded in April–May. Temperatures become more equable moving southward. In the coastal regions of the southern peninsula and Sri Lanka they range only between 30°C in July and 25°C in January.

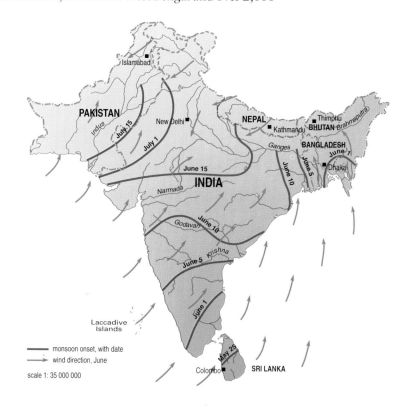

monsoon onset, with date
wind direction, June

scale 1: 35 000 000

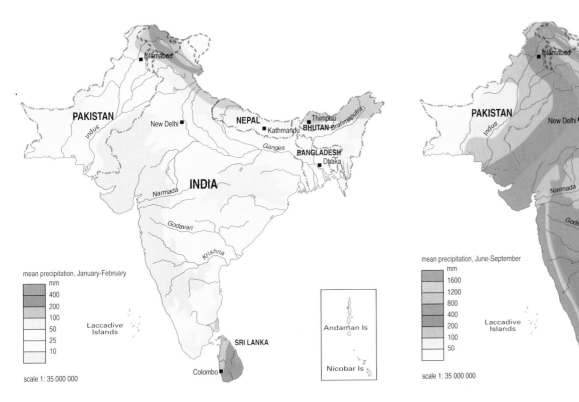

mean precipitation, January-February

mm
400
200
100
50
25
10

Laccadive
Islands

scale 1: 35 000 000

mean precipitation, June-September

mm
1600
1200
800
400
200
100
50

Laccadive
Islands

scale 1: 35 000 000

Mean precipitation (*above*)
Rainfall is governed by the two seasonal rain-bearing winds, the northeast monsoon (December to February) and the southwest monsoon (June to December). Nearly all the subcontinent, except for the northwest, benefits from the summer monsoon, with the heaviest amounts falling in the northeast and the Western Ghats. Sri Lanka and eastern coastal areas benefit from the winter monsoon. Winter precipitation in the Himalayas is in the form of snow.

The summer monsoon (*left*)
During the early summer, when the sun is directly overhead, the Indian land mass warms up quickly, creating a low-pressure center, while the Indian Ocean remains relatively cool, generating a high-pressure center. Moisture-laden air moves from the high-pressure area to the low, and the winds, deflected to the right by the effect of the earth's rotation, become southwesterly. The disappearance of the upper-level westerly jet streams south of the Himalayas in April–May causes a high-level trough to form over the Bay of Bengal. Upper-air easterlies replace the westerly jet stream and the rain-bearing winds are deflected up the Indo-Gangetic plain.

Right The Thar Desert in Rajasthan rarely receives more than 100 mm of rain in a year, as the summer monsoon winds from the Bay of Bengal have lost most of their moisture by the time they reach the area. This arid tract of land has long formed a barrier to communication. Too dry for more than scant settlement by man, it is home to many desert creatures including the black buck, the desert fox, the chikara and numerous species of eagle.

mm in northeast Bangladesh. The monsoon rains reach their climax in the hills of Assam: 11,430 mm has been recorded at Cherrapunji in Meghalaya, one of the wettest places on earth. As the winds proceed westward up the Gangetic plain the amount of rainfall gradually diminishes. About 600 mm falls on Delhi, and around 900 mm in the wettest parts of Pakistan, the region of the Punjab around Lahore and Islamabad. It dwindles to less than 200 mm in southern and western Pakistan, and rarely reaches more than 100 mm in Rajasthan in northern India.

In winter, a powerful high-pressure system builds up over the Asian landmass, establishing a flow of dry air into the subcontinent from the northeast. Most of northern India is protected from these winds by the mountain ranges, and those that do reach the surface of the subcontinent are no longer composed of cold polar air. The northeasterlies that reach Sri Lanka and the southeast coast of India, however, have picked up moisture from the Bay of Bengal; southeastern India (in the rainshadow of the summer monsoon) receives most of its rain between October and December from the winter monsoon, as do northern and eastern Sri Lanka. The island's wettest zone, in the southwest, receives around 700 mm in the winter monsoon and 800 mm between April and June.

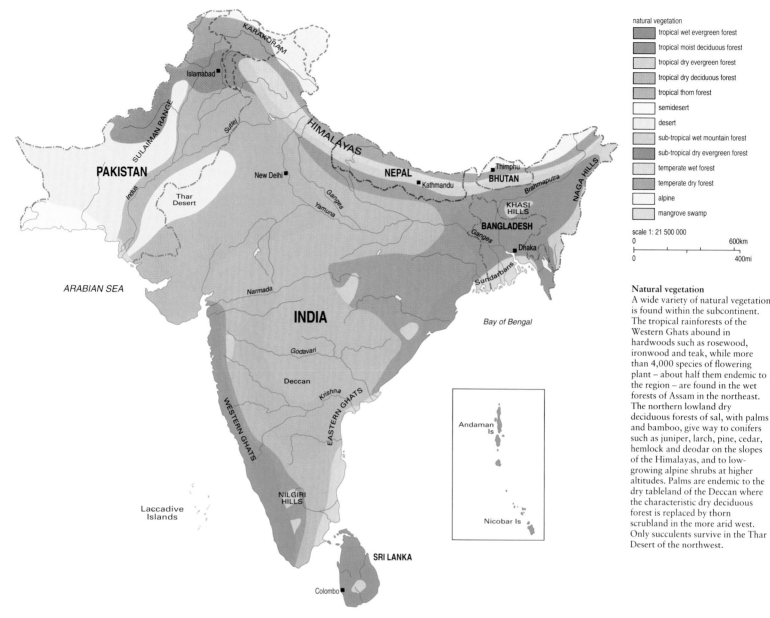

natural vegetation

- tropical wet evergreen forest
- tropical moist deciduous forest
- tropical dry evergreen forest
- tropical dry deciduous forest
- tropical thorn forest
- semidesert
- desert
- sub-tropical wet mountain forest
- sub-tropical dry evergreen forest
- temperate wet forest
- temperate dry forest
- alpine
- mangrove swamp

scale 1: 21 500 000

0 ——————— 600km

0 ——————— 400mi

Natural vegetation
A wide variety of natural vegetation is found within the subcontinent. The tropical rainforests of the Western Ghats abound in hardwoods such as rosewood, ironwood and teak, while more than 4,000 species of flowering plant – about half them endemic to the region – are found in the wet forests of Assam in the northeast. The northern lowland dry deciduous forests of sal, with palms and bamboo, give way to conifers such as juniper, larch, pine, cedar, hemlock and deodar on the slopes of the Himalayas, and to low-growing alpine shrubs at higher altitudes. Palms are endemic to the dry tableland of the Deccan where the characteristic dry deciduous forest is replaced by thorn scrubland in the more arid west. Only succulents survive in the Thar Desert of the northwest.

December and January are the coolest months in the subcontinent. Along the coastline of Pakistan the land retains some warmth, falling to around 10°C, but north of Karachi the temperature drops to below 5°C in January. As altitude increases, days and nights become very cold indeed. Temperatures fall below 10°C in the northern plains of India, and in Bangladesh range between 10°C and 15°C. In the south, seasonal temperatures show less variation. In summer, temperatures in the Deccan may rise to 35°C or 40°C, but in winter rarely fall below 20°C. Sri Lanka is more equable still, with temperatures of 20°C to 30°C throughout the year.

Manmade landscapes

The natural vegetation of the subcontinent is predominantly tropical deciduous forest (trees that drop their leaves in the hot season, when conditions are arid). There is tropical humid forest in areas where annual rainfall exceeds 1,300 mm, and vegetation is reduced to dry scrubland and drought-resistant plants in the Thar desert and other arid expanses. As in all regions of the world with a long and continuous history of human settlement, however, there is virtually no part of the natural landscape that has not been significantly altered by human intervention. Even where large areas of forest are still found, the original cover has been

replaced by secondary forest growth of scrubby trees and plants that suggest climatic conditions somewhat drier than those actually encountered. This is because human activity, repeatedly clearing and burning off the land to allow for the spread of cultivation and to make provision for domesticated animals, has caused soil erosion and degradation. Both the land and the vegetation it supports have lost their ability to retain moisture.

Satellite reconnaissance shows that over 55 percent of the land in India and up to 75 percent in Bangladesh is under cultivation. Between 1973 and 1982, the area of natural forest declined from 17 percent to 12 percent in India alone (about 375,000 square kilometers in all). In Bangladesh less than 15 percent of the country is forested. Deforestation is being carried out at unprecedented rates in the Himalayan region. It is the tropical deciduous forests of the densely settled Indo-Gangetic plain that have been most extensively cleared for cultivation; what little that remains, mostly along river banks, is degraded. Two of the deciduous trees of the subcontinent stand out as having particular economic importance: sal (*shorea robusta*), which grows mainly in the northeast, in the Terai (the lowland belt of jungle adjacent to the Himalayas) and in Nepal, and teak (*tectona grandis*), confined to the western parts of the subcontinent. Both species are

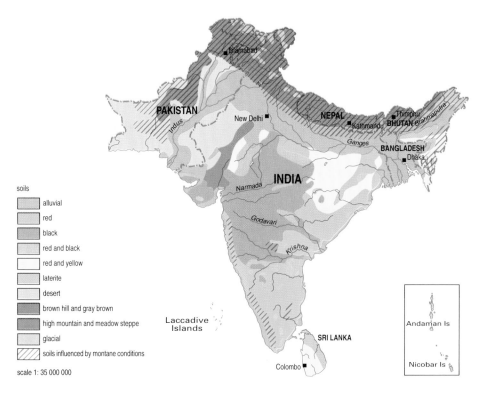

soils

	alluvial
	red
	black
	red and black
	red and yellow
	laterite
	desert
	brown hill and gray brown
	high mountain and meadow steppe
	glacial
	soils influenced by montane conditions

scale 1: 35 000 000

Soils
Of the many different soil types found in the subcontinent, three are most widespread: alluvial, red and black. The alluvial soils of the Gangetic plain – rich in potash but low in nitrogen and organic matter – provide good agricultural land, as do the black soils of the western Deccan. The red soils, light in texture and easily drained, are not so suitable for farming.

much of the natural vegetation to little more than thorn scrub. In areas of low rainfall, for example in the Aravalli Range, drought-resistant shrubs such as gum arabic, acacia, khejri and tamarisk are found. Savannah grasslands interspersed with palmyra palm predominate in inland areas of the south. All around the coast, palm trees, especially the coconut palm with its multifarious products and uses, are common. The Ganges delta has one of the world's largest mangrove forests, the Sundarbans, covering an area of 10,000 square kilometers.

The great Himalayan mountain ranges contain a variety of forest trees. From the eastern margins through to Bhutan and Nepal, woods of chestnut and oak grow at heights of between 1,000 and 2,000 meters, giving way to subtropical pines toward the west. Higher up, temperate pines, cedars, firs, spruces and deodars give way in turn to alpine forests of rhododendron (particularly dominant in Nepal above 2,500 meters) birch and juniper, while poplars grow from Kashmir to Bhutan, larches from Bhutan to Nepal. In the far eastern Himalayas are forests of bamboo, and bamboo and other grasses cover the foothills of the mountains and are to be found along the northern ranges of the peninsula. Eastern Bangladesh contains more than 150,000 square kilometers of semi-evergreen forest and bamboo jungle.

Agriculture and soils

The Indian subcontinent supports a predominantly agricultural way of life. As many as 93 percent of the workforce are employed in farming in Nepal and Bhutan, 75 percent in Bangladesh, 70 percent in India, 55 percent in Pakistan and 53 percent in Sri Lanka. Most are peasant cultivators of small plots of land. In the Indian Punjab, for example, an average holding is about 4 hectares, divided into four or five plots; in Bangladesh, it may be as small as 1 hectare, divided

resistant to burning, and both tend to occur in relatively large stands, which makes them suitable for cultivation in managed forests. Teak is traditionally used in shipbuilding and, being termite resistant, in the construction of buildings and furniture.

On the wetter margins of the subcontinent – in the hills south of Bombay, at heights of between 500 m and 1,400 m, and in Assam at lower altitudes – a rich diversity of tropical evergreen rainforest survives, but where the rainfall becomes lighter, or the dry season lengthens, degraded forest becomes more typical. In many places, overgrazing by livestock has reduced

Right The vast majority of farmers in the subcontinent are cultivators of small plots of land who rely on their traditional knowledge of local soil and climatic conditions. Farmers in Ladakh, which lies high in the Himalayas of Kashmir and receives little rainfall, could not raise crops without irrigation. Water from the spring snowmelt is captured and stored, to be fed through channels to the growing crops in the fields.

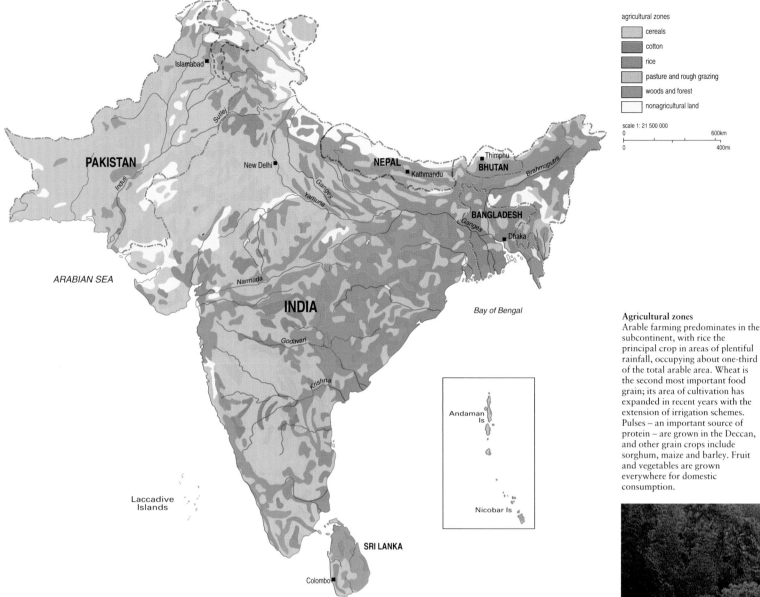

agricultural zones

- cereals
- cotton
- rice
- pasture and rough grazing
- woods and forest
- nonagricultural land

scale 1: 21 500 000

Agricultural zones
Arable farming predominates in the subcontinent, with rice the principal crop in areas of plentiful rainfall, occupying about one-third of the total arable area. Wheat is the second most important food grain; its area of cultivation has expanded in recent years with the extension of irrigation schemes. Pulses – an important source of protein – are grown in the Deccan, and other grain crops include sorghum, maize and barley. Fruit and vegetables are grown everywhere for domestic consumption.

into as many as 12 or 15 plots. The land is farmed using mainly traditional methods and relying on a knowledge of local environmental conditions, including soils and climate, which has been passed down over the generations.

A wide combination of factors affects the nature of the soil, and determines its suitability for cultivation – the type of parent rock of which it is made up, the drainage and lie of the land, animals and vegetation (which add nutrients and organic matter) and climate. Soils may vary enormously from village to village, and even within villages. Consequently, the cultivator's knowledge of which soils will grow the highest yielding crops and which require irrigation and other forms of management is of major importance in ensuring farming success.

Red soils, formed from the basement Archaeon rocks, are the largest category of soil in the Indian peninsula. They are generally sandy and easy to work, but do not retain moisture well. In some places, for example in Sri Lanka, such soils are subject to the leaching that is typical of tropical rainforest areas, whereby minerals and nutrients are washed out by rainwater, leaving the soils sterile. In the northwest Deccan are black soils – the regur or cottonsoils, so-called because cotton is grown here – formed of volcanic lavas. These retain water well and are potentially rich, but they become heavy and clayey, making them difficult to work and to irrigate: in the dry season they have a tendency to crack badly.

The alluvial deposits of the densely populated Indo-Gangetic plains and the coastal deltas have provided the basis for settled agriculture throughout historic times. However, they vary greatly in quality and pose cultivators with a series of complex problems of management. In and close to the deltas, the soils are renewed annually with the deposit of new silt by floodwater. In Bangladesh the coarser silts left at higher levels are ideal for the cultivation of jute. Older deposits, however, become less fertile and areas beyond the reach of the floods may be poor in organic materials, and therefore lack nutrients. Elsewhere in the Gangetic plain, large-scale irrigation has led to waterlogging and salinization of soils. This is still more of a problem in the arid lower Indus valley where the river deposits are coarse and sandy, and evaporation gives rise to large expanses of salt.

Water management

Over thousands of years, the farmers of the subcontinent have had to find ways of managing the resources of land and climate in order to realize to the full their potential for agriculture. Rice is the most important foodcrop of the subcontinent. It takes 6 months to ripen and year-round warmth means that, potentially, two crops can be grown a year. However, a minimum of 1,000 mm of rainfall is required for cultivation: the seedlings are planted in the rainy season (*kharif*), and grown in flooded paddyfields, standing in depths of 50 to 100 mm of water. Loss of surface water through evaporation is at its greatest at the time the rice is growing. This is also the period of heaviest rainfall, and much water is also lost in runoff from the saturated soil. Without methods of storing water, and of deploying its use through systematic irrigation, only one crop a year can be grown in most places.

On the whole, the higher the rainfall (say, above 2,000 mm a year) the better the chances of securing a good harvest – though, in such regions, there is always risk from flooding. The lower the rainfall, the more precarious agriculture becomes. Once rainfall is below around 350 mm, water resources must be managed, and it becomes impossible to grow crops without some form of irrigation. Over the centuries, different methods have been developed to exploit local environmental conditions. In hilly parts of Rajasthan, for example, a form of water-harvesting is traditionally employed that depends on the building of dam-like structures (*johads*). These are constructed along the contour lines of a watershed to trap the monsoon rains before they run off the surface of the land, causing soil erosion. The water then soaks into the ground to raise the water table and replenish the wells.

The pattern of farming

The lower Gangetic plain, which receives reliable supplies of monsoon rain, and the rainy coastal plains of the peninsula are the most important rice-growing areas. Rice is also cultivated in the interior Deccan, wherever irrigation tanks have been constructed, and in the fertile, irrigated valleys of the west and central Himalayas; hardier crops such as maize and barley as well as fruit – almonds, apricots and apples – are grown on higher slopes. Wheat is the most important cereal crop of the drier upper Ganges and of the Indus valley; it is heavily dependent on irrigation, provided through an extensive network of canals. However, some 22 percent of Pakistan's irrigated land is now unusable as a result of waterlogging and salinization. Since the 1960s, new high-yielding rice varieties have been introduced to these areas.

Pulses – mainly gram (chickpeas) and lentils – millet and cotton are grown in arid parts of the south. The warm, wet slopes of Sri Lanka are ideal for the cultivation of plantation crops such as tea, rubber and coconuts: pepper and other spices are also grown for export. India is a major producer of tea, pepper, groundnuts, sugar cane, cotton and jute for export. Jute – a source of fiber for sacks and ropes – is Bangladesh's single most important commercial crop, grown on tiny plots by small peasant producers.

The cow, a holy and protected animal, is essential to the agriculture of the subcontinent, and India has the largest population of cattle in the world: they provide draft power for plowing, haulage, threshing crops and raising water from wells. Dried cattle dung is used as a fuel for cooking and, mixed with mud, as a building material. Buffaloes, goats and sheep are also widespread. The scarcity of fodder increases pressure on pastureland: in arid and semi-arid areas overgrazing leads to desertification – the reduction of productive land to a sandy or dusty waste.

Below Rice is a vital source of food throughout the Indian subcontinent. It occupies about one-third of all the land under grain, but can only be grown in areas of high rainfall, as the seedlings need to be planted in standing water of at least 50 mm. In the Gangetic plain the flat land is easily prepared for planting, but in the Western Ghats of the southern peninsula farmers have had to carve the steep hillsides into an intricate pattern of terraced paddyfields that add great beauty to the landscape.

PEOPLE, RELIGION, SOCIETY

Counting heads

There is a wealth of statistical and demographical information about India and its peoples that goes back more than a century. The government of India conducted its first major census in 1872. A second was held in 1881, and thereafter it became a decennial event throughout the period of British rule. Independent India has maintained the sequence, the most recent count of its citizens taking place in 1991. Pakistan, Bangladesh and Sri Lanka also conduct regular full-scale counts. Every one of these censuses has taken the form of a major sociological enquiry – at different times, the people of the subcontinent have been classified by caste, religion, language or occupation, assessed according to their levels of literacy, divided into town- and country-dwellers, or listed to show their ability to pay different sorts of tax.

In such huge and populous countries it requires a tremendous administrative effort to collect even these simple facts. Shri Pedatala Padmanabha, the Registrar-General and Census Commissioner responsible for the 1981 Indian census, has described the way the task was carried out: "In 1980 our enumerators went round and listed every residence in the country.... It was a complicated undertaking, because many houses had no numbers. In such instances, we painted numbers on their doors. That was an operation almost as vast as our actual nose count, which began on February 9th ... and ended on March 5th. Sunrise on March 1st was our reference point. We counted everybody, I hope, between February 9th and February 28th, and then we went back over the same ground between March 1st and March 5th to check on new births and deaths. That was true for all of the country except the

northern state of Jammu and Kashmir – which we covered last fall, before much of the area became snowbound – and the state of Assam, which is in demographic chaos because of the influx of immigrants from Bangladesh....Our field strength - enumerators and supervisors – came to 1 million 350,000 people, nearly all of them government employees, and ninety-five percent of them schoolteachers." A particular problem, tackled afresh in 1981, was the attempt to count the city sidewalk-dwellers. Padmanabha explained: "We had enumerators in all the railway and bus stations, counting the people who were sleeping there. We persuaded the motion-picture theatres to shut down early, so as to get people in there to leave and go wherever they usually bedded down." This latter category was estimated to come to between 2.5 and 3 million people.

Once the raw statistics of the census have been collected, they are processed, summarized and published in reports. Given the huge numbers involved and the many practical difficulties that the enumerators have to face in the field, it is not surprising that errors and inaccuracies are introduced. It is not always possible to compare like with like when looking at the information from different years. Between 1951 and 1961, for example, the urban population of India appeared to fall by 4.4 million as a result of changes made in the way towns were classified. Time and again the census operation has been subjected to political pressure, and this has had significant effect upon the figures. In 1931, for example, the civil disobedience campaign run by the nationalist leaders undoubtedly resulted in some deliberate understatement of numbers in households. A decade later the census was taken at a time

Left About one-seventh of the Indian population belong to social groups previously held to be untouchable by brahminic religion. These include people whose employment was considered ritually polluting – sweepers and cleaners, those tending the dead or coming into contact with blood, leather-workers and certain other craft occupations – as well as some ethnic or racial groups. The earliest Vedic texts do not mention untouchability, and both the concept and its social realization appear to have been developed and refined during the two millennia before 1,000 AD. Protests against untouchability have been vigorous since the time of the Buddha and are a recurring theme throughout Indian history. The constitution of the Republic of India made the concept of untouchability illegal and put laws and policies in place to end discrimination against untouchables (also known as Harijans or Dalits). Such measures have done much to improve the social and economic lot of some of the poorest people in Indian society, but have also met with opposition, especially from those whose livelihoods are threatened by the use of quota systems that reserve a percentage of government and public-sector jobs for untouchables and lower castes. Often this has spilled over into violence.

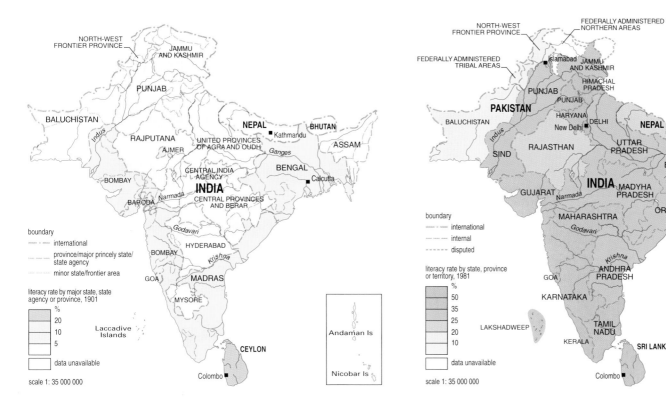

Levels of literacy

The wealth of statistics gathered since the first census in 1872 makes it possible to study information about India's population over a period of time. With regard to levels of literacy, for example, it is clear that Sri Lanka had reached a position of eminence in the subcontinent by the early 20th century, which it still retains today; Kerala's leading position in India was also apparent in 1901, and was explained by the fact that the ruler of Travancore had been a supporter of primary school education as early as the 1860s. Levels were high in the coastal presidencies – Bengal, Madras and Bombay – too, giving the literate classes from those regions a pre-eminence in certain professions (especially government service) across the whole subcontinent. By 1981 – though levels of literacy remain generally low – considerable improvement had been made everywhere, but regional differences were still very marked. Most notable was the addition of provinces in northwest India to the list of the more literate regions. Moreover, even within regions there are great disparities between town and village, and parts of rural Bihar count among the most backward areas in the subcontinent.

when feelings between Hindus and Muslims were running high, so that each community sought to exaggerate its size.

Despite such problems of interpretation, what emerges with stark clarity from the census reports is the magnitude of the subcontinent's population and its very rapid rate of growth in the 20th century. In 1900, there were just about 300 million people living there. By the early 1990s the number had risen to over 1,000 million. Though some parts of the subcontinent have been relatively densely populated throughout historic times, the really dramatic increase in population is a modern phenomenon and, indeed, dates back only as far as the 1920s.

Many reasons have been put forward for this sudden growth. There have been fewer massive natural disasters in the shape of flood, drought and epidemic than in the previous half-century. Much new land has been opened up for settlement. But undoubtedly the most important factor has been a pronounced drop in the death-rate, accompanied by little or no decline in the average rates of birth. In 1921, the average life expectancy of an Indian male on birth was 20 years; by 1941 this had risen to 32 years, by 1961 to 46 years and by 1991 to 59 years. The decline in the death-rate in all parts of the subcontinent can be attributed in part to improved public health measures implemented since the 1920s, including mass inoculation against small pox and the increasing application of preventive and curative medicine, such as DDT, which has eradicated the malaria-carrying anopheles mosquito in many places, and the use of antibiotics.

The widening gap between birth and death rates is reflected in the extreme youthfulness of the subcontinent's populations: in all countries more than 50 percent are aged less than 20 years. Birth rates are thus set to climb still higher: if present trends continue it has been reckoned that the population of Bangladesh (122 million in 1992) will have reached between 140 and 175 million by the end of the century. The Indian government's commitment to a vigorous program of

birth-control and planned parenthood has done little to halt the rise. Between 1981 and 1991 the population grew from over 688 million to 834 million.

An uneven distribution of people

The subcontinent contains some of the least as well as some of the most populated regions in the world. Baluchistan, for example, has large tracts that hold less than 5 people to the square kilometer, while a similar area of fertile farmland may support more than 580 people and in cities such as Calcutta densities can be more than 27,000 people per square kilometer. Such figures, however, are meaningless unless related to the capacity of the land to support life at a reasonable level. Mountains and desert regions are inimical to human settlement, while fertile alluvial plains are capable of sustaining large populations. With the development of towns and of urban economies the ability of a region to maintain human activity is significantly increased.

From earliest times, the peoples of the subcontinent have lived in greatest number on the rich alluvial soils of the Indo-Gangetic plain. Today, approximately half of the total population is found there, with the highest densities in those areas of regular, reliable rainfall, extending from eastern Uttar Pradesh through Bihar into rural West Bengal. The Brahmaputra valley in Assam and, in the south, the coastal plain of Kerala also support large rural populations. Paradoxically, these naturally fertile and populated regions are also areas of great rural poverty and underemployment. They are particularly vulnerable to the occasional failure of the monsoon, there is little urbanization, and there are few, if any, alternative resources to fall back on in time of scarcity.

Population is also high in areas where permanent irrigation has freed agriculture from the vagaries of the climate and where there are the resources to support some industrial development – for example in western Uttar Pradesh, Haryana and Punjab; in the east down the coast of Andhra Pradesh and inland

Indo-European
- Indic
- Iranic
- Dardic

- Dravidian

Austroasiatic
- Munda
- Mon-Khmer

Sino-Tibetan
- Tibeto-Burman
- Tai

- unclassified
- uninhabited

TAMIL major language
(BRAJ) Hindi subdivision

scale 1: 21 500 000
0   600km
0   400mi

Distribution of languages
Given the sheer number and
diversity of people in the
subcontinent, it is no surprise that
it is a place of many languages.
Those of the Indo-European family
are dominant in terms of the
numbers speaking them, their
historical influence and their
geographical spread: they include
both Sanskrit- and Iranian-derived
languages, as well as the Dardic
group of the upper Indus valley.
The Dravidian languages of
peninsular India and northern Sri
Lanka form the second largest
group. Their much wider
distribution at an earlier time is
indicated by the survival of related
languages in central India and by
Brahui in Pakistan. The states of
the south have consistently resisted
attempts to promote Hindi as a
national language.

across Tamil Nadu; and in the west extending inland
from Bombay to Pune and northward to the plains of
Gujarat. But in some hilly areas of central India and in
a swathe of rocky land, desert and saltflat running
westward from the northwest Deccan into Rajasthan
and Kutch soils are too poor to support crop farming,
even with irrigation. Inaccessible areas of the
Himalayas, the wet, forested districts of the northeastern frontier states, and the arid northwest are also
all very sparsely populated. (Nevertheless, Rajasthan
supports nearly 60 times the population of the desert
state of Nevada in the United States where the physical conditions are very similar.) Within all of these
broad regions there are, of course, local variations –
the desert has its oasis cities, the mountains their pockets of fertile valley floor, and in the rich plains good
land lies cheek by jowl with stony or waterlogged
soils.

Human pressures on the environment
It is in the less densely settled areas that rates of population growth have been highest in recent years. The
lowest rates have been in the fertile agricultural plains
that were already densely populated by the early 20th
century. The implications of this are inescapable –
much of the best land in the subcontinent has for long
supported what must be reckoned to be its maximum
sustainable human load, and the brunt of the population increase has had to be borne on areas of marginal
land made more productive by high investment in irrigation and modern agricultural techniques, and by the
development of industrial towns. There are limits,
however, to the amount of new land that can prof-
itably be brought into production: a very high proportion of the subcontinent's cultivable land has
already been claimed for use. Agricultural production
can only be increased by improving the control and
use of water and fertilizers on existing land and by
developing higher-yielding, pest-resistant varieties of
food plants, better husbandry and better management
of the land. To be successful, this requires very considerable investment in agriculture, as well as the diffusion of new knowledge and new resources among
cultivators and easier access to capital and markets.
Without proper management and knowledge, uncon-
trolled agricultural development presents enormous
dangers to the subcontinent's fragile ecologies and
puts at risk its very ability to sustain human life.

Even in areas where the total population is very
small, the human relationship with the environment is
delicately poised. In many of the more marginal pastoral or herding areas, or in settlements in the hills, it

takes a very small increase in the human population, or a change in the use of natural resources, to upset the local ecology and to wreak havoc on human society. Population pressure on land in the foothill areas of the Himalayas, for example, has led over the past 50 years to extensive deforestation to provide fuelwood and free land for farming. Cleared of trees, hill slopes are easily eroded. This has important consequences not only for the local economies, but affects the areas where soil washed down from the hills is deposited, the densely populated plains, where siltation of the river channels increases the risk of large-scale flooding during heavy rainfall.

The importance of religion and worship

The peoples of India experience great uncertainty in everyday life and feel the capriciousness of the universe. In their religion they show respect for vast unseen forces and adopt strategies to try to come to terms with them. The vast majority of the population of the subcontinent are followers of Hinduism. Its great strength is that its theologies, philosophies, and modes of worship make some sense of the world and its impossible uncertainties, and it provides a justification for a moral social order that is not too far out of line with contemporary social realities.

Hinduism is so complex, and the forms it assumes are so variable, that it is impossible to give it a precise definition. The product of many centuries of growth and compromise, Hinduism, like other faiths, is a composite religion made up of many different and sometimes conflicting elements. It has, over the centuries, been responsive to current social needs, and social and political forces have in turn helped to fashion religious belief. Hinduism does not distinguish at all sharply between this world and the next, between the earth and the heavens, or between the human and the divine. Though the gods are immortal, they sometimes behave as if they were ordinary men and women, while in some contexts ordinary men and women become like the gods. At worship, the Hindu seeks to glimpse divinity and become part of it; at wedding ceremonies the bride and groom are worshiped by their family and friends as divine beings.

According to one ancient sage, Hinduism is a religion of some 330 million gods, some of whom are greater than others. They reach from the great gods like Brahma, the original creator, or Shiva and Vishnu who came to prominence within Hinduism 2,000 years ago, to minor gods and lesser spirits who may inhabit a single place. These latter are incorporated into the grander scheme of things by being seen as a manifestation of a greater god, or they may become part of the divine order, as dozens of local female deities are, by marriage to a great god. Moreover, the pantheon keeps growing as new manifestations of the divine are recognized and worshiped. Sometimes these may be actual historical figures – there are accounts even of British officers being included – or they may represent new abstract ideas – in one of the most recent temples at Varanasi the nationalist concept of Mother India (Bharat Mata) is worshiped in the form of a map of the subcontinent – or they may be new incarnations of the living god, as in the case of the recently popular cult of the Hindu goddess Santoshi Ma, a figure unknown thirty years ago. The literature of India, classical and vernacular, ancient and modern, is filled with stories of the gods, their relationships with each other and with the temporal world. They

fight and make love, they compete and co-operate, they express the noblest ideals of the ascetic, they exhibit the finest of morals and the highest of characters, and they can behave as the most licentious of libertines.

Yet in Hinduism the gods are but different aspects of a single supreme being. They have many forms and numerous names. Shiva, for example, is known as Nataraja (Lord of the Dance) and Mahakala (Great Black One); at Varanasi he becomes Vishwanath (Lord of All), at Madurai he is Sundareshwara (Beautiful Lord), and throughout India he is recognized by dozens of other names besides. But just as one deity can become many, so a multitude of deities can become one, and Hindu polytheism can be seen as a species of monotheism too.

The gods are worshiped and offered sacrifices because they are not separate from the world but are powerful within it, capable of determining the day-to-day fortunes of mankind. While many gods are generally beneficent, a number are not, and even the best may be angered by neglect. A proverb from Kathiawar advises "Pay reverence once to a benign god, for he may do you good, but twice to a malign power in order that he may do you no harm", and an old brahmin pandit recorded that in his daily worship he first made an offering to Vishnu, his own chosen deity, and then scattered a handful of rice for the other deities for "it was his hope that by thus recognizing the existence and authority of these, though there were no clear notions in his mind concerning any of them, he would keep them in good humor towards himself."

The gods may be found anywhere and in any form throughout creation. A 19th-century Sanskrit scholar put it thus: "Rocks, stocks, and stones, trees, pools, and rivers, his own implements of trade, the animals he finds most useful, the noxious reptiles he fears, men remarkable for any extraordinary qualities – for great valor, sanctity, virtue or even vice – good and evil demons, ghosts and goblins, the spirits of departed ancestors, an infinite number of semi-human, semi-divine existences . . . each and all of these come in for a share of divine honor or a tribute of more or less adoration." The gods may be worshiped simply by repeating their names, or a particular god might be enshrined in some way – as an image, or in plants or a pile of wayside stones. A river-worn ammonite stone with spiral markings might be thought to resemble the discus of Vishnu and be offered prayers and oblations; Shiva is most commonly worshiped as a phallic pillar – a lingam, symbolizing energy and potential, and the mystery of generation – as well as in human form. But it would be wrong to interpret this as simple idolatry. The French traveller, François Bernier, visiting Varanasi in 1665, was told by some learned pandits there, "We have indeed a great variety of images. To all we pay great honor, prostrating our bodies and presenting to them, with much ceremony, flowers, rice, scented oil, saffron, and other similar articles. Yet we do not believe that these statues are themselves Brahma or Vishnu, but merely their images and representations. We show them deference only for the sake of the deity whom they represent, and when we pray, it is not to the statue, but to the deity. Images are admitted in our temples because we conceive that prayers are offered up with more devotion when there is something before the eyes that fixes the mind; but, in fact, we acknowledge that God alone is absolute, that He only is the omnipotent Lord."

Below While most of India's people continue to live in the countryside, towns and cities provide rapidly increasing opportunities for employment, often complementing rural incomes rather than replacing them altogether. Much of this employment is casual and short-term or seasonal in nature, with people returning to their villages at sowing or harvest time. Housing is at a premium, and the low-paid are driven to find shelter in shanty-towns on the edges of urban areas. Events such as religious festivals and cattle fairs may also draw large numbers of people to a particular town, making it difficult for them to find accommodation. This overspill tented city is on the outskirts of Udaipur in Rajasthan.

Shiva

The Hindu god Shiva is surely one of the most powerful and ambivalent figures to be found in any of the major mythologies of the world. His character is massively complex and self-contradictory, and the newcomer to Hinduism does best to face this fact head-on. It has been well observed that Shiva "embodies *all* of life, in *all* of its detail, at every minute". Nothing is alien to Shiva; as a consequence, whatever Shiva is, he is also its opposite.

One of the most striking paradoxes is that Shiva is at one and the same time both highly erotic and highly ascetic. He is notorious for his sexual avidity, exercised not merely with his wife Parvati but also with numerous other women; as a result of one such episode he was cursed to be worshiped in the form of a *linga*, a phallic emblem (illustrated on facing page, *far right*). And yet the same Shiva is celebrated as the chaste lord of ascetics, who sits deep in meditation on Mount Kailas, his hair matted and his body smeared with ashes.

There are other stark contradictions in his character. He is the god who saved the world by drinking the deadly poison that threatened to consume it, and he is the god who dances it to destruction. He is an entrancingly handsome young man, and he is a snake-covered habitué of the burning ground. He is a drunken reveler, leader of troops of goblins, and he is the supreme lord of the universe.

Unlike Vishnu, who regularly intervenes in human affairs, Shiva is thought of as remote and aloof, not to say alarming. But he is also a family man, father of Skanda the war-god and the elephant-headed Ganesha, lord of favorable beginnings.

Right This 11th-century South Indian bronze shows the god Shiva standing in a relaxed posture, leaning against his bull Nandi (the image of which has been lost). Shiva wears nothing but a loincloth, a few ornaments and, running across his body from the left shoulder, the sacred thread of the high-born. The matted hair of the lord of ascetics has been reworked to suit the image's mood of grace and authority by being coiled round his head like an elegant turban.

Left This man's high caste is indicated by his sacred thread, his position as a *sadhu* (holy man) by his unkempt hair and beard. The three horizontal lines marked on his forehead, shoulders, arms and chest show that he is a devotee of Shiva, as does the rosary of *rudraksha* berries around his neck.

Left When depicted in anthropomorphic form, Nandi is Shiva's chief attendant, who acts as his door-keeper and heads his goblin-troops. More often, however, he is shown as a white bull, the "vehicle" (*vahana*) of the god. In temples to Shiva, an image of Nandi is stationed just outside the inner chamber housing the icon or phallic *linga* of the deity; the bull gazes in at his master with adoration.

Below left Shiva as *nataraja* (king of dancers) is probably the best-known form of the god's image. Hair wildly disheveled, he is depicted in the midst of a circle of flames as he dances the *tandava* dance that brings the world to the end of a cycle of existence, whilst trampling underfoot the demon of ignorance.

Below Vishnu and Brahma were once arguing as to which of them was greatest of the gods when a huge flaming *linga* (phallic emblem of Shiva) appeared. Vishnu tried to find its bottom, Brahma its top, but both failed, and they were forced to acknowledge the supremacy of Shiva, shown here in majesty between his unsuccessful rivals.

41

Vishnu

Vishnu was already worshiped as early as the time of the Rig Veda (around 1000 BC). In the hymns of that text he appears as a minor solar deity, and is associated almost exclusively with the movement of the sun: he is the wide-striding god whose three steps correspond to the three worlds (earth, air and heaven). Later his solar connection waned, and from the latter part of the first millennium BC he came to be regarded above all as the great god who repeatedly takes incarnate form to resolve earthly crises. (In one such incarnation the old story of his wide strides was given new and specific form in his incarnation as a dwarf who rescued the earth from the domination of the demonic king Bali: he begged from Bali as much land as he could cover in three strides, then resumed his normal colossal size.)

Two of Vishnu's incarnations far outstrip all the others in popularity amongst his devotees. These are Rama and Krishna, whose stories first came to be told in the Sanskrit epics *Ramayana* and *Mahabharata*. Rama is revered as the virtuous god-king of Ayodhya who became incarnate to overthrow the wicked demon Ravana. With his wife Sita and faithful brother Lakshmana he was banished to the forest, where he fought successfully against Ravana with the aid of the monkey-god Hanuman and his forces. Krishna's career was more complex: as soon as he was born he was handed over to a cowherd family to conceal him from the wicked king Kamsa, who had vowed to kill him. He grew up as a cowherd boy, but later became a divine king, and played a great part in the war between the Pandavas and the Kauravas described in the *Mahabharata*. His devotees worship Krishna in several forms: as a "difficult" toddler, as a handsome teenage lover, and as the supreme lord of all.

When Vishnu is conceived of in his own form, the bird-god Garuda acts as his "vehicle" and his wife Lakshmi (also known as Shri), the goddess of good fortune, often accompanies him. His other consort is Bhu, the goddess Earth, whom Vishnu rescued from the sea in his incarnation as a boar.

The incarnations of Vishnu

According to ancient Hindu texts, Vishnu became incarnate on ten occasions. His incarnations (*avataras*) took the following forms:
1 Matsya (fish)
2 Kurma (turtle)
3 Varaha (boar)
4 Narasimha (man-lion)
5 Vamana (dwarf)
6 Parashurama (Rama-with-ax)
7 Rama
8 Krishna
9 Buddha
10 Kalkin (future incarnation on a white horse. He will bring the present age of the world to an end).

Below The serpent demon Kaliya lived in the river near where Krishna grew up: his venom had polluted not only the water but the land nearby and the air overhead. The boy Krishna entered the river and fought Kaliya, trampling him underfoot; then he released the half-dead demon, who became Krishna's devotee.

Left Every Hindu god must have a "vehicle" (*vahana*) to travel on: Ganesha has a rat, the great Goddess a tiger, and so forth. Vishnu's "vehicle" is the bird-god Garuda, the divine eagle who takes him where he wishes to go. Garuda's form is winged, but he is depicted as part-bird, part-man.

Right Rama and his wife Sita are worshiped as the respective embodiments of male and female virtue. Rama's calm acceptance of banishment by his father is held to be exemplary, as is Sita's wifely devotion. In art, Rama is often identified by the great bow that he broke in order to win Sita's hand.

Below A *sadhu* is a holy man, one who has given up all worldly ties in the quest for liberation from the cycle of rebirth. Wearing ocher robes and with matted, uncut hair, *sadhus* may adhere to any of Hinduism's cults: the shape of the mark on this *sadhu*'s forehead reveals him to be a devotee of Vishnu.

Below Vishnu's third incarnation was in the form of a boar. The demon Hiranyaksha had thrown the earth into the sea; Vishnu fought and defeated him, and raised the earth up, supporting it on his tusks.

Right In this South Indian bronze, Vishnu is shown as having four arms, as is usually the case in images depicting him in his own form rather than as one of his incarnations. The god's two upper arms hold a discus and a conch-shell, two of the emblems associated with him, and with his lower right hand he is making the characteristic *abhaya* gesture, with which he grants security to his worshipers.

Puja (worship of Hindu gods and goddesses) takes a number of different forms – it may be through the performance of rituals and the making of sacrifices, through a quest for knowledge and a concentration of mind and spirit in finding god (often achieved by reciting the sacred Vedic scriptures), or through devotion and love expressed in adoration, pilgrimage and festival. These modes of religious behavior are not necessarily mutually exclusive, though some people may prefer one way rather than another. What they all have in common is the determination to find the deity and to catch a glimpse of the divine. So the performance of religious duty is highly personal, and though it may gain special merit by being performed in a particular way or in a particular holy place, it can just as well be done in the home or in the fields.

Even worship in a major temple is not a congregational matter: the temple is a sanctuary of a god or goddess and divine service consists not of common prayer but of ceremonies performed by priests ministering to the deity. The ordinary worshiper comes to see the god when he is ready to give audience. The following description of the daily round of ceremonies at the temple of Jagannath at Puri, in Orissa, may serve as an example: "It begins with a hymn warning the gods [Jagannath, his brother, and his sister] to leave their couches as the sun is about to rise, and is followed by setting some camphor on fire and waving blazing torches. The gods are then presented with cakes made of rice, flour and water, and a gong is beaten. After this they are supposed to bathe and dress. Bathing is done by proxy, i.e. attendants sit in front of some brass plates, in which the images are reflected, and pretend to clean their teeth and rinse their mouths, and water is poured into brass tubs. The images are dressed and then the gods give audience, i.e. the public are admitted and allowed to see the images and present offerings. Early breakfast follows, i.e. fried rice covered with sugar and clarified butter is put in the front of the images. At about 10 a.m. the breakfast proper, which consists of such things as rice, vegetables and cakes, is served, and, when this has been done, betel-nut is presented for chewing and the clothes on the image are changed (as is also done after other meals). After a midday meal cots are brought and placed before them, so that they may have an imaginary siesta. They enjoy an evening meal at between 8 p.m. and 9 p.m., and an hour or two later are anointed. At midnight they are garlanded from head to foot with wreaths of flowers, and sweet-smelling flowers are put to their noses to smell. Finally they are given a light repast, with music and hymns, and are put to bed, couches being brought and placed before the throne."

The maintenance of a large temple-complex is expensive and besides the offerings of visitors, requires the protection of a patron or king who will assign to it land and revenues for upkeep. To build a temple is said to free from the endless round of reincarnation eight generations of ancestors. Some places in India are endowed with particular sanctity, and they became cities of temples or centers of pilgrimage and festival. Those fortunate enough to die at Varanasi, or to have the appropriate funeral rites

Above From the very earliest times, Hinduism has contained an ascetic tradition of religious renunciation and social withdrawal. In some regards, the ascetic who eschews the world, thus reminding others that the principal objective of life is to escape from all future lives, sits at the top of the religious hierarchy. Ascetic practices and mortification of the flesh also bring about heightened religious consciousness. This miniature painting shows a yogi at his ashram first meditating and then prostrating himself before an appearance of Vishnu, who is seen in the upper left of the picture flying about on his mount, the bird-god Garuda. It dates from around 1800 and comes from Rajasthan, most probably from Jaipur.

performed at Gaya, for example, go straight to heaven, but it is only in relatively modern times, with the improvement and cheapening of transport, that these cities have become places of mass religious activity. Besides, everywhere in India is special – hills, land and water.

Theologies without dogma

Hinduism is a source of many sophisticated theologies and philosophies. Its religious texts and commentaries, written in both the classical and vernacular languages, explore the meanings of the universe and the nature of creation in as deep, as elaborate, and as critical way as those of any other major religion. But Hinduism lacks definite dogmas, and does not have a central controlling authority. In a sense, then, nonconformity can scarcely be said to exist. New ideas, new sects and cults, new social elements are constantly being brought under the Hindu umbrella. This does not mean that there are no disputes, nor is Hinduism without occasional sectarian violence, but what is orthodox is fluid and generously construed. Hence

there is a capacity to retain reform movements within the system, broadly defined. It is a mistake to see Hinduism as progressing from one state to another, from primitive forms of belief to more complex and cultivated ones, or making permanent shifts from, say, worship by sacrifice through mysticism and devotion.

While unmatched in its capacity for speculation about the universe, Hinduism is also concerned with the temporal order. Two powerful themes, in some degree of tension with each other, have persisted throughout the course of its history. One is the belief in fate and the transmigration of the soul. The soul survives the disintegration of any particular body and passes through a number of existences, said by some to number 8,400,000. These may vary in form across the whole range of creation – from rocks and stones to vegetable, animal and human existences. Moreover, a soul's state in any particular life is determined by actions (*karma*) in previous lives – there is a clear cause and effect. Goodness will lead to rebirth on a higher plane, wickedness will lead to demotion. All will try to achieve, in proper time, release from the burden of

Madurai

Below Though Madurai's great temple is formally dedicated to both Minakshi and Sundareshvara, this architectural detail depicts a Ratha Devi, a manifestation of the goddess, and reflects Minakshi's rather than her husband's, local pre-eminence. In Madurai, Minakshi enjoys ritual centrality in most temple festivals.

Right The Hindu temple is a "crossing-place" (*tirtha*) where divine and mundane realms intermingle and where deities are most accessible. Towered gateways known as *gopuras* symbolically control access to these potent locales. In the past only those of high social status could enter.

Far right The plan of the Minakshi-Sundareshvara temple reveals a series of boxes nestling one inside each other, at the center of which lies Minakshi's sanctuary.

The city of Madurai in Tamil Nadu is dominated architecturally by the massive temple dedicated to the goddess Minakshi and her consort Sundareshvara (Shiva), and the ritual life of the city is largely articulated by brahmin priests who minister to the thousands of residents and pilgrims who visit the temple every day. Madurai is regarded as one of India's great "holy places", the quintessence of the subcontinent's deep religiosity. In the past, however, Madurai was also an important seat of government, and this gave it a royal as well as a religious character. Not only were royal palaces important landmarks in the city (the 17th-century palace of Tirumala Nayaka is the most striking surviving example) but the Minakshi-Sundareshvara temple itself was built with royal patronage as well as priestly participation, and as an expression of dynastic greatness.

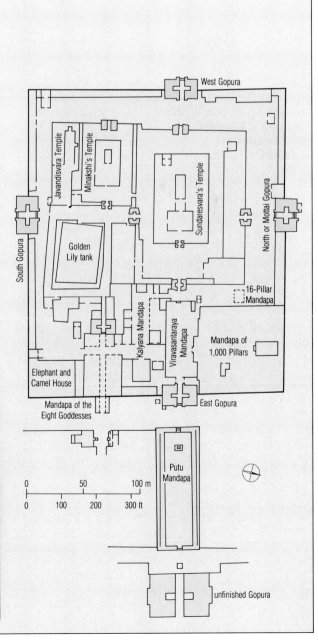

Sacred Architecture

Differences in religion and cult fail to obscure the underlying principles regulating the forms of sacred architecture in India. The temple is basically a house of god, a place where the deity inhabits a stone or metal icon placed inside a sanctuary. This image or emblem is not intended as a symbolic representation – rather, it is a visualization of an actual celestial presence. Elaborate rituals are required to persuade the divine force to inhabit the icon, and to "wake" the deity when worshipers are ready to make offerings and recite prayers.

By extension, the temple itself is identified with the god or goddess to whom it is dedicated. Its fabric, whether of stone, brick or wood, is a *prasada*, a seat or platform where the god or goddess is manifested. Devotees pay homage to the building by performing a clockwise circumambulation, or *pradakshina*. This rite takes architectural expression in an ambulatory passageway proceeding around the focal shrine. Otherwise, the exterior of the sacred building serves this purpose, being cloaked in images of celestial beings and mythological stories.

The forms of the temple affirm the connection with the heavens. The tower soaring above the sanctuary is a model of Meru, the mountain that supports the heavens. Clusters of pinnacles and finials imitate the silhouettes of celestial peaks. The sanctuary is conceived as a cave inside the cosmic mountain, and is invariably dark, massive and undecorated. Cave and mountain are linked by an axis that proceeds vertically from the image or emblem housed in the sanctuary to the auspicious finial capping the tower above.

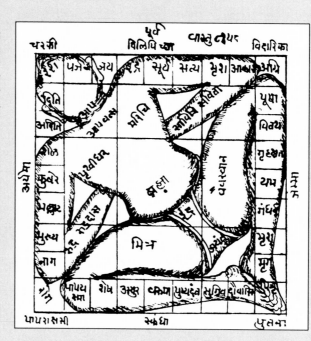

Above The image of cosmic man, known as *mahapurusha*, underlies the layouts of sacred buildings. He is identified with the universe, embodying all the known world on his outstretched body. This anthropomorphic vision of the cosmos is incorporated into the geometric diagrams that determine sacred buildings. The different parts of the *mahapurusha* are made to correspond to the forms of the temple by superimposing his body onto the temple diagram, which is known as a mandala (*right*). This is intended to replicate the mathematical structure of the universe, and also accommodates the planetary deities and the creator-god Brahma.

Right This watercolor rendition of the Ranganatha temple at Srirangam in Tamil Nadu comes from a 19th-century manuscript. It shows the main shrine in the middle housing Ranganatha, the reclining form of the god Vishnu, capped with a domed roof. The shrine is surrounded by seven enclosures, the inner four with colonnades and subshrines, the other three with houses. Gateways are positioned in the middle of each side. This arrangement of concentric rectangles provides a geometric model accommodating the residences of deities and devotees. Srirangam is only one of many sacred cities in south India that provide architectural settings for priests and ordinary people to live together in the presence of the gods. Perhaps more than in any other part of the country, Tamil Nadu witnessed the development of the temple-city into a major urban feature. Religious sites were greatly expanded in the 16th and 17th centuries when shrines came to be surrounded by streets, markets and houses laid out in accordance with the geometry of the focal shrine. Chariot festivals and other religious ceremonies regularly take place outside the walls of the religious monument, thereby confirming the ritual interaction between temple and town. There is, therefore, no essential spatial distinction between the world of the gods and that of man.

Above The importance of measurement in sacred buildings is indicated by this drawing of the architect holding a surveyor's road on a palm-leaf manuscript from Orissa in eastern India. Temple plans and elevations are regulated by a strict system of numbers that created a sacred geometry. Only if the temple is well measured can it serve as a suitable place for the gods on earth. Proportional systems regulating building forms employ a unit, known as the *tala*, which governs the extent and height of the temple, giving it an overall mathematical unity.

Below and right The shrine at Mamallapuram known as the Dharmaraja Ratha dates from the 7th century. Though unfinished, it demonstrates the successful application of geometry to sacred architecture. The plan (*below*) shows concentric squares containing a central octagon; the elevation (*right*) is based on a series of superimposed equilateral triangles that fix the capping cornices of each level. This geometric control confirms the mathematical basis of the universe, providing a means of linking architecture with the heavens.

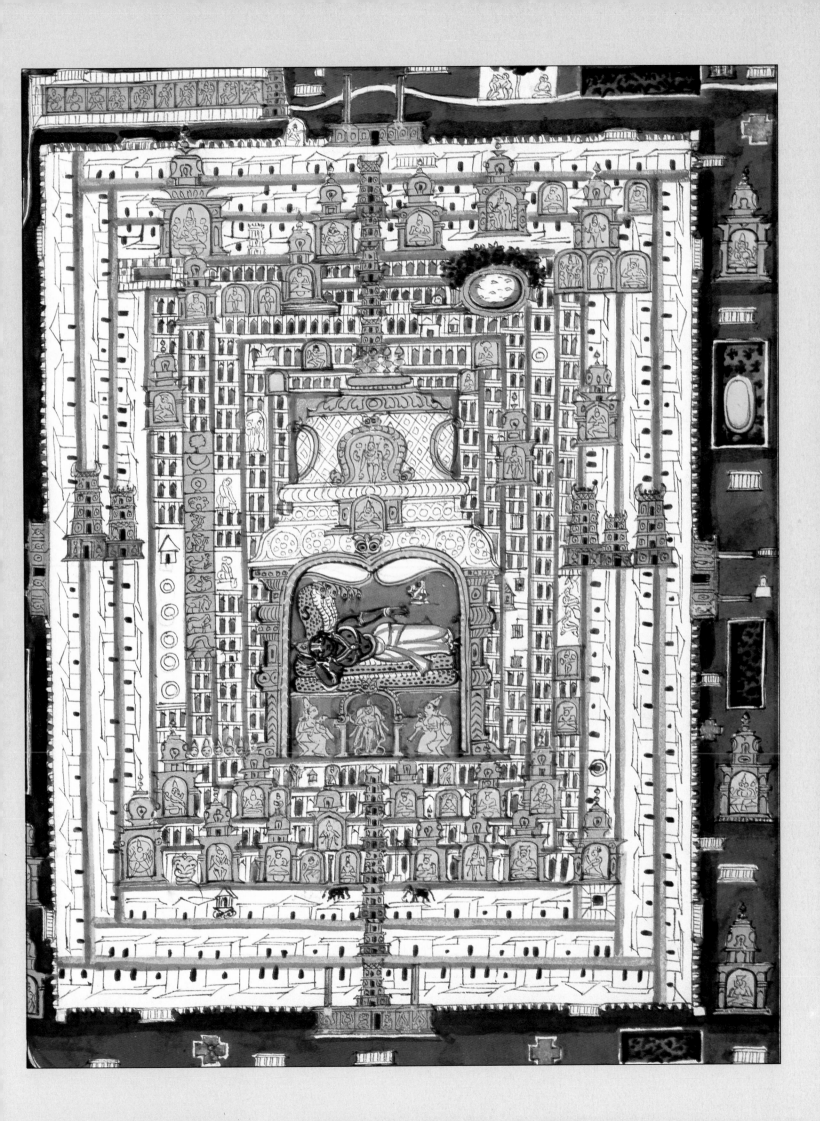

Festivals

Festivals play a very important part in Hindu religious practice. But, inevitably in so widespread and diverse a religion, there are many different types of festival. The commonest are annual celebrations, but there are also major festivals that follow a slower timetable – such as the massive Kumbh Mela, held four times every 12 years and rotating between Allahabad, Hardwar, Ujjain and Nasik. The Allahabad festival, the most important, is attended by literally millions of worshipers. In terms of geographical spread, the range is from festivals restricted to a single village temple, through others that are observed over a larger or smaller regional area, to those that have achieved more or less pan-Indian status.

The best-known annual festivals, those that are most widely celebrated, are relatively few in number and strikingly different from one another. Navaratri ("the nine nights") is celebrated throughout India in September or October to commemorate the great Goddess Durga's victory over the buffalo-demon Mahishasura; it culminates on the tenth day, which also marks Rama's victory over Ravana. The celebration usually concludes with the burning of an effigy of Ravana on a huge bonfire. Not long after Navaratri comes Divali, the festival of lights. Less formal and more domestic in character, Divali is characterized by the lighting of numerous small oil-lamps on a moonless night, as well as by feasting and fireworks held in honor of the goddess Lakshmi and in celebration of Rama's return from exile. The Holi spring festival, celebrated throughout northern and central India, is famous for its role-reversals, in which women and members of lower castes gain a brief revenge over their day-to-day masters.

Left In the city of Puri, Orissa, a major annual festival takes place during the Hindu month Ashadha (June/July), which draws massive crowds from many parts of the country. The celebrations culminate with the image of Krishna as *Jagannatha*, "Lord of the world", being placed in a huge mobile temple built on a cart and paraded through the city.

Below In the following month Shravana (July/August) there occurs a very widespread and important festival in honor of snakes, which in Hindu eyes are holy as well as dangerous. Snake-charmers show off their cobras (as here in Shirala, Maharashtra), and members of the public feed them delicacies in hopes of winning safety against snakebite.

Below right Spring festivals and nature fertility rituals have been part of Indian religious observance since earliest times. Here, in Madhya Pradesh, a special ceremony is held to mark the transplanting of the new corn crop.

Above Lakshmi (also known as Shri) is the consort of Vishnu. She is the goddess of good fortune and is worshiped in particular at the Divali festival. As well as the lighting of lamps, the celebration of Divali involves the offering of a great and varied range of food – fruit, grain, spices and so on.

Left The usually good-tempered anarchy that characterizes the Holi spring festival finds its best-known outlet in the hurling of colored powder and the squirting of colored dye – the faces and clothes of the men at this tea-stall in Orissa have been stained pink and purple. Alcohol and cannabis are consumed in quantity. Village worthies are mocked, men are beaten by women, and obscene dances and mimes are performed as everything is turned upside down – for a single day.

endless re-birth. This doctrine grapples with the riddle of existence and provides explanation for differences and inequality.

The second major theme that runs through much of Hindu thinking is the supreme importance of doing one's duty (*dharma*) according to the position in which one has been put. It is more virtuous to do what you should be doing, according to some given role or status, than to attempt to do something apportioned to someone else. For many this means in practice that strict obedience to sets of social rules prescribed by birth will reap the greatest reward. These rules include those that govern food, marriage, occupation, social intercourse, and dress. *Dharma* reinforces an ideology that takes inequality as read, for it simultaneously explains and remakes social hierarchies.

Distinctions of class and caste

All societies exhibit degrees of economic and political inequality, and social status may be acknowledged in a number of ways, even if the prevailing social theory rests on notions of the fundamentally equal worth of each individual. Indian religious and social ideals, however, accept and sustain inequalities quite explicitly and they justify and maintain an hierarchical social order, running from brahmins at the top to the Harijans (Gandhi's re-naming of the untouchables as "the children of god") or Dalits ("the down-trodden", as they now prefer to call themselves) at the bottom. The rank order of classes between the top and bottom is not always without dispute, and is affected by a multitude of local variations in detail.

The divisions in Indian society are usually explained first by reference to *varna* and then by mention of caste. The *varna* classification provides an ideal model of society divided into four classes or groups. These classes are ranked in a hierarchy, but they are also interdependent and mutually supportive. There is scriptural justification going back to the oldest Vedic texts for considering an ideal society to be one led by those with religious knowledge, the brahmins (not, it must be stressed, necessarily restricted to those who

can perform certain religious rituals), protected by rulers and warriors (kshatriyas) in the second class, with a third class responsible for agriculture and trade (vaishyas), and a fourth (shudras) acting as the servants of all. This four-fold classification of the ideal society (not in essence dissimilar from models used in other cultures) was translated into a table of social respect and as it became more refined – perhaps representing the values of colonizing and conquering peoples – the model also allowed for the existence of people found beyond these four fundamental categories. They were marked as outsiders and had no status within the civil society being formed. Yet by engaging in some sort of intercourse with them, their degraded existence gave further validation to the respectable people.

Caste is a word brought into common usage by early Portuguese explorers in India. Nowadays it is used interchangeably with the Indian word *jati* to mean "genera", "breed", "race", "lineage" and it describes a society composed of definable and closed corporate groups, formed through descent and marriage and often associated with particular occupations. There are thousands upon thousands of such kinship groupings in India and each of them will claim for itself a place within one of the four broad classes set out in the *varna* model of the ideal society. Such claims have to be recognized by others, and there may be dispute as to whether a particular caste or *jati* does indeed deserve to be regarded as, say, a kshatriya or a shudra. Moreover, since many different *jatis* are necessarily included within one of the four orders in the *varna* system, there is enormous scope for the establishment of pecking orders between *jatis* within each of the broader classes.

A person cannot join a caste other than by birth, but *jatis* may be subdivided in a number of ways into smaller clan or family units, and even among those reckoned to be of the same blood there may be quite complex rules and conventions that govern their relationships with each other, giving rise to relative rankings within the same group. Ties of blood determine

Below The Devanagari script – written from left to right like the Greco-Roman based alphabets of Europe – has enjoyed widespread use in northern India for at least a thousand years. It is the script in which the classic Vedic texts were written, and is today used for Hindi, Marathi and Nepali as well as Sanskrit. Like the Roman alphabet, Devanagari is a phonetic sign system in which there is a one-to-one correspondence between symbol and sound. At least ten other scripts of indigenous origin are used in the subcontinent: Gujarati, Bengali and Oriya all have their own scripts. The scripts of south India are distinctive in style, originally being incised on palm-leaf manuscripts for subsequent inking in, as opposed to the northern scripts, which were written with pen on paper. Each of the four major Dravidian languages (Tamil, Telugu, Kannada and Malayalam) has its own script. In Pakistan, a cursive Perso-Arabic script, running from right to left, is used for Urdu, the principal language of the subcontinent's Muslim populations, and for the country's other languages.

	VOWELS			CONSONANTS							
	Diphthong-forming simple vowels	Nondiphthong-forming simple vowels	Diphthongs	Voiceless stops		Voiced stops		Nasal	Semivowels	Sibilants	Breathing
	short long	short long	short long	unaspirated aspirated		unaspirated aspirated					
Velar	अ a आ ā			क k	ख kh	ग g	घ gh	ङ ṅ			ह h
Palatal	इ i ई ī		ए e ऐ ai	च c	छ ch	ज j	झ jh	ञ ñ	य y	श ś	
Retroflex		ऋ ṛ ॠ ṝ		ट ṭ	ठ ṭh	ड ḍ	ढ ḍh	ण ṇ	र r	ष ṣ	
Dental		ऌ l (ॡ) (l̥)		त t	थ th	द d	ध dh	न n	ल l	स s	
Labial	उ u ऊ ū		ओ o औ au	प p	फ ph	ब b	भ bh	म m	व v		

patterns of marriage within a caste, thus maintaining a purity of line and providing forms of social cohesion. Moreover, over wide geographical areas *jatis* of the same name may coalesce into larger social units and deploy their bigger numbers for political and economic purposes – though again there are likely to be minor discrepancies in standing and arguments about relative social worth. Thus a social theory that appears to propose a rigid framework for society, and kinship arrangements that appear to place greatest emphasis on maintaining the purity of the blood-line, interact with each other in practice in a much more ambiguous way. This begins to explain the apparent paradox that Indian society, often characterized as fixed, hierarchical and unchanging, is in fact flexible and fluid. The mere existence of hierarchy and jealously protected social segments does not of itself preclude social mobility and social change. Over the centuries, India society is revealed as a social system of quite extraordinary resilience with a capacity to adjust, to survive, and to reproduce itself.

Ideas of purity and pollution
Arguments about the precise place anyone may occupy in the caste hierarchy turn in part on notions of ritual purity and pollution. In general, brahmins are the least ritually polluted – hence their place at the top of society – while Dalits and other marginal groups are at the bottom because they are considered in some way unclean. Ritual pollution comes from many sources: all bodily emissions and waste matter are reckoned to be polluting in some way or another, and natural happenings, such as birth, death and menstruation also affect the purity of individual and family. Pollution is controlled by daily bathing and by other forms of ablution, by participation in rituals, and by acceptance of a variety of social restrictions to prevent the transmission of impurities. Menstruating women, for example, may not be allowed to prepare food, normal social intercourse will be set aside while a family works through a period of mourning, physical contact between people widely separated across the spectrum of pollution will be minimized. From this results the exclusion of those at the bottom of the social scale from access to certain wells or entry to temples. The ritually clean can be protected from pollution by allocating to specialist, low-ranking social groups specific sorts of polluting work: cleaning and sweeping, barbering, laundering, cobbling. This gives rise to the paradox that brahmin priests – that is, those who perform ritual duties – can be of low status because in making their intercessions with the gods they rub up against so much human sin. To go further, those priests whose duty it is to deal with the dead and conduct funerary rites are amongst the most unclean members of society.

In many societies there tends to be a convergence between possession of wealth, political power, and social status. But this is not necessarily the case in India. Just as the gods may appear in many forms and play many parts, so too social hierarchies can be reformulated and ambiguities between different versions of rank order exploited. Much of the religious literature of India, and its classical laws, present a society in which the brahmin is to be venerated above all others in all hierarchies. But very often this simply reflects a brahmin view of the matter. Alternative positions can be adopted. For example, it may be argued that the person who gives up everything but his begging-bowl deserves to be given the highest social status, for through renunciation of the world he is seeking liberation from rebirth. Again, while a kshatriya may accept that the brahmin has a special position in society, he would also argue that in reality it is the king who guarantees the social order. Harmony in society, and indeed harmony in the wider universe, depends on the kshatriya being in charge. Moreover, the kings are the earthly regents of the gods and are therefore also the essential patrons of worship. These notions are transformed into less speculative social reality by the claim of most dominant land-holding castes in the countryside to be of kshatriya status and to function at the local level as little kings. Politically and economically powerful non-brahmins may, therefore, be rather ambivalent about brahmin pre-eminence: in their eyes such people are menial cooks, bottle-washers and priests whom they have to feed and care for.

Social organization
Most of the population of South Asia – well over three-quarters of them – live in more than half a million villages scattered across the subcontinent. A marked feature of this rural society is its inegalitarian nature. Not only is wealth and social power distributed very unevenly, even among the poor, but village society is riddled with complex hierarchies that impinge on the ordinary transactions of daily life. A number of *jatis* may be found living in any given village, but the houses of distinct groups or sub-groups will be clustered together, there will be demarcated areas for different people to meet, and the use of wells, temples and public eating places will be governed by custom and regulation disbarring people of lower caste from using the facilities of the higher castes. On social occasions, such as a wedding, people arrange themselves in separate caste lines and food is served in order of rank; at religious festivals or in public processions people play a role befitting their local standing. The way people dress, talk or walk reveals their caste and status. Within the village, everyone knows everyone and every act makes explicit the social order. But even here the harmonious stable ideal is rarely attained: change is forced on the village by continual shifts in family circumstance. A dispute, a death, a change of material fortune or a re-alignment of political patronage and faction – all make possible the re-arrangement of social ranking.

Caste-standing goes some way toward determining occupation; though here again matters are not so inflexible as at first they seem. In practice some occupations, especially those that carry low status in the service and artisan sectors, are specific to particular castes, and washermen, carpenters, temple drummer-boys and the like enjoy a virtual monopoly of their trade within their caste. But while it is rare for someone of another caste to engage in this sort of occupation, it is common for those born, for example, to be sweepers or oil-pressers to find an occupation outside that traditionally assigned to them. Moreover, most agricultural work is not divided up and made specific for particular castes, and almost all occupations in the modern sectors of the economy are caste-free. Thus, a society theoretically ranked in part by occupation has its rigidities dissolved by the ordinary process of occupational mobility.

According to virtually all traditional Hindu authorities (in common with almost all other societies before the later 20th century) women are inferior to men.

The Mahabharata

The *Mahabharata* is a vast Hindu epic composed sometime in the middle of the first millennium BC. It tells the story of complex dynastic problems in the royal line of the Kurus, the consequent hostility between two sets of rival cousins – the virtuous Pandavas and the wicked Kauravas – and the catastrophic war of annihilation that followed. Overseeing and participating in these events is Krishna, incarnation (*avatara*) of the lord Vishnu, who has taken human shape to ensure that right prevails.

It seems certain that the *Mahabharata* was originally the property of the kshatriyas, the class of rulers and warriors, who favored the "new" deity Krishna. The epic would have served to spread knowledge and worship of the god (a function that oral epics of modern hero-deities perform to the present day) but over the course of many centuries the brahmin priests took control of the cult and its associated text. By the middle of the first millennium AD, the *Mahabharata* had been radically changed, both in nature and length. As well as many expansions in the narrative itself, numerous long didactic passages were added, the most famous being the *Bhagavad Gita*, the sermon preached by Krishna to the Pandava hero Arjuna before the great battle at Kurukshetra. The end result was the longest work of literature in the world: a poem of about 100,000 stanzas, eight times the combined lengths of the Greek epics, the *Iliad* and the *Odyssey*. Though generally outstripped in popularity by the other great epic, the *Ramayana*, the *Mahabharata* has retained its potency as myth. Over the centuries, the story has been recounted in many different Indian languages, and episodes from it illustrated in numerous forms – in sculpture, painting and drama. In a recent retelling it was serialized at great length by the Indian state television service Doordashan.

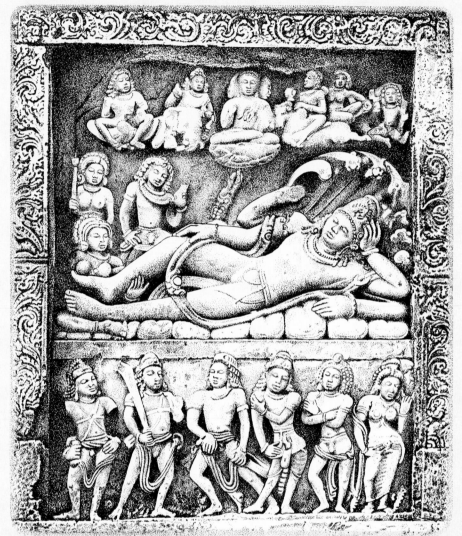

The central theme of the *Mahabharata* is the eternal conflict between the gods, who became incarnate as the Pandava heroes, and the demons, incarnate as their Kaurava enemies. (*Left*) In a sculpture from a 6th-century temple, the great god Vishnu, who took human form as Krishna to help the Pandavas, is shown with various gods: below him are the Pandavas with their joint wife Draupadi. The Kauravas tricked the Pandavas out of their kingdom in a crooked game of dice, a scene depicted (*below left*) in a 16th-century illustration from Nepal, and the Pandavas had to endure 12 years' exile in the forest. On their return the Kauravas still refused to return their kingdom to them. War became inevitable and the opposing forces gathered at Kurukshetra. Krishna acted as charioteer to the Pandava hero Arjuna, and the two are shown facing their enemy Karna in a 19th-century painting from Garhwal (*right*). A still from the Doordarshan television serial (*below right*) portrays the moment when the Pandava leader Yudhishthira paid his respects to his elders Bhishma and Drona, who found themselves fighting on the Kaurava side. Finally the terrible battle began, a scene illustrated (*below*), in an 18th-century Chamba wall hanging. With Krishna's help, the Pandavas triumphed, but at an appalling cost in human carnage.

The Ramayana

The *Ramayana* – the second of the two great epics of Hindu India – was, like the *Mahabharata*, composed in Sanskrit. It also tells of an earthly episode in the unending cosmic conflict between the gods and the demons: once again, Vishnu assumes human form in order to take charge of events. Scholars, however, are generally agreed that the *Ramayana* came into being rather later than the earliest form of the *Mahabharata* – being composed in perhaps the 3rd or 2nd century BC – and that it is chiefly the work of a single author, the poet Valmiki.

The story tells of Dasharatha, the king of Ayodhya. He was childless, and to secure an heir he performed a great sacrifice. As a result, his wife Kausalya bore a son, Rama. Rama was in fact an *avatara* of Vishnu, who had determined to take human form in order to overthrow Ravana, the demon king of Lanka, invincible against all beings except men. Rama grew up with his brothers Bharata, Lakshmana and Shatrughna. In his teens he traveled to Mithila where the king had a bow that no one could bend. Rama not merely bent it, but succeeded in breaking it altogether, and so won the hand of the princess Sita. Dasharatha now decided to make Rama prince regent over his kingdom of Ayodhya. But on the eve of his consecration his stepmother Kaikeyi insisted that her son Bharata be awarded this rank instead, and that Rama be exiled for 14 years. Rama and Sita, together with Lakshmana, accordingly left Ayodhya and set out into the forest where the princes proceeded to wage war against the many demons who lived there. Meanwhile, Dasharatha died of grief.

Shurpanakha, sister of Ravana, approached the two brothers and attempted to seduce them. Repulsed and disfigured by them, she complained of her treatment to Ravana, who devised a plot to avenge her by abducting Sita. The scheme succeeded, and he carried Sita off to his kingdom of Lanka. Rama, desperate to regain his wife, made a pact with the monkeys of the forest, including the mighty Hanuman, who became his most faithful follower. It was Hanuman who located Sita in Ravana's palace in Lanka and subsequently led Rama, Lakshmana and the monkey forces there. A great battle took place, in which Ravana was killed and Sita freed. After undergoing an ordeal by fire to prove her unsullied chastity, she was reunited with Rama and they returned to Ayodhya, where Rama at last became king.

The story of Rama is enormously popular throughout India, and there exist a very large number of retellings in various languages. Rama and Sita are held to represent the exemplary husband and wife, and Rama's kingship in Ayodhya is regarded as the model for earthly rulers. Like the *Mahabharata*, the *Ramayana* was broadcast on Indian state television in serialized form in the 1980s when as many as 80 million people are believed to have seen it. A great number of viewers accorded the television set and its moving pictures the same religious respect they would give to a shrine containing holy icons.

Left The monkey-god Hanuman combines utter faithfulness to his lord Rama with an impetuous aggression. For instance, when Rama and Lakshmana were wounded in the battle and needed medicinal herbs, Hanuman went to the mountain of herbs to fetch them. Unable to find what he wanted, he simply broke off the top of the mountain and carried it away to the battlefield. Shrines and images of this benevolent but fierce deity are often placed where they will serve to protect a temple or even a whole village. This 18th-century sculpture shows Hanuman about to kill a demon.

Below left This small 17th-century Rajput miniature shows the final battle in all its frenetic activity. Ravana, identified by his 10 heads and 20 arms, appears twice, in his court at the center and standing above among the battlements. Round him his warriors, some human in appearance, others demonic, do battle with Rama's allies, the monkeys and bears.

Above An 18th-century miniature from the Punjab state of Kangra shows the scene just after Rama has broken the "unbendable" bow of the king of Mithila. Princess Sita, supported by her ladies, is placing the garland of victory around Rama's neck and shoulders. Behind the triumphant prince stands his brother Lakshmana and the white-turbaned figure of the king.

Below Another 18th-century Kangra miniature depicts an episode described in some northern texts of Valmiki's *Ramayana*. The god Indra, accompanied by Sleep (Nidra), visits Sita in the palace garden of Lanka shortly after she is taken captive. Sleep overpowers the guards, and Indra gives Sita reassurance and celestial food.

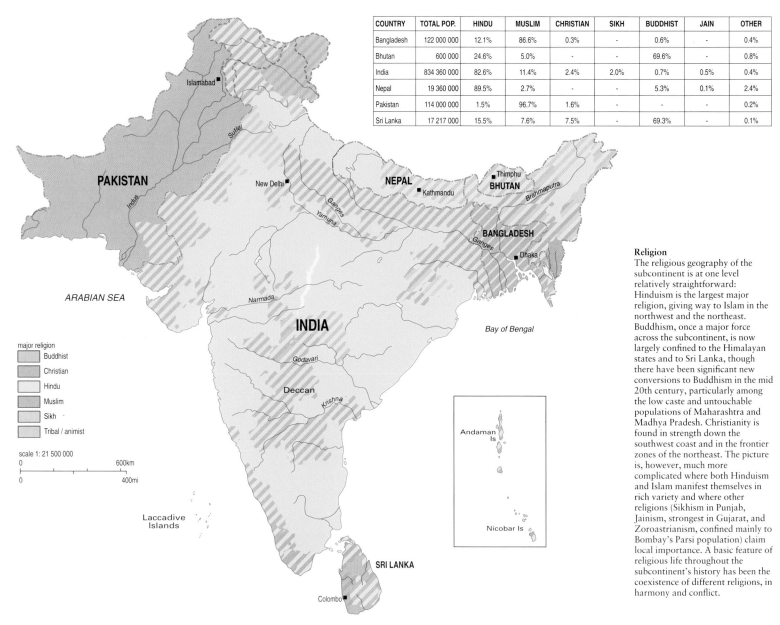

COUNTRY	TOTAL POP.	HINDU	MUSLIM	CHRISTIAN	SIKH	BUDDHIST	JAIN	OTHER
Bangladesh	122 000 000	12.1%	86.6%	0.3%	-	0.6%	-	0.4%
Bhutan	600 000	24.6%	5.0%	-	-	69.6%	-	0.8%
India	834 360 000	82.6%	11.4%	2.4%	2.0%	0.7%	0.5%	0.4%
Nepal	19 360 000	89.5%	2.7%	-	-	5.3%	0.1%	2.4%
Pakistan	114 000 000	1.5%	96.7%	1.6%	-	-	-	0.2%
Sri Lanka	17 217 000	15.5%	7.6%	7.5%	-	69.3%	-	0.1%

Religion
The religious geography of the subcontinent is at one level relatively straightforward: Hinduism is the largest major religion, giving way to Islam in the northwest and the northeast. Buddhism, once a major force across the subcontinent, is now largely confined to the Himalayan states and to Sri Lanka, though there have been significant new conversions to Buddhism in the mid 20th century, particularly among the low caste and untouchable populations of Maharashtra and Madhya Pradesh. Christianity is found in strength down the southwest coast and in the frontier zones of the northeast. The picture is, however, much more complicated where both Hinduism and Islam manifest themselves in rich variety and where other religions (Sikhism in Punjab, Jainism, strongest in Gujarat, and Zoroastrianism, confined mainly to Bombay's Parsi population) claim local importance. A basic feature of religious life throughout the subcontinent's history has been the coexistence of different religions, in harmony and conflict.

Though they always had rights of maintenance and residence, until relatively recent times, with few exceptions, they had no legal claim on property and no civil rights. A verse from the laws of Manu summed up the woman's position: "In childhood subject to her father, in youth to her husband, and when her husband is dead to her sons, she should never enjoy independence". The duty of a wife lies with her husband, and she must honor him as a god. But here again multitudinous discrepancies arise between the ideal enshrined in text and custom and the social and economic reality. Many women, particularly in later life, exercise enormous influence in the household, arranging marriages, organizing work, buying and selling property. And class distinctions complicate the way in which women are viewed. Family status may turn on the sort of work a woman does: the higher the status of the family, the more likely it is that the woman will stay at home, be veiled to go out, and do no work other than to supervise the household routine. Lower down the social scale, a woman will have to do her own housework and lend a hand in the fields at sowing and harvest times. The very lowest are those women who have to go out to work as servants, field laborers, on construction sites or at factory benches.

But even here there are exceptions. Women of high caste, with all the advantages of wealth, education and broad social contact, are able to become formidable professional people in their own right. The women of fishing communities are responsible for taking the catch to market and this places them in a crucially important position within their families' domestic economies. Nor has being a woman in South Asia been a bar to wielding political power: India, Pakistan, Bangladesh and Sri Lanka have all had women leaders in the past forty years. Once again an apparently timeless set of laws and attitudes is revealed as being not quite what it seems. Practice is often out of step with precept, and besides, as an Indian proverb has it, "A man does not make public his defeat or the thrashing he receives from his wife."

Many common perceptions of India's religions and its societies are grounded in notions of rigidity, continuity, and quite remarkable lack of change. But these notions do not stand up to testing. Indians have elaborated a number of complex religious and social ideals; they stress that the divine and the temporal are interconnected, they try to explain inequality and to justify hierarchy. But these ideas have been subject to reinterpretation over time, and Indian societies, whatever their ideal form, have shown no lack of creative dynamism to meet the challenge of human survival.

PART TWO
THE PAST

PREHISTORY AND EARLY HISTORY

Stone Age peoples

An enormous number and range of Stone Age sites have been identified in the Indian subcontinent. None can be dated earlier than 500,000 years ago, and it seems reasonable to suppose that the ancestors of *homo sapiens* did not spread south of the Himalayas before then. Stone Age sites throughout the subcontinent are mostly found along the banks of shallow streams and on the margins of lakes, jungles and deserts. Though capable of sustaining only small populations, all these places would have offered particular advantages for the exploitation of wild life by groups of nomadic hunter–gatherers. Excavations at sites in the Aravalli Hills, for example, suggest that they were occupied only in the wet season when animals would have congregated in large numbers at watering places, and plant life was abundant.

Around 20,000 years ago, in places far distant from each other in the subcontinent, the use of multi-purpose stone axes began to give way to smaller, sharpened stone tools designed for specialist tasks and fitted with handles: arrow-heads, variously shaped cutting and piercing implements, as well as axes and scrapers have all been found. There is evidence, too, that people were beginning to find more permanent settlement in the shelter of caves and rock-faces, and were developing economies that combined hunting and fishing with trade or barter, with simple forms of animal husbandry, and even the limited cultivation of wild grasses and grains. This does not imply, however, that old technologies were completely abandoned for new ones, nor that a uniform shift from one way of life to another occurred throughout the subcontinent, or even within a particular locality. The mixture of artifacts discovered at some sites in the Narmada valley suggests that the use of early Stone Age implements extended into later periods of occupation.

About 10,000 years ago, cave dwellers at Bhimbetka and other places along the Vindhyan escarpment were decorating the walls of their caves with scenes of domesticated animals, hunting, dancing and warfare. They also drew geometric designs. Some pictures that appear to show landscapes in plan form may be a diagrammatic representation of their vision of the universe. Though it is hard to interpret this cave art with any degree of certainty, it does suggest the development of complex ideas of religion or magical belief, as well as the desire to express thoughts and emotions in artistic form.

Early settled societies

The evidence for early settled societies begins to become more plentiful and its interpretation more certain after about 7000 BC. The first indications of major change in the way that people lived comes from the northwest of the subcontinent. At Mehrgarh on the Bolan river in Baluchistan, in the area where the Indus plain runs up against the hills, a settlement has been excavated that gives evidence of having been continuously occupied for over 4,000 years. Sheep and goats were husbanded, and by about 4000 BC humped cattle had become the most common domestic species of animal. Wheat and barley were cultivated; at first stone cutting tools were used to cut the stems, but later – as knowledge of metallurgy developed – they were made of copper. Buildings containing a number of rooms were constructed out of mud bricks, and the dead were buried in graves. Handmade pottery was first produced about 5000 BC; the introduction of the potter's wheel about 3500 BC led to a great increase in the number and variety of vessels that were made. By about 3000 BC, the settlement at Mehrgarh spread over an area of approximately 75 hectares; examples of its distinctive black-on-red decorated pottery have been found in Baluchistan, Sind and southeast Afghanistan.

As yet, no sites similar to that at Mehrgarh have been found in neighboring regions outside the subcontinent, and this leads to the supposition that it developed independently. Similar settlements, though none so ancient, have been discovered in the Quetta valley north of Mehrgarh, and perhaps also in the Bannu basin in the North-West Frontier Province. At Kechi Beg in Quetta, Amri and Kot Diji in Sind, and Sothi in northern Rajasthan, pottery in similar styles to that found at Mehrgarh, but showing distinct regional differences, begins to put in an appearance between 3000 and 2500 BC. In all these places the development of a more sophisticated technology led to the production of a fine gray pottery. It was in this context of related, but distinct, social and ethnic groups in Baluchistan and the greater Indus valley region that the Harappan, or Indus valley, civilization emerged around 2,500 BC.

The Indus valley civilization

It was in the early 1920s that archaeologists working at two sites – Harappa in eastern Punjab and Mohenjo-Daro in Sind – first unearthed evidence of a major civilization in the Indus valley. This, they believed, had lasted for over a thousand years. Urban-based, it was as advanced and sophisticated as the civilizations of Egypt, Mesopotamia and China that had flourished at about the same time. Further investigations appeared to support the view that a distinctive and remarkably uniform society had held sway over an area of more than 1.3 million square kilometers. Its main centers were in the Indus plain, but it reached westward into Baluchistan and along the Makran coast toward Iran, southeastward through the marshes of Kutch and the Kathiawar peninsula to the Narmada valley, and eastward as far as Alamgirpur in the Ganges-Jamuna doab, the westernmost edge of the Gangetic plain. There was a distant outpost at Shortughai on the Amu Darya in northern Afghanistan. The mainstay of the civilization was agriculture. The annual floodwaters of the Indus were utilized to irrigate crops of wheat, barley, pulses, sesame, mustard, dates and vegetables, and possibly rice. Domesticated animals included cats and dogs as well as livestock:

Top Evidence of early human settlement east of the Jamuna river in the Ganges delta depends in part on the discovery of a number of copper hoards. These date from the end of the 3rd millennium to the end of the 2nd millennium BC, and are therefore contemporary with the mature Indus valley civilization. The objects found so far, including this short sword, are made of impure copper with traces of tin, lead and arsenic. The copper may have come from the Rakha mines of Bihar. The range of tools found suggests a more limited range of technology than was present in the Indus valley.

Above Dating from the 1st millennium BC, this high-necked jar, with a rolled lip, a sharply angled shoulder and rounded base, comes from an excavated tomb complex near Palambati in Coimbatore district, Tamil Nadu. It is 18.3 centimeters high and 22.3 centimeters in circumference, and is made of a gritty red pottery with a black core and white decoration.

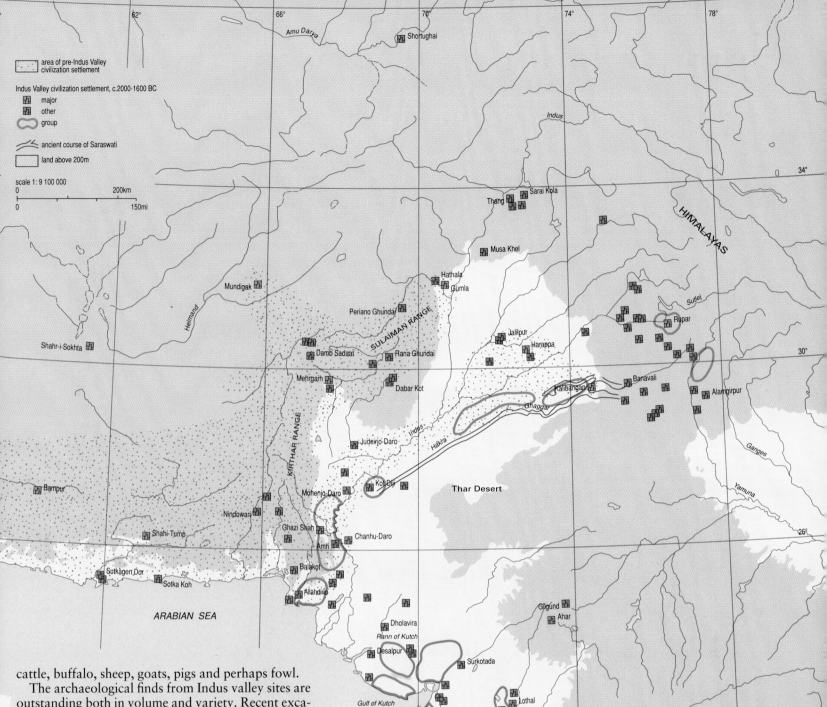

cattle, buffalo, sheep, goats, pigs and perhaps fowl.

The archaeological finds from Indus valley sites are outstanding both in volume and variety. Recent excavations at Dholavira in Gujarat, for example, have yielded over 20,000 artifact fragments – seals, beads, copper tools and weapons, terracotta figures, bone, ivory, stone, and baked-clay items, and immense quantities of pottery. Almost all the sites so far identified (over a thousand in all) have been located on rivers and streams. Most covered an area of between 0.8 and 2 hectares, suggesting that their populations were no more than 5,000. However, some of the bigger centers may at times have supported 40,000 people, and Mohenjo-Daro possibly even more.

The bigger towns all appear to be arranged with a high mound, or citadel, on the west side containing the settlement's public structures, and a larger area to the east, laid out in a grid pattern, showing evidence of residential occupation with different areas of specialized craft production. The towns had highly developed drainage and sewerage systems, and were fortified with thick mud and brick walls. Weights and measures display accuracy and standardization across the whole region. The pottery is remarkably uniform. The existence of numerous kilns show that it was produced locally, but the commonest form – a hard ceramic ware, covered with plum-red slip and then

The Indus valley civilization
The civilization that flourished in the Indus valley between about 2500 BC and 1800 BC evolved from agricultural settlements of much greater antiquity and of considerable diversity. It is the world's largest known urbanized Bronze Age civilization, and its numerous sites have been found across a huge area that straddles the borderlands of present-day India and Pakistan. It contains two major geographical regions – the Baluchistan plateau and associated highlands, with the passes that link it to Iran; and the lower Indus valley running down to the delta. Through this region once flowed the river Saraswati, mentioned in classical texts but which dried up sometime in the 1st millennium BC.

Mohenjo-Daro

Recent discoveries suggest that Mohenjo-Daro, 400 kilometers north of Karachi in Pakistan, was one of the largest Bronze Age cities in the world. It was protected from the annual flood waters of the nearby river Indus by being built on gigantic mud-brick platforms. Today an area of about 100 hectares of the city is visible as a hill rising above the level of the surrounding alluvial plain, and about a tenth of this area was excavated in six different sites in the 1920s. It is estimated that a further 200 hectares lies buried under alluvial deposits of the Indus.

Right and below The northern part of the citadel was thoroughly excavated in the 1920s when remains of the bath and the so-called granary were uncovered. A Buddhist stupa was built on the site in the 2nd century AD. The densely built areas of the lower city show the limited space that was available. The houses and streets were laid out on a north–south orientation. At least one major north–south thoroughfare, 10 meters wide, bisected the lower city. Lanes zigzagged across the site from east to west.

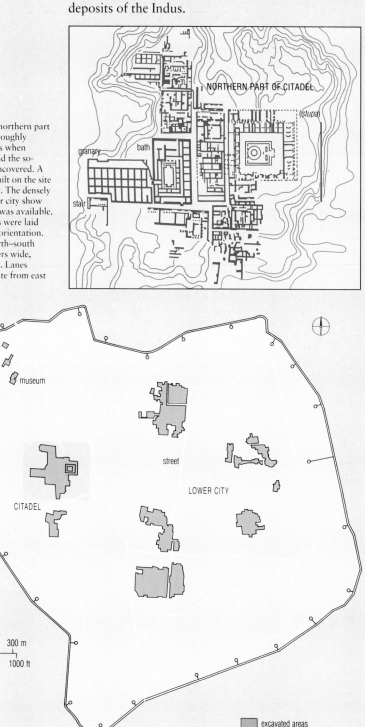

excavated areas

The city itself is divided into two parts: a western higher "citadel" measuring 200 by 400 meters, and the "lower city" in the east. They are separated by an unbuilt area 200 meters in width. This arrangement is typical of other cities of the Indus valley civilization. All buildings were constructed of bricks made to a uniform ratio of 1:2:4 (height, width, length), corresponding to the proportions of modern standard bricks. No evidence of a palace or temple has been identified, but it is highly probable that the structures of the citadel had some form of religious function – for example, a tank measuring 7 by 12 meters, described as the earliest public bath, was uncovered here. In the lower city large houses of more than 800 square meters in area may have been inhabited by rich families who perhaps formed a ruling elite. The houses contain lavatories and bathrooms, and there was a sophisticated water-supply and sewerage system. The builders of Mohenjo-Daro were skilled engineers who clearly understood the natural hazards of the site. As well as having flood defenses, the city had more than 600 wells which would have kept the inhabitants supplied with water should the river have shifted its course.

Left The writing system of the Indus valley civilization is known to us from the texts incised on stamp seals – small squares of steatite - but has not been deciphered. Many of the seals also bear fine naturalistic depictions of animals – shown here are a rhino, elephant and zebu – and were probably used as identification tokens.

Above This view shows the citadel crowned by the crumbling remains of the Buddhist stupa. Beyond lies the lower city with the river Indus in the far background. All the structures of Mohenjo-Daro were made of baked mud brick.

Left The "Priest King", a bust fragment made of steatite, measures only 17.7 centimeters in height. It was found in a small house in the lower city. The figure wears an arm ring and a head fillet, and the edge of his cloak is decorated with a trefoil pattern. These, and the man's look of mysterious solemnity, have given the bust its name.

Right This clay model, and others like it found in Mohenjo-Daro and other Indus valley sites, show that wheeled carts drawn by zebu cattle were in use. However, no actual wheels have been found. Boats are depicted on many seals, and it seems likely that most transportation was by water.

decorated with black floral, fishscale and geometric motifs – is found everywhere.

Particular skill went into making the engraved rectangular steatite seals that have been found all across the region, many of them with repeated designs. Some of the pictorial and symbolic motifs seem to draw their inspiration from mythology: they include composite animals and fabulous beasts along with heroic figures in combat with wild animals. Among the most attractive of the seals are those depicting animals, which are drawn with amazing accuracy. Geometric designs include swastikas and equal-armed upright crosses. The seals have pierced bosses on the back to carry a string: they may been used to secure objects, or were perhaps worn as amulets. Some of the seals, some pottery and a few copper tablets have writing on them, but scholars have not yet been able to decode it. No inscription discovered so far consists of more than 21 signs, and most have only five or six. They are generally agreed to be pictographs.

Nothing had prepared the archaeologists who first came upon these settlements for the existence of so major a culture at such an early date in the subcontinent, and one that lasted for such a long span of time. At first it was argued that new settlers must have moved into the Indus valley from the northwest, bringing with them more advanced technological skills and a higher degree of social organization than yet existed in the subcontinent. In line with the then current thinking about the ancient civilizations of Mesopotamia and Egypt, the Indus valley settlements were claimed to belong to a highly organized central state, probably hierarchical and theocratic in form and ruled from the twin settlements at Harappa and Mohenjo-Daro. As this empire declined it came under attack from the invading Aryan peoples who moved rapidly into the Indian subcontinent about 4,000 years ago – a line of argument that owed a great deal to contemporary theorizing about the rise and fall of civilizations.

These early hypotheses have not stood the test of time. It is now generally accepted that the Indus valley civilization did not come about through the diffusion of ideas and peoples from outside the region. But whether over a millennium or so, starting about 5,500 years ago, this complex and relatively dense pattern of human settlement evolved gradually out of existing settlements such as those at Mehrgarh or Kot Diji, or whether an abrupt change took place within the span of two or three generations to bring it into existence about 4,500 years ago, is still the subject of lively debate. While some sites show evidence of continuous occupation and development, others appear to have been occupied at one period and not at another, while some displayed the characteristics of a particular phase at a much later period than elsewhere. It may reasonably be inferred, however, that the region was able to sustain a growing population – perhaps because of improving climatic conditions and the development of better methods of managing water resources and increasing agricultural production – and that more and more land was opened up for colonization. In this way, people were brought into contact with other hitherto scattered settlements and a wide network of communication was established across the entire region.

Most of the materials used by the craftsmen of the Indus valley were local in origin. However, copper came from Rajasthan, semiprecious stones from the Narmada valley or Badakhshan in the upper Amu Darya region, and gold probably from southern India. A well-developed network for the exchange of goods within the Indus valley was supplemented by far-reaching connections beyond it. Indus valley seals and other objects have been found at sites in the Persian Gulf, Mesopotamia and Iran, while the Harappan outpost at Shortughai almost certainly owed its existence to the trade in lapis lazuli. Such an extensive movement of artifacts would surely have been accompanied by a similar traffic in ideas and skills.

What archaeologists have so far failed to uncover, amidst all the impressive Indus valley remains, is any convincing evidence that the settlements contained temples or palaces. The excavation of funerary remains gives no indication of sharp divisions of rank or wealth. High quality pottery, seals and metal objects are widely found, even at very minor sites. All this suggests a more even distribution of wealth or status than is commonly ascribed to the civilizations of Egypt or Mesopotamia. In the Indus valley there were no great court-temple complexes where the wealth of a servile countryside was accumulated and where priest-kings were buried surrounded by sumptuous treasures. Mohenjo-Daro, the largest of the Indus valley sites, does not appear to have exercised imperial power over the rest, though it probably formed some sort of administrative center. There were also sizable settlements at Harappa, Dholavira, Ganweriwala and Rakhigarhi.

Most archaeologists today would argue that the agrarian and pastoral societies that inhabited the greater Indus valley and the surrounding areas between 4,500 and 3,000 years ago resembled a loose federation of peoples rather than a unified state. An early impression of uniformity gives way on closer scrutiny to one of diversity. Over time, settlements expanded and contracted, or were even abandoned and later resettled and abandoned again. While the evidence still points to what, for the ancient world, was an almost unparalleled uniformity in the material culture, this is now most convincingly explained by the establishment of effective networks of trade within the Indus valley, or by the wide dispersal of skilled craft groups responsible for the specialist manufacture of particular types of artifact.

The Aryan myth

Until the major settlements of the Indus valley were first excavated in the 1920s, Indian history proper was commonly believed to begin somewhere in the 2nd millennium BC with the Aryans, a people thought to have originated in the steppes of Central Asia. It was through the study of philology and linguistics that theories about the supposed Aryan invasion of the subcontinent first took shape. As early as 1786 Sir William Jones had shown that Sanskrit, the language of the Vedic classical texts, was closely related to Greek, Latin, German and Celtic, and consequently concluded that all these languages were derived from a common Indo-European language. The oldest Sanskrit texts were difficult to date, but arguments were put forward to suggest that they were compiled early in the 2nd millennium BC (some scholars argued for an even earlier date) and that they had been passed down by word of mouth for many centuries before being set down in writing sometime around the 4th century BC. The Vedic texts – a mixture of myths, philosophical treatises, commentaries on ritual and

Above The Indus valley site of Harappa lies on the left bank of a former course of the river Ravi in Pakistani Punjab. The vast mounds beneath which it lay buried were first commented on in the 1820s, but it was not until after 1920 that the Archaeological Survey of India began excavation here. Among the discoveries was a series of 12 circular platforms, each of which consists of a single course of four continuous concentric rings of brick-on-edge masonry with a hollow in the center equal to the length of three bricks. Mud was used as the mortar, and the pointing is of gypsum. The platforms are laid out in a double row running east–west, with a distance of approximately 6 meters between each pair, measured from the centers. It is not known what purpose the platforms served, though it is assumed that they constituted some form of public building.

instructions for conducting rituals – were believed to represent the actual language of India at the time of their first composition, and it was thought that their contents revealed much of the history of that period.

Study of the literature appeared to suggest that it was concerned with the affairs of a group of strong tribes who – with the advantage of fire, horses and chariots – conquered a dark-skinned, flat-nosed and phallus-worshiping primitive people. The invaders were guided by their god Indra, and the Vedic texts were seen to contain the earliest elements of Hinduism. It was from here an easy step to conclude that India's distinctive history began in the migration of enterprising warriors from Eurasia into the north of the subcontinent. Possessing both technological skills and philosophical sophistication, they used their superiority to overcome the more primitive indigenous Dravidian peoples of the subcontinent, driving them south into the peninsula.

The discovery of Harappa and Mohenjo-Daro seemed to put this version of events in doubt. However, evidence uncovered in 1920s and 1930s suggested that the Indus valley civilization had come to an abrupt and violent end. City walls had been destroyed and sometimes burnt, and the people who inhabited them overwhelmed by sudden death. An obvious explanation was that the ancient cities had fallen to invaders from outside the region. There was disagreement about the precise timing of these events, and no one seemed certain of where the Aryans had originated. But for a time it was accepted by many that the Indus valley civilization had been destroyed by military conquest and its peoples killed or subjugated by a fair-skinned race of invaders.

It is only recently that scholars have begun to disprove these earlier theories. Archaeologists have shown that a distinctive Indus valley culture, spreading out from its original centers, survived much later into the 2nd millennium BC than had been thought.

Moreover, while the earliest excavations were of towns that seem to have come to a sudden end about 1800 or 1700 BC, other settlements, particularly those at the outer edges of the Indus valley, have since been shown to have continued beyond this date and to have spawned new colonies. Major climatic and environmental changes may have occurred in the region of the Indus valley early in the 2nd millennium BC: there is evidence that conditions became more arid and that at least one major river-course dried up. Some people have suggested that the very success of the Indus valley civilization upset the environmental balance: there may have been overgrazing, or mismanagement of water supplies, or excessive deforestation. The destruction of walls and buildings (some of which are known to have been sloppily repaired) were perhaps caused by earthquake. While it remains unclear what caused the major cities to become deserted, it seems very far from being the case that the Indus valley civilization was extinguished overnight.

Vedic society and religion

Around 1500 BC invading tribes – the so-called Aryan people – appear to have moved into Punjab from Afghanistan or into Sind through the Bolan pass. No doubt fighting with each other as well as with indigenous tribes, they made their way stage by stage through the densely forested countryside of the Gangetic plain, settling in one place to the life of the sedentary agriculturalist, living elsewhere as semi-nomadic pastoralists, and everywhere making accommodations with those they found already in place. From the number of peoples and leaders named in the early Sanskrit literature it seems that several groups were involved in colonizing the land, sometimes co-operating with each other, sometimes fighting.

The first successful settlements appear to have been along the rivers of eastern Punjab, from where a push was made into the plains of Kurukshetra, lying to the east of the old Sarasvati river. This region, today the modern state of Haryana, has remained a holy place of great significance to Hindus throughout Indian history. At some stage, however, following the drying up of the Saraswati, it became inadequate to support a growing population and a move was made across the Yamuna onto the Doab, the land lying between the Yamuna and the Ganges. From there, settlement pushed eastward into modern Bihar and finally into Bengal and the mouth of the Ganges.

The Aryan culture that became established on the Gangetic plain over a period of a thousand years or so was village-based and overwhelmingly rural and agrarian. Sanskrit was the common language of culture, but there was no over-riding political imperial entity, rather a scattering of tribal communities. There is early fragmentary evidence of an emerging hierarchical social organization, with settlements such as those at Ayodhya, Kashi and Mithila coming under the domination of clans of warrior-priests (kshatriyas). Notions of kingship began to take hold. These were not related to territorial possessions, but were based on the king's authority to maintain the cosmic order and secure the fertility of the earth through the performance of appropriate sacrifices and rituals.

The early literature gives an impression of a life beset by strife and filled with hazard. One poet put it thus: "I feel depressed by my helplessness, by nakedness and want. My mind wanders like a bird which is chased hither and thither. Like rats gnawing their tails by sorrows are gnawing at me." In this insecure and harsh environment, people turned to pondering questions of morality, and began to have doubts about the power of the gods. Later Vedic philosophy explored notions of an immutable law whereby everybody was accountable for his deeds, not just in the present existence but in future rebirths. Greater emphasis was placed on the correct performance of sacrificial rites, and brahmins – priests who could interact with the gods – became of central importance.

The unequal organization of society in which people were allocated status and role by birth and by the history of their previous existences became more clearly specified, while social and economic differences were underlined and reinforced by ritual behavior. The developing corpus of Hindu beliefs was never the expression of a rigid orthodoxy, but absorbed many points of view. There were always some who resisted the claims of monarchical authority and priestly privilege. Moreover, its philosophical ideas were subject to change. Belief in the trauma of a single life, which might be mitigated by the correct performance of magical rites, broadened to the horrific prospect of an endless series of lives – a constant scheme of rebirth, with one's lot (karma) in any particular existence being determined by behavior and fate in an earlier unremembered one. This was a bleak philosophy, but the vision of endless incarnations, in which the quality of existence in each was only partly determined by personal action and morality, was made easier to bear by the possibility of individual liberation from the material world that would lead to an escape from life into unity with the divine source, or godhead. By playing down the unlimited power of the gods to determine the fate of the universe, such ideas undermined the power of the brahmin as the earthly intercessor and performer of necessary propitiatory acts. They are most clearly stated in the teachings of Vardamana Mahavira and of the Buddha.

New beliefs: Jainism and Buddhism

Born into a noble family in the eastern Gangetic plain, Mahavira – the great exponent of Jainism – led a normal life until he was 30, when he renounced the world and became an ascetic. After 12 years he achieved enlightenment and spent another 30 years taking his message through the countryside before achieving final liberation (moksha) by his death. Jains believe this to have happened in 527 BC, but there are arguments to place his death as late as 468 or even 447 BC.

The ideas that Mahavira propounded can be seen to have grown out of the anti-brahminical beliefs about reincarnation that were already developing within Hinduism. Jainism urges asceticism upon its followers as the means of attaining enlightenment and teaches sympathy and compassion for all forms of life. At the core of the Jain cosmology lies the idea that time endlessly repeats itself like a great cosmic wheel, with six spokes on the ascendant and six on the descendant. In the middle two spokes of each ascent and descent 24

Above A sculpture from the stupa at Amaravati, on the river Krishna in modern Andhra Pradesh, which was the most important Buddhist site in south India from the 3rd century BC to the 14th century AD. The stupa, which was reconstructed and refurbished during the rule of the Satavahana dynasty in the 2nd and 3rd centuries AD, surpassed other Buddhist monuments of its time in size and sculptural elaboration. Today, its uniquely beautiful sculptures are preserved in museums in India and Britain. In this panel, the Buddha is shown in human form standing at the gateway to the stupa, being worshiped by snake-kings and other humans. The representation of the dome of the stupa, its supporting slabs, and the gateway include richly carved narrative scenes. The space above the dome is filled with naturalistic human figures and spirits.

Tirthankaras (ford-makers) or Jinas (conquerors, and hence Jains) are born to bring Jain teaching to humanity. In the present revolution of the wheel the first Jina, Rishabha, lived millions of years ago, and after a succession of preachers came the 22nd Jina who was a cousin of Krishna. Parshva, the 23rd Jina, is reckoned to be an historical figure of the 9th century BC; Vardhamana Maharira is the 24th, and hence the last Jina in the current era.

Jainism, because of its anti-brahminical leanings, was attractive to those involved in commerce and trade, who gave their support to Jain communities and promoted Jain teaching. The Jains also won strong political backing from the powerful ruling dynasties that emerged from the expanding societies of the Gangetic plain at the end of the 1st millennium BC: the Mauryans, who became the dominant power there in the late 4th century BC, supported them, and so did the rulers of Kalinga to the east. Jainism spread quickly across India. Mathura on the Yamuna river become an important Jain center, and further west Jains held prominent positions in the principal courts of Gujarat and the Kathiawar peninsula; money flowed into great temple complexes at places like Mount Abu. In the northwestern Deccan Jain communities were supported alongside Hindu temples and Buddhist monasteries. Centers of Jain devotion were also established in the south and Sri Lanka as Jain monks and traders carried their ideas down the east coast. By 300 BC they had become a significant presence in Karnataka, where they were closely associated with several ruling dynasties and exercised a major influence on the development of Kannada literature.

Buddhism, the other great non-brahminical Indian religion, came into being at about the same time and in the same part of India as Jainism. It was based on the life and teachings of Siddharta Gautama who – like Mahavira – rejected domestic life for that of a wandering ascetic. After attaining enlightenment he called himself the Buddha ("the enlightened one") and is believed to have died, or obtained *parinirvana* (complete enlightenment) about 461 BC.

The Buddha's teaching reached out to all sorts and conditions. His main message was very simply that it is misknowledge (misunderstanding of the self and of nature) that causes all suffering by giving rise to violent emotions and evil actions, and that these lead to rebirth in misery. To achieve the understanding that will allow them to escape from eternal rebirth and suffering people have to observe the life of himself and other Buddhas, adhere to absolute truth (the *dharma*) and form enlightened societies of mean and women (the *sangha*). The Buddha propounded a clear ethical code that prohibited killing, stealing, adultery, lying, slander, abuse, frivolity, greed, malice and false ideologies, and encouraged the saving of life and the sharing of gifts.

Like Jainism, Buddhism proved very popular in the expanding society of the central and eastern Gangetic plains, providing opportunities for those excluded from Vedic rituals to participate in a communal religious life that found no place for priestly mediation. With its emphasis on social service and its ability to create wealthy corporate institutions that went far

Below The two summits of Satrunjaya hill, rising 600 meters from the plain just 2 kilometers south of Palatana in Gujarat, boast the largest Jain temple-city in India. According to local tradition, Adinatha, the first Tirthankara, visited the hill several times, and the first temple was built by his son Bharata. The complex was the object of Muslim attacks in the 14th and 15th centuries, and consequently little building survives from before the 16th century. The numerous temples and shrines on the hill, most of which have been endowed by wealthy Jain merchants, are visited by large numbers of pilgrims who ascend to the top each day – a climb of almost two hours – returning to the bottom by nightfall.

The Story of Buddha

Buddhists believe that there have been several Buddhas over the ages (the name means "the enlightened one") but the one known as the Buddha was a man called Siddharta Gautama, who was born c.563 BC. Though a historical figure, there is nothing known of him that is historically recorded, and the many stories arising from his life have formed a body of legend similar to those surrounding the life of Christ. According to these legends, the story of the Buddha began when, as a young brahmin, he took the vow to achieve *nirvana* (enlightenment), many lifetimes before the birth of Siddharta in the 6th century BC. He thus became a *Bodhisattva*, one who has the intent to become enlightened but who remains behind in the cycle of rebirths to help others. Thus he passed from life to life performing virtuous deeds until his last birth, which was to the ruler of a clan called the Sakyas whose homeland was in northern Bihar (hence one of the Buddha's titles, "Sakyamuni").

It was obvious from the miraculous nature of the child's birth that his was to be a spiritual life, but his kshatriya father wanted his son to be a prince and did his best to ensnare him with material wealth. Under his influence, Siddharta married a very beautiful woman and had a son. Through various encounters, however, he realized that the reality for all beings was suffering, and that no material thing would bring him satisfaction. At the age of 29, therefore, he abandoned his worldly life.

He went from one teacher to another, but found no doctrine that would lead him to *nirvana*. He then spent six years practicing severe austerities and fasting, but this, too, failed to lead to enlightenment. He eventually decided to relax his ascetic disciplines and to take food and, sitting beneath a *bodhi* tree, vowed not to move until he attained enlightenment. In response to his earlier realization that suffering was universal, when enlightenment came it was as a revelation of the Way of Salvation. This became the essence of the Buddha's teaching, consisting of the Four Noble Truths followed by the Eightfold Path. The Four Noble Truths are the fact of suffering; that suffering has a cause; that it can be ended; and that it can be ended by following the Eightfold Path of right views, right intention, right speech, right action, right livelihood, right effort, right mindfulness and right concentration. This leads in time to *nirvana*, which is the cessation of desire and liberation from the cycle of rebirth.

These representations of the life-cycle of the Buddha are from Gandhara in the northwest of the subcontinent, and were made in the early centuries of the Christian era when the first images of the Buddha began to appear. Sacred art tends to be fixed and conservative in form, with little room for change, but the arising of Buddhism gave the opportunity for new art styles to flourish. Gandharan sculptors were greatly influenced by their contacts with Greco-Roman culture and their art is a striking fusion of western classical and Indian styles.

Below The Buddha died in Kusinagara, in modern Uttar Pradesh, after eating a meal of pork. He had ordained that his body should be burnt on a funeral pyre, and that a stupa (funerary mound) should contain his ashes. However, after the cremation, a quarrel broke out over the remains, with several people claiming them.

It was resolved by a brahmin called Drona who, as shown in this relief, divided the ashes into eight parts. Stupas were built as giant reliquaries over the Buddha's scattered remains, the earliest being at Sanchi.

Left Siddharta Gautama was one of a line of Buddhas. When a young brahmin in a previous birth, he prostrated himself before the Buddha called Dipamkara and spread out his hair for the master to walk upon. Dipamkara promised the fulfillment of the vow of the *Bodhisattva*, and the young brahmin rose into the air. In this relief of the 2nd century AD the figure on the ground has eroded. The sculptor's delight in fabric folds is typical of the Gandharan style.

Below Both the conception and the birth of Siddharta was miraculous. He was conceived in a vision when his mother Maya dreamt that a white elephant entered her right side. When it came to the delivery, the child was born from her right side. There were signs upon him which, after interpretation by the priests, led to his being named Siddharta – "he whose purpose is accomplished". In this relief of the 2nd–3rd century AD, the elephant – an incarnation of the *Bodhisattva* – is shown entering Maya.

Above The young Siddharta, having become a monk, spent six years in the company of five ascetics. Together they practiced various disciplines of self-mortification, which were so severe as to lead to the emaciation of the body. Such disciplines are still practiced by ascetic holy men (*sadhus*) in India today, but in spurning them the Buddha established the Buddhist way of a moderate half-line between worldliness and austerity, and a preference for contemplation. The skeletal figure of the emaciated *Bodhisattva* occurs often in Buddhist art. When Siddharta relaxed his disciplines, the five ascetics deserted him and went to Sarnath near Varanasi.

Above After enlightenment at Bodh Gaya, the Buddha went is search of his fellow ascetics and found them at a deer garden in Sarnath. There he preached his First Sermon, the text of which survives. Shown in this Gandharan relief is the seated Buddha in the characteristic cross-legged *padmasana* pose. Other iconographical details of the Buddha are the top-knot, which indicates his origin in the warrior caste, the mole between his eyebrows, and his extended ear lobes. Below is the symbol of the Wheel of the Doctrine flanked by deer, indicating the location where the wheel was first set in motion. Beside the Buddha are the ascetics who were to become his first disciples.

Sanchi

The earliest phase of Buddhist architecture and art is nowhere better illustrated than in the monuments at Sanchi, a remote site in central India, dating from the 3rd century BC. Sanchi has no known connections with the life of Buddha himself, but the shrines here received patronage from the emperor Ashoka as well as local craftsmen, such as ivory-workers from the nearby town of Vidisha. Sanchi is known for its solid hemispherical features known as stupas. Originally intended as funerary mounds encasing holy relics of Buddha and his followers, Sanchi's stupas also symbolize the life and teachings of the Master. Veneration was paid by proceeding around the stupa in clockwise motion. Other forms of worship at this site took place in temples. That monks actually lived at Sanchi is indicated by a number of monastic complexes.

Below The most important monuments at Sanchi are located on the flat top of a hill surrounded by a perimeter wall. The group is dominated by stupa 1, but there are also smaller versions, including stupa 2. They are surrounded by apsidal-ended shrines, structural temples, monasteries and commemorative columns.

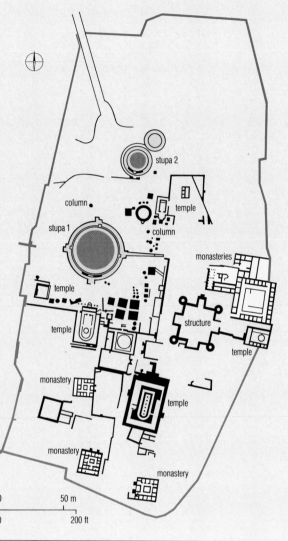

beyond the narrow ties of family and tribe, it must have been attractive to those who were pushing forward the colonization of new land in the east, beyond the frontiers established by the tribal royal supremacies. The rise of Jainism and Buddhism should not be separated from a longer process of social and economic change that took place in the Gangetic plain in the 6th and 5th centuries BC, which manifested itself particularly in the building of new towns. There is also evidence for public buildings and religious monuments including, by the 5th century, Buddhist stupas. Coins and weights have been discovered, and after 500 BC a new kind of pottery – the northern black polished ware – became widely distributed. Literary sources (particularly Buddhist and Jain chronicles) paint a picture of growing political rivalry as chieftains established new settlements and attempted to consolidate their hold on them. In time these agricultural communities banded together in tribal federations, increasingly identified with particular areas and territories. By the beginning of the 5th century BC, Buddhist sources speak of 16 major realms or domains (*Mahajanapadas*) in India.

The kingdoms in the northwest of the subcontinent came increasingly into the orbit of their neighbors in southwest Asia. In 530 BC the area was invaded by the Achaemenid emperor Cyrus, who made Gandhara (corresponding to northwestern Pakistan and eastern Afghanistan) a satrapy, or administrative division, of his empire. Successive Persian rulers exploited the wealth and manpower of the Indus region to extend their power in southwest Asia. In 327 BC Alexander the Great of Macedon (356–323 BC), who had brought about the downfall of the Achaemenid empire four years earlier, led his conquering Greek army into Gandhara and overran the area of Punjab, but was forced to withdraw after two years.

At the eastern end of the Gangetic plain an indigenous center of power began to emerge in the area of Magadha (contemporary Bihar). The region's agricultural wealth and mineral resources (particularly iron) allowed its Nanda rulers to dominate its neighbors and then extend their authority south and west. For a century or so, from around 340 BC, the Nandas even made the Magadha region pre-eminent over the whole of the Gangetic plain.

Below Scenes of Buddha's life are frequently illustrated on the Sanchi portals. A favorite episode is the worship of the *bodhi* tree beneath which Buddha sat when he gained Enlightenment. In this early phase of Buddhist art the Master himself is never shown. His presence here is indicated merely by the empty throne.

Far left Stupa 1 is a massive hemispherical mound of masonry. At the summit is a small square railing and a multi-tiered, umbrella-like finial. This marks the point in which a reliquary casket was buried deep inside the stupa. A paved pathway defined by stone railing surrounds the stupa. Portals in the middle of four sides have stone posts and lintels imitating wooden construction. The carvings that cover these elements contrast with the unadorned surfaces of the stupa and railings.

Right The cave-temples and monasteries at Ajanta in Maharashtra cover a span of more than 600 years from the 2nd century BC, and contain some of the finest examples of early Buddhist art in India. Particularly impressive are the mural paintings depicting scenes from the life of the Buddha and other divines. The most numerous are in cave 17, from which this detail comes, and date from the 5th century AD, Paintings in this cave include an unusual composition of the Wheel of Life and a panel showing Indra flying through the clouds, accompanied by a troupe of celestial beings, as well as elaborate representations of Buddha figures and scenes from the Jakata stories.

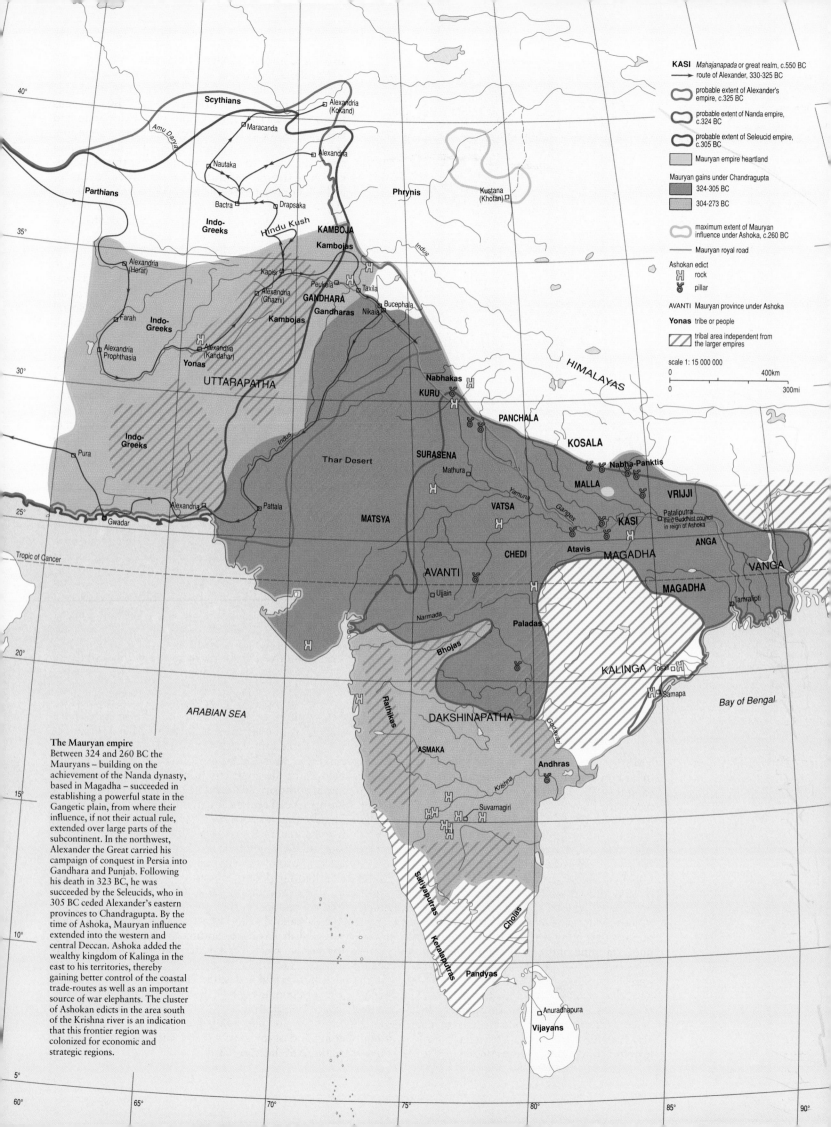

40°

Scythians

Alexandria
(Kokand)

Amu Darya

Maracanda

Parthians

Alexandria

Phrynis

Kustana
(Khotan)

Nautaka

Indo-
Greeks

Bactra   Drapsaka

35°

Hindu Kush   KAMBOJA

Indus

HIMALAYAS

Kambojas

Alexandria
(Herat)

Kapiṣi   Peukela

Taxila

Alexandria
(Ghazni)   GANDHARA

Bucephala

Indo-
Greeks

Kambojas   Gandharas   Nikaia

Farah

30°

Alexandria
(Kandahar)

Nabhakas

Alexandria
Prophthasia   Yonas

UTTARAPATHA

KURU

PANCHALA

KOSALA

Indo-
Greeks

Pura

Indus

SURASENA   Nabha-Panktis

MALLA

VRIJJI

Mathura

Thar Desert

Yamuna   Pataliputra   ANGA
third Buddhist council
in reign of Ashoka

VATSA

Ganges   KASI

Alexandria   Pattala

25°

MATSYA

CHEDI

Atavis   MAGADHA   VANGA

Gwadar

AVANTI   MAGADHA

Tropic of Cancer

Ujjain   Tamralipti

Narmada

Paladas

20°

Bhojas   KALINGA   Tosali

Samapa

Rathikas   Bay of Bengal

ARABIAN SEA   DAKSHINAPATHA   Godavari

The Mauryan empire
Between 324 and 260 BC the
Mauryans – building on the
achievement of the Nanda dynasty,
based in Magadha – succeeded in
establishing a powerful state in the
Gangetic plain, from where their
influence, if not their actual rule,
extended over large parts of the
subcontinent. In the northwest,
Alexander the Great carried his
campaign of conquest in Persia into
Gandhara and Punjab. Following
his death in 323 BC, he was
succeeded by the Seleucids, who in
305 BC ceded Alexander's eastern
provinces to Chandragupta. By the
time of Ashoka, Mauryan influence
extended into the western and
central Deccan. Ashoka added the
wealthy kingdom of Kalinga in the
east to his territories, thereby
gaining better control of the coastal
trade-routes as well as an important
source of war elephants. The cluster
of Ashokan edicts in the area south
of the Krishna river is an indication
that this frontier region was
colonized for economic and
strategic regions.

ASMAKA

Andhras

Krishna

15°

Suvarnagiri

Satiyaputras

10°

Cholas

Keralaputras

Pandyas

Anuradhapura

Vijayans

5°

60°   65°   70°   75°   80°   85°   90°

KASI *Mahajanapada* or great realm, c.550 BC

route of Alexander, 330-325 BC

probable extent of Alexander's
empire, c.325 BC

probable extent of Nanda empire,
c.324 BC

probable extent of Seleucid empire,
c.305 BC

Mauryan empire heartland

Mauryan gains under Chandragupta

324-305 BC

304-273 BC

maximum extent of Mauryan
influence under Ashoka, c.260 BC

Mauryan royal road

Ashokan edict

rock

pillar

AVANTI Mauryan province under Ashoka

Yonas tribe or people

tribal area independent from
the larger empires

scale 1: 15 000 000

0   400km

0   300mi

Right This capital, carved from a polished sandstone, dates from c.250 BC. It originally headed a stone column more than 15 meters high, erected at Sarnath where the Buddha preached his first sermon, on which were displayed edicts of Ashoka, proclaiming him to be the world-conquering righteous king. The magnificent capital, with its four majestic lions, looking north, south, east and west, was fittingly adopted as the symbol of the Republic of India in 1948.

The Mauryan empire

In 321 BC Chandragupta Maurya seized the Nanda capital of Pataliputra (modern Patna) and took control of the Nanda state. He launched his bid for power from the frontier region of the northwest, where he had been fighting against the military outposts left by Alexander of Macedon. Tradition has it that his principal colleague and advisor in these campaigns was Kautilya, the author of the *Arthashatra*, a famous treatise on statecraft, and that both men had fallen out of favor with the Magadha court and had been exiled to the northwest. The *Arthashatra*, written in the form of a manual of advice to a ruler, is remarkable for its understanding of the working of politics and its timeless psychological insight into human political behavior. The successful ruler, according to Kautilya, had to have fine personal qualities, choose good and intelligent ministers, and pay close attention to the condition of his provinces, his city, his treasure, his army and his allies. He would be a man who understood how to build up his power while at the same time

striving to undermine that of his rivals.

As ruler, Chandragupta's first aim was to secure the northwestern district, and by about 311 BC the Indus had been fixed as his frontier. In 302 BC Seleucus Nicator (d. 281 BC), the satrap of Babylon who had emerged as the ruler of Alexander's eastern empire, became active in the region, but in 305 Chandragupta secured a treaty in which, among other things, Seleucus ceded to him Alexander's eastern provinces east of Kabul in return for an alliance and a corps of 500 war elephants. With this settlement both the Indus and the Gangetic plains came under the nominal control of a single ruler for the first time.

Chandragupta received at his court at Pataliputra an ambassador from Seleucus, Megasthenes, whose account of his embassy is preserved in later classical texts. He describes a thriving society, supported by an organized government and divided into several social orders. Megasthenes believed that the king owned all the land. In return for protection, the farmers not only paid rent for their fields but handed over a quarter of their produce in tax. According to Jain writings, Chandragupta became an adherent of their beliefs and gave up his royal power to become a wandering ascetic. Some time during the 290s BC his son Bindusara became ruler. By the time of his death in c. 272 BC Mauryan influence had been extended into the Deccan as far south as Karnataka.

Bindusara was succeeded in 268 or 267 BC by his son Ashoka, who was to be the greatest of the Mauryan kings. Ashoka at once turned his attention towards the kingdom of Kalinga (present-day Orissa). Kautilya had written that "Victory for a king depends primarily on elephants", and had also reported that some of the finest war elephants came from the forests of Kalinga. Ashoka now determined to capture the kingdom in the east, which was an area of great wealth and strategic importance, able to control the coastal trade-routes. Kalinga had so far resisted Mauryan attempts to dominate in, but it was unable to withstand the violence of Ashoka's assault in 261 BC. According to his own accounts, 100,000 men were killed in battle and over 150,000 people forcibly resettled elsewhere in Mauryan territory.

The capture of Kalinga marked the limit of Mauryan military conquest. Ashoka is supposed to have showed such contrition at the human havoc wrought in the fiercesome battle for Kalinga that he became a Buddhist, abjuring further violence and, as a ruler beloved of the gods, conquered only by virtue of his moral authority. In a number of carved edicts set up in his provincial centers and in the frontier regions of his kingdom he laid out his principles for a just government. Officials toured his domains to see his edicts were obeyed, and Mauryan delegations (no doubt making use of the expanding networks of Buddhist and Jain missionaries) took the same message to the independent courts of the south and of Sri Lanka, and to the kingdoms beyond the northwest frontier.

Ashoka died in 233 BC. The empire he did so much to establish may have continued to function effectively for about another 50 years before succumbing to internal factionalism and external pressures. The elaboration and widespread dissemination of imperial ideology conducted by Ashoka was unparalleled in the ancient world. It was also shrewd and politically realistic. No previous ruler had managed to gain such command of the subcontinent and none would do so again until the Mughals.

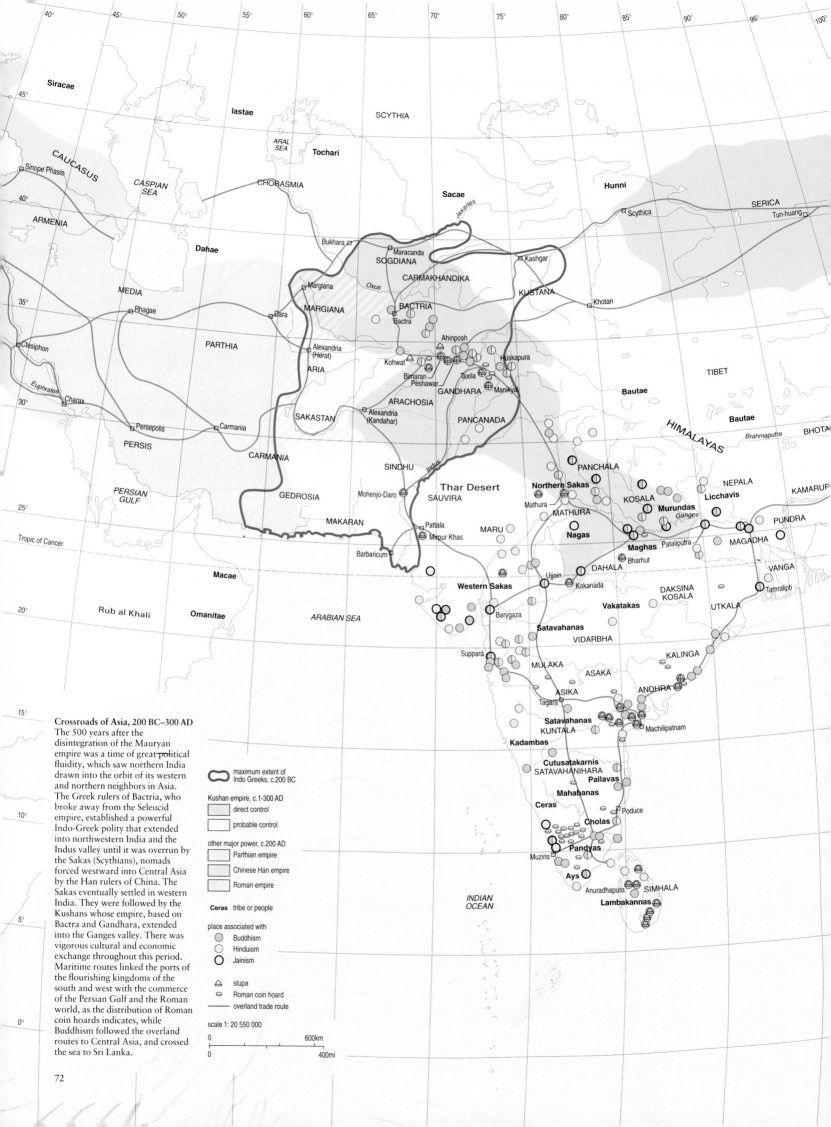

Crossroads of Asia, 200 BC–300 AD
The 500 years after the disintegration of the Mauryan empire was a time of great political fluidity, which saw northern India drawn into the orbit of its western and northern neighbors in Asia. The Greek rulers of Bactria, who broke away from the Seleucid empire, established a powerful Indo-Greek polity that extended into northwestern India and the Indus valley until it was overrun by the Sakas (Scythians), nomads forced westward into Central Asia by the Han rulers of China. The Sakas eventually settled in western India. They were followed by the Kushans whose empire, based on Bactra and Gandhara, extended into the Ganges valley. There was vigorous cultural and economic exchange throughout this period. Maritime routes linked the ports of the flourishing kingdoms of the south and west with the commerce of the Persian Gulf and the Roman world, as the distribution of Roman coin hoards indicates, while Buddhism followed the overland routes to Central Asia, and crossed the sea to Sri Lanka.

maximum extent of Indo Greeks, c.200 BC

Kushan empire, c.1–300 AD
direct control
probable control

other major power, c.200 AD
Parthian empire
Chinese Han empire
Roman empire

Ceras tribe or people

place associated with
Buddhism
Hinduism
Jainism

stupa
Roman coin hoard
overland trade route

scale 1: 20 550 000
0 — 600km
0 — 400mi

886666868888888888888

Above A gold pendant showing a Roman emperor, perhaps Constantine (280–337 BC) or one of his sons, with a Latin inscription on the obverse, and the goddess Ardochsho with a Bactrian inscription in Greek script on the reverse. The obverse appears to have been copied from a Roman coin current in the first half of the 4th century AD, and the reverse derives from coins of Kanishka current in the 2nd century AD. The pendant has been described as "a fantasy, a creation of some fanciful jeweler" who worked in northwest India in the late 4th century.

The Gupta empire (*right*) During the 4th century AD the Guptas, based in the central Gangetic plain, reestablished an imperial state that included most of northern India as far as the Himalayas. Their period of rule is rightly regarded as a cultural highpoint in the history of the subcontinent, when some of the finest Buddhist and Hindu monuments were built, a rich courtly literature in Sanskrit was developed, and Hinduism began to take on its recognizably classical form. However, it was extremely difficult to hold together such a vast and diverse state, and it proved unable to withstand the challenge of the Hunas (Huns) from Central Asia. The Vakatakas, closely linked to the Guptas through marriage alliances, appear to have dominated the northern Deccan, while farther south a number of local lineages contested power with each other.

Political fragmentation

The Mauryan empire gave way to a rapid succession of smaller principalities, partly resulting from the new movements of peoples from Central Asia and the Hellenic world into the northwest. The most successful were of these the Kushans, nomads originally from northwest China who by c.128 BC were in evidence to the north of the Amu Darya (Oxus) river, from where they conquered Bactria and Sogdiana. Moving through the passes of the Hindu Kush into India, their influence in the 1st and 2nd centuries AD extended as far east as Varanasi and southward into Malwa and Gujarat. Drawing on the agricultural wealth of the fertile Amu Darya, Indus and Gangetic river valleys, the Kushan territories also straddled the lucrative trade-routes that carried silk overland from China to the Mediterranean, and they accumulated large amounts of gold. Their great leader Kanishka issued coins that used Chinese, Parthian, Indian and Roman titles to proclaim his sovereignty and displayed Hindu, Buddhist, Greek, Persian and even Sumerian-Elamite images of gods.

Theirs was not an integrated empire, but a loose federation of small kingdoms and chieftains, and the Kushans adopted the languages, scripts and cultures of the people they ruled. Wide-ranging in their patronage, they vigorously promoted Buddhism and employed the artists of Gandhara, who were much

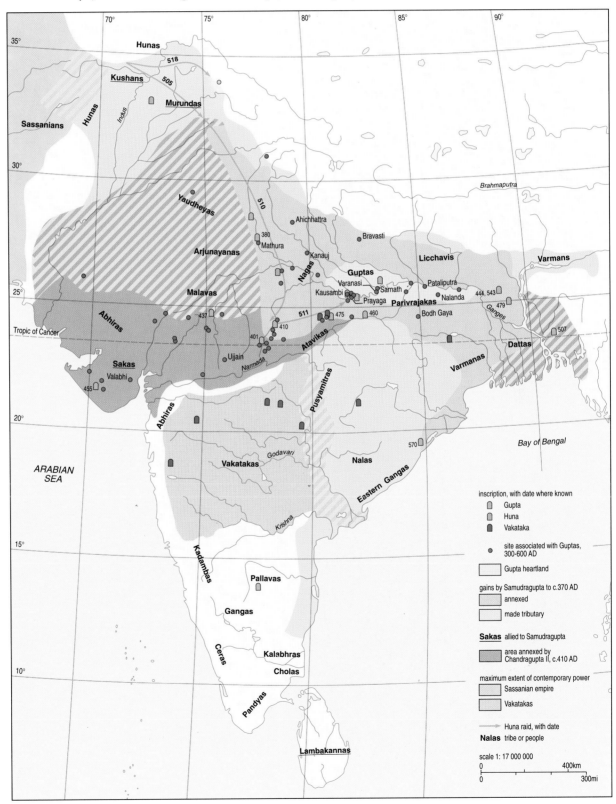

influenced by Hellenic styles, as well as Indian artists centered on Mathura. Poets and philosophers were made welcome at their courts and camps, and Sanskrit literature blossomed during this period.

By the 3rd and 2nd centuries BC, a steady stream of migrants had begun to travel south in search of wealth and trade, bringing with them the religions and ideas of the north, and peninsular India began to assume a more complex social character as new populations settled alongside those already established. The building of artificial ponds and lakes (tanks) for irrigation allowed the area of settled agriculture to increase, and the populations of the valleys and deltas grew. Ports were established on the coasts, with connections with the more sparsely populated inland areas along the rivers and by sea with other coastal regions. Longer distance journeys were made, and overseas maritime trade became an important aspect of south Indian life. During the 1st millennium AD, a number of distinct centers of power were to emerge as successive dynasties such as the Pandyas (based on Madurai), the Pallavas – a northern brahmin dynasty that became established in the south with their capital at Kanchipuram – and after them the Cholas, who established an ascendancy along the Kaveri river in the 8th and 9th

centuries, took control of trade and for a time became the dominant power over a wide area outside their own locality. But, despite claims to overlordship, political boundaries were never securely fixed, and no one dynasty, and no one linguistic or economic region could ever truly claim to dominate the peninsula.

Greek geographers writing in the 1st century AD give us some idea of the scale and value of international trade in the ancient world, and of India's place in it. Towns in the northwest like Taxila linked the complex networks of overland trade; ports on the west and east coasts acted as entrepots for maritime trade. Indian muslins found their way into Africa in exchange for ivory and gold; the island of Socotra in the Arabian Sea traded Indian rice, wheat, textiles and slaves for tortoise-shell; the Persian Gulf imported Indian copper, sandalwood, teak and ebony. Ports in south India handled silks from China, oils from the Gangetic plains, precious stones and spices from Southeast Asia.

Trade was often run by powerful merchant guilds associated with Buddhists and Jains, and major Buddhist and Jain monuments – stupas, rock-cut caves and monasteries, adorned with paintings and sculptures – were constructed in the centuries around 500

goods traded

- ● import
- ● export
- ✚ cloth
- ⊝ coin
- ✳ dye
- ⊟ glass
- △ incense
- ✎ ivory
- ☆ metal
- ✪ precious stones
- ① rice/wheat
- ⊓ silk
- ⚲ slaves
- ◇ spices
- ⊞ timber
- ◎ tortoise shell
- ↘ weapons
- ⚜ wine

scale 1: 30 000 000

0   600km

0   400mi

Left Mamallapuram was the principal port city of the Pallava dynasty who were the most powerful rulers of the Tamil region of south India in the 7th and 8th centuries. It contains many fine monuments. This elephant (with a lion beyond) belongs to a sequence of 7th-century monoliths known as the Pancha Rathas (the five chariots). They were not completed nor used as actual places of worship, and may have served as shrine models of different architectural design.

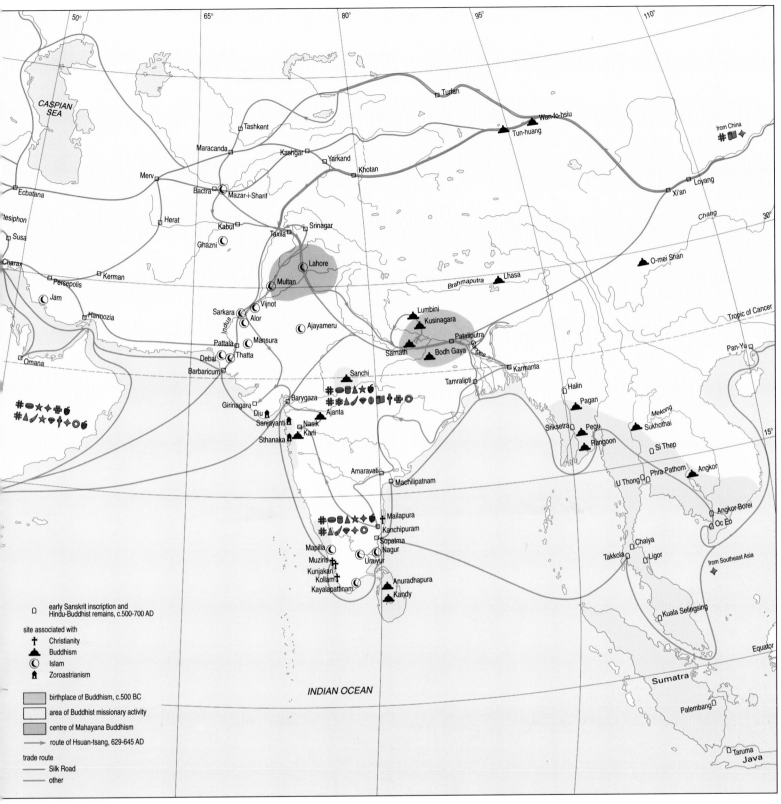

50°   65°   80°   95°   110°

CASPIAN
SEA

Ecbatana
•tesiphon
Susa
Charax
Persepolis
Kerman
Jam
Harmozia
Omana

Merv
Bactra   Mazar-i-Sharif
Herat
Kabul   Srinagar
Ghazni   Taxila
Lahore
Multan
Sarkara   Vijnot
Alor
Ajayameru
Pattala   Mansura
Debal   Thatta
Barbaricum

Tashkent
Maracanda
Kashgar   Yarkand
Khotan

Turfan
Wan-fo-hsiu
Tun-huang
from China
Loyang
Xi'an
Chang

O-mei Shan

Brahmaputra   Lhasa

Tropic of Cancer

Lumbini
Kusinagara
Pataliputra
Sarnath   Bodh Gaya
Karmanta
Tamralipti

Girinagara   Barygaza
Diu
Sanjayanti   Nasik
Ajanta
Sthanaka   Karli
Sanchi

Amaravati
Machilipatnam

Mailapura
Kanchipuram
Sopatma
Mapilla   Nagur
Muziris   Uraiyur
Kunjakari
Kollam
Kayalapattinam
Anuradhapura
Kandy

Halin
Pagan
Sriksetra   Pegu
Rangoon
Mekong
Sukhothai
Si Thep

U Thong   Phra Pathom   Angkor
Angkor Borei
Oc Eo

Chaiya
Takkola   Ligor   from Southeast Asia

Kuala Selingsing

Pan-Yu

INDIAN OCEAN

Equator
Sumatra
Palembang
Taruma
Java

Ω early Sanskrit inscription and
   Hindu-Buddhist remains, c.500–700 AD

site associated with
✝ Christianity
▲ Buddhism
☾ Islam
⌂ Zoroastrianism

☐ birthplace of Buddhism, c.500 BC
☐ area of Buddhist missionary activity
☐ centre of Mahayana Buddhism
→ route of Hsuan-tsang, 629–645 AD

trade route
—— Silk Road
—— other

India's place in the world

By the 1st millennium AD, the subcontinent had developed far-ranging cultural and commercial links. Routes through the passes of the northwest brought cultural contact and exchange with the peoples of Central Asia and beyond, to both east and west; sea passages through the Persian Gulf and the Red Sea facilitated trade with the Mediterranean and Africa, and were the means by which Christianity and Islam first entered the subcontinent. Trade from India's eastern ports carried western and Indian influences to Southeast Asia.

AD. Rulers as well as mercantile families showed their devotion by generous religious benefactions. Buddhism was particularly well entrenched in the northwest, while the Jain influence was strong in the west and the Deccan. But there was also a gradual resurgence of brahminism and sacrificial Vedic religion, together with the growth of theistic Hindu sects. Gods of both pre-Aryan and of non-Aryan origin found their way into the evolving Hindu pantheon: at Madurai, for example, the local goddess Minakshi became a wife of Shiva. At the same time, notions of social stratification and of purity and impurity became more rigidly codified. In many parts of India the new Hinduism won popularity and princely patronage.

The Guptas (c.320–455 AD)

In the 4th century the Gupta dynasty emerged as a new power in the Gangetic plain. From its heartland in the area around Allahabad and Varanasi its territories were extended by marriage and military conquest until, by the reign of Chandragupta II (375–415), the Gupta empire extended from the Ganges delta to that of the Indus and from the high mountains of the north to the Narmada valley. Its influence ran far beyond the territories that came under its direct rule. As an inscription on an old Ashokan pillar at Allahabad detailing the achievements of Samudragupta, Chandragupta's father, records, rulers as far distant as Sri Lanka "pleased the emperor by offering him various

Rock-cut Monuments

Temples and sacred monuments carved into cliffs and rock-faces are found widely distributed throughout India. Large amounts of solid rock had to be excavated and removed before sculptural treatment could begin, and the Indian masons who created these complex structures demonstrated remarkable technical skills and ingenuity in overcoming this and other difficulties. The earliest rock-cut monuments, such as those at Junnar, Nasik, Ajanta and Udayagiri, date back to the 2nd century BC and are associated with early Buddhism and Jainism. They take the form of monastic establishments, known as viharas, in which groups of small cells to accommodate monks have been cut directly into cliff faces. They are mostly found in close proximity to chaitya halls – prayer chambers with colonnaded aisles leading to the model stupas (funerary mounds housing relics of the Buddha) that provided a focus for prayers. A particular feature of these chaitya halls are the arched vaults with curving ribs, such as that roofing the great chaitya hall at Karli (*bottom right*).

By the 4th and 5th centuries AD, it was permitted to worship images of the Buddha, and the makers of the rock-cut temples made use of a lively figural imagery in which icons of the Master were placed in shrines at the end of halls and corridors. Painted imagery also came to cover the walls of rock-cut temples, and the frescoes in the 5th-century viharas at Ajanta are world famous. Hindu rock-cut architecture responded to these technical advances with the result that there exists a series of excavated shrines at 7th-century sites such as Ellora, Badami and Mamallapuram. These temples have central halls with side shrines to accommodate different deities for worship. The interiors are enlivened with richly sculptured panels that illustrate the gods and goddesses of the Hindu pantheon in the company of guardian figures, attendant maidens, dancers and musicians.

A parallel, though slightly later, development is the preference for monolithic temples that were cut out of solid rock but stood open to the sky. Famous examples are to be found at Mamallapuram, built by the Pallavas in the 7th and 8th centuries, but others also exist. The largest and most elaborate is the Kailasa at Ellora, illustrated below, a project unsurpassed in the history of Indian architecture.

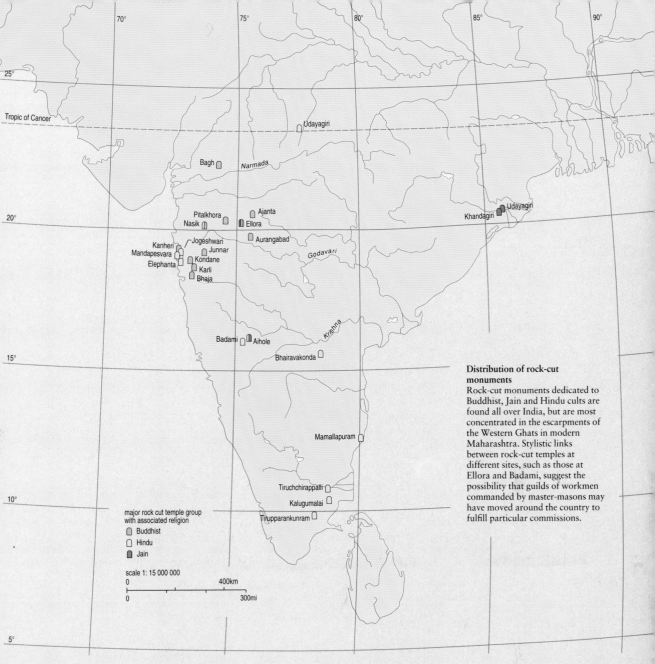

Distribution of rock-cut monuments

Rock-cut monuments dedicated to Buddhist, Jain and Hindu cults are found all over India, but are most concentrated in the escarpments of the Western Ghats in modern Maharashtra. Stylistic links between rock-cut temples at different sites, such as those at Ellora and Badami, suggest the possibility that guilds of workmen commanded by master-masons may have moved around the country to fulfill particular commissions.

major rock cut temple group
with associated religion
- Buddhist
- Hindu
- Jain

scale 1: 15 000 000
0   400km
0   300mi

Above That excavated temples were actually part of the "living" rock did not dissuade architects from fashioning them in the likeness of actual buildings, complete with the structural apparatus of columns, brackets, beams and ceilings. The interior of the 6th-century AD cave-temple on Elephanta island in Bombay harbor shows lines of elegantly conceived columns. The tops of the shafts and the capitals have swelling fluted forms.

Left The Kailasa monument at Ellora was constructed under the direction of the 8th-century AD Rashtrakuta ruler, Dantidurga. A deep trench was first cut out of a cliff face to leave a mass that was then carefully whittled away to give the semblance of an actual built form. In the foreground is a standing elephant and a decorated victory pillar, both monoliths, with the walls of the main shrine behind. The sides of the surrounding trench are still visible.

Right Rock-cut architecture was directly derived from built wooden forms, as is revealed in this cut-away drawing of the chaitya hall at Karli in the Western Ghats. This 1st-century BC Buddhist monument has teak ribs set into its rock-cut vault, thereby suggesting the actual wooden hall that it imitates.

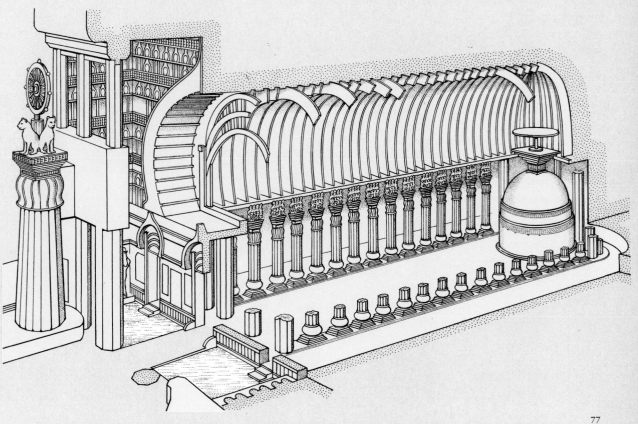

Khajuraho

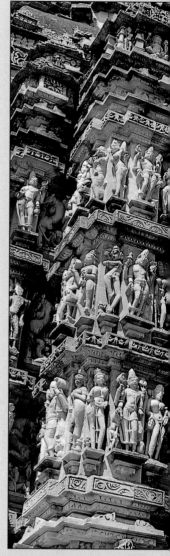

The Chandellas were one of several lines of rulers that dominated central India between the 9th and 11th centuries. Yet little is known about them, and virtually no remains belong to their period other than religious buildings. The largest and most impressive temples stand at the remote site of Khajuraho, sometimes identified as the Chandella capital. There are around 30 monuments at Khajuraho dedicated to different Hindu cults and even the Jain saviors. The temples demonstrate a distinctive and coherent evolution marking the culmination of the central Indian style. The chief characteristics are the soaring towers that develop from single spires into complex clustered arrangements with multiple elements crowding around a central mass. This sustained emphasis on superstructures reflects the symbolic function of the temple as an evocation of Meru, the cosmic mountain.

Below and plan The Vishvanatha Temple erected in 1002 AD is one of the finest in the complex at Khajuraho. It stands on a broad terrace surrounded by minor shrines, and is approached through an entrance porch reached by flights of steps. Its exterior is dominated by a curving tower that soars over the sanctuary. The molded basements on which the temples are raised are enlivened with carvings of guardians, attendants and divinities, as seen on the right of the picture.

Below Some of the temples display sculptures of couples in erotic and sexual postures, as here on the Parshvanatha Temple. The meaning of these figures is puzzling. On the one hand, they may illustrate esoteric tantric practices intended for initiates only; on the other, they may be merely imaginative realizations of courtly love. A clue to the magical and protective power of these couples may be seen from their locations on the most ritually vulnerable parts of the temple – the junctions of halls for worshipers and sanctuaries for gods. The sculptures on the Vishvanatha Temple (*right*) are arranged in ascending tiers crowded with divinities, attendants and devotees.

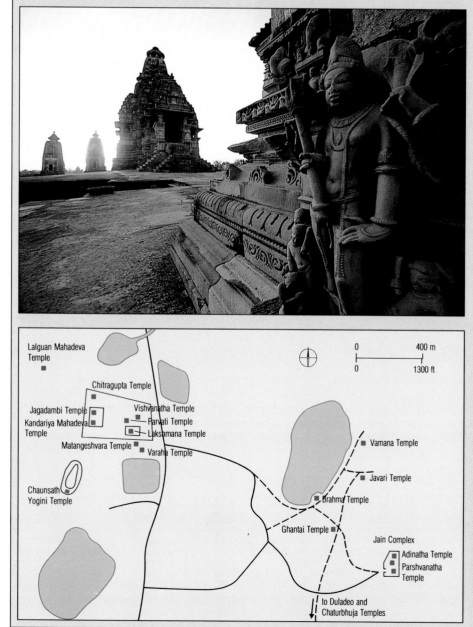

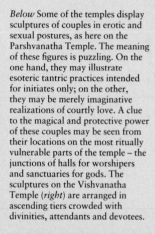

Lalguan Mahadeva Temple

Chitragupta Temple

Jagadambi Temple
Kandariya Mahadeva Temple

Vishvanatha Temple
Parvati Temple
Lakshmana Temple

Matangeshvara Temple
Varaha Temple

Chaunsath Yogini Temple

0   400 m
0   1300 ft

Vamana Temple

Javari Temple

Brahma Temple

Ghantai Temple

Jain Complex
Adinatha Temple
Parshvanatha Temple

to Duladeo and Chaturbhuja Temples

Above A polished sandstone image of Nandi, the bull mount of Shiva, is placed in front of the Vishvanatha Temple. The animal is decked in ceremonial garlands and bands, but is otherwise depicted naturalistically. The pavilion in which Nandi sits is roofed with a corbelled dome constructed from ascending rings of stonework.

The dynastic politics of Sri Lanka often entwined with those of south India. These frescoes come from the palace of Sigiriya, built for the Sri Lankan ruler Kasyapa after he murdered his father in 473. His brother deposed him in 491 with the help of a Tamil army, leading to a significant south Indian presence at the Sri Lankan court.

personal services, presents, girls in marriage, and by applying for charters entitling them to the enjoyment of their own territories".

The Guptas were supporters of the resurgent Hinduism. Samudragupta made much of restoring old Vedic sacrifices associated with kingship. One of his magnificent gold coins displays a sacrificial horse on one side and his chief queen on the other with the legend, "After conquering the earth the Great King of Kings with the strength of an invincible hero is going to conquer the heavens." The Chinese Buddhist pilgrim Fa-hsien who visited Chandragupta's court reported in his journal (a valuable source of information about life in northern India at this time) that when people "enter towns or markets they strike a piece of wood to announce their presence, so that others may know they are coming and avoid them" – apparently referring to the enforcement of elaborate caste rules.

Some of the main features of Hinduism such as image-worship and the devotional *bhakti* tradition came into being in this period, with the temple becoming a central institution of social and religious life; Shiva and Vishnu were placed at the head of the Hindu pantheon. The *Ramayana* and the *Mahabharata*, along with the main *Puranas*, were cast in their final form, and Sanskrit literature reached new heights with the poetry and plays of Kalidasa, which celebrate nature, conjugal love and family life. Treatises on law and books on religion and philosophy were written, while advances were made in astronomy and mathematics – later the use of the cipher and Indian numerals would be adopted by the Arabs and introduced by them to Europe. During these years Indian culture was transmitted to Southeast Asia, following commerce and trade, and contacts with China were frequent.

Succession disputes and local rebellion weakened the Gupta state in the late 5th century, and it was unable to withstand the incursions of the Huns from Central Asia. Northern India was to remain politically fragmented for another 500 years, though a brief hegemony over the Gangetic plain was established by Harsha (reigned 606–47). He supported Buddhism, particularly the great center of learning at Nalanda in Bihar, but also patronized Sanskrit writers and once every five years presided over a great distribution of treasure at the sacred confluence of the Ganges and Yamuna. As in the south, the ensuing centuries witnessed the rise of a number of locally important dynasties. In the northwest a number of small but vigorous Rajput principalities emerged, often based on kin-groupings. These chieftains set about building fortresses in the hilly country of modern Rajasthan and providing havens for crafts, trade and religion. On

35°
65° 70° 75° 80° 85° 90° 95°

Kabul □

Peshawar □ 🕌   Srinagar □ 🕌
30°
KALANAU
Gujrat □ 🕌 Sialkot 🕌
Chhani Sahnpal □ 🕌
Chiniot □ 🕌 Lahore □ 🕌
Kasur □ 🕌 **LAHORE** Sukhet □
Multan 🕌 Hujra □ 🕌 Sirhind 🕌
Ghazni □   **SAMANA** Sadhaura □

Indus
MULTAN Bhatnair □ **KUHRAM** Hardwar □
Uch □   Panipat □ 🕌 Gangoh 🕌
SARSUTI **HANBI** Meerut □
Delhi □ 🕌 Miyath □
SIWISTAN **UCH** **DELHI** **BADAYUN**
25°
Nagaur □ 🕌
Sikri □ 🕌 **KANAUJ** **AWADH**
Yamuna
Gwalior □ 🕌 Jais □ 🕌 Sultanpur □ 🕌
Jaunpur □ 🕌
KARA Jaunpur □ **JAUNPUR** **BIHAR**
Manikpur □ 🕌 **1394**
Brahmaputra
Ganges
Gagraun □ 🕌 Gaur □
MALWA
Tropic of Cancer **1392** Sarangpur □ 🕌 **BENGAL**
1341
Ahmadabad □ 🕌 Narmada Garha □
GUJARAT
1396 **GONDWANA**
KHANDESH Ratanpur □
1382
Thalner □ Burhanpur □ 🕌 **JAJNAGAR**
20°
ARABIAN SEA **BERAR** Canda □ *Bay of Bengal*
Daulatabad □
Aurangabad □ 🕌 **DEVAGIRI**
AHMADNAGAR
BAHMANI KINGDOM **GOLCONDA**
1347 **BIDAR**
Gulbarga □ **TELLINGANA**
BIJAPUR
Krishna
15° **TALANJ**
Vijayanagara □
DVARASAMUDRA
VIJAYANAGARA
1340

10° **MA'BAR**
MADURAI
1334

Jambudoni □
Gampala □

Rayigama □
5°

0°

Delhi sultanate

⬭ area controlled by Mamluks, 1206

▨ extent at beginning of Tughluq rule, 1320

▢ gains by 1330

MALWA Tughluq province with date region
1392 rebels against sultanate

→ invasion route of Timur, 1398

▨ empire of Timur, 1405

— Deccan sultanate boundary, 1490

⬭ maximum extent of Lodi sultanate, 1519

Vijayanagara state, c.1485

▨ maximum extent

▢ tributary area

🕌 major *sufi* shrine

scale 1: 15 000 000
0   400km
0   300mi

the Bundelkhand plateau in Madhya Pradesh the Chandella dynasty came to prominence in the 9th century and built a magnificent city of palaces and temples at Khajuraho. In the east a succession of ruling families dominated the coast of Orissa, sometimes extending their power from the mouths of the Ganges to those of the Godavari. Some of the finest temple complexes in the subcontinent were built at Bhubaneswar, Puri and Konarak which – combining worship of local deities with the great gods of Hinduism – attracted pilgrims from all over the country.

The Muslim invasions

In the 11th century a new militant force made itself felt in the subcontinent when, between 1000 and 1025, the Muslim leader Mahmud of Ghazana (971–1030) raided India no fewer than 17 times from his base just south of Kabul in Afghanistan. He attacked towns as far south as Khajuraho and Gwalior, sacked the temple of Shiva at Somnath in Kathiawar, breaking up the stone lingam with his own hands, and carried off as much as six and a half tons of gold on one expedition alone. He made no attempt to assert a permanent rule in India, but its wealth enabled him to build at Ghazana one of the most wonderful cities of the time. For more than 150 years after his death the frontier remained quiet, but at the end of the 12th century Muhammad of Ghur (d.1206) began campaigning in India, once more from Afghanistan. He defeated the Hindu rulers of Delhi in 1192 and moved on to take Kanauj, Varanasi, Gwalior and Ajmer, and so through to Gujarat. Wherever he went, mosques were built on the ruins of Hindu shrines.

The Muslim armies that operated in India were professionally organized. War was one way to make converts to Islam, and their soldiers spent their whole lives in the field. Their rapidly moving cavalrymen were armed with hand-weapons and formidable bows and arrows, and they drilled continuously. Men of any ethnic origin might serve in the army, and many had joined it as slaves: a military career was often the path to wealth and political advancement. After Muhammad's death his general Qutb ud-Din Aibak (d. 1210), a Turkish-born former slave, established the sultanate of Delhi, but its real founder was his son-in-law Iltutmish (d. 1236) who succeeded him as sultan and made himself master of much of northern India from Punjab as far as Bihar.

In the course of the 13th and 14th centuries Muslim influence was extended more widely. The Deccan was invaded, and some of its rulers forced to accept the overlordship of the Delhi sultans. An increasingly bureaucratic system of government brought more and more revenues into their hands and deprived their Hindu subjects of property and political influence. In 1320 the Tughluqs succeeded as sultans. The founder of the dynasty Ghyas ud-Din (d. 1325) was the son of a Turkish slave officer and an Indian Jat mother. He was assassinated by his son Muhammad bin Tughluq (d.1351), who determined to make the Deccan an integral part of the Delhi sultanate and embarked on an ambitious campaign of southern expansion. Accordingly, he moved his center of government to Daulatabad. However, despite his fame in the field, Muhammad bin Tughluq never quite managed to subdue the south fully, while his operations in the Deccan tended to weaken his hold in the old lands of the sultanate in the north. By the end of his reign he was forced to return to Delhi, leaving the Deccan in the

care of governors. By the end of the 15th century it had broken up into five independent sultanates.

The Delhi sultanate now began to lose its hold on the provinces in its northern heartland. Virtually independent rulers appeared in Gujarat, Malwa and at Jaunpur near Varanasi, and its vulnerability was apparent when, in 1398, Timur (Tamerlane the Great, 1336–1405) led a Mongol army into northern India and sacked Delhi itself. In 1451 the Lodis, an Afghan dynasty, captured Delhi and took control of the sultanate. However, though they regained lost positions in the Gangetic plain and threatened Gwalior from the fortress at Agra, they were unable to restore the sultanate's former prestige.

Muhammad bin Tughluq's advance into the south had halted at the Tungabhadra and Krishna rivers in 1346. Here the city of Vijayanagara became the center of a powerful Hindu kingdom that for the next 200 years – until its destruction in the Deccan wars of the mid 16th century – not only drew a line against further Muslim expansion but united the numerous petty rulerships of the south in a species of Hindu military theocracy. New lessons of warfare were learned, and fulltime armies equipped with horse and elephants were raised and paid for. Though Vijayanagara sat at the center of a new state that was capable of raising resources and waging war, it did not develop into a fully centralized government. Rather it took the form of a confederacy of military chieftains serving as was expedient under a single overlord, and was always prey to internal dissensions. For this reason the rulers of Vijayanagara gave great importance to elaborating notions of Hindu kingship and called upon divine sanction to legitimize their rule. The city itself – the "city of victory" – was built as a fortress, but at its heart lay a temple and palace complex, symbolizing that it was an abode of the gods as well as a seat of kings. A Persian visitor in 1443 described it as being "of enormous magnitude and population, with a king of perfect rule and hegemony whose kingdom stretched more than a thousand leagues....The city of Vijayanagara has no equal in the world," and Portuguese visitors in the next century were to testify to Vijayanagara's wealth and bustle, and to its wide commercial enterprise.

India at the beginning of the 16th century presented a bewildering richness of cultures. It had become the homeland of numerous peoples, mingling and interacting with each other in creative tension. Nowhere was there uniformity, not even in the Muslim north. It was the nature of the Muslim regimes in India that the sultan shared power with his principal military officers. The ruling elite tended to draw on talent wherever it was to be found in the Islamic world. While the early Delhi sultanate was Turkish at its core, by the 15th century the Islamic presence in India included Iraqis, Persians, Afghans and many others. Though all were bound by a common faith, Muslim beliefs and practices had developed different forms in different countries, and it was possible for an ambitious ruler to play men of different ethnic background and Islamic persuasion off against each other within the army and the government. The Muslim rulers borrowed Abbasid and Persian models of government, but accommodated themselves to the Indian administrative systems they found in place, as well as experimenting with the forms deployed by the Mongols in Central Asia. The pattern of Muslim rule in India before the advent of the Mughals was diverse in the extreme.

The Muslim invasions
Islam was introduced to the coast of Sind and Gujarat by Arab traders from the Middle East during the 8th century, but it was in the 11th century, with the invasion of Mahmud of Ghazana from Afghanistan, that it first made itself felt as a militant force in the subcontinent. Successive invasions followed, and by the 14th century military adventurers from every part of the Islamic world had established themselves across much of northern India. The Tughluq dynasty, ruling in Delhi, carried Muslim power into the Deccan plateau, but the Hindu state of Vijayanagara, which now arose as the dominant power in south India, prevented its further expansion. By the end of the century the now weakened Delhi sultanate had lost territory in the northwest to the empire of Timur, based at Samarkand, and Delhi itself had been sacked by his Mongol armies. The Lodis, an Afghan dynasty, established themselves as the rulers of Delhi in the mid 15th century and regained some of the sultanate's former positions in the Gangetic plain.

Vijayanagara

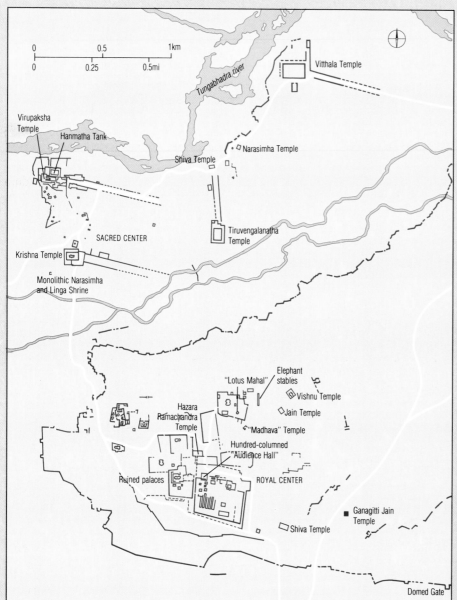

Vijayanagara, whose name means City of Victory, was the capital of the most successful Hindu dynasty in south India between the 14th and 16th centuries. The rise to power of Vijayanagara is partly explained by the devastations of this part of the country by the conquering troops of the Delhi sultanate at the turn of the 14th century. The Muslims defeated the Hoysala, Kakatiya and Pandya kings who governed most of India at this time, and then established themselves at Daulatabad in the Deccan and at Madurai in the far south. The rulers of Vijayanagara, no more than local chiefs to begin with, succeeded in recapturing the lands lost to the Muslims in the south and expelled them from Madurai. However, the sultans of the Deccan, who soon claimed independence from Delhi, proved more difficult to dislodge. War between Vijayanagara and the Muslim states to the north was a constant feature of political life for more than 200 years. The conflict ended only with the disastrous defeat of the Vijayanagara army in 1565 and the consequent sack and abandonment of the capital.

The Vijayanagara territories expanded throughout the 14th and 15th centuries until they encompassed almost all of the peninsula south of the Krishna river. During this period the Vijayanagara kings built up their capital as a showpiece of imperial magnificence. Persian, Italian and Portuguese visitors attest to the conspicuous wealth, ostentation and formality of the Vijayanagara court. Their accounts of the Mahanavami festival, the most spectacular annual event at the capital, describe the elephants, horses, troops and bejeweled women commanded by the Vijayanagara rulers. However, absence on campaigns of war and pilgrimages to temples meant that the king and army spent only a fraction of each year in Vijayanagara.

Far left The city of Vijayanagara is laid out in clearly distinguished zones in a rocky landscape to the south of the Tungabhadra river. The Sacred Center incorporates the holy village of Hampi with its Virupaksha temple dedicated to an aspect of Shiva. Some 2 kilometers distant from the river, at one end of the fortified urban core, is the Royal Center. Ruined standing structures mark the residential and ceremonial headquarters of the Vijayanagara royal household and the elite members of the court.

Left Each major monument in the Sacred Center is distinguished by a long colonnaded street serving as a market. This leads up to entrance gateways capped with pyramidal towers, or *gopuras*. That of the Virupaksha temple – still a popular place of worship – was rebuilt and renovated in modern times.

Above Among the religious complexes in the Sacred Center are several enshrining different forms of Vishnu. They include the Tiruvengalanatha temple, with its concentric arrangement of rectangular enclosure walls, viewed here from the nearby Matanga Hill.

Right One of the shrines in the Vitthala temple is fashioned as a chariot, complete with stone wheels.

Above Narasimha, the fierce man-lion avatar of Vishnu, was evidently a popular deity at Vijayanagara, especially when shown as a seated yogi. This monolith, 6.7 meters high, was hewn out of a granite boulder by royal order in 1528, in what must have been one of the most remarkable technical feats of the era.

THE MUGHAL PERIOD

Babur's invasion

The Mughals acquired northern India by conquest, and their rise signaled not just the incursion into the subcontinent of yet another invading people from Central Asia – this time the Chaghatai clan from what is now southern Uzbekistan – but also the establishment of a new dynasty, the Timurids. The Turkic-speaking Timurids traced their ancestry back to the great Mongol conquerors of Asia, Chengis Khan (?1167–1227) and Timur. The latter was the great-grandfather of Babur (the name, meaning "tiger" in Arabic, that is customarily given to Zahir ud-Din Muhammad). When he turned his attentions toward Punjab and northern India in the early 1520s Babur was ruler of Kabul in Afghanistan, having acquired it through conquest in 1504. He had, however, lost his hereditary principality of Fergana to the Uzbeks, and had abandoned any hope of recovering the great city of Samarkand, Timur's former capital.

By 1525 Babur had invaded Punjab three times, but had been unable to hold it. In November of that year he and his comrades swept down into India with an army of 12,000 men. In April 1526, their superior horsemanship and military technique, deploying matchlockmen and field cannon, defeated the much larger army of Ibrahim Lodi, the last sultan of Delhi, whom they killed on the battlefield of Panipat, 80 kilometers north of Delhi. Babur's victory was celebrated by the construction of a mosque at Panipat; though built by local architects and artisans, it displays elements in its design that are resonant of the Timurid buildings in Samarkand. After the battle, Babur immediately sent his son Humayan to seize the royal palaces and treasure of the Delhi sultans at Agra. The treasure he distributed according to custom among his followers, and he made Agra his capital.

Babur's successful incursion into northern India came at a time when the Lodi dynasty and the Afghan chieftains who had settled in India were in conflict with a number of other military interests – especially the Rajputs. Babur was able to turn this situation to his own advantage. For the next two years his army was constantly on the move, attacking Rajput strongholds and capturing treasure; in 1527, it defeated a confederacy of Rajput chieftains under the leadership of Rana Sanga of Mewar, and the next year stormed the fortress at Chanderi, killing its garrison.

These military operations ensured the pre-eminence of the Mughal forces in northern India. Meanwhile, acting under Babur's general orders, two of his companions built mosques at Sambhal and Ayodhya, sites which both had significant religious associations for Hindus. Such forceful assertions of overlordship suggest that by the time of his death in December 1530, Babur had decided that, rather than withdraw to Kabul and treat his expedition to northern India as a single successful plundering raid, his best long-term interests lay in strengthening his hold over the fertile lands and wealthy cities of the Gangetic plain. At the outset of his campaign this had by no means been a

foregone conclusion. Babur noted in a famous passage in his *Memoirs* (the *Baburnama*): "Hindustan is a country of few charms. Its people have no good looks; of social intercourse, paying and receiving visits there is none; of genius and capacity none; of manners none; in handicraft and work there is no form or symmetry, method or quality; there are no good horses, no good dogs, no grapes, musk melons or first-rate fruits, no ice or cold water, no good bread or cooked food in the *bazars*, no hot-baths, no colleges, no candles, torches or candlesticks."

These were the impressions of a prince for whom Samarkand (which he had occupied briefly, in 1497 and 1501), with its magnificent gardens, mosques, madrasas (Muslim colleges) and tombs, and with its patronage of some of the finest workmanship of the 15th century, was the cultural capital of the Islamic world. Babur also deeply admired the great city of Herat in northern Afghanistan, which under the rule of Hussein Baikara (1469–1506) had witnessed a marvelous flowering of Islamic humanism. "The whole habitable world", Babur was to recall "had not such a town as Herat had become under Sultan Hussein Mirza . . . filled with learned and matchless men. Whatever work a man took up, he aimed and aspired to bring it to perfection."

As Samarkand had fallen, so too was Herat taken by the Uzbeks in 1507. Babur was destined to replant amid the drab heat of the plains of northern India the Timurid inheritance from Samarkand and Herat that he so cherished. But he preferred to live in great tents pitched in gardens rather than reside in cities, and his wealth was portable, in the form of treasure, carpets, artifacts, manuscripts, and attendants. Babur's was a society that had to move to survive, and that drew part of its sustenance by exacting tribute from wealthy areas of settlement, or by levying charges on the prosperous long-distance caravan trade of Asia. Babur was amazed by the great size of India which he found to be "full of men, and full of produce" with "masses of gold and silver". The peasant farmers of the Gangetic plains grew a great variety of food-grains and other crops. Despite chronic political unrest, parts of the settled land were watered in a controlled way by wells or by grander schemes of irrigation, and its produce was marketed and exchanged for cash. The diverse economies supported specialist centers of manufacture – particularly of textiles – for sale in a number of markets. By the early 16th century the productive parts of the subcontinent, though still only patchily settled, were linked together by overland trade-routes, and goods were carried between the Indian regions by sea. Cloth, spices and other high-value commodities were exported to Southeast Asia, East Africa, the Middle East and, increasingly in the course of the 16th century, Europe, in exchange for precious metals, war horses, slaves, ivory and exotica. In short, the subcontinent was a territory ripe for raiding.

The forging of an empire

The lands of northern India that fell to Babur as a result of four years' campaigning and plundering were transformed by his successors through warfare, diplomacy and political innovation into one of the largest and most successful centralized states in early modern world history, greater in extent than the empires of either Persia or Turkey. At the height of their power, the Mughals would lay claim to 3.2 million square kilometers of territory and command a population of between 100 and 150 million people. Arguably only the Ming dynasty in China exceeded the greatness of the Mughal emperors.

The Mughals benefited from the fact that for centuries much of the subcontinent, especially in the north, had been subjected to repeated conquest and settlement by Muslim peoples. Babur and his successors were able to portray their actions as part of an established tradition. When the occasion suited them they would claim to be fighting a *jihad* (holy war) in the cause of Islam, thus establishing the legitimacy of their rule among the Muslim elites already entrenched in the country. They would seek to include the old nobility in their court and government and give financial and political support for Muslim religious leaders and institutions already thriving in India. At other times, however, the Mughals – echoing the policies of earlier governments – would attempt to come to terms with the Hindu military and landed elites who made up the bulk of the resident armies and controlled much of the agrarian economy. Since rule by Muslim dynasties of one kind or another had been the norm for so long, many important Hindu groups already accepted the legitimacy of Islamic political power. In return for being allowed to continue to dominate the countryside, Rajput, Maratha and Telugu warriors saw no difficulty in putting their martial skills at the disposal of a non-Hindu king: and many who lived by their wits and their pens, such as kayasths, khatris or Kashmiri pandits, were able to reconcile their Hindu religion comfortably with service to a Muslim lord. The fabled riches of the Mughal emperors found expression in the development of a sophisticated courtly culture and in the lavish patronage of architecture and the arts. It was acquired through the effective appropriation of revenue from the land. But it is notoriously difficult to assess and collect taxes levied on crops in the fields. Naked force was used to transfer the product of peasant labor from the countryside to the imperial treasury, and it had to be threatened or applied year after year. Not the least part of the Mughal achievement was the creation of political and administrative procedures that allowed them to manage productively the very lands and peoples that their soldiers might destroy from day to day.

In the 16th and 17th centuries no political connection could be taken for granted. The Mughal state depended for its operation on its ability to organize and manage its wealth so that its military and administrative elite could be adequately rewarded; sharp punishments were needed to call into line those who were tempted to seek alternative paths of preferment. Assassination, intrigue, war and diplomacy marked the politics of the empire. The bulk of its revenues were expended on the army. Mughal armies were in the field full-time, often to give the appearance of force rather than for action. Though there were times of great blood-lettings and massacres, particularly when recalcitrant opponents threatened to undermine the authority of the state, or when the succession to power was in dispute, it is surprising how effectively the Mughals established order and reduced casual violence. They eroded the independence of some of the localities and improved communications across the subcontinent.

Above all, the Mughals levied and collected taxes on a grander and more rational scale than any of their predecessors. Successive emperors revealed a keen appreciation of the need to maintain a balance

Left Babur's *Memoirs* were written in Turkic, in a terse but lucid style that conveys an impression of a cultivated and perpetually inquiring mind. There was a long Timurid tradition of composing chronicles and genealogies, but Babur's autobiography stands in a class of its own in its revelation of an exceptional and arresting personality. In 1589, during the reign of Akbar, Babur's *Memoirs* were translated into Persian and lavishly illustrated. A number of copies were made and the manuscripts used to promote an imperial image of the Mughal dynasty that stretched all the way back through Babur to Timur, emphasizing its Central Asian origins. Here Babur is pictured at a banquet held in Herat in 1507 where he is being entertained by his cousin Sultan Hussein Mirza. Babur recalled "At this party they set a roast goose before me but as I was no carver or disjointer of birds, I left it alone. 'Do you not like it?' inquired the Mirza. Said I, 'I am a poor carver.' On this he at once disjointed the bird and set it again before me. In such matters he had no match."

between a free-standing imperial elite and locally entrenched aristocracies. The line between these two categories was never clear cut. A large part of the politics of the period turned on the tensions that arose when those originally bound to the emperor by personal ties carved out for themselves some independent power in the districts or when those who possessed their own influence in the towns or the countryside were recruited into the Mughal nobility. The history of the Mughals shows that military victories were never permanently decisive, that boundaries were never fixed, that politics were never settled and that administrative reforms required constant attention.

After Babur: failure and success
No one could have predicted, on Babur's death in 1530, the eventual success of the Mughal empire. It was not the Timurid custom for a father's lands to be passed easily and uncontroversially to a single heir: Babur's eldest son Humayan (1508–56) had to share parts of the diverse territories, stretching from Central Asia to Bihar and as far south as Gwalior, that Babur had brought under his single rule, with his four brothers. In Afghanistan, Mirza Sulaiman obtained Badakhshan in the north, while Kamran governed Kabul and Kandahar; within India, Askari and Hindal were each given large districts to administer. By custom, too, it was almost inevitable that the heirs would fight among themselves for their father's possessions and, within a year, Askari and Kamran had formed an alliance with each other to take over the Punjab from Humayan's governor. Throughout the period of Mughal rule, succession disputes of this sort spawned one political crisis after another. And the quarrels to the death between contending heirs gave the nobility the opportunity to re-assess their allegiance and the localities the chance to bid for their independence. Thus at each handover from one generation to the next the very survival of the Mughal state was regularly threatened.

Beside the challenge of his brothers, Humayan faced serious resistance to his overlordship from Afghan chieftains in the eastern districts of his domains, while in the south Bahadur Shah, the sultan of Gujarat, drew Humayan's enemies to his camp and gained possession for a time of the wealthy and strategically important kingdom of Malwa. Almost overnight the complex of revenue-producing lands held by Babur had become a territory contested on all sides. For most of the 1530s, Humayan tracked back and forth across northern India in the attempt to maintain his hold on his possessions. At the end of the decade Sher Shah Sur (?1486–1545), an Afghan chieftain with a power-base in southern Bihar, opened a campaign that by 1540 had given him the wealth of Bengal and most of the central Gangetic plain. Eventually Delhi, too, fell to him. He succeeded in bringing these districts under his own very effective revenue and policing administration and, had he not failed to pass on his conquests to the next generation on his death, the Mughals would have faded from the history of India.

As it was, Humayan – denied refuge by his brothers in Punjab and Kabul – found uneasy political asylum with Shah Tahmasp of Persia. The years of exile exposed Humayan to the art of the Safavid court, and to the architecture of Herat and Samarkand, thus reinforcing the Timurid-Safavid Persian cultural traditions that Babur had so admired. In 1553, supported by the Shah, Humayan was able to seize Kabul from a

newly established position in Kandahar, and deposed and blinded his brother Kamran. The following year he launched a new campaign in India, recapturing Delhi in the summer of 1555. Barely six months later Humayan, upon hearing the call to prayer, fell to his death down the steep stone steps of his library in the citadel at Delhi. The event was kept secret for 17 days while the nobles at Delhi determined the succession: eventually Akbar, Humayan's young son (1542–1605), was crowned under the title Jalal-ud-din Muhammad Akbar. It was during his 50-year reign that the Mughal empire was created.

Akbar – the early years
During the first four years of Akbar's reign, effective power was in the hands of Bairam Khan, a noble of Persian origin and a Shia Muslim, who assumed the role of regent. Facing the new government was the immediate problem of armed opposition from the heirs of Sher Shah Sur. Bairam Khan, with Akbar at his side, led the Mughal army to victory, again at Panipat just outside Delhi, against formidable forces commanded by Hemu, a Hindu general. Then Akbar's army made its way successively into the Punjab, Rajputana (present-day Rajasthan), and eastward toward Bihar. By early 1558, he had secured firm control of a compact region between Lahore, Delhi, Agra and Jaunpur. This gave him districts of great agricultural and commercial wealth – the old heartland of Muslim political and military power in northern India, which was to be the bedrock of the new Mughal empire.

Bairam Khan fell from power in 1560, and shortly afterwards Akbar was strong enough to free himself from the factional struggles of court politics to take full charge of government. Dispensing with the office of chief minister, he divided the business of the state between four separate departments responsible for financial, military, household and religious affairs, an important innovation that gave him strategic control over public affairs and made it more difficult for a rival to emerge in opposition to his own authority. Through the coming years Akbar consolidated his authority by continually deploying his armies to secure his home base and extend his frontiers, by constant diplomatic and political activity, and by initiating and carrying through an unprecedented program of administrative reform. An ambitious inquiry was undertaken into the productivity of the lands he ruled: fields and villages were measured and arranged into groups, districts and provinces. This careful gathering and recording of information made possible the establishment of administrative routines, facilitating the regular collection of taxation and the dispensation of justice.

In order to achieve all this, in what remained a fluctuating polity whose fortunes were still very dependent on that most fickle of political assets, continuous and successful military enterprise, Akbar had to build support from among the military and landed classes. When Humayan had returned to India from exile in Iran he had brought with him a small cadre of 51 officers, nearly all of whom came from outside India – there were 27 high-status Chaghatai or Uzbek clan leaders from Central Asia, and 16 Persian Shias. Akbar steadily increased the number of nobles in imperial service so that it had reached 222 by the time he had ruled for 25 years, at the same time reducing the relative influence of men from Central Asia, even though many of them could claim some degree of blood-relationship with the royal house. In the mid

Above This unusual and informal pencil drawing is inscribed on the reverse in Persian as "the emperor Akbar", and has often been regarded as a contemporary portrait. However, the style of the drawing, particularly the naturalistic effect achieved by the artist, suggests a date of composition later in the 17th century than the death of Akbar, and many scholars now question whether it is an actual portrait of the emperor.

Above The ruined fortress of Chitor, formerly the capital of the Rana of Mewar, the most prominent of the Rajput rulers to defy Akbar. In September 1567, Akbar besieged Chitor, built on a hill 200 meters above the plains, which housed a garrison of 5,000 soldiers. The initial Mughal assaults were repulsed with heavy losses but on the night of 22 February 1568 siege cannon breached the walls in several places; Akbar killed Jaimal, the fortress commander, with a musket-shot. The morale of the besieged was broken and the next day the Rajput garrison began killing their families in preparation for their own deaths in battle. Virtually all the defenders were to die in the hand-to-hand fighting that followed. Akbar destroyed the fortress, and it remained deserted thereafter. Though the Rana remained at large until his death four years later, the destruction of Chitor, and of the fortress at Ranthambor the next year, effectively ended serious Rajput military opposition to Mughal rule.

1560s Akbar found himself seriously opposed by a group of Uzbek nobles. There is some evidence to suggest that these leaders, who formed the core of the original Mughal incursions into India, were disaffected by the increasing complexity of Akbar's mode of government in India, which deviated more and more from traditional Central Asian pastoral and raiding habits. In particular, they disliked the loss of comradely equality, fostered by life in the steppes, as Akbar centralized power in his hands and behaved less and less as the first among equals.

Akbar attracted a number of capable Persians to his service to balance the Central Asians, so that by 1580 there were 47 Persians to 48 nobles of Central Asian origin in key positions in the Mughal state. Perhaps more important, he recruited to the nobility several of the Muslim warriors already settled in northern India, such as the Sayyids of Baraha, originally adventurers from Iraq, who had arrived in India in the 13th century. They had been at a discount during the years of the Delhi sultanate but now found enhanced opportunities for employment with the expanding Mughal state. About the only Muslims who did not find favor with Akbar were the Afghan chieftains whose lands stretched across the Himalayan foothills from Kabul to Dhaka and who proved a constant thorn in the side of the Mughals, and others whose ancestors had served the Delhi sultanate. They were either killed off or reduced to minor status, destined to sulk on poor land around the edges of the prosperous empire.

The alliance with the Rajputs

Akbar also found ways of incorporating into his empire certain Hindu warrior groups that had been excluded from power by the Lodis. Arguably the most important of these were the Rajput chieftains – indeed, had he not effected an alliance with these conservative Hindu warriors on his southwestern flank it is doubtful that he would have succeeded in establishing the Mughal state. By reaching an accommodation, not only did he secure the services of some of the ablest men of the time, but he also solved, at least temporarily, the nearly intractable political problem of how to pacify a dangerously ambiguous frontier of empire.

In the 16th century the arid terrain of the Aravalli Hills supported fiercely independent pockets of settlement; in a region of poor communications, virtually impregnable forts and watering-places overlooked the important military and commercial routes that linked northern India to Gujarat and the west coast. Dominant families controlled small areas of the region and were often at war with each other, but the more ambitious Rajput lords attempted to weld together larger political organizations and sometimes raided northward into the richer plains. Often they applied pressure on those wishing to move goods and men across their country, and their great fortresses were havens for political dissidents from the north. No government could feel truly secure in the Gangetic plain without having come to some sort of accommodation with the Rajput princes.

Rajput Courts

Below left Rajput rulers, like their Mughal overlords, reinforced their authority over subordinates by regularly calling them to a *durbar*, as depicted in this miniature of a "minor" Rajput ruler and his courtiers (painted in the Ajmer area c.1790). Though both official business and more pleasurable pursuits were transacted at *durbars*,

The Rajputs were one of the principal non-Mughal groups that were co-opted into the Mughal empire in northern India. This enabled prominent Rajput leaders to rise to positions of importance in the Mughal army and civil administration. While remaining nominally subservient to the Mughals, several Rajput lineages took advantage of their imperial associations to establish semi-autonomous polities in central and western India, in the region of Rajasthan today. Here they set up courts that blended Mughal and non-Mughal aesthetic forms. Though the term "Rajput" derives from the Sanskrit *rajaputra*, meaning "son of a king", apparently reflecting the belief that all Rajputs are descended from kings, in the pre-Mughal era genealogical descent was not as important in defining Rajput status as it became first under Mughal, and then British, power. During this earlier period (prior to the late 16th century), the term "Rajput" was generically applied to any horse-soldier, trooper or headman of a village, regardless of bio-genetic origin, who achieved his status through his personal ability to force a wide network of alliances as a result of military service and marriage. But under Mughal domination, elite Rajputs, taking advantage of the opportunities afforded them within the empire, tended to close ranks in order to consolidate their new-found positions. In the process, the more successful lineages increasingly used the language of descent and kinship to legitimize their social status. The British, in the late 19th century, consolidated this tendency by categorizing the Rajputs as a "martial race (or caste)", thereby linking their notional identity as warriors to biological inheritance.

their fundamental purpose was to establish ritually the ruler's charismatic authority over his followers and thereby confirm the unity of his dominion. Public displays of royal charisma were also translated into Rajput architecture. Take, for example, the richly ornamented *Huwa Mahal*, or "Palace of the Winds" (*bottom*

left), built by Maharaja Pratap Singh of Jaipur in 1799. This royal residence, constructed on one of Jaipur's busiest commercial streets, consists of six stories of clustered, honeycomb-like oriel windows, each surmounted by a curved roof and golden finials. This ornamentation is the visual expression of the bursting surfeit of

wealth, vitality and energy possessed by the dynasty that resided therein. Similarly, the schools of painting patronized by Rajput rulers favored lively, expansive and exuberant styles, as represented in the *Vasanta raga* (*below*), a celebration of the coming of spring.

Akbar's policies towards them went beyond the formation of simple alliances and the assertion of Mughal over-rule. Initial contact was by battle, some of which were particularly bloody: in 1567 and 1568, for example, Akbar declared *jihad* on Udai Singh Sisodia, the Rana of Mewar. The fall of his citadel at Chitor and the capture of Udaipur by the Mughal army led to the slaughter of perhaps 25,000 people. Having made plain his capacity to damage the Rajput principalities, Akbar was quick to make diplomatic overtures, offering to accept incorporation into the Mughal state. Individual rajas or chieftains (whose local position was often challenged by kin and neighbors) would be invited to head a contingent of their own kinsmen and subjects to serve in the Mughal army. In return Akbar would guarantee them possession of their ancestral lands, partly as a tax-free benefit but also in part as a salary for becoming a Mughal noble. This recognition enhanced their local status, helping them to establish a pre-eminence amongst their own kinsmen.

The Rajputs were allowed by the Mughals to retain their beliefs and their customs; in particular their honor as Hindu warriors was respected. Moreover, service with the Mughals offered an opportunity to the Rajput chieftains to acquire more power and wealth by participating in the larger world of the Mughal empire. Both parties benefited: the emperor was able to win over thousands of loyal soldiers, while at the same time pre-empting the formation of a Hindu-led anti-Mughal coalition on a dangerous frontier. The Rajput chieftains drew on Mughal political support to strengthen their hold on land and people, and their service abroad was the means of bringing new wealth to the region. Often the compact was sealed by the marriage of a Rajput princess into the Mughal royal household; the intermingling of Hindu and Islamic elements in the arts and architecture from the later 16th century is a longer-lasting legacy of the alliance.

The military elite

Whatever the social composition of its members, Akbar succeeded to a remarkable degree in creating an aristocracy of merit rewarded by performance. Status and pay depended on the emperor: he could promote and demote, and no title or rank necessarily descended from a man to his son. Akbar's nobles derived their personal position from a numerical rank (*zat*) which was related to the size of the military contingent they were required to command. These could range from as few as 20 men to well in excess of 5,000. Though the nobles were assigned land-revenues as a salary and to cover their expenses, this did not entitle them to become landholders in an ordinary way; revenues were accounted for separately and the books audited by centrally appointed government officials. Precisely which lands would be assigned for their upkeep was also at the discretion of the emperor, and in the 16th century these were changed regularly, to prevent too close a connection developing between a noble and the territories that produced his income. The number of a noble's rank did not always equate with the actual number of men he had to maintain for active military service, but by the 1590s, a second numerical rank (*suwar*) had been added to a noble's *zat* ranking. This reflected an additional number of armed heavy cavalrymen he had actually to maintain, and carried with it an additional stipend to make this possible.

A list of nobles and other office-holders drawn up for 1595 shows that the military and service elite at the end of Akbar's regime was composed of 1,823 men, of diverse origin, in command of at least 141,000 followers, who served as heavy cavalrymen with their own horses and equipment. Their importance to the regime was more than military. They established homes and households throughout the empire that copied the social life of the court and diffused to lower levels the imperial ideologies of the Mughal state. Furthermore, noblemen and senior civilian servants stimulated economic activity in a number of small towns and cities across northern India, spent money on new buildings and through their patronage encouraged a flourishing of the arts.

The practice of religion

By the mid 16th century the permanent presence of Islam was an accepted fact across much of northern India. Muslims accounted for perhaps up to a fifth of the population in some places, and had long occupied dominant political and economic positions. But, despite the proselytizing energies of Muslim saints and preachers, and despite Islamic missionary activities being backed by military and political authority, the peoples of the Gangetic plain were still overwhelmingly Hindu. No doubt this was partly because Hinduism had adapted to the centuries of Muslim rule by finding expression less in ostentatious public worship at great temples and more in quiet popular devotional *bhakti* movements that stressed the relationship of the individual to God and the importance of personal piety. But Indian Muslims, drawing on the richly diverse heritage of Islam itself, and because they had lived in the subcontinent for many generations, showed a degree of accommodation to its other religions and cultures. Hindu and Islamic mystics, scholars and teachers actively sought common ground between the great faiths. The great 15th-century mystic poet Kabir of Varanasi, a Muslim by birth, proposed the unity of Hinduism and Islam under one God, and other poet-saints in the *bhakti* tradition combined elements of Hinduism and Islam in their worship, while rejecting the formalism of both. Religious teachers on either side of the divide found that their practices were not so dissimilar from each other. In Punjab, Guru Nanak (1469–1539), the founder of Sikhism, was explicit in his intention to create a synthesis between Hinduism and Islam. At the grass roots, where people in villages and small towns lived next to each other, there was a substantial pooling of customs, ceremonies and beliefs. Shrines and holy places were often shared, fierce village gods like the smallpox goddess Sitla were worshiped by Hindu and Muslim alike, and local festivals were celebrated in common.

Undoubtedly the process that had brought several cultural and religious movements together by the 16th century was a major factor in Akbar's creation of an unusually open and tolerant state for the time. The Mughal emperor nonetheless faced a formidable political problem. He needed the support of powerful religious elites to give legitimacy to his regime, but even among Muslims theological and religious opinion about what constituted orthodoxy differed widely. Moreover, how could he maintain his status as a good Muslim ruler, support Islam, its laws and its powerful religious establishments, without provoking the vast majority of his non-Muslim subjects into dissidence and revolt? Akbar at first solved this problem by emphasizing his religious orthodoxy and by balancing

the different Islamic interests at court. Then, as his political position strengthened and his own theological beliefs matured, he enacted reforms that treated all his subjects in a more even-handed way and allowed him to evolve a distinctively new imperial ideology.

Akbar early asserted his political authority against those Muslim religious leaders who expected him to impose Islamic law in the most uncompromising fashion. In 1563 he abolished the tax his predecessors had levied on Hindu pilgrims when they gathered on festival occasions. He also allowed them to repair aging temples, and even to construct new ones. Even more disturbing, for those who expected him to interpret the *sharia* strictly, was an order permitting those who had been forcibly converted to Islam to return to their original faith and escape the death penalty that Islam ordained for apostasy. Akbar also prohibited the

Below A picture from an *Akbarnama* of c. 1590 shows Akbar seated on a horse while he watches two rival Hindu sects in Punjab do battle with each other. Akbar's soldiers are restoring order, making the point that the king has a duty and a right to intervene in religious disputes and to arbitrate, with force if necessary, when things get out of hand. The picture was composed by Basawan, himself a Hindu (as were most of the painters in Akbar's workshops). Akbar's biographer, Abul Fazl, ranked Basawan fourth in his list of the top painters at court, noting that "in the drawing of features, distribution of colors, portrait painting and several other branches, he is most excellent. . . ."

Fatehpur Sikri

Below In the middle of the south wall of the *Khanqah*, the religious compound housing Shaikh Salim Chisti's tomb and the Jami mosque, stands the Buland Darwaza, a huge gateway. It probably commemorates Akbar's military successes in Gujarat in 1573, when the capital gained its name of Fatehpur ("City of Victory") Sikri.

Bottom In Akbar's capital the center of worship was laid out next to the palace complex where the buildings of government – the *Diwan-i amm* (hall of public audience) and *Diwan-i Khass* (hall of private audience) – lie clustered together with the emperor's residential quarters, a serai, workshops and nobles' houses.

During the height of Mughal power, the empire's capital shifted repeatedly in order to be closer to areas of imperial expansion. Indeed, for much of this period the administrative center of the empire was the emperor's immense, movable tented city (complete with palaces, bazaars, and a royal mint). However, when the Mughal capital did rest for a time at such cities as Delhi, Lahore, Agra and Fatehpur Sikri, the Mughals demonstrated a great flair for monumental architecture. The emperor Akbar's choice of Fatehpur Sikri as his capital in 1570 was unusual only insofar as no pre-existing urban settlement occupied the site. The city was constructed from scratch in less than 15 years but was quickly abandoned when Akbar moved his government north to Lahore to be nearer at hand to cope with unrest in Afghanistan.

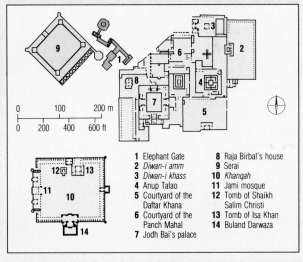

1 Elephant Gate
2 *Diwan-i amm*
3 *Diwan-i khass*
4 Anup Talao
5 Courtyard of the Daftar Khana
6 Courtyard of the Panch Mahal
7 Jodh Bai's palace
8 Raja Birbal's house
9 Serai
10 *Khanqah*
11 Jami mosque
12 Tomb of Shaikh Salim Christi
13 Tomb of Isa Khan
14 Buland Darwaza

enslavement of prisoners of war and the involuntary conversion of non-Muslim slaves.

These measures were followed by a more sweeping change in 1579 when Akbar abolished the *jiziya*, an annual graduated property tax that was levied exclusively on non-Muslims who were legally classified as client groups tolerated and protected by Muslim rulers. This had a direct impact on nearly all his Hindu subjects, and implied that the unequal distinction between Muslim and non-Muslim was also abolished. Akbar's policy in these areas was bitterly resented by orthodox Muslims. The emperor also made a show of celebrating at his court some of the major Hindu festivals, such as Divali, which appealed especially to his entourage of Rajput nobles; he followed customs of charitable giving that had their roots as much in Hinduism as in Islam, and he provided support for religious causes other than strictly Muslim ones.

But it was difficult to deny that Akbar was a faithful Muslim, even though he expressed great interest in other religious philosophies and was tolerant of other beliefs. At the heart of his new capital at Fatehpur Sikri was the tomb of the widely revered *sufi* saint, Shaikh Salim Chisti, who died in 1571. Akbar worshiped

publicly in an orthodox way, sweeping the floor of the mosque, for example, and acting as a prayer leader under the tutelage of Shaikh Abdul Nabi, the *qazi*, or chief jurist of the empire. He demonstrated his piety by making regular pilgrimages on foot from Fatehpur Sikri to the tomb of Khwaja Muin-ud-Din Chisti (d. 1236), another of the great *sufi* saints, which was situated strategically at Ajmer, the gateway to the region of the Rajputs. In choosing to associate himself with the Chisti order of *sufi* saints, renowned for its austerity and rejection of secular political power, Akbar aligned himself with the broadest and most appealing form of *sufi* devotionalism. Significantly, he did not identify himself with the stricter and more orthodox Naqshbandi order, which originated in the old Timurid lands of Central Asia, despite his family's long association with it. After the conquest of Gujarat in 1574 gave the Mughals control of ports on the west coast, permitting direct access to the holy cities of Arabia, Akbar actively organized and paid for annual pilgrimages to Mecca and Medina; the first such caravan, setting out from Agra in 1576, included his aunt, the empress Salima Sultan Begum, and other high-ranking ladies of the court.

Throughout his mature life, Akbar encouraged religious discussion and patronized the translation into Persian of Hindu holy books so that his court could be instructed in the religion of his subjects. In 1575 he built a large hall at Fatehpur Sikri specifically to house debates in religion and theology. At first, these discussions were confined to Muslim divines, but after 1579 participants included Jains, Hindus and Parsis. In 1580, two Jesuit priests, Father Aquaviva and Father Antonio Monserrate, visiting the Mughal court from Goa (a Portuguese enclave since the beginning of the century) were invited to explain Christianity to Akbar and his colleagues.

Akbar and orthodox Islam

Inevitably, Akbar's apparent open-mindedness in religious matters, coupled with his tolerance of non-Muslim practices and a refusal to insist on rigorous discrimination against Hindus and others not of the faith, brought him in time into open political conflict with the *ulema*, the guardians of Islamic law. The *ulema* looked to the emperor to set a good example of piety and devotion, and they expected him to provide adequate state funding for the upkeep of mosques, colleges, other charitable trusts, and pilgrimages. Religion was thus seen as an essential part of the fabric of the state. Just as Akbar had needed actively to take in hand his support from among the warriors and nobility, so too he had to devise policies to scrutinize, manage, and control the religious establishments of the state. Division among the Muslim clergy allowed the emperor to balance and then arbitrate between the parties competing for royal patronage. During the 1570s, Akbar investigated the assignment of tax-free lands to religious men and institutions. His inquiries showed that many charitable grants were being misused, or had been illegally acquired or wrongly passed on from father to son. A sizable number of tax-free estates, especially in Punjab, had been given out to pious Afghans by the Lodi or Sur rulers. In 1578, Akbar ordered a wholesale inspection of lands granted for religious purposes, and any whose title was not strictly in order were taken back. He strictly prohibited the practice of automatic right of inheritance, and limited the area and number of grants made. Much to the disgust of the orthodox, he also provided support for some non-Muslim learned men.

Akbar consistently refused to sympathize with the more narrowly fundamentalist of the Muslim religious leaders and tended instead to throw his weight behind liberal and heterodox theologians and lawyers. From the point of view of the most orthodox, the greatest threat to the enforcement of the *sharia* came from those claiming to be within the life of Islam – most *sufi* masters and other mystics were suspect, not to mention Shia Muslims, whether of the Persian branch or the Ismailis found in the coastal cities of Gujarat. Then, with the approach of the Islamic millennium (the thousandth year of the Hijra began on 27 September 1592), a number of strictly heretical sects began to gain significant followings. Prominent among these was the Mahdawi sect, founded by Sayyid Muhammad Jaunpur in the late 15th century. He preached from the tradition that after a thousand years Muhammad would rise from his grave and return as the *mahdi* to redeem the world. Despite recurring persecution by orthodox *ulema*, Sayyid Muhammad's movement took hold especially in Gujarat, Sind and parts of northern India. Not only

did Akbar not move against the Mahdawis, but he invited their preachers to explain and defend their position in the religious debates at court.

It is difficult to determine how much of Akbar's religious policy-making derived from his own convictions, how much from motives of genuine toleration, and how much was forced on him by political necessity. In order to expand and maintain his new state he needed to accommodate his Hindu subjects, and this he achieved not only by the amelioration of discriminatory laws but by demonstrating his authority in ritual and symbolic ways that would make sense to them: this was of particular importance in regard to key supporters in his army and civil service. Moreover, the mix of Sunnis, Shias and mystics at court, and the lack of any clearly dominant Islamic party, inevitably meant that Akbar had to steer a cautious way between the rival groups, creating between them conditions at least of armed neutrality, if not real toleration.

A major breach between Akbar and the more orthodox groups occurred in 1578. Despite the emperor's disapproval, Shaikh Abdul Nabi insisted on carrying

Above The setting for this picture is Ajmer, where an annual festival was held to commemorate the *sufi* saint Muin ud-Din Chishti, whose tomb is located in the city. According to *sufi* belief, ecstasy – found through music, singing and dancing – is the means by which the soul communicates directly with God. In this picture – probably painted for Dara Shukoh, the eldest son of Shah Jahan, between 1650 and 1655 – Muslim mystics engaged in ecstatic dancing and singing are watched by Mughal courtiers; next to them stands a row of *sufi* saints who extend in an unbroken chain linking one master to another back to the Prophet. Along the bottom are seated a number of unorthodox popular Hindu mystics; they have in common their devotion to the name of god and their rejection of brahmanical ritual and authority. The picture is unique among survivals of Indian art for its depiction of both Muslim and Hindu holy men.

out a death sentence on a brahmin tried in his court for insulting the name of Muhammad. The following year, Akbar assumed sweeping powers in religious matters, publishing an edict that asserted the Mughal emperor's prerogative to be the supreme arbiter of religious affairs within his realm. In other words, if scholars and jurists disagreed on a point of law, the emperor would decide which opinion would be binding on all. The edict also claimed for Akbar authority as the caliph, or secular successor to the Prophet, with leadership of the entire Muslim world. Before the edict was issued, Akbar forced the leading office-holders and jurists to sign it; the only one to do so willingly was the distinguished liberal Shaikh Mubarak.

Humiliated, Shaikh Abdul Nabi and Maulana Abdullah, the *sadr* (chief court theologian), took sanctuary in a mosque, claiming that they had been coerced into signing Akbar's edict. At the same time, rebellion broke out among a group of imperial officers in the eastern districts. They killed the governor of Bengal and proclaimed the ruler of Kabul, Mirza Muhammad Hakim, Akbar's half-brother, as the legitimate emperor. An orthodox judge in Jaunpur added fuel to the rebellion by enjoining all good Muslims to rise against Akbar as an infidel. In response, Akbar sent his finance minister, Raja Todar Mal, with an army to regain control of Bengal and Bihar (which took nearly five years to achieve completely); he himself marched on Kabul and deposed his half-brother. The two campaigns were backed by harsh punitive measures against any jurists or scholars who had supported the uprising. At Agra, Akbar removed Shaikh Abdul Nabi and Malauna Abdullah from office and sent them to exile in Mecca by appointing them joint leaders of the pilgrimage caravan in 1579.

Below Akbar's friend and most able minister, Abul Fazl, is seen here presenting the emperor with the first volume of his official memoir of Akbar's reign, the *Akbarnama*. Abul Fazl was also responsible for the compilation during the 1590s of the *Ain-i-Akbari*, a statistical account of the Muhgal empire designed to help administer the state.

The apotheosis of the Mughal emperor

As his reign progressed, Akbar and his close associates – especially Abul Fazl (d. 1602) and his brother, the poet Faizi (d. 1595), who emerged as his principal advisers during the 1570s – began to justify, beyond mere heritage and conquest, the Mughal emperor's right to rule India. This new ideology found expression in politics, art, literature, and in public ritual: it was embodied in Abul Fazl's official chronicle of the emperor's life, the *Akbarnama*. A key element in the ideology was the importance given to the emperor as a superior being, existing closer to God and to true reality. He was the recipient of superior knowledge and authority, greater than that of the recognized interpreters of Islamic law, or of the most saintly *sufi* masters, or even of the eagerly anticipated *mahdi*. In pictures, this was represented as divine light passing to Akbar from God through a chain of dazzling angels; and from this period, just as the life-enhancing image of the flow of water through the gardens of paradise was a recurring theme in Timurid thinking, so the Mughal rulers after Akbar became particularly associated with wisdom and righteousness manifested by the radiation of light.

From the early 1580s, Akbar began to use this ideology in a political context. He developed a formalized social life at his camp and court, and required his followers to wait on him there. In keeping with his need to manage a large number of powerful men of assorted backgrounds and cultures, Akbar appeared to move farther away from conventional Islamic practices. He gave up sending pilgrimages to Mecca and Medina, and after transferring his capital from Fatehpur Sikri to Lahore in 1585 played down his devotion to the Chisti saints. He began openly to worship the sun in a series of new rituals, and abstained from excessive meat eating, alcohol and sexual intercourse. Such behavior was in keeping with the daily world of Hinduism, and was especially compatible with the ethos of his Rajput nobles.

Akbar now began to build up around his person an inner core, or order, of nobles. Selected members were initiated into this new order at ceremonies associated with the worship of the sun and light. They swore to put their lives, property, religion and honor at the service of the emperor, and those that were Muslim

signed a declaration repudiating the bonds of orthodox Islam. Throughout the ceremony, the initiate lay
prostrate before the emperor, placing Akbar's feet on
his head. As a sign of membership of this inner group
a nobleman would be given a special turban, a medal-
lion embossed with a picture of the sun, and a miniature portrait of Akbar to wear. Eventually most of the
Mughal *amirs* (military commanders) had joined this
select group. It proved a very effective way of assimi-
lating a heterogeneous body of nobles and ensuring
their loyalty to the throne. This development in fact
drew on several respectable Islamic traditions such as
that of the slave-soldier, represented by the elite corps
of Janissaries at the Ottoman court and a common
institution also in both Central Asia and Muslim
India, or the relationship between the *sufi* master, the
pir, and his devotees. Similar forms of courtly behavior and submission to the emperor by the nobility had
long been established at the Persian court.

Akbar went beyond earlier Mughal court practices
by holding formal sessions at which the ritual made
explicit the social and political ranking of the nobles,
who were forced to cooperate with the emperor if they
wished for advancement. They sought places near to
the emperor, and on formal occasions gifts were
exchanged that marked their current position. High
favor was shown by ritually presenting a noble with a
robe of honor. Akbar would dress himself in a fine and
richly embroidered garment that he then took off and
draped on the recipient – thus symbolically enclosing
the servant in the body of the master. Such development of the ideas of kingship, and of the divine origin
of rule, had moved far beyond the bluff philosophy of
conquest propounded by Babur and his comrades as
they swept on their horses into northern India. It
allowed the Mughals to develop a monarchy appropriate for ruling a huge, multiregional and largely non-
Muslim population.

Mughal India in the reign of Akbar
Babur's invasion left the Mughals
with only a tentative foothold in
the prosperous Indo-Gangetic
plain, which his successor,
Humayan, had difficulty in
retaining. It was during the long
reign of Akbar that the Mughal
position in northern India was
consolidated and extended. By
1600, a number of sub-provinces
had been established capable of
producing a regular
revenue, and a powerful network of
fortresses gave the Mughals
military dominance. Even so, the
Mughals claimed, with some
justification, to rule a far more
extensive territory than they could
hope to administer on a daily basis.
The success of their enterprise
depended as much on their political
pragmatism as on their military
capability and administrative
sophistication.

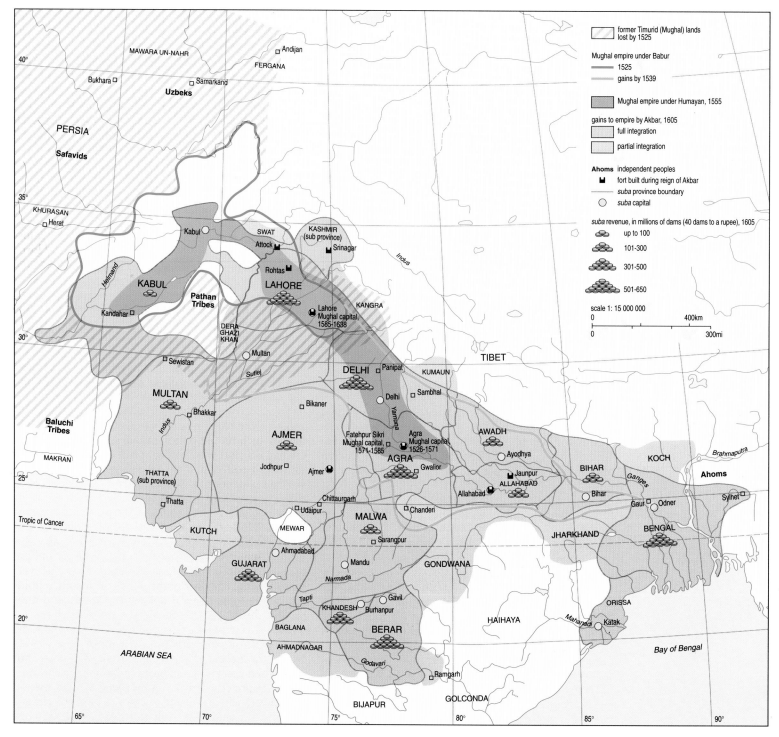

94

revenue from many of the lands to which he laid claim. At the time of his death in 1605 the imperial treasuries contained reserves worth between 139 million and 166 million silver rupees. During the 1590s, revenue receipts were running at the order of 99 million rupees. The emperor spent about 5 percent of the total revenues on his own household and palaces (quite a modest proportion of the whole). A unified coinage, minted under Akbar's direct control, was in use throughout much of his domains, and some progress had been made with the establishment of uniform weights and measures. Many lands had been surveyed and their productivity recorded.

The paradoxes of Mughal rule

The empire remained, however, shot with interesting qualities and paradoxes. At the end of the century it was no less a military state than it had been at its beginning. Perhaps as much as nine-tenths of revenue collected went directly or indirectly on military expenditure. The government was constantly at war, within its own territories and in those of its neighbors. This was a military culture devoted to constant expansion by the sword. Politics turned on the control of men, forts and armaments. As much was achieved by show as by actual fighting, but hardly a season went by without real battles being fought somewhere or other. In some districts, and often for lengthy periods, Mughal rule was firmly riveted in place and hardly challenged: stable centralized administration was often accompanied by substantial benefits such as economic growth and the maintenance of law and order. But changing fortunes in the field could easily upset what remained a delicate balance: if the emperor had a good campaigning season, men complied with his demands and attended his court; if the emperor lost a campaign or was attacked from without, local lords were less supportive and stayed at home to watch the outcome.

Though appearing to be a fully bureaucratized and centralized state, run according to recognizable administrative procedures by technically proficient salaried officers, the Mughal empire was at heart a different kind of managerial enterprise. It deployed military authority to cow local lords and peasant cultivators into remaining at peace and into producing revenue. A number of checks and auditory systems, controlled from the court, were placed in position, but overlapping them lay a series of intermediaries such as the major military commanders and civilian officials who had the right under certain conditions to collect and dispose of public wealth. The vast sums of money extracted from the countryside did not flow in a straightforward way from the fields to the capital, there to be redistributed as the emperor wished. While Akbar spent around 10 million rupees a year on his own troops and heavy artillery, an enormous amount of the total revenue, some 81 million rupees (or more than eight-tenths of the total), was placed by the emperor in the hands of the office-holders for the more general upkeep of the Mughal military machine.

This was a practical necessity, for, without some such decentralized structure, resources could never have been successfully mobilized in the first place, but it required constant vigilance by the imperial authority to ensure continued control. Serious competition for power, whether from within the political elite or inspired by a challenge from beyond Mughal domains,

Above Akbar's great fortress at Agra, begun in 1565 and completed around 1571, replaced an earlier brick-built Lodi fort. Its buttressed and crenellated walls were constructed of red sandstone with white marble detailing. With the massive main gate, they were designed to convey visually the immense power and authority of the emperor; they stood 22 meters high and enclosed a semicircular area about 2.5 kilometers in circumference. Abul Fazl records in the *Ain-i-Akbari* that more than 500 stone buildings were put up within the walls of the fort. The most notable of these to survive is a palace overlooking the river known as the Jahangir Mahal. However, much of the interior of the fort was rebuilt by Akbar's successors, particularly Shah Jahan who was himself held prisoner here at the end of his life.

Military power

During his 50 years of rule, Akbar made the Mughal presence a fixed reality in northern India, establishing a military overlordship across the Gangetic plain. Early on in his reign he realized the strategic importance of constructing a network of major forts. These not only served the purpose of overawing the localities in which they were placed and acting as barracks and arsenals, but were also cities of tombs, mosques, treasuries and palaces. The first was at Agra where, in 1565, work began on strengthening the city's defenses by erecting a new fort on the banks of the Jamuna. Akbar subsequently built two other huge new fortresses, one at Allahabad, controlling the confluence of the Ganges and Jamuna rivers and the eastern part of the Gangetic plain, and the other at Lahore, in Punjab, the first line of defense against invasion from Central Asia. These major military cities were reinforced by other castles, at Ajmer, guarding the route into Rajput country, Attock and Rohtas in the northwest, and at Jaunpur in Bihar. All were repositories of wealth and weapons, and provided secure places for the royal family. Their commanders were directly appointed by the emperor, and the villages immediately around their walls were assigned to maintain them and to defray their costs. The Mughals would come eventually to occupy and garrison many famous strongholds as they extended their military rule in the subcontinent, but the great strongholds in northern India remained the base of their power to the very end of their empire.

The degree of centralization achieved by Akbar can be judged by the relative ease with which he collected

Left This picture comes from the Genealogy of Hari, a supplement to the *Mahabharata* dealing with the life of Lord Krishna. Akbar commissioned a translation of the *Mahabharata* by assembling a number of Hindu scholars at Fatehpur Sikri and having their recitation of the story copied down and then roughly translated. Faizi, brother of Abul Fazl and a considerable poet, then produced a polished Persian version, which was lavishly illustrated. The work was complete by 1586. A similar project to render the *Ramayana* into Persian was initiated about 1584. A number of copies of these works were made for wide distribution. Akbar's interest in the Hindu classics was no doubt stimulated by the fact that many Rajput chieftains had become fully part of Mughal court life, though the Sidosia dynasty of Mewar continued as a thorn in the side of the Mughals into the reign of Jahangir.

could transform the material position of the emperor overnight – one day he could claim to be rich and at the head of a large army, the next his wealth and men could be commanded by enemies in the provinces. Thus the art of imperial control was to manage the localities, the intermediaries and the court nobility. The emperor wielded great power, but was also politically constrained. Hence the paradox of the grandeur and solidity of Mughal rule, and the instability and occasional bloody tumult of its politics. Hence, too, its need to survive by constant expansion – itself productive of long-term problems – and the chronic uncertainty about the degree of control exerted over its lands and the precise limits of its frontiers.

Despite the ring of fortresses established by Akbar, he and his successors had constantly to be in the field against their political foes. The Mughal emperors were as much at home in their court-camps as in their cities of sandstone and marble. When moving around the country with his army we are told the emperor processed at the head of some 50,000 cavalry, 500 elephants and supporting infantrymen. Advance parties were sent out to reconnoiter the best route, make sure that supplies were available and set up the emperor's pavilion at the next camp-site. At night a flaming torch would be set on a tall mast in the camp to act as a guide for stragglers. As the array moved across country, heralds informed the local populations that they would come to no harm if they supported the emperor and would be richly rewarded when he returned from his successful campaign. They could, moreover, bring grain and goods to the bazaars in his camp for sale, free from taxes. The progress of a huge army and movable city-court was purposely designed to impress and to overawe.

The accession of Jahangir
In part, Akbar achieved so much because he lived for so long. The last four years of his life were full of dissension as opposing parties at court, grouped around the persons of Akbar's son Salim and his eldest grandson Khusrau, began to maneuver for the succession. During the late summer and fall of 1605 Akbar fell ill with dysentery. In his weakened state he recognized Salim as his successor, presenting him with a turban and the sword of Humayan. He died on 25 October 1605 and was buried in the magnificent tomb he had built for himself at Sikandra, just outside of Agra. Khusrau's adherents found that they could not muster sufficient support to make him emperor. After a week of mourning, Salim declared himself emperor with the title Nur-ud-din Jahangir Padshah Ghazi. After an unsuccessful bid by Khusrau the following year to dispossess his father, Jahangir had him blinded and his supporters executed. The immediate political crisis was over, and no full-scale war of succession occurred – a rarity in the history of the Mughal empire.

Jahangir's reign saw the need for constant political vigilance and perpetual military activity to keep the inheritance he had received from Akbar intact. The Sidosia dynasty of Mewar, based in the hilly country around Udaipur, who had always been the most conditional of Akbar's allies, once again seized the opportunity to display their independent spirit. In 1613, after a series of indecisive campaigns, Jahangir ordered his son Prince Khurram at the head of an army into Rajput country, where he set up garrisons in the hills, previously thought inaccessible by the Mughal generals. Jahangir himself moved to Ajmer for the

final stages of the campaign, and as Khurram harassed the Rana of Mewar's forces, made hostages of his family, and finally forced him to capitulate, Jahangir impressed the local Hindu population with a display of Mughal power.

The Rana's defeat was celebrated by holding a hunt along the banks of the sacred tank at Pushkar and visiting some of the Hindu temples there. Upon discovering one place belonging to the Rana's uncle that contained an image of Vishnu in his incarnation as Varaha the Boar, Jahangir ordered his followers to "break that hideous form" and throw it into the lake. He also ridiculed the local religious belief that the tank was bottomless by having it measured and establishing it to be "nowhere deeper than 12 cubits". Jahangir later built a small hunting lodge on the banks of the tank at Pushkar with an inscription stating that it celebrated his victory over the Rana of Mewar. It became one of his favorite hunting spots. To the numerous Hindu devotees who came to this holy site, where all life was held to be sacred, there could have been no clearer demonstration of the political reality of Mughal power. Having re-asserted imperial authority, Jahangir was willing to make a political compromise: the Rana, after agreeing to "choose obedience and loyalty", was forgiven and his titles to land and rulership restored. Karan, his son and heir, was brought to the emperor at Ajmer to be given lavish presents and other marks of esteem and appointed to high office within the Mughal nobility.

Other frontiers of the empire continued to remain problematical throughout Jahangir's reign. He still harbored his predecessors' ambitions of restoring the Timurid family to power in northern Afghanistan and their ancestral lands in Central Asia. He was thwarted in this, not just by the continuing turbulence of the various peoples across this broad but economically and strategically important zone, but also by the complexities of Mughal-Persian relations. Much military and diplomatic effort was spent on ventures that produced many local shifts in the balance of power but no long-lived results.

In the northeast, too, Jahangir faced difficulties in defining the limits of his state. The Mughal expansion through Bengal and into Assam had come up against the expansion of the Ahoms, a Shan people from upper Burma who, since the early 15th century, had been pressing down the Brahmaputra valley, dispossessing or incorporating into their polity the tribal and Hindu populations settled there. The Mughals regarded these Asian invaders as savages: Lahori, a mid 17th-century chronicler, wrote: "The inhabitants [of Assam] shave the head and clip off beard and whiskers. They eat every land and water animal. They are very black and loathsome in appearance. The chiefs travel on elephants or country ponies; but the army consists only of foot soldiers." Nonetheless, they proved a formidable enemy: the Ahoms were used to fighting from boats, were adept at throwing up mud and bamboo fortifications, and adopted surprise tactics such as attack by night. The Mughals responded by developing river-boats with cannon mounted in the bows, and deploying matchlockmen as well as cavalry. Meanwhile the frontier remained indeterminate, the scene of constant activity, providing opportunities for Mughal soldiers to serve their emperor. Along the whole range of the northern Himalayan foothills, as well, petty rajas had constantly to be kept in line, and on occasion major expeditions had to be sent to

Natural History Painting

Though the first Mughal emperor, Babur, appreciated India's wealth, he did not like the people he encountered there and wrote in his *Memoirs* that they had "no genius, no comprehension of mind, no kindness or fellow feeling, no ingenuity or mechanical invention...". He was, however, fascinated by the country's flora and fauna and his *Memoirs* are replete with detailed descriptions of India's natural wonders. This ardent interest in nature was shared by his successors who commissioned some of the world's most beautiful wildlife studies. While these paintings are notable for their naturalism and closeness of observation, they were more than scientific or clinical investigations of nature. The Mughal emperors followed in the tradition of India's Hindu rulers, who were not perceived as having authority only over the world of human affairs and politics but were considered to be prime movers in the natural (as well as in the supernatural) world, responsible for such phenomena as the coming of the monsoon or plagues of smallpox or locusts. Indian theories of governance did not encompass the existence of a dichotomy between nature and culture, and representations of plants and animals symbolized the emperor's mastery over the natural domain. The paintings reproduced here show a profound respect for their subject matter, but the emperor's authority over nature also had a dark side. This is displayed in another genre of painting favored by Indian artists – that of the hunting scene. Paintings depicting the *gamargh*, or mass slaughter of wild animals within a small enclosure, are perhaps the most striking example of this. It is the blurring of the boundary between the social and the natural that "animates" these paintings in a way that distinguishes them from their European counterparts, and it is thus unsurprising that they bear compositional similarities to the single-figure portraits that the Mughal emperors often commissioned of their courtiers.

Right In the late 18th and early 19th centuries, after the substantive demise of the Mughal empire, the British continued to commission Indian artists to paint natural history subjects. The pair of Indian gerbils (*top*), was painted by Haludar, who was employed by the Barrackpore Menagerie, c.1804–5. The Sarus crane (*bottom*) was painted in Calcutta c.1780–82 by Shaikh Zain ud-Din for Mary, Lady Impey, wife of Sir Elijah Impey, chief justice of Bengal from 1777–83. It was part of a collection of more than 200 studies produced for Lady Impey by three native artists. Zain ud-Din, the most talented of the three, was originally from Patna and trained in the Mughal tradition, perhaps at Lucknow. However, he adapted his style to suit the taste of his European patron for more "scientific" and "dispassionate" observation.

Right and above Mughal wildlife painting reached its zenith under the patronage of the emperor Jahangir. Artists focused their attention on exotic species, such as the Himalayan *markhur* ("serpent-eating goat) painted by Inayat c.1615 (*right*), and more common animals such as the *nilgai* ("blue bull") painted by Mansur c. 1610–15 (*above*). Because it was a popular quarry of royal hunters, the *nilgai* was a particularly favored subject, and Mansur depicted it several times. More generally, Mansur made his reputation in painting wild animals, birds, and flowers. He is known, for example, to have completed over 100 floral subjects (of which only a handful, alas, survive), and his work was so greatly esteemed by Jahangir that he granted the artist the title of *Nadir ul-asr* (Wonder of the Age).

remind princes like the Raja of Kangra of the powerful overlord on the plains.

Religion and politics

During his bid for the succession in 1605, Prince Khusrau went up into Punjab and at the prosperous town of Goindwal, then one of the Sikhs' centers, received the support of Arjun, the fifth Sikh Guru. Jahangir took a dim view of this popular religious figure who had won converts among both Hindus and Muslims. He ordered Arjun's capture and execution, along with the confiscation of his property. Arjun thus became the first Sikh martyr. His young son Hargobind survived to become recognized as the sixth Guru, but was forced to shift his center of operations to Bilaspur in the Himalayan foothills. There he held court on the margin of the Moghul state, promoting Sikhism and drawing support from followers in the Punjab plains.

On the whole, however, Jahangir effected no significant departure from the religious policies of his father. Those who actively stirred up religious controversy or cultivated large popular followings could expect to feel imperial displeasure or, like the Sikh leader, suffer persecution, but provided no political threat was evident, the emperor was willing to treat religious leaders generously and with courtesy. The Englishman, Sir Thomas Roe, James I's ambassador to the great Mughal from 1615 to 1618, went so far as to observe that Jahangir's religion "is of his own invention; for he envies Muhammad, and wisely sees no reason why he should not be as great a prophet as he, and therefore professes himself so . . . he has found many disciples that flatter or follow him . . . all sorts of religions are welcome and free, for the King is of none." Akbar's encouragement of religious debate was continued. Jahangir sought out the more quietist religious teachers, much as his father had done, and made several visits to Gosain Jadrup, a widely venerated Vaishnava ascetic who lived in a cave on a hillside near Ujjain.

The emperor's title, Nur-ud-din, meant "light of the faith", and Jahangir gave every indication of developing still further his father's view that as a monarch he was a special person, linked with the great light of the sun, and capable of greater knowledge and power than ordinary men. Like his father, too, Jahangir gathered around himself an inner circle of disciples – even extending it to include such people as Sir Thomas Roe – who in return for close and loyal service to the emperor received from him many presents, including the right to wear his miniature portrait. Younger members of the nobility, brought up within Jahangir's household, looked to him for preferment and honor.

Such actions were unlikely to win approval in orthodox Islamic circles. However, Jahangir showed some sensitivity toward the Muslim clerical establishment. As was particularly fitting in someone whose birth had been prophesied by a Chisti saint, he resumed the practice, abandoned by Akbar, of showing public favor to the Chisti order. In 1614, while recovering from a bout of illness, he paid a visit to the tomb of Khwaja Muin-ud-din Chisti at Ajmer and declared his own discipleship of the saint by piercing his ears and hanging lustrous pearls in each. Jahangir gave away 732 pearls to those of his officers who followed his example. Such devotion to Islam was not enough to satisfy Shaikh Ahmad Sirhindi, a prominent member of the orthodox Naqshbandi order. From the early 1590s he been prominent in evolving a radical

Mughal Gardens

Though there was a tradition of landscape architecture in India prior to the Mughals' arrival, it was under their rule that gardening was raised to a sublime art form. The first Mughal emperor, Babur, left little behind in terms of monumental architecture, but we know from his *Memoirs* that he was an avid builder of gardens – an interest he brought to India from his Central Asian homeland. The city of Samarkand was famous for its gardens embellished by Babur's illustrious ancestor Timur. Only a few ruined fragments of Babur's gardens survive today, but his interest in landscape architecture was continued by his successors, especially Jahangir and Shah Jahan. The name of Shah Jahan's Shalimar garden in Kashmir remains synonymous with a terrestrial, second paradise. Indeed, the gardens built by the Mughal emperors were specifically intended to evoke an other-worldly setting befitting a dynasty whose legitimacy to rule was based in part on claims of divine sanction. While these gardens are idylls of great serenity and beauty, in an era when military campaigns and royal progresses were ubiquitous, they also doubled as military and imperial caravanserais. Though the early gardens may have initially incorporated few permanent buildings, with time they increasingly included architectural features such as pavilions, baths and audience halls. Moreover, they became constituent elements of monumental structures such as palaces and royal mausoleums.

Right Babur is often credited with introducing to India the *char bagh* – a quadripartite garden formed by water courses intersecting at right angles, which evoke the rivers of paradise. A posthumous painting by Bishandas and Nanha (c.1590) depicts Babur supervising the construction of such a garden.

Below The *char bagh* design was elaborated upon by later emperors, particularly Shah Jahan. He used this form as the basis of the gardens fronting the Taj Mahal, depicted below in 1828 by C.A. Hodgson, the Surveyor-General of India.

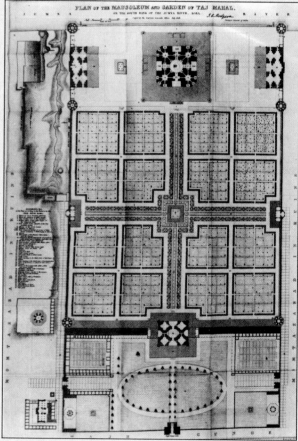

Left The gardens of the alpine valley of Kashmir were favored hot season retreats of the Mughals, prized both for their beauty and bounty. In addition to fruit trees, other luscious garden crops, especially melons, thrived there. However, because the valley bottom was largely covered by lakes and marsh, arable land remained scarce. Thus, as shown in a Kashmiri painting, horticulture was commonly practiced on floating islands tended by farmers on small boats known as *shikaras*.

Right The *char bagh* may have had a Central Asian origin, but its formal qualities harmonized well with Hindu cosmological designs such as the mandala. Therefore, Hindu rulers readily adapted the design, as in this garden at the Amber palace of the Maharaja of Jaipur. However, because the mandala represents a total universe in which the natural, the supernatural and the social are thoroughly interconnected, the similar Rajput and Mughal designs may have been imbued with somewhat different meanings.

conservative response to the religious trends in evidence at the Mughal court, denouncing the participation of non-Muslims in the state and calling for the humiliation of the Hindus and their false religion. Underlying his numerous letters and treatises could be detected anxieties about the ways in which state patronage was diverted from Muslims to other religious groups, coupled with fears for spiritual loss and a weakening of the sense of Muslim community. While Sirhindi's views were not unchallenged, even by other impeccably orthodox teachers, he gathered some support for his ideological position, particularly in Punjab.

After his death in 1624, Sirhindi's followers compiled and kept in circulation volumes of his writings, and glorified his role as a persecuted champion of Islam (he had been imprisoned for a time at Gwalior by Jahangir to cool his enthusiasm). Sirhindi remains a controversial religious figure. His significance lay in the fact that his teaching heralded the resurgence of a more aggressive strain of Muslim orthodoxy, and his continuing popularity indicated the degree of concern amongst some Muslims in India at the political and cultural compromises being made by the Mughals. Though stating in an extreme way the orthodox position, he persuaded many Muslims to reconsider their own religious position and his anti-Hindu sentiments echoed down throughout the century, sharpening communal divisions in the subcontinent.

The arts of the Mughal court

In 1611, Jahangir married Mehrunissa, the widow of a Mughal officer killed in action in Bengal. She rapidly became his favorite wife and exercised great influence at court for the rest of his reign. Regarded as extremely beautiful, Mehrunissa had a strong personality and was tremendously capable. Of refined taste, her skills extended to the design of gardens, golden ornaments and palace interiors. She arranged great feasts and wrote poems in Persian. She excelled in the hunting field. Jahangir gave her the title Nur Jahan, or "Light of the World". Her father, a high-ranking Persian nobleman at court, was promoted to chief minister, and her equally able brother, Asaf Khan, strengthened the family's position through the marriage in 1612 of his daughter Arjumand Banu to Jahangir's son Khurram (1592–1666). For over a decade, this group dominated the court and ran the affairs of Jahangir's government. While they worked together, no other faction could stand effectively against them, though some dissident nobles did begin to form a party around Jahangir's blinded son, Khusrau.

Jahangir displayed none of the great military and organizational talents of Akbar; and some criticism was voiced of his capriciousness and cruelty, his love of luxury, and his sentimentality and generosity. But the relative security of his regime, coupled with the practical business skills of Nur Jahan and her party, allowed the emperor time to develop a courtly culture. During Jahangir's reign Agra was re-established as the imperial capital. The emperor did not engage in any major new building projects, but he was responsible for the creation of a number of new gardens, especially Shalimar Bagh, Achabal, Vernag and Nishat Bagh, all in Kashmir. Testimony abounds to Jahangir's knowledge as a plantsman, and as a person interested in understanding nature as a whole.

He was also a lavish patron of the arts, especially painting. Artists working for him and for other noble

Abu'l Hasan

Abu'l Hasan (b.1588) was the son of a distinguished Persian painter Aqa Riza who had entered the household of Prince Salim, the future Mughal emperor Jahangir, and it was there that he was brought up. In their incessant demand for illustration for new manuscripts, Mughal patrons drew upon a wide range of talent: painters with different artistic backgrounds were attracted from Persia and Central Asia to join the workshops of indigenous Indian artists. Artistic work was a communal activity conducted under the supervision of a senior master, who would impose a coherent style on the work issuing from the studio. European art, carried to India largely in the form of prints, also influenced Indian painting in the 16th century. Besides the exotic Christian subject-matter, Mughal artists were interested in the way the Europeans gave depth and realism to their pictures, and they studied the techniques that allowed human figures to take on weight and volume.

By the 1580s, individual painters began to achieve recognition, though the promotion of originality conflicted with the traditional practice of imposing artistic unity on a manuscript to which many people had contributed. Jahangir, however, who was noted for his connoisseurship and the delight he took in collecting a wide variety of pictures, boasted of his ability to distinguish one artist from another. He prized individual expression and had little interest in pictures that were the product of more than one hand. During his reign a number of artists flourished as individuals, each exhibiting some degree of specialization in their work: Mansur concentrated on animals and flowers, Govardhan drew different types of holy men, musicians and eccentrics, Abu'l Hasan and Bishan Das emerged as imperial portraitists. Of Abu'l Hasan, Jahangir recorded: "His work is perfect", and in 1618 he honored the young artist with the title *Nadiru-z-zaman* – "Wonder of the Age".

Left The drawing of *St John the Evangelist* was executed in 1600 when Abu'l Hasan was 12 years old. Abu'l Hasan, in copying from Albrecht Dürer's *Crucifixion* (1511), makes skillful use of light and shadow to create physical bulk and texture.

Above In *Jahangir embracing Shah Abbas I* (c.1615) Abu'l Hasan symbolically presents the Mughal ruler as the greater of the two monarchs: the lamb of the Iranian shah is lying down with the lion of the Mughal emperor. In fact the two rulers never met, and Shah Abbas remained a threatening neighbor of Jahangir's.

Right Perhaps the best-known of Abu'l Hasan's works is *Squirrels in a plane tree* c.1615. The realistically painted squirrels recall values of European art, while the pattern created by their tails, together with the tree, creates a decorative surface composition evoking the finest Persian ideals.

households painted many of the finest Mughal miniatures. Some of these projected the political ideology of the ruling dynasty – the association of the emperor with light, the rituals of the court – or gave explicit pictorial form to the imperial political point of view. But naturalistic trends in Mughal painting also reached their apogee during these years. Jahangir was famed for his close observation of nature, and to this period belong many outstanding studies of animals, plants and birds.

Expansion into the Deccan

In the declining years of Jahangir's reign, succession politics at court began to interact with wider events, particularly in the Deccan. A pattern of political conflict emerged that was to endure throughout the 17th century, with the Deccan becoming the focus of the most intense concern. The Mughals' attempt to extend their power southward over the independent sultanates of the Deccan met with resistance, but once involved in the region's shifting politics they were unable to extricate themselves. It was the need to expand their boundaries constantly to capture new sources of revenue and men that prompted the Mughals to claim overlordship of the sultanates in the Deccan at the end of the 16th century. At Jahangir's accession, Khandesh, Berar, and part of Ahmadnagar accepted some sort of Mughal supremacy, but neither Bijapur not Golconda to the south had done so. Moreover, within Ahmadnagar, Malik Ambar, an Abyssinian general in service with the sultan, spearheaded resistance to the Mughals.

For more than a decade, the Mughals carried out a desultory campaign against Malik Ambar. In 1616, the Mughal army razed the new city, but even this did not break the Abyssinian general's successful resistance from Daulatabad. Sent to deal with him, Khurrum waged a brilliant campaign, forcing Malik Ambar to surrender control of Berar and Ahmadnagar. Nothing in Deccani politics, however, was ever made permanent during these years. Mughal military success would be followed by an apparently decisive political settlement, only to be undone by kaleidoscopic changes in the political alignments of the Deccan. Renewed violent resistance to Mughal overlordship would provoke further Mughal military intervention, and the whole political cycle would start again.

As a reward for his successes in the Deccan, Khurram was awarded a new name – Shah Jahan, King of the World – and given new privileges. But he also began to behave more and more as if he had already succeeded to the throne of the ailing Jahangir. This opened a breach in the alliance between him, Nur Jahan and her brother Asaf Khan, who remained attached to Khurram, his son-in-law. In 1620, partly as a response to the prince's growing power, Nur Jahan arranged a marriage between Shahryar, Jahangir's 16-year-old youngest son, and Ladili Begum, her daughter by her previous marriage. This had the effect of creating at least three major factions at court grouped round the persons of Khurram, the disabled Khusrau (whom many nobles believed still to be Jahangir's favored heir), and Shahryar (who was now Nur Jahan's preferred candidate).

Outbreak of hostilities

In 1621 after Jahangir had suffered a serious illness, Khurram arranged the death of his elder brother Khusrau, whom he had earlier held prisoner in his camp in the Deccan. The main political contest was now between Khurram and Nur Jahan. The loss of Kandahar in southern Afghanistan to the armies of the Shah of Persia in 1625 provided an opportunity for Nur Jahan to send her protégé, Shahryar, northwest at the head of a large army. This was partly paid for by taking over revenues previously assigned to Khurram. He promptly revolted, but was forced to flee to the Deccan. Here he formed an alliance with, among others, his erstwhile enemy, Malik Ambar. But he failed to carry the day in the field, and was compelled to remain as governor of the Deccan, sending his sons as hostage to court.

Jahangir's death on 28 October 1627 set in motion a quite extraordinary sequence of events. Asaf Khan successfully prevented Nur Jahan from exercising any significant influence over affairs by confining her to the camp beside the body of the dead emperor. He then proclaimed Dawar Bakhsh, one of the sons of the late Prince Khusrau, as the new emperor – by this means provoking Shahryar to battle, whom he defeated and captured. By the turn of the year, Khurram had made his way from the Deccan toward Agra, and by 19 January 1628 the political position was sufficiently secure for Asaf Khan to proclaim Khurram emperor under the title Shah Jahan. Within days of this announcement, Asaf Khan had arranged the killing of Shahryar, Dawar Bakhsh, Dawar's brother, and another two cousins of Shah Jahan. The way cleared for him by his father-in-law, the new emperor entered Agra in triumph on 24 January 1628. Asaf Khan was proclaimed chief minister and Nur Jahan accepted retirement with a pension of 200,000 rupees a year. Living for another 18 years, the enterprising queen devoted herself to good works and to the construction of Jahangir's tomb at Lahore.

The empire of Shah Jahan

Shah Jahan had seized from his rivals a large and rich empire. The removal of his brothers and nephews by Asaf Khan had ensured that there was no serious challenge to his authority at court and for the next 30 years he set about consolidating Mughal rule. The Rajputs were kept more or less in order, and continuing thrusts into the Deccan stabilized relations with the now only semi-independent sultanates. In the northeast, a political compromise with the Ahom kingdom resulted in Mughal authority extending as far, but no farther than, Kamrup. Shah Jahan shared the Mughal dream of retaking the Timurid lands in Central Asia, but expeditions through northern Afghanistan to Balkh showed that this was impractical. In 1647 a treaty with the Uzbeks advanced the Mughal frontier a few kilometers but effectively ended Mughal aspirations to repossess Bukhara or Samarkand. A similar limitation was set on Mughal expansion to the west when military attempts to regain Kandahar failed.

Nonetheless, the Mughal territories, divided into 22 *subas*, or provinces, and some 4,350 *parganas* (as the main administrative sub-divisions were called) constituted a very large empire. Shah Jahan was able to call upon about double the amount of revenue raised at the time of Akbar's death, partly as a result of the territorial aggrandizement that had taken place since 1605. But part also came from the increased productivity of some of the empire's key districts. The countryside around centers such as Lahore and Agra, for example, were capable of producing revenue in excess of a million rupees a year, and Mughal officials had made

strenuous efforts, particularly important in a country where land was still relatively plentiful, to encourage settlement and cultivation. Moreover, districts falling directly under the central administration had increased in number, and Akbar's systems had become more effectively applied. Shah Jahan's share of the revenues was a seventh of the total – a significant increase on the proportion raised in the previous century. During his father's reign, cash reserves had become run down, but despite continued large-scale expenditure, Shah Jahan had succeeded in restoring them to around 95 million rupees by the mid 1640s.

The officer elite

The number of senior imperial officers also increased. A list of all the *amirs* and *mansabdars* with a rank of 500 *zat* and above drawn up in 1647 shows that there were 445 such senior officers – approximately double

Above This portrait of the three younger sons of Shah Jahan – Shah Shuja, Aurangzeb and Murad Bakhsh – was painted by Balchand around 1635. Balchand's career spanned the reigns of Akbar, Jahangir and Shah Jahan. He became best known for his portraits but (as in this composition) showed himself to have an accurate eye for animals, birds and plants as well. The brotherly friendship implied in this portrait did not last long: by the 1650s, Shuja, Aurangzeb and Murad, together with their elder brother Dara, were locked in an intense and increasingly bloody struggle for the succession.

Right This white nephrite jade wine cup belonging to Shah Jahan is carved out of hard stone, but is nonetheless translucent in places like mother of pearl. Its shape is based on a halved gourd, tapering at one end to form the neck and head of a wild goat. The cup stands on a base of an open lotus flower from which acanthus leaves radiate across the lower surface. The Mughals probably brought the skills and traditions of jade carving to India from their Timurid homelands of Turkistan and eastern Iran: both Akbar and Jahangir are known to have had carved jade cups. A Persian inscription on this cup gives Shah Jahan's title in monogram and a date equivalent to 1657. The title used is "The Second Lord of the Conjunction", thus linking Shah Jahan directly with Timur, who had styled himself "Lord of the Conjunction" in reference to an auspicious conjunction of planets that brought him fame and fortune.

the number of 50 years before. However, the distribution of power and revenues among them was very uneven. Just 73 officers were responsible for nearly half the troops and accounted for some 37.6 percent of the entire revenues of the empire. The four sons of Shah Jahan alone, each appointed to lucrative governorships, controlled forces that absorbed more than 8 percent of the total revenue take. Moreover, most of the lands from which they drew their resources were in the richer, more productive and more securely administered parts of the empire.

Muslims accounted for four-fifths of the 445 senior officers, half of them of Persian ancestry. But the early 17th century saw some changes in the composition of the Mughal elite. Noticeably more Afghans were being admitted – 26 of them in 1647 – signaling the incorporation into the state of a number of the Afghan chiefdoms of the Himalayan foothills. Some 65 nobles were Muslims of Indian origin, 8 of them from the Deccan. Rajputs accounted for 73 officers, but there were great differences between them: a handful of houses – those of Marwar, Mewar, Ambar, Gaur – stood out above the others, and another five clan heads held rank of 2,500 *zat* or above. In a real sense, these dynasties had used Mughal recognition to achieve positions of power within Rajputana.

Not all the officers recruited from the Deccan were Muslims: Shah Jahan had ten senior officers who were Marathas. As in Rajputana, the Mughals needed to penetrate the local social structures of the Deccan in order to tap new sources of revenue, and they could do so only by recruiting locally dominant families and clans. But social organization in the western Deccan was so fluid, and its economy so perilously poised between dearth and plenty, that, as in Rajputana, there was no real certainty nor guaranteed continuity in the membership of the dominant elites. Mughal intervention in this area, therefore, represented as much an opportunity for certain individuals and families to achieve power and be maintained in it, as it revealed the need of the Mughal state to draw upon and make compromises with the societies it found established there. The apparatus of the state machine under Shah Jahan was not very different from the blueprint laid down by Akbar, but it was bigger and more complex.

The revival of Islam

The decades between 1630 and 1660 saw some of the greatest artistic achievements of the Mughals, while Shah Jahan, presiding over an increasingly formalized courtly culture, presented himself as an idealized and aloof king. During these years the orthodox Muslim reaction to the eclectic religious policies of Akbar and Jahangir began to have an effect on public affairs. By the 1630s prominent groups of orthodox Sunni teachers, including the Shattari and Chisti orders and a number of laymen, had joined members of the Naqshbandiya *sufi* order in voicing their concern about heresy within Islam and about the dangers posed by the assimilative capacity of Hinduism.

Unlike his father and grandfather, Shah Jahan was obliged to pay more attention to the call for greater orthodoxy and he gradually aligned himself more closely with mainline Sunni teachings. He first accepted that official policy should be guided by the *sharia*, as interpreted by one of the four legal schools of Islam, rather than arrogating to himself as emperor any special superior religious authority. From 1633

Shah Jahan banned the construction or repair of non-Muslim places of worship and, on hearing that wealthy Hindus wished to complete work on major temples in Varanasi, he ordered a number to be pulled down. After this initial move, however, his new policy does not seem to have been applied very rigorously, though a number of Hindu shrines were damaged or destroyed in the course of military campaigning.

It was in his active support of Islam that Shah Jahan differed most markedly from his father and grandfather. He began to pay greater attention to Islamic festivals and resumed generous support for Muslim holy men and Muslim holy places. The birth of the Prophet was marked with lavish and pious celebrations, and pilgrimages resumed to the Chisti center at Ajmer. Imperial sponsorship of pilgrimages to Mecca and Medina also began again on a large scale. Above all, his reign saw the building of many new mosques under his sponsorship.

The buildings of Shah Jahan

Shah Jahan's lasting fame rests on the huge sums he spent on new building (over 28 million rupees by some calculations), and on the refinement of his architectural taste. As well as rebuilding much of Agra and Lahore, he was responsible for laying out a new capital city at Delhi. His architecture was carefully conceived and, while drawing on earlier traditions, achieved an unprecedented grandeur and formality. During the 1620s there had been increasing use of white marble in prominent buildings, often delicately carved or inlaid with colored stones, and this became characteristic of Shah Jahan's new work. His buildings reached a pitch of perfection, establishing at once a classic Indian style but one destined not to be matched by later architects.

Shah Jahan's enthusiasm for buildings was evident from the earliest days of his reign. At Ajmer he sought to commemorate his earlier victories over the Rana of Mewar by adding gardens and pavilions to the buildings at the main Chisti shrine. But his chief work was

the Jami mosque, constructed entirely of white marble quarried from nearby Makrana and placed just to the west of the tomb of Khwaja Muin-ud-din Chisti. The mosque's east facade consists of 11 equal-sized arched openings supported on elegant slender piers, while beneath the eaves is carved a lengthy inscription in Persian, not only recording when the building was finished (1637–38), but explaining that Shah Jahan had long resolved to build a mosque, aligned with the mausoleum, as a thanksgiving for his victory over Mewar in 1615. The precise placing of the mosque was also a considered decision: when at prayer it allowed the emperor to be positioned auspiciously between the saint's tomb and the wall of the mosque facing Mecca.

Until the building of the new capital at Delhi, Lahore remained the second city of the empire. It was where Jahangir was buried, and where the tombs of Asaf Khan (died 1641), and of Nur Jahan (died 1645) were later built. Shah Jahan added a large 40-pillared hall for public display and ceremonial to the buildings in the fort, and completed the courtyard that enclosed the imperial palace. At Agra, the main seat of government from 1628, Shah Jahan tore down nearly all the structures within the fort, replacing them with buildings made of white marble or covered with stucco, and enclosed within walled courtyards. Work began during the first year of his reign, and the buildings were ready for public use by 1637. They included a new *Chehil sutun* (Hall of Public Audience), a new quadrangle with terraces and pavilions, and a new *Diwan-i khass* (Hall of Private Audience), as well as private residential quarters for the emperor. Two small mosques were constructed in the fort early on in the

rebuilding program, but in 1653 the emperor finished the Jamia mosque, known as the Moti or Pearl mosque, which is reckoned to be the most majestic of all Mughal mosques. In part, the design follows that of the mosque at Ajmer, but the Moti mosque was surmounted by domes and *chattris* like those at Akbar's mosque at Fatehpur Sikri. The lengthy decorative inscriptions in Persian, executed in black marble beneath the eaves, describe Shah Jahan as ruler of the world and use paradisiacal and sacred imagery to describe the mosque's features.

Shah Jahan's most famous building at Agra – perhaps the most renowned Indian building in the world – is the Taj Mahal, the tomb he built for his favorite wife, Asaf Khan's daughter, known as Mumtaz Mahal. Building began in 1632 and appears to have been substantially completed four years later, though work was still being carried out in 1643. The tomb itself consisted of a domed white marble structure, flanked by four slender minarets and situated on a high plinth. To the west of the tomb was built a mosque in red sandstone, and facing it on the east a building that is its mirror image and is usually described as a guest house. The walled grounds were laid out to evoke the gardens of paradise; the architects achieved the remarkable sense of balance evident in the buildings and in the grounds as a whole by working the design according to a series of geometrically related grids.

Even with all these improvements, Agra proved to be an inadequate capital for the Mughal ruler. The fortress was too cramped to accommodate either the business of government or the ceremonial of the court;

Right Shah Jahan's palace fort at Delhi covers more than 50 hectares and is enclosed by massive sandstone walls rising to between 18 and 22 meters in height. A full range of public and private imperial buildings, gardens and ponds was laid out within them – a French traveler recorded that the fort contained workshops of every kind, for the manufacture of paper, textiles, swords, perfumes, the preparation of food and the painting of fine pictures. Shown here is the pavilion in the women's section of Shah Jahan's private apartments. Water once flowed into the centrally placed marble pool carved to resemble an open lotus flower, and gilt and polychrome inlay originally covered the marble walls. Beyond are the imperial sleeping quarters.

Left Universally regarded as one of the finest monuments anywhere in the world, the Taj Mahal was built by Shah Jahan as a magnificent tomb for his wife Mumtaz Mahal who died after giving birth to their 14th child at Burhanpur in June 1631. A site 1.6 hectares in extent was purchased on the banks of the river Jamuna, and the revenues from 30 villages were assigned to the construction and maintenance of the tomb and its garden.

the city was overcrowded, and additional constraints had been placed on new building by the construction of the Taj Mahal. After consulting architects, builders and astrologers, Shah Jahan decided in 1639 to move his capital to a site just south of Delhi, on a bluff overlooking the river Jamuna. The city had many associations for pious Muslims. It had long been a great religious center. The landscape round about was littered with tombs, mosques and shrines, attracting thousands of pilgrims who made their way there on the anniversaries of the deaths of numerous Muslim saints. Delhi had political associations, too, for many decisive battles for the control of northern India had been fought there or in its immediate vicinity, and it had served as the capital for earlier Muslim dynasties.

The foundations for the new city, to be called Shahjahanabad, were begun on 29 April 1639. Nine years later, and after the expenditure of over 6 million silver rupees, Shah Jahan's new fortified palace, the Red Fort, was ready for occupation. On an eminence opposite the fortress, Shah Jahan built the Jama Masjid, the largest communal mosque in India with space for thousands of worshipers. Alongside were hospitals and colleges. By 1653 nearly 2,600 hectares had been enclosed within the new red sandstone walls of the city. Eleven gates provided points of entry to the new city, and the walls were topped by 27 towers. Shahjahanabad had grown to a magnificent city of 400,000 people.

Descent into civil war

Shah Jahan's rise to power had been accomplished by intrigue and bloodshed, but that was as nothing compared to his fall. It was a strange irony that what to many would have seemed a desirable and wonderful achievement in a father – the survival to manhood of four capable and energetic sons – should have resulted in a bitter civil war and Shah Jahan's close confinement in the fort at Agra. Once again the failure of Timurid law to provide either for the simple handing on to the eldest son of the property and rights of the father or for the equal distribution of such an inheritance between all the children ensured that the sons of the emperor would fight each other for possession of the Mughal throne.

Shah Jahan's eldest surviving son, Dara Shukoh (1615–59), was kept for most of the time near his father at court. Some saw this as an indication that he was the emperor's favored successor, but others suspected that the emperor wished to prevent him from becoming too powerful in his own right. Prince Dara was a man of considerable intellectual gifts, and he came to represent in court politics the more open and eclectic ideology that had been followed with such success by Akbar and, to a degree, by Jahangir and Shah Jahan. He was an active disciple of two leading liberal Shaikhs of the Qadiri *sufi* order, and was attracted by the mystical strains in Islam. During the 1640s, on the grounds that Muslims ought to know more about Hinduism, he translated the Upanishads into Persian, employing some brahmins to help him, and had the manuscript copied and distributed widely. Though Dara remained a convinced monotheist, and considered himself within the house of Islam, his disregard of more orthodox practices and rituals made him suspect in the eyes of the growing number of *ulema* who wished to restore and reinvigorate the Sunni tradition. Dara also proved to be an ineffective commander in the field, and many nobles found him to be arrogant.

From an early date Aurangzeb (1618–1707), the third son of Shah Jahan and Mumtaz Mahal, projected a different image. He proved to be the most gifted soldier and administrator of all Shah Jahan's sons, and he was ambitious for the succession. He stressed his fundamental orthodoxy by not drinking wine and by observing all the regular public rituals of Islam. His theological inquiry did not take him along esoteric paths but into discussion with teachers and lawyers soundly based in the orthodox Naqshbandi order. He was an avid reader of the Qu'ran and of legal treatises, and he cared little for art or music. He was, therefore, an ideal champion for those wishing to see a return to mainline Sunni belief and practices.

As the sons of Shah Jahan took on more military and governmental responsibility, and as they showed their paces diplomatically and in the field, so the tensions between them, and between themselves and their father, grew. The political crisis, long in brewing, finally came to a head in the late summer of 1657. Aurangzeb, stationed as governor of the southern provinces of the Deccan, and his other brothers, Muhammad Shuja, then governing Bengal, Bihar and Orissa, and Murad Bakhsh, who was in charge of Malwa and Gujarat, were increasingly resentful of the favors being shown to Dara by Shah Jahan. Constantly at his father's elbow in Delhi or Agra, he was vigorously supported in family politics by Jahan Ara Begum, Shah Jahan's favorite daughter. When the emperor became seriously ill and failed to make his customary daily appearances in public, rumors abounded that he was dead or dying. Dara moved to prevent any news leaving court, thereby fueling the rumors further, but in fact Shah Jahan made a partial recovery. Whereupon, raising Dara to an unprecedented height in the ranks of the nobility, he handed over authority to him and retreated to the fort at Agra.

As one of the chroniclers put it later, it seemed to Dara's brothers, lingering in the provinces, that the prince was "endeavoring with the scissors of greediness to cut the robes of the Imperial dignity into a shape suited to his unworthy person." In Bengal, Muhammad Shuja declared himself emperor and began to move his forces up the river toward Agra; in Gujarat, Murad Bakhsh murdered his finance minister and ransacked the port of Surat for treasure before similarly declaring himself emperor. Aurangzeb held his hand for the time being, accumulating money and troops in the Deccan and engaging in secret diplomatic correspondence with his brothers and with other key commanders. As a result, when the fighting started, Aurangzeb proved to have prepared the strongest position and to have mustered the most support. Leaving the other armies to fight each other, Aurangzeb did not move north until February 1658, when he immediately inflicted losses on the imperial army. By the end of May he had occupied the city of Agra. Negotiations with his father failed, and on 8 June, he forced Shah Jahan to surrender to him. Seizing the treasure in the fort, he then pursued Dara to the northwest, stopping in Delhi on 21 July to crown himself emperor with the title Alamgir, or "world-seizer". Shah Jahan was kept a prisoner until his death in 1666.

Aurangzeb now turned on his brothers. Over the next 12 months Dara's forces were harried and pursued, and as defeat followed defeat his supporters defected from him. He was finally delivered to Aurangzeb by Malik Jiwan, an Afghan officer whom Dara had saved from execution some years earlier. Brought to Delhi with his 15-year-old son Sipihir, Dara was paraded in rags through the streets and bazaars. On 30 August 1659 he was executed in prison on the grounds of being an apostate and idolater. Aurangzeb, on being presented with his brother's head, was reported as saying "As I did not look at this infidel's face during his lifetime, I have no wish to do so now." Prince Shuja proved more difficult to run to ground. Aurangzeb's forces had to fight a difficult campaign against him as he retreated eastward through Bengal, but by May 1660 he was forced to flee from Dhaka. He found temporary refuge with the king of Arakan, but Aurangzeb used diplomatic intrigue to secure his death. Murad Bakhsh, the third brother, had been imprisoned in Gwalior since January 1659. An abortive attempt was made to rescue him in early

1661, and in December of that year, on the petition of the son of an officer he had killed in Gujarat at the start of the war, Murad was executed in accordance with the Islamic law of retribution.

The triumph of Islamic orthodoxy

Aurangzeb ruled until his death, aged 90, in 1707. His reign was effective, long and eventful. It marked a decisive shift in imperial culture, as the emperor, continuing the policies begun by Shah Jahan, pushed the Mughal empire into becoming more of an Islamic state, conforming more to the *sharia*, and having as its aim the benefit of the community of believers. New effort was put into defining Islamic thought and practices more closely, and into the attempt to win converts to the Muslim community.

Aurangzeb himself set the example: over seven years he learnt the Qu'ran by heart, and he secured legitimacy for his seizure of power by resuming close contact with the holy places of Islam in Arabia. He abandoned as un-Islamic Akbar's practice of appearing on a balcony at sunrise for all who wished to worship him. He ceased to patronize chronicle-writing and book illustration and closed artistic workshops at court. Few new public buildings were ordered and those he did construct – tombs and mosques – were neither grand nor ornamented. A number of social events were dropped from the calendar, and court musicians were dismissed; nor did the emperor encourage informal conviviality.

Aurangzeb turned instead to the promotion of Islamic learning. He summoned a group of jurists to work on and publish a major legal textbook, the *Fatawa-i 'Alamgiri* – designed to bring some order and uniformity to judicial rulings and aimed at making the general Muslim public act according to the legal decisions and precedents of the theological scholars of the Hanafi school. This major undertaking won acclaim in India and beyond as the definitive guide to the law for orthodox Muslims. State support was restored for Muslim schools, mosques and shrines, and a serious, though incomplete, attempt made to enforce *sharia* prohibitions against blasphemy, wine-drinking and gambling, and other heretical or idolatrous behavior in public. Hindus came under increasing restrictions. A tax on Hindu pilgrims was reinstated, and after 1665, Hindus had to pay internal customs duties at a higher rate than Muslims. In 1672 Aurangzeb initiated the cancellation of tax-free grants of lands to Hindus (though this was not fully enforced), later making the grant of such lands to Muslims fully hereditary. In 1679 he restored the *jiziya* levied on non-Muslims, though the measure was so unpopular that it was even argued against within the government. Orders were also given to replace Hindus with Muslims in public service wherever possible. A new edict of 1669 ordered that recently built or repaired Hindu temples should be destroyed. It was, of course, impractical to do this everywhere, but the ruling was fully enforced whenever it was felt necessary to quell growing disaffection among his Hindu subjects and allies.

Shifting balances of power

Such a determinedly Islamic orientation to the empire, however much tempered in practice, did little to make the task of governing the subcontinent easier. But Aurangzeb may have had little choice other than to try to tighten up the ideology of the state. The very success of his predecessors in expanding the physical

Right Dating from about 1680, this portrait shows the emperor Aurangzeb in full armor and holding a gold lance. He is mounted on a charger protected by chain mail. Aurangzeb was not noted for his patronage of painting – art historians usually suggest that there was a movement of artistic talent away from the imperial court to the households of other princes and to the provincial centers, accounting both for the rise of new schools of painting and a corresponding decline in Mughal court taste. Nevertheless, this portrait reveals no diminution in the desire of the emperor to be represented with all the trappings of royalty, nor any lack of technical or aesthetic skill in the artist employed to paint it.

boundaries of the empire, and of incorporating within it a bewildering diversity of peoples and their cultures, had begun to make it unwieldy. While initially this allowed for the effective development of a new Indian state, by the mid 17th century it had created new tensions of its own. As the Mughal state became more present in everyday life – as it lay more heavily on the countryside and in the districts around the great cities of the heartland – so did resistance to its demands for tax and service become more articulate. Moreover, as the century wore on, discernible shifts in the balance of economic power between the regions and between different social groups began to make themselves felt. People started to resist further absorption into the larger whole, or sought to define and build upon a sharper community identity for the better promotion of their interests. Much of the conflict underlying the politics of the late 17th century took on explicitly religious overtones: people were to be made to obey the state because it was a righteous Islamic government; secular resistance in the provinces might well be justified on anti-Islamic grounds. Consequently, in Punjab, so near to the crucial Delhi base, disaffection was made the more bitter by the fact that local politics took on the shape of Islam embattled against Sikhism. Revolts by the Rajputs and Marathas, who had recently emerged as an important force in the northwestern Deccan under their leader Shivaji (1630–80), were given additional vigor as they invoked the support of indigenous religion against the impositions of a "foreign" overlord.

Yet nothing was totally clear-cut. Hindus remained an integral part of Aurangzeb's more overtly Islamic state, and Muslims were prominent among the opponents of Aurangzeb, both within and outside the territories he laid claim to. In the political mosaic of the Deccan, they served with distinction even in non-Muslim regimes. Undeniably, something had been lost by the narrowing of the Mughal state. Yet the different cultural layers had by now become so interwoven with each other, sometimes coalescing, sometimes separating, that far from being threatened with annihilation, they simply found new means of expression. As opportunities for patronage diminished at the great court of the Mughal, so they opened out in the great households of the empire. Architects, painters, writers and musicians found employment in noble households or at the newly emerging centers of power in Awadh (Oudh), Bengal and Hyderabad. The Rajput courts, soon to enjoy almost unprecedented wealth and independence, turned to patronage of the arts on a large scale. Maratha power expanded beyond the northwestern Deccan onto the Gangetic plain and encouraged the rebuilding of the Hindu holy city of Varanasi. There was a great flowering of minor courtly culture among the tiny polities in the Punjab hills.

During the 1660s and 1670s Aurangzeb attempted, like his predecessors, to expand Mughal authority beyond the northeastern and northwestern frontiers of the subcontinent, but these drives ended in failure; the Mughal empire was an Indian state. But it still depended on territorial expansion for survival. Aurangzeb was forced to turn more and more to the Deccan to find additional men and money. This policy met with mixed results. Undoubtedly, the Mughals had considerable success in extending their military and administrative systems through most of the Deccan, except the districts in the far south, but they paid a high price and the net benefit was far from clear. Nei-

ther war nor diplomacy were able to bring lasting stability to the politics of the Deccan.

The Mughal state had become badly overstretched. Greater territorial commitment required enhanced revenues to support the state. The older, well-established provinces began to prove unequal to the task of subsidizing the empire at large, and some of the new provinces did not produce enough surpluses to bring relief. It became increasingly difficult to keep order in most places for most of the time, encouraging resistance among the emperor's subjects. As it became harder to find enough money to meet the expenses of the state, so the senior officers and their dependants began to settle down in their districts, retain more of the revenue locally, and resist demands that they serve the empire on some other, far distant frontier.

At the end of his life, Aurangzeb was still a great emperor, and on paper his state was still fabulously wealthy. The administration was effective, and revenues were collected. But the center had lost some of its ability to manage and direct affairs in the regions, and consequently effective power began to be exercised away from the Mughal court. The empire did not dissolve into anarchy; rather it gave way to a more decentralized political order born of the contradictions inherent in the structure of the empire itself.

Above One of the schools of painting that developed in the late 17th century was that of the Rajput court of Kota. This posthumous painting shows Majarao Durjan Sal of Kota (ruled 1723–56) hunting lions. Hunting scenes – not restricted to the pursuit of lions – loom large in the corpus of Kota painting, and superb examples exist going back to the earliest days of the school. Hunting demonstrated the ruler's claim to be master of the natural world as well as lord of human society, besides being an aristocratic pursuit that fitted men for the field of battle. Here the artist has painted a picture brimful of action and vitality, but his conception is not original – he is reworking a stock composition that had been in continuous use by artists at the Kota court for more than 100 years. The genius of the artist lies in his creativity in painting a startling variation on a familiar theme.

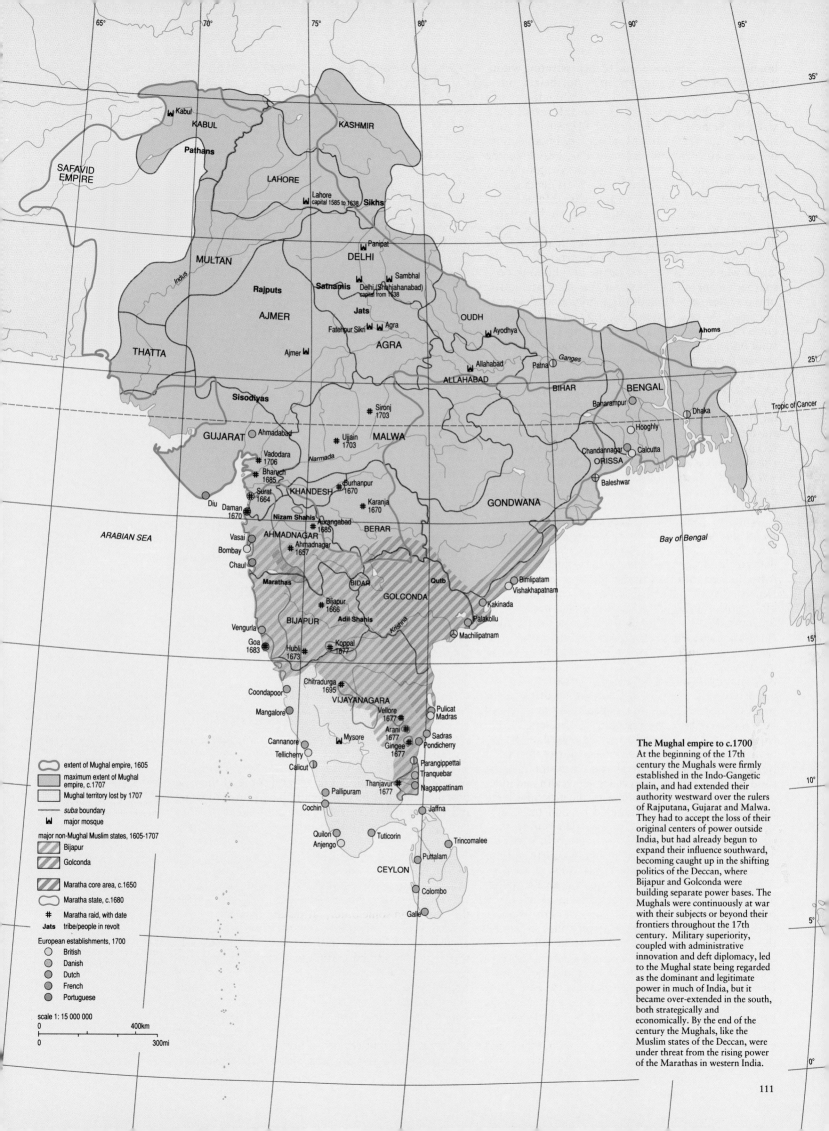

65° 70° 75° 80° 85° 90° 95°

35°

30°

25°

Tropic of Cancer

20°

15°

10°

5°

0°

SAFAVID
EMPIRE

KABUL

Kabul

Pathans

KASHMIR

LAHORE

MULTAN

Indus

Lahore
capital 1585 to 1638   Sikhs

DELHI

Panipat

Rajputs

Satnamis

Sambhal

Delhi (Shahjahanabad)
capital from 1638

AJMER

Jats

OUDH

Ahoms

THATTA

Ajmer

Fatehpur Sikri   Agra

AGRA

Ayodhya

Allahabad

Patna   Ganges

ALLAHABAD

BIHAR

BENGAL

Sisodiyas

GUJARAT

Ahmadabad

Sironj
1703

Baharampur

Dhaka

MALWA

Ujjain
1703

Hooghly

Narmada

Vadodara
1706

Chandannagar   Calcutta

ORISSA

Bharuch
1685

Burhanpur
1670

KHANDESH

Karanja
1670

Baleshwar

Surat
1664

GONDWANA

Diu   Daman
1670

Aurangabad
1685

BERAR

Nizam Shahis

Vasai

AHMADNAGAR

Ahmadnagar
1657

ARABIAN SEA

Bombay

Bay of Bengal

Chaul

Marathas

BIDAR

Qutb

Bijapur
1666

GOLCONDA

Bimlipatam
Vishakhapatnam

BIJAPUR

Adil Shahis

Kakinada

Krishna

Palakollu

Vengurla

Koppal
1677

Machilipatnam

Goa
1683

Hubli
1673

Chitradurga
1695

Coondapoor

VIJAYANAGARA

Mangalore

Vellore
1677

Pulicat
Madras

Arani
1677

Sadras

Cannanore

Mysore

Gingee
1677

Pondicherry

Tellicherry

Parangippettai

Calicut

Tranquebar

Thanjavur
1677

Nagappattinam

Pallipuram

Cochin

Jaffna

Quilon
Anjengo

Tuticorin

Trincomalee

Puttalam

CEYLON

Colombo

Galle

Legend

extent of Mughal empire, 1605

maximum extent of Mughal empire, c.1707

Mughal territory lost by 1707

— suba boundary

ᕫ major mosque

major non-Mughal Muslim states, 1605-1707

Bijapur

Golconda

Maratha core area, c.1650

Maratha state, c.1680

✛ Maratha raid, with date

Jats tribe/people in revolt

European establishments, 1700
○ British
○ Danish
○ Dutch
○ French
○ Portuguese

scale 1: 15 000 000

0   400km

0   300mi

The Mughal empire to c.1700

At the beginning of the 17th
century the Mughals were firmly
established in the Indo-Gangetic
plain, and had extended their
authority westward over the rulers
of Rajputana, Gujarat and Malwa.
They had to accept the loss of their
original centers of power outside
India, but had already begun to
expand their influence southward,
becoming caught up in the shifting
politics of the Deccan, where
Bijapur and Golconda were
building separate power bases. The
Mughals were continuously at war
with their subjects or beyond their
frontiers throughout the 17th
century. Military superiority,
coupled with administrative
innovation and deft diplomacy, led
to the Mughal state being regarded
as the dominant and legitimate
power in much of India, but it
became over-extended in the south,
both strategically and
economically. By the end of the
century the Mughals, like the
Muslim states of the Deccan, were
under threat from the rising power
of the Marathas in western India.

THE EXPANSION OF THE MARATHAS

As the Mughals extended their authority across the Gangetic plains and southward into the Deccan they provoked resistance among the populations settled there. Sometimes it was crushed, more often neutralized through accommodation, but in the process new social and cultural forces were released among those they subjugated. The new regime did not simply impose itself without let or hindrance on Indian society, but economic activity was stimulated within the towns and villages drawn into its administrative systems, and networks of communication opened up across the broad geographical zones of the subcontinent. Moreover, the activities of the great empire precipitated change within the old ruling groups as they adjusted to altered circumstances. Even as rajas and chieftains, clan-heads and village officials in the provinces and districts accommodated themselves to the expanding imperial authority, they were defining themselves against it. The courts of Rajputana, the Hindu and Muslim kingdoms of the Deccan and, as time went by, the separate headquarters of the directly administered Mughal provinces themselves, took advantage of membership of the larger authority to build up their own wealth, play their own political game, and support their own distinctive cultures.

There is no more striking an example of this phenomenon than the rise, during the 17th and 18th centuries, of the Marathas of the northwestern Deccan, who carried their rule through much of western and central India, eventually penetrating the heartland of the Mughal state itself. Variously interpreted as a sustained Hindu rising against Islam, as the resistance of the south to the north, as a revolt of landed gentry unwilling to meet the revenue and military demands of an overmighty imperial government, or even as the first stirrings of a linguistic and cultural nationalism, the creation of the Maratha state is best seen as part of the perpetual interplay of cultural forces within the subcontinent. The rise of the Marathas to prominence in India as a whole was prompted both by regional change and by the development of intricate relationships forged between themselves and others within the framework of the Mughal empire.

The land of the Marathas

The area from which the Marathas sprang – roughly corresponding to the modern state of Maharashtra – is composed of a large triangular-shaped territory lying south of the Tapti river in the northwestern Deccan. It was not the most promising base from which to launch a bid for pre-eminence in India. However, from the 16th century onward its peoples exhibited such tremendous drive and social mobility that by the 18th century they had mounted a formidable challenge for control of the subcontinent as a whole. They were able to do so partly because of social and economic developments within their own districts, and partly because they were able to exploit the opportunities for advancement offered by broader political change within the Deccan as a whole.

To the north lie the Satpura and Vindhya mountain ranges and the Malwa plateau; though difficult to cross, these do not make defensible frontiers. To the south and east there are no obvious physical barriers to movement. But if open to invasion from the north and very vulnerable to attack from the rest of the Deccan, the land of the Marathas nonetheless constituted a recognizably distinctive region, with its own products, trading patterns, marriage customs, and pilgrimage centers. It was, and is, divided into three quite distinct regions: the Konkan, the long narrow coastal strip, running from just north of Bombay as far as Goa, with a coastline broken by creeks and inlets that gave harborage to numerous small craft; the mountains of the Western Ghats, which rise abruptly from the narrow plain with steep separated peaks and few passes, a land dotted with forts that sought to impose control over the countryside to either side; and the Desh, part of the great plateau of peninsular India that lies partly in the rainshadow of the Ghats. It is not very fertile, but becomes more easily habitable toward the east and in the basins of the three main river systems – the Purna-Tapti, the Godavari, and the Krishna-Bhima – that drain into the Bay of Bengal.

In the past, the economies of these three regions complemented each other. Coconuts (an extremely versatile crop, since the fruit was eaten both fresh and dried, the husk made into matting and rope, the oil used for cooking and for dressing hair), mangoes, jackfruit, and betelnut grew only in the Konkan. The coastal strip alone produced dried fish, salt, herbs and honey from the forested areas, some rice, sea-shells for ornament, timber and bamboo. The Desh was the sole source of sugar cane, cotton, onions, garlic, tobacco, turmeric, and pulses (an essential component in the rice-based diet of the coast). But achieving the easy exchange of these goods, given the unreliability of the region's agriculture, the lack of a coin-based economy and the difficulties of transportation, was far from straightforward. Much depended on who was able to secure surpluses in kind, and who controlled the routes across Maharashtra and to the sea.

Maratha society was far from settled: even in the 17th and 18th centuries it was remarkable how few families could claim distant ancestry. Villages would flourish and then disappear through natural or man-inflicted disaster. Settlers had to be encouraged to take on risky agricultural ventures, or would flee into difficult, economically unproductive terrain to escape the attentions of a predatory overlord. Rates of mortality were high and families simply disappeared from sight. Where land was settled successfully, inheritance laws meant that viable farms were divided equally between all the members of the family (including females – the Marathas were one of the few peoples of India who allowed women to inherit land, wield power and lead armies). Eventually individual shares would be so reduced that a plot could no longer support one person. To avoid the most basic level of subsistence and survival, alternatives had to be found to living off the land, and successful families and individuals would combine agriculture with service, almost invariably of a military nature, with a protecting lord.

Muslim intervention in the Deccan

When in 1327, Muhammad bin Tughluq, the Muslim ruler of northern India, shifted the capital of his sultanate from Delhi to Daulatabad, a rock fortress in northern Maharashtra, the move signaled his clear intention to stamp his authority throughout the Deccan. However, barely 20 years later, Hasan Gangu, the governor left in charge of the Deccan when events required Muhammad bin Tughluq's return north, revolted successfully against him and established the Bahmani sultanate with its capital at Gulbarga, in present-day Karnataka. At the same time the Vijayanagara state, based in the Tungabhadra valley, began to build up a substantial military presence to resist the Muslim armies and to prevent their further expansion into the southern Deccan.

For the next two centuries there was almost constant warfare in the Deccan. This provided its inhabitants with plentiful opportunities for employment and military service; by taking advantage of this situation, new local lineages began to achieve a dominance in the countryside. This was a volatile process. As elsewhere in India, it was as often as difficult to keep hold of position and possessions as it was to obtain them in the first place. However, the fragmentation of the Bahmani kingdom at the end of the 15th century into five independent sultanates – the Imad Shahi sultanate of Berar (1484–1574), the Adil Shahi sultanate of Bijapur (1489–1686), the Nizam Shahi sultanate of Ahmadnagar (1490–1636), the Barid-Shahi sultanate of Bidar (1492–1609), and the Qutb Shahi sultanate of Golconda (1512–1687) – multiplied considerably the sources of patronage.

Unlike northern India, Muslims in the Deccan always constituted a minute proportion of the population. Islamic conquest was not followed by substantial settlement of Muslim peoples, and neither the Bahmani kingdom nor its successor sultanates set much store on conversion to Islam. Hence, the Muslim states of the Deccan were even more dependent than the Mughals and their predecessors in northern India on coming to a working agreement with the Hindu populations. Certainly, they built mosques and tombs, patronized Muslim holy men and introduced Persian technical terms into the government, the military and the revenue systems, keeping the core of the administration in the hands of Muslims based in the towns and forts. Brahminical ideologies and rituals disappeared from court, and the sultans tended not to arbitrate in caste disputes. But they evolved a new court language that combined Persian and the local vernacular, be it Maratha, Kannada or Telugu, they continued government support of Hindu establishments, and depended on Hindus for local administration, particularly for collecting taxes. Above all, they recruited their armies from the local populations. Thus, from the 15th century onward, certain families, lineages and castes began to consolidate themselves within Deccan society. Some Deshastha brahmins moved into the literate occupations of government and some even became officers; farmers moved into soldiering. Within Maharashtra, the Maratha soldier clans began to differentiate themselves from the mass of ordinary *kunbis* (peasant farmers) and from the numerous specialist artisan castes of the region through their martial traditions and through the rights they exercised in the countryside as a reward for military service.

Maharashtrian society was particularly well placed to respond to the cultural and religious challenge of Islam. Though it boasted a well-developed language of its own, it was open to many influences. Long before the Muslim invasion of the country, Hindu *bhakti* movements had swept into Maharashtra from the

Left Daulatabad – the fortress that Muhammad ibn Tughluq made the center of his operations in the Deccan – is built on a conical rock on the top of a hill that rises almost perpendicularly from the plain to a height of 142 meters. The outer wall, which formerly enclosed the ancient city of Deogiri, the capital of the Yadava dynasty, is nearly 4.5 kilometers in circumference: three lines of fortification lie between it and the upper fort. After the Delhi sultanate was forced to abandon its ambitions in the Deccan, Daulatabad was held first by the Bahmani sultans and then by the Nizam Shahis of Ahmadnagar before falling to the Mughal emperor Shah Jahan in the 17th century. Technically, the fort was very advanced: its multiple defensive walls secured ascending passageways carved through solid rock, and it was able to withstand artillery fire.

south. These emphasized the importance of pure and fervent devotion to the gods, usually to Krishna, as the essential feature of religion and opposed over-formal ritualistic Vedic Hinduism. The *bhakti* movements also encouraged people to meet together to sing hymns and worship the gods, and stressed the importance of making mass pilgrimages – especially to sacred sites within Maharashtra such as Pandharpur. There was a great flowering of devotional literature, all in the Marathi language. Namadev, a 14th-century poet-saint of Maharashtra, a tailor by profession, wrote of the all-embracing love of God; he rejected caste-based restrictions in formal worship (such as limiting the roles people could play in ritual), and set no store on caste status as an indication of spiritual development. Quietist, fervent and anti-caste in orientation, the *bhakti* movements were also syncretic, combining elements from both Hindu and Muslim teaching. Among the radical saints revered in Maharashtra were brahmins who preached the opening of temple culture, as well as Muslim poets, notably Shah Muntoji Bahmani of the royal house of Bidar and Husain Ambarkhan who wrote a commentary on the *Bhagavadgita* and was an ardent follower of Ganpati (Ganesha), Maharashtra's most popular god. Moreover, Maharashtrian Hindus could be found worshiping Muslim *pirs*, and Muslim shrines were included among Hindu places of pilgrimage.

The organization of Maratha society

Short of man-power, the Muslim rulers of the Deccan did not have the capacity to reshape the precarious economy or the society of Maharashtra in any radical way. They had to operate through the leading families they found in place. But the unreliability of harvests in the region's harsh physical environment meant that these cultivators were by no means secure within their localities and needed the support of whatever state there was to help them keep direct control of agricultural surplus, the only form of wealth there was. Rulers and ruled were thus interdependent. Families would be encouraged to settle a village or establish a new village. They would be rewarded with secure title to some of the best land and encouraged to maximize its potential by being given privileged rates of taxation, incremental over a number of years. In turn, the leading village families would be given rights and powers over other laborers and artisans who would have to provide them with goods and services in kind.

Within Maharashtra (as within other parts of India with a similar geography) office-holding in the villages, not hereditary ownership of land, became the prime objective of ambitious individuals and families. Offices such as the *patel* (village headman), or the *kulkarni* (village accountant and record-keeper), needed to be recognized and confirmed by political authority. Much sought after, they involved the village

Above One of the states in the northwest Deccan with whom Maratha soldiers were able to find service was the sultanate of Bijapur, ruled by the Adil Shahi dynasty since 1489. To the west of the city of Bijapur, just beyond the Mecca Gate, stands the Ibrahim Rauza, a group of buildings that includes the tomb of Ibrahim Adil Shah II (d.1627) and other members of his family. The complex is surrounded by a high wall pierced by a tall gateway with corner minarets. Shown here is the mosque that faces the tomb on its west side. Its five elegant arches are surmounted by finely detailed cornices with stone chains carved from single blocks of stone. Ambitious Marathas such as the Bhonsle family were able to use the political rivalries between Bijapur and the other Deccan sultanates, particularly Ahmadnagar, to forward their own position and influence.

establishments in wider social and political ties: court and village became part of each other. No pre-modern government could hope to deal effectively with a society of villages , even if it had to recognize that the village was the basic building block of the state. And so villages became grouped together, anything from 20 to 100 of them depending on locality, in a bigger administrative unit, the *pargana*. The village offices were replicated at the *pargana* level: there would be a *deshmukh* who was head of the district and responsible for taxation and a wide range of government services, and a *deshpande*, who would keep the books. These officers similarly would be paid in kind in both goods and services, and if they were skillful managers they might build up substantial military resources and administrative skills with which to bargain on the grander political stage.

Many who became Maratha soldiers, or who harbored political ambitions, sought first to become a *patel* and then a *deshmukh*. In this impoverished rural society, the rights of a *patel* were so substantial as to give real power. Many documents survive from the 17th century onward listing these rights, for by then office and its perquisites had become both hereditary and saleable. In 1726, for example, Jannojee Bin Dutojee, the *patel* of a village in Phultan *pargana*, was forced by economic circumstances to sell part of his office to Beemajee Bin Assajee, a richer *patel* from Pune district. The deed of purchase, which sets out in great detail the partition of rights, provides a vivid account of social and political organization at village level. Each man was to receive half of the *patel*'s material entitlement from the village. The deed showed that this fell into 16 different categories – including rights to grain and pulses of various kinds, vegetables and garden produce, oil from the oilman, cotton and woolen cloth from the weavers, a share of the goods coming into the village market, a share of the well, of revenue-free and of revenue-privileged lands, the services of village servants, of payment levied on travelers, and a division of the presents given to the *patel* by the government in the completion of each tax-round. In addition, the purchaser was to have half the use of the old *patel*'s house, the gift of goats on various ceremonial and sacrificial occasions, the right to a pair of shoes annually from the village cobbler, as well as customary presents from other members of the community, or from the itinerant pastoralists who grazed their flocks on village fields.

As the new *patel* increased his material wealth, he was buying political power as well. The deed went on to specify how the two men would divide between them social privileges, marks of dignity and precedence. At the Holi festival, for example, "it will be customary for both to bake bread. The musical instrument players should come to my house first, and go playing before me till I arrive at your house, when we shall both set out, my bread being carried on the right of your bread, and on arriving at the place of worship . . . I shall tie up yours under it. We shall then, together equally go through the worship, and the rest of the ceremony conjointly and at the same time." At the main festival praising Hanuman, both men's bullocks would set off at the same time and walk equally in procession round the image of the god; but, and here some vestige of the older right was recognized, "the music shall precede my bullocks home, while yours remain until it returns, when you shall bring your bullocks home with music also." Similarly at village weddings, the original *patel* was to be invited first, and to be received at the celebrations first, though the presents given to him would be shared equally.

The path to power

It has been calculated that up to half the surplus produce of the villages went in taxation and to those who held office-holding rights. At *pargana* level, the package of benefits from the villages beneath could be very substantial; in addition, the ruler apportioned taxes and particular lands and perquisites to pay for the administration and upkeep of troops. By the 17th century complex rights and obligations were set out in contracts between rulers and *deshmukhs*, and with *patels*, detailing financial, military, judicial and social obligations. The art of survival came to turn on the way in which an individual or a family could accumulate a number of *patels*, or shares in them, or win appointment as a *deshmukh* in one or more *pargana*. While village officials pure and simple tended to be somewhat protected from political changes, *deshmukhs* were not. Unlike the *patels*, their assignments were not hereditary and depended for their continuance upon satisfactory performance of their duties and on good political behavior. Even so, because emoluments tended to come from widely dispersed villages and districts, security of title depended on luck as well as on good management: a standard ploy of a hardpressed ruler was to grant to a new supporter revenues already assigned to someone else. This created a vibrant polity, in which family feud and faction played a major role.

Being a *deshmukh* was a high-risk enterprise, but provided a rising Maratha chieftain with virtually the only route to power open to him, apart from meritorious military service. Once in a position to combine his village with service to a distant ruler, a political aspirant would fortify his house and press his young menfolk into military service. He would then seek to be accommodated in one or other of the sultanates and in return would expect to build up further wealth through the assignment of rights and privileges. These rights were both geographically dispersed and often shared. The nimble chieftain would move his loyalty from one ruler to another, seeking confirmation of rights across the whole Deccan from the currently favored court. He would have to watch with care the maneuvering of the main armies and the current play of factions at court, but looked at from the point of view of the rulers, he was someone at once essential to the state but difficult to control.

Ramchandra Nilkanth, a high-serving Maratha official, said of the *deshmukh* families in the 17th century: "They are no doubt small but independent chiefs of territories. The weak manage to exist by rigidly maintaining the tradition of power though decreasing from the Emperor downwards. But they are not to be considered as ordinary persons. These people are really sharers in the kingdom. They are not inclined to live on whatever *watan* [rights] they possess, or act loyally towards the king who is the lord of the whole country and to abstain from committing wrong against anyone. All the time they want to acquire new possessions bit by bit, and to become strong; and after becoming strong their ambition is to seize forcibly from some, and to create enmities and depredations against others. Knowing that royal punishment will fall on them, they first take refuge with others, fortify their places with their help, rob the travelers, loot the territories and fight desperately, not even caring for their lives. When a foreign invasion comes they make peace with the invader with a desire for gaining or protecting a *watan*, meet personally with the enemy, allow the enemy to enter the kingdom by divulging secrets of both sides, and then becoming harmful to the kingdom get difficult to control. For this reason the control of these people has to be cleverly devised."

The rise of the Bhonsle family

The remarkable rise and development of Maratha power emerged in the particular conditions of the 17th century Deccan, in the interplay of politics between each of the Deccan sultanates, and between the Deccan sultanates and the Mughals as they extended their power southward. The first great Maratha leader was Shivaji Bhonsle (1630–80), a man of extraordinary ambition and skill, who perceived how an independent Maratha state might be created out of the most uncompromising and impoverished terrain. Very little is known of his forebears. His grandfather, Maloji, is the first to appear in the records. The family were *patels* of a village named Verul, located near Daulatabad and the Ellora caves. Maloji served as a petty horseman under the command of fellow Marathas, the Jadhavs of Kindkhed, who held grants for military service from the sultans of Ahmadnagar: at about the same period at the end of the 16th century another branch of the Bhonsle family was serving in the army of the rival kingdom of Bijapur.

In the confusion following the death of the sultan of Ahmadnagar in 1594, Maloji, like many other Maratha soldiers, transferred his allegiance to Malik Ambar, the Abyssinian general who took control of Ahmadnagar's affairs and, despite losing in battle to the Mughal Prince Khurram (later Shah Jahan) in 1616 and 1620, succeeded in extending the kingdom's influence at the expense of both the Mughals and the Deccan sultanates. By 1621, (a year before he was killed in battle at Indapur), Maloji Bhonsle was responsible for collecting revenue in the disputed area of Kanad Khore. His son, Shahji, then 26 years old, was one of the minor commanders in the Ahmadnagar army. For a brief period after 1624, Shahji entered the service of the sultan of Bijapur, though he retained *jagir* rights in Pune district, which was claimed by both Ahmadnagar and Bijapur. The careers of Maloji and his son show how military service could enhance family prospects and allow the building up of positions of power in rural society. They also reveal the very fluid nature of political allegiance in the Deccan.

For almost a decade from the mid 1620s the politics of the north Deccan were in a state of great confusion. After the death of Malik Ambar in 1626 and of Ibrahim Adil Shah of Bijapur the following year both courts were thrown into factional turmoil. When, in 1630, the Mughals invaded the Deccan to deal with disloyal commanders and to assert control over Ahmadnagar, Shahji's position in the army had been weakened by the assassinations of key members of his faction. He took service briefly with Shah Jahan (who employed him in his campaigns in the Deccan), but when he was denied adequate reward, defected to Bijapur, taking with him some of the defeated Ahmadnagar army as well as the somewhat tenuous control of districts in the south of that kingdom.

After further military campaigning and several twists and turns of policy, the government of Bijapur and the Mughals concluded a treaty in 1635. In effect,

this recognized Mughal rule across the northern part of Maharashtra, leaving the major forts and cities of that region in Mughal possession; Bijapur retained Pune and its nearby forts, much of central Maharashtra, and the Konkan. It was agreed that Shahji, as one of the significant local chieftains in the north, should be employed by Bijapur outside the area where he had been building up his power-base. Given a new stability on the northern frontier, Bijapur then turned its attention to further southward expansion, into the lands across the Krishna and Tungabhadra rivers. Shahji played a major part in this enterprise, and though his subsequent political career was not without occasional set-backs, remained an important figure in the Bijapur government until his death in 1664.

Shivaji: founder of the Maratha state

Shivaji (1630–80) was the second son of Shahji and his wife Jijabai. He was born in the hillfort of Shivneri in Pune district at a time of great political disturbance, exacerbated by famine. In the political maneuvers of the early 1630s, Jijabai's own family remained attached to the Mughals, and she was estranged from her husband. Consequently, when Shahji moved to the south in the service of Bijapur, Jijabai and Shivaji remained in the Pune region, where the young boy was

Above This posthumous picture of Shivaji, gouache and ink on a decorated page, was probably painted in Golconda in the 1680s. According to James Grant Duff, a British army officer in India who collected Maratha records and family traditions in the early 19th century in order to write the first history of the Marathas, Shivaji "was a man of small stature, and of an active rather than strong make; his countenance was handsome and intelligent; he had very long arms in proportion to his size, which is reckoned a beauty among Mahrattas." He is shown here in Deccani dress, but his martial attributes are emphasized by the sword he is carrying and the gauntlet he wears.

Right From the late 15th century the Bahmani kingdom of the Deccan fragmented into five separate sultanates of which Bijapur and Golconda were the largest and proved the most successful. They recruited senior officials particularly from Iran, thereby strengthening the position of Shias within Indian Islam and bringing new Persian literary and artistic tastes to the Deccan. But the sultans also made efforts to reduce the barriers between themselves and their Hindu subjects: in Bijapur, Marathi and Kannada speakers were brought into government; in Golconda, the army and public service drew heavily on Telagu-speaking farmers and warriors. Moreover, the defeat of Vijayanagara in 1565 prompted the migration of artists, skilled craftsmen and artisans from the devastated Hindu capital to the thriving aristocratic households of Bijapur and Golconda. During the next century the arts flourished in the Deccan, playing synthesizing variations on Indian and Iranian themes. Sultan Abdullah Qutb Shah, shown here, who ruled Golconda between 1626 and 1672, was particularly noted for his patronage of fine calligraphy.

brought up. Subsequently it was agreed that Shivaji should be recognized as holding his father's interests in northern Maharashtra, though they were to be administered by Dadaji Kondev, an officer appointed for the purpose by the government of Bijapur. What was involved were the hereditary patelships of three villages in Pune district, the *deshmukh* rights of Inda-pur, some 112 kilometers southeast of Pune, and other, more general rights to revenue in an area that corresponded roughly to the Pune district of later times. This in time would become the basis for the new Maratha state.

Throughout the 1630s and 1640s, the Pune region was in a devastated condition. Dadaji Kondev set about encouraging resettlement and restoring its pro-ductivity. He also sought to bring the whole region more directly under his control, in particular making good his claims on the *deshmukh* families. This was not done without violence: hardly had he begun his work when the *deshmukhs* in Pune "were seized and taken in hand, the refractory among them were put to death". When Dadaji Kondev died in 1647 the 17-year-old Shivaji assumed control of affairs in Pune. From then on his strategy was clear. He continued the old steward's work of encouraging agriculture, kept up the pressure on the other *deshmukhs* in the district, and set about capturing, either by force or diplomacy; a number of hillforts in the Western Ghats. Significant among these were Sinhagad, overlooking the city of Pune itself and Chakan which commands the northern route into the city.

From these strongholds Shivaji began to raid nearby towns and build up a substantial following. By the mid 1650s he had consolidated his position in the Pune region, and by 1656 had begun to expand beyond it into Satara district to the south, taking over the inter-ests of other major landholders such as the More fam-ily, partly by conquest, partly by stirring up disputes within the family, and partly by going directly to the *pargana* and village office-holders below them and offering better terms if they defected to him. South of Satara, the fort of Torna was emptied of its treasure in order to build a new fort on a hilltop 8 kilometers to the east, which Shivaji named Raigad. This was to serve as his capital for over a decade. By 1660, Shivaji was in possession of 40 forts and controlled 8 passes through the Western Ghats, giving him the Konkan below Pune and Satara. He maintained a force of 7,000 cavalry and about 10,000 infantry and employed a further 3,000 independent troopers. Inter-estingly, his forces included a group of 700 Muslim Pathans who came over to him from Bijapur, and at least two Muslim officers are known to have risen to high command in his army. Shivaji also employed Muslim officials in his civilian administration, partic-ularly on the judicial side. Rajputs, too, took service with him. He had become a chieftain of whom notice had now to be taken.

Most offended by Shivaji's success was the kingdom of Bijapur, from whom Shivaji had taken territory in the second half of the 1650s, partly because the Bijapur court was either occupied with other more pressing concerns or consumed by faction. By 1659 a new agreement with the Mughal emperor Aurangzeb had taken some of the external pressure off the king-dom. Ali Adil Shah, newly established as sultan, decided to move against the unruly Maratha chieftain in northwest Maharashtra. An army of about 10,000 men under the command of Afzal Khan set out to call Shivaji to obedience. The plan was for Afzal Khan to draw on local support once he reached Shivaji's terri-tory, for after all grants and privileges to *deshmukhs* and *patels* in the region stemmed in the main from the Bijapur government. For some reason, however, and despite the fact that his army included several Maratha auxiliary units and mounted skirmishers, Afzal Khan sought to make a political display on entering the Pune region by ordering the desecration of some of the Hindu holy places at Pandharpur. This was out of line with established Bijapur policy and almost certainly it lost him the support of some of the local *deshmukhs*.

Nevertheless, Afzal Khan's army was a formidable force, consisting of well-equipped heavy cavalrymen, artillery and infantry and accompanied by a full sup-port staff. It was well placed to inflict defeat in any conventional battle-plan. But it was slow moving, and Shivaji, learning from the earlier successes of Malik Ambar in this same region, had developed a smaller but much more mobile military force. The art was to avoid coming to formal battle, where the bigger and more heavily equipped army would win, but rather to harass the enemy's camp, drawing him deeper into the countryside, and then threaten his lines of communi-cation and supplies by deploying lightly-armed but fast-moving cavalrymen from the forts in the fast-nesses of the mountains. This was how Shivaji had built up his power, and it was now used with good effect against Afzal Khan.

By the end of the year there was a military stalemate. Shivaji had withdrawn to his fort at Pratabgarh, with other forces dispersed over the surrounding hillsides and jungle. Afzal Khan was stationed beneath the hills, with an army that could not maneuver well within them. Shivaji knew he could not win a straight-forward battle in the open field, nor could he expect to hold out in Pratapgarh indefinitely. But Afzal Khan also had problems: he did not have the capacity to destroy the mountain fort, nor could he deal effec-tively with the constant harassment of his camp. Fur-thermore, he was hampered by a lack of supplies – the result of Shivaji's activities and of his own political folly in alienating local support. So it was agreed to negotiate under a truce at a place beneath the fort. Both men came armed to the meeting, not without jus-tification: Shivaji was known to be ruthless, and Afzal Khan had earlier broken a similar truce to imprison the opposing general. Shivaji wore chainmail under his clothes, a metal cap under his turban, and carried a short sword in one hand. In the other was a set of iron claws to be worn over the fingers. The exact sequence of events has never been established, but it is certain that the two men fell to fighting hand to hand, and Shivaji succeeded in disemboweling the Bijapur commander with his metal claws. Shivaji then gave a signal for his forces to fall on the leaderless Bijapur army, which was quickly routed.

Shivaji followed up his success by raiding through Satara district into northern Karnataka, capturing the fort at Panhala near Kolhapur. Bijapur was slow to respond, but eventually an army under the command of Sidi Jauhar managed to pen Shivaji in at Panhala. He escaped in dramatic circumstances to the safety of Vishalgad, a small band of his followers holding a pass in the mountains with great tenacity and bravery. Bijapur's campaign against Shivaji thus ended incon-clusively. By now a new conflict was opening up, this time with the Mughals.

Above This fine 18th-century Maratha helmet from Gwalior is made of damascus steel, embossed and parcel-gilt. It has a sliding nose-guard and two upright plume holders. A coif of chainmail would have been suspended from the sides of the helmet to protect the neck. The high quality of the piece suggests it was part of the uniform of an elite unit and was probably used for ceremonial occasions. Though the Maratha armies are conventionally portrayed as consisting of ill-equipped peasant soldiers, from the start they boasted armament and armor of the highest quality, as an inventory taken at the time of Shivaji's death shows.

Right Tiger claws – a weapon consisting of four or five curved blades fixed to a cross-bar with rings for the fingers – were carried concealed in the palm of the hand, and were used for close hand-to-hand fighting. The claws could inflict multiple lacerations with a single blow, but were often used to grapple and hold an enemy in order to finish him off with a sword. This was the weapon famously used by Shivaji in his deadly encounter with the Bijapur general Afzal Khan.

The war with the Mughals

Much of the territory actually held by Shivaji was land originally claimed by the sultan of Ahmadnagar, seized by Bijapur and then, under the terms of their agreement with Bijapur, ceded to the Mughals. Shivaji had conducted a diplomatic correspondence with Aurangzeb while the latter was still governor of Deccan, offering him his services in return for confirmation of his rights in northern Maharashtra. These overtures were ignored in the early part of the civil war that engulfed the Mughal court at the end of Shah Jahan's reign, but once secure as emperor Aurangzeb determined to send an army under the command of Shaista Khan to deal with Shivaji. At first it met with relative success, devastating lands around Pune and retaking some of the old Ahmadnagar districts, but in April 1663 Shivaji executed a daring attack by night, in which Shaista Khan's son and a number of his senior officers were killed.

Shivaji followed up this success with a raid on the great Mughal port of Surat, from which he carried off substantial wealth. His attitude toward the Mughal court changed. Besides wanting recognition of his ancestral holdings in the Pune region, Shivaji sought the right to collect a quarter *(chauth)* of the Mughal empire's assessed revenue in a number of *parganas*, and a tenth *(sardeshmukhi)* over a much wider area. As part of his continuing negotiations with Aurangzeb, he pointed to the repeated failure of the large, well-equipped Mughal armies to bring him down: "My home," he wrote, "unlike the forts of Kaliani and Bidar, is not situated on a spacious plain, which may enable trenches to be run [against the walls] or assault to be made. It has lofty hill ranges . . . everywhere there are *nalas* [watercourses] hard to

cross; sixty forts of extreme strength have been built, and some [of them are] on the sea coast."

In response, Aurangzeb sent a much larger army to the Deccan under the command of the Hindu Rajput Jai Singh, one of the most able generals of the day. He was more systematic in his approach, preferring to secure territory and take forts as he went, rather than simply pursuing the Maratha leader through difficult terrain. By June 1665, Jai Singh had managed to restrict Shivaji's movements, isolating him from the other Deccan kingdoms, and had won over to the Mughal army some of Shivaji's officers and their units. From this much stronger position, the Mughal general then set about trying to make a political settlement. Shivaji was forced to surrender more of his forts and his territories, and he had to agree to wait upon the Mughal emperor in person at Agra, accompanied by his son and a small detachment of troops. Jai Singh guaranteed his personal safety.

Shivaji's visit was not a diplomatic success. It was clear that Aurangzeb regarded him as a minor refractory landholder who would be beaten into submission within the wider political context of the collapse of the kingdom of Bijapur. Shivaji was assigned a lowly place in the *durbar* (the emperor's formal court), and effectively put under house arrest. Aurangzeb was believed to be prepared to offer him a station in Kabul, but refused to negotiate to restore Shivaji to any sort of position in the Deccan. Finding his position at Agra growing more precarious by the day, Shivaji effected an escape in July 1666. He eluded pursuit by traveling through the backwoods of eastern Malwa, reaching Maharashtra the following month.

The breakdown of discussions between Shivaji and Aurangzeb was to prove a turning point in the history of India. Had they been able to come to some sort of accommodation, Shivaji might never have been spurred on to reshape his polity in Maharashtra, and Aurangzeb might never have become so embroiled in Deccan politics. One of Aurangzeb's unlucky generals described the Maharashtrian landscape through which his army dragged its cannon as "a specimen of hell" in which "all the hills rise to the sky, and the jungles are full of trees and bushes."

Expansion out of Maharashtra

Between his flight from Agra in 1666 and 1669 Shivaji made no attack on the Mughals. He continued to offer his formal submission to Aurangzeb and sent his son to the Mughal court to be enrolled as a *mansabdar*. But he set about restoring his position within Maharashtra in a number of small campaigns and when the fighting season opened in 1669 felt secure enough to meet the renewed demands of the Agra court with a series of quite stunning challenges. First, his men recaptured the fort at Sinhagad, scaling the walls at night by means of rope ladders and conducting hand-to-hand fighting within the walls to secure the citadel. This success was followed by the capture of another four major forts, and in October 1670 Shivaji again sacked Surat.

Throughout that year, Shivaji sent expeditions into the Mughal provinces of Khandesh, Berar and Baglan, in some cases simply carrying off wealth, but in others demanding payment of *chauth* and *sardeshmukhi*. He put the Mughals on the defensive in Khandesh by taking the fortresses that controlled the road through the province to the entrepot at Surat. On a more southerly front, he succeeded during 1671 in pushing the Mughals from their remaining positions around Pune and Nasik, carrying his campaigns first into Bijapur and then across Golconda. Throughout most of the 1670s, helped by the preoccupation of both Bijapur and the Mughals with wars on other fronts, Shivaji's forces met with success in nearly every quarter, and he extended his power as far south as Jinji on the east coast. He both fought and negotiated with his half-brother Ekoji for possession of the fortress at Vellore, southwest of Madras.

Shivaji's expansion in the 1670s went beyond simple raiding. He understood the need to restore productivity to ruined agricultural land, and – while he was a sufficient pragmatist to recognize that he had to continue to work through the agency of *deshmukhs* and *patels* – he made strenuous efforts to expand the amount of productive land under his own direct administration. He built forts and deployed his highly mobile cavalry units to compel obedience, but he appreciated the dangers of embarking on purely destructive campaigns in the countryside and consequently sought to protect, so far as possible, the heartland of his power-base by directing his raiding forces into neighboring territories.

Even here, he followed up the punishing raids of his army by strategies designed to win political consent. A notable feature of his move into the relatively well-governed Mughal provinces was the exaction of documents from the village authorities in the path of his armies that agreed to pay Shivaji or his officials one-fourth of the yearly revenue due to the government. Receipts issued upon payment served to exempt the villages from pillage. Sir John Malcolm (1769–1833), the British soldier and administrator who got to know the Marathas well, observed that they chose this way

of insinuating themselves into the share of the management of a district or a country rather than use force. "They were content at first to divide the government as well as revenues, with . . . the military class they found established, trusting to time and intrigue for their gradual reduction."

During this final decade of his life, Shivaji greatly enlarged the size of his army. Beside his forts, which provided a base for infantry and artillery, he now maintained over 30,000 horses, which suggests that there were between 15,000 and 20,000 fully equipped cavalry on his payroll. An army of such magnitude allowed him to enforce his will over much of the Pune region at least – it was certainly enough to overawe the most recalcitrant *deshmukh*. Yet even here, Shivaji resorted to other means to get his way. Some privileged landholders who failed to recognize his rule paid for their opposition with their lives; he married into other families, each occasion providing an opportunity for acquiring shares in privileged tenures. Sometimes, as in the case of the regions beyond Maharashtra, Shivaji subverted the authority of free-standing landholders by going behind their backs and offering a better deal to village headmen beneath them, or else his officials simply bribed the villagers to bring them into the new polity.

A new Hindu kingship

Shivaji's impressive run of victories, the increasing wealth from plunder and taxation that flowed into his treasury and his achievement at restoring some level of prosperity to a part of Maharashtra, led him to translate his wealth and might into an assertion of his ritual status as a great Hindu king. But it was not sufficient simply to state his claim to Hindu kingship; he had to make it good by having it recognized throughout Maharashtra. And here there were problems to be overcome. It was well-known that Shivaji's father had been in the service of Bijapur and that his family was of quite humble agricultural origin. On occasion, both Shivaji and his father had represented themselves as being of Rajput descent but they had not pressed this point; nor had they followed the rites and ceremonies traditionally assigned to kshatriyas, the ruling and warrior caste. Shivaji and his immediate ancestors may have proved themselves to be good warriors, but it was difficult to link them to families of impeccably high status. In fact, they seemed to have behaved, in religious terms, as if they were merely sudras (farmers). No brahmin in Maharashtra could find a way round this difficulty, so Shivaji sent to Varanasi, the holiest city of Hinduism. There Gagabhat, a distinguished brahmin philosopher and a Maharashtrian by origin, solved the problem by supplying a genealogy that traced Shivaji's ancestry back to Rajput origins in Rajasthan. According to Gagabhat, the Bhonsle family had migrated south during the Muslim invasions of the 13th century.

Gagabhat devised new kingship ceremonies, based on a reading of ancient texts. The rituals were performed over a period of several weeks in the summer of 1674. They began with Shivaji paying homage to the family deity and undergoing penance for not having lived as a kshatriya performing kshatriya rites. He and his son were invested with the sacred thread of the twice-born, and he went through new marriage ceremonies with his wives in accordance with kshatriya customs. The coronation rituals themselves extended over nine days, beginning with fasts and sacrifices to

The expansion of the Marathas Under Shivaji, the Marathas revived ideals of a Hindu polity that had last found expression with the rulers of Vijayanagara. Making the most of the political uncertainties in the Deccan that resulted from the decline of Mughal power, Maratha influence expanded, not necessarily through territorial conquest but by gaining rights to shares of revenues. This allowed the Marathas to penetrate a number of administrative systems and lay claim to partial sovereignty over large expanses of India. In the early 18th century the Maratha kingdom was transformed into a more complex political structure of chieftains. Though nominally under the leadership of the *peshwa* at Pune, these chieftains were as much concerned to look after their own interests as to serve the needs of a larger Maratha confederation. In this way Maratha power spread throughout central and western India and into the Gangetic plain, checked – but not seriously halted – by defeat at the hands of the Afghans on the field of Panipat in 1761. The most effective barriers to their influence came from Hyderabad (established as a separate kingdom by the Mughal governor of the Deccan in 1724 and ruled by his successors, the *nizams*) in the eastern Deccan, from the rulers of Mysore in the south, and from the British in Bengal and Bihar. Between 1800 and 1820 the East India Company effectively contained the Maratha princes by confining their power to small and separate states.

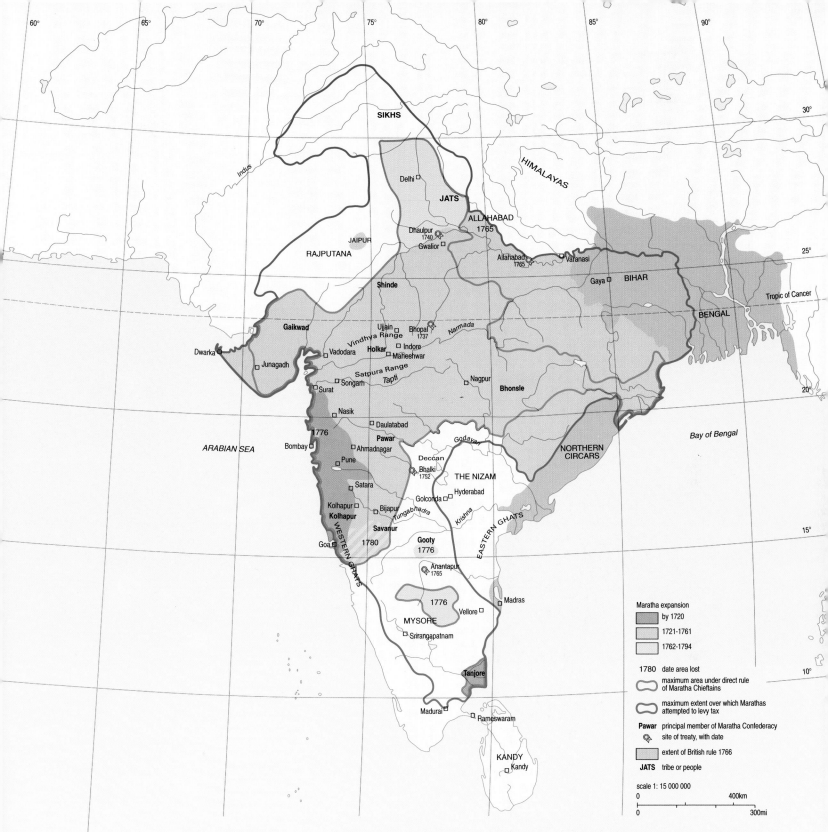

the sacred fire, and the ascending of a small throne. Shivaji held *durbar* and announced the start of a new era and the beginning of a new calendar. Then he was ritually cleansed by a series of ceremonial bathings in water and oil, anointed with earth from sacred places, and bathed again in honey, milk, curds, ghee and sugar. A further bathing and anointing with sandalwood powder made him the representative of Indra on earth. The participation of brahmins in these ceremonies showed that they accepted him as king with authority over them. Shivaji distributed presents to the brahmins and, seated in a chariot of Indra, received bows, arrows, horses and elephants that had been blessed. The coronation ceremonies reached their climax when Shivaji ascended a second throne, made of gold and covered with lion and tiger skins, and

received presents from the nobility. His principal officers poured gold coins over him before retiring to declare their fealty in private. The coronation came to an end with a great public *durbar* at which Shivaji announced his kingship and distributed presents. From now onward, Shivaji would emphasize that he was a fully independent ruler, able to negotiate with others on a footing of equality.

The coronation was followed by further expeditions into Khandesh and Berar, and then to the Konkan and the south. Shivaji died in 1680, leaving a full treasury, over 100 forts in the Ghats, a well-run homeland and more tenuous possessions and rights beyond it. He had worn down the independence of many lineages and *deshmukh* families, and out of an unpromising territory on the margins of the Muslim

Maratha Hill-forts

The mountain ranges of western India lend themselves naturally to defensive fortification and there is evidence of such use going back to at least the 1st century BC. By the 16th and 17th centuries, however, rulers were better able to control the region through the great fortress-cities such as Daulatabad, located in centers of agricultural production. The advent of heavy cannon also worked to render the small hill-fort obsolete in military terms. The particular genius of Shivaji was to restore a network of neglected hill-forts and to build new ones in order to carve out for himself a political domain within Bijapur territory, and then to hold it against the Mughals. This strategy was particularly well-suited to a leader with only limited resources at his disposal, and its success enabled Shivaji to exercise quite disproportionate political influence in the region. For a time in the 17th century the Marathas were able to exploit their position in the hills: once a Maratha army was in occupation of a hill-fort, it provided a difficult target for a large conventional army to attack. The enemy would be forced to lay siege to the fort, whereupon the Marathas would mount lightning attacks upon their opponent's immobilized and extended lines of communication. Though Shivaji suffered major military reverses in the field, he was able, through this network of hill-forts, to maintain strong defensive positions against the Mughals and other Deccan rulers to the north and east, and against the coastal principalities and the Portuguese to the west. After the Marathas had expanded out of their original core region in the 18th century, the hill-forts became redundant and fell into disuse.

Above Since the late 19th century, Shivaji has been for Maharashtrians a potent political symbol against foreign oppression, and there are many statues of him. They mostly show him mounted on a horse, but this mid 20th-century statue – at Raigad, his principal hill-fort – has him seated on a throne with all the trappings of kingship. The sculptor has drawn upon ancient Buddhist and Indo-Bactrian representations of royalty as well as modern European traditions in the iconography, and Shivaji is holding a European rather than a Maratha sword.

Left Sinhagad overlooks the important town of Pune: Shivaji's forces recaptured it from the Mughals in a particularly daring raid in 1669 when a band of soldiers scaled the walls at night by means of rope ladders – an event still recalled in Marathi ballads.

Right Pratapgarh was Shivaji's first new fort. The military engineers have skillfully exploited the natural defensive advantages of the site to construct the walls: cisterns for water and cellars for storing food were cut into the rock. It was below this fortress that Shivaji killed Afzal Khan, the Bijapuri commander, in 1659.

states of northern and central India had created a new kingdom. He had, moreover, revived Hindu kingship in India. Of course, his heirs quarreled at his death, and the kingdom was not passed on to his son Sambhaji intact. Factionalism destroyed the coherence of his territories, and Aurangzeb was able to seize the chance divide and rule among some at least of Shivaji's followers. But sufficient remained of his actual achievement to survive into the 18th century and to form the foundation for a new political expansion from Maharashtra.

In the longer historical perspective Shivaji came to exercise an influence over generations unborn: his deeds were recorded in Maharashstrian histories and, more importantly, in numerous popular songs and ballads. They told of his audacity and courage, and of the dramatic events of his remarkable life. So he became a potent symbol in modern times: a great soldier and statesman who had successfully thrown off the rule of foreigners, a great Hindu who had stemmed the progress of Islam, and a great Maratha who had restored true religion to his country, who had promoted pilgrimages and protected brahmins. An idealized warrior king, his memory would inspire many in the building of contemporary India.

Factionalism and civil war

In the decades immediately after the death of Shivaji in 1680, the Maratha polity was wracked by conflict within the royal family. Pressed from without by the Mughal emperor Aurangzeb, many officials and privileged landholders changed allegiance more than once to protect their positions, choosing one or other of the Maratha factions or offering their services directly to the Mughal court in return for confirmation of their local privileges. Some of those who had been prominent in Shivaji's day were unable to keep on top of the shifting political situation, and lost out. Some supported Shivaji's son, Sambhaji, who with the aid of the skilled administrator Ramchandra Nilkanth kept together a semblance of a kingdom until he was captured by a Mughal force in 1688. Brought to Aurangzeb, he was executed and his immediate family, including his young son Shahu, held prisoner thereafter in the Mughal camp.

A number of Maratha gentry threw in their lot with a younger son of Shivaji, Rajaram, who continued to resist the Mughal presence after Sambhaji's death. When he, too, died power passed to one of his queens, Tarabai, who ruled for a decade in the name of her young son Shivaji II. But hers was a weakening government. Failing to win over a sufficient number of the Maratha leaders at the outset, she was forced to make concessions to her supporters thereafter as a price of their continued loyalty. Aurangzeb and his generals began to meet with some success in their drawn-out campaigns against the Maratha strongholds. Though at no stage looking likely to win a definitive victory, they were sufficiently part of the Maharastrian scene to draw large numbers of Maratha gentry into their service.

The deleterious effect of these developments on the Maratha state were well analyzed by Ramchandra Nilkanth in the first decade of the new century. Writing of the civil turmoil in Maharashtra from the point of view of one who had consistently resisted the Mughal intrusion, he said that many soldiers "went to heaven whilst fighting in the cause of their master. . . . Some, having lost their armies, got confounded in their valor and went over to the enemy. Some, seeing their master given up to vices like the enemy, usurped, with the idea of holding them independently, parts of territories and forts which had been made over to their possession . . . In various places persons, rising like the crescent moon owing to the weakness of government, began to quarrel against one another. During these adverse times minor chiefs . . . got firmly rooted. The remaining parts of the country became desolate, and forts got exhausted of military provisions. Only the idea of the state remained."

The death of Aurangzeb in 1707 triggered a major war of succession within the Mughal state from which the central government never really recovered. One consequence of Aurangzeb's death was the release from captivity of Shahu, Shivaji's grandson, who returned through Malwa to Maharashtra. For the next few years, the politics of the region took the form of a three-cornered civil war between the Mughals, Shahu and Tarabai, still acting as regent for Shivaji II. None of these parties was able to command the loyalty of the Maratha chieftains for long periods, and quarrels about *deshmukhi* and other rights continued to bedevil stability. By 1718, however, Shahu's group had gained decisive control of the Maratha state, and his position was confirmed and enhanced the following year by treaty with the Mughal court.

The first *peshwa*

In part, Shahu owed his success to the support of a small number of the older families who had risen to eminence with Shivaji in the formation of the original Maratha state. Just as crucial, however, was the allegiance of several families who, having no previous connection with Shivaji's family, had emerged as significant figures during the recent civil war. Many of these came from village *patel* backgrounds and had succeeded during the turmoil of civil war in displacing some of the older lineages. The most important family to emerge during this period was the Bhats. They had been small landholders in the Konkan and were the hereditary *deshmukhs* of Danda Rajpuri, about 96 kilometers south of Bombay. Ballaji Vishwanath Bhat became Shahu's *peshwa* (chief minister) in 1713. Under his heirs, the *peshwas* became the de facto rulers of the Maratha state in the 18th century.

Ballaji Vishwanath Bhat is a classic example of the energetic young man who makes his way to the top by his own skill and enterprise. In his late teens he left the Konkan, where he had a post as clerk in the saltworks at Janjira, to seek his fortune in the Deccan, becoming the *subahdar* (head administrator) first of Pune district and then of Daulatabad. He proved himself to be an excellent administrator and an extremely competent soldier as well. As one of those opposed to Tarabai, he was quick to throw his weight behind Shahu and was instrumental in mustering fresh supporters for him. After his appointment as *peshwa*, Ballaji Vishwanath sealed Tarabai's fate by detaching the powerful Kanoji Angria from her party.

Some of Ballaji Vishwanaths's successes were due to military skill – he led Shahu's army against the Mughal forces in 1713–15 – but he was also an accomplished diplomat and negotiator, as became clear in 1716 when he entered into negotiation on Shahu's behalf with the much-weakened Mughal court. He sought a *sanad*, or treaty, that would grant to Shahu the right to a *chauth* and *sardeshmukhi* of government revenue throughout the six Mughal provinces of the Deccan

(Ahmadnagar, Berar, Bidar, Golconda, Bijapur and Khandesh), the right to collect *chauth* in Malwa and Gujarat, recognition of the independence of Maharashtra and the return to Shahu of several forts still held by the Mughals, and confirmation of recent Maratha conquests in Berar and Gondwana. In return, the *peshwa* undertook to uphold law and order, to pay for 15,000 troops for the Mughal governor of the Deccan, contribute 10 percent of the *sardeshmukhi* collected to the Mughal treasury, and to pay an annual tribute of 100,000 rupees. The *peshwa's* proposal amounted to nothing less than the ending of direct Mughal power south of the river Tapti. At first it was resisted, but after further campaigning, Ballaji Vishwanath brought his own troops to Delhi, enlisted with the Sayyid brothers – one of the factions then seeking to gain the Mughal throne – and, on the back of their success, had the treaty ratified in 1718.

Ballaji Vishwanath Bhat returned to Maharashtra in triumph. The civil war was quickly brought to an end, largely through the alliance of a number of newly emerged Maratha and Brahmin gentry families whose position had been consolidated by the *peshwa's* military and diplomatic skills and, in particular, by the way in which he had established renewed political legitimacy for the Maratha polity within the old Mughal shell. It was no simple matter to implement fully the treaty between the Marathas and the Mughals, for claims continued to be tested both locally and regionally. Nevertheless, the treaty provided the *peshwa* with moderate real assets and with huge potential assets. These he was able to dispense to loyal followers to build the Maratha state further.

The consolidation of Maratha power

Ballaji Vishwanath Bhat, who died in 1720, was succeeded as *peshwa* by his son Bajirao (1720–40) and in turn by his son Ballaji Bajirao (1740–61). These men were the real rulers of Maharashtra. Shahu withdrew to his seat at Satara, and there held court; after his death in 1749, his heirs were effectively held there as state prisoners, to give the required ritual and ceremonial sanction to public affairs when required. Pune, where the hereditary line of *peshwas* was settled, became the center of real power, and in the course of the 18th century was transformed from a small town to a major city. The Maratha government, however, continued to face the major problem that Maharashtra was a relatively poor land. While the grant of substantial revenue rights over the war-torn Mughal provinces of the Deccan added considerably to their resources, there remained problems of collecting revenue due from dispersed and contested rights. The solution was to expand. Already a branch of the Bhonsle family was beginning to build up a new state to the east in Berar. They would become the rajas of Nagpur, and during the 18th century would extend Maratha power to coastal Orissa and threaten Bengal.

From the 1720s the *peshwas* turned their attention to the north – to Gujarat (where eventually a Maratha regime would be established at Baroda under the Gaikwads), and into Malwa, Bundelkhand and the Gangetic plain itself. To begin with, the expansion ordered by Bajirao amounted to little more than raids on neighboring provinces. Malwa was a prime target because it was relatively rich, producing around 10.2 million rupees in revenue in the early 1700s. Year after year, following the Dasserah festival that marked the end of the monsoon, Bajirao organized expeditions

Right This portrait of the *peshwa* Madhav Rao II, shown seated with his chief minister Nana Phadnis on the right, was painted in 1792 by James Wales, probably for the *peshwa* himself. In the complex politics of the court at Pune in the late 18th century, Madhav Rao had been installed as *peshwa* in 1774, only weeks after his birth. Nana Phadnis was his guardian, and for the next 20 years was the real power at Pune until his position was undermined by the accidental death of the young *peshwa* in 1795. Nana Phadnis died on 13 March 1800, aged 58, "and with him", wrote Colonel Palmer, the English East India Company's ambassador at Pune, "has departed all the wisdom and moderation of the Mahratta government."

into Malwa. The Maratha armies were composed partly of troops under the *peshwa*'s own direct command and pay, supplemented by forces brought to the field under the command of other energetic captains. Those who responded most enthusiastically to the call of the *peshwa* were not drawn primarily from among the powerful vested interests of Maharashtra but were soldiers of fortune who had come up through the ranks during the time of Ballaji Vishwanath Bhat.

They claimed no ancient lineage, nor had their ancestors been prominent in the affairs of the 17th century. They depended for their rise on their success in the field, and on their competence to hold and administer the rewards they were given. On his initial raids into Malwa, the *peshwa* not only seized and carried off revenues by force, but also came to agreements with local lords and village establishments for a regular share of revenue in the future. Bajirao combined military and political operations on the ground with high-level diplomacy at neighboring courts and with the Mughals. By the early 1730s, the Delhi emperor, the pleasure-loving Muhammad Shah (1702–48), had conceded the office of governor of Malwa to the *peshwa*. Some of the major local lords were left in place so long as they recognized Maratha supremacy and paid an agreed annual charge. The rest of the province was divided between the *peshwa* and his main supporters.

Independent rulers

The Maratha expansion enabled families like the Gaikwads, the Shindes, the Holkars, the Pawars, the Ghorpades and the Nimbalkars to establish themselves in Gujarat, Malwa, Rajasthan and beyond. Though these chieftains owed their positions to the *peshwa*, the simple facts of geography and politics meant that they became rulers in their own right. In the second half of the 18th century the Marathas were a political and military force to be reckoned with, on more than one occasion successfully defeating in battle growing British aggression in central and northern India. By the end of the century, the two most powerful Maratha dynasties were the Shindes and the Holkars, both based in western Malwa. Their rise to power had been helped in part by the failure of the *peshwas* to avoid debilitating quarrels within their own family after 1761 (when their army suffered a terrible defeat at the hands of the Afghans at Panipat) and in part by their own successes in turning motley collections of rights and interests into something approaching coherent territorial power-bases. As the later *peshwas* faced increasing political troubles at Pune and in the Deccan, the Shindes and Holkars exploited the situation in the north to build up their own positions.

After 1764, Mahadji Shinde (whose ancestors had held a patelship in a village in Wai district, and whose father had served as slipper-bearer in Ballaji Vishwanath's household) regrouped his forces in Malwa and from his capital at Ujjain began systematically to increase his power in central and north India. Mahadji Shinde was a skilled general. He expanded his army and, using the best available technical expertise, built up its infantry and artillery to the highest standards. He recruited widely among the military classes in Rajasthan – both Rajput and Muslim – and his forces included 16 battalions of regular infantry, 500 pieces of cannon and 100,000 horse. Nearly two-thirds of Malwa and parts of the Deccan were held by him in *jagir*, and in the 1780s he became effective ruler of Delhi, giving him control of vast swathes of territory in northwest India from Agra to the Sutlej river.

The puppet Mughal emperor was forced into making a humiliating treaty with the Maratha state by which the *peshwa* became viceregent of the whole Mughal empire, and Shinde his deputy. Mahadji traveled at the head of his army from Delhi to Pune to bring the new charter to Madhav Rao, the young *peshwa*. His troops surrounded the *durbar*, leaving no one in any doubt as to who was the real master of affairs, while Mahadji Shinde took up a position in one of the lowliest places in the assembly. The *peshwa* arrived and desired Mahadji to be seated. But the latter objected on the ground that he was unworthy of the honor. Untying a bundle that he carried under his arm, he produced a pair of slippers, which he placed before Madhav Rao saying "This is my occupation, it was that of my father." The Shinde government survived a serious succession dispute on Mahadji's death in 1794 and was strong enough, under Daulat Rao Shinde, to present the British with a grave military challenge in both northern India and the Deccan. But the revenues built up by Shinde were inadequate to support his expensively modernized army, and by the early 19th century the family – though accorded prestige under British rule – was much reduced in independence, territories and revenues.

The ancestors of the house of Holkar had not even been cultivators, but shepherds, before one of their number had come to the notice of a Maratha nobleman. The family had then entered the service of the *peshwa* and served Bajirao especially well in both the Konkan and Malwa. By the middle decades of the 18th century, Holkar, along with Shinde, was overawing the princes in Rajasthan and pushing up into Punjab. The real founder of the Holkar fortunes, however, was Ahilyabai, the widowed daughter-in-law of Malhar Rao Holkar who, having demonstrated formidable administrative and political skills during her father-in-law's lifetime, on his death in 1767 successfully petitioned the *peshwa* to be allowed to manage the Holkar estates. When her own young son had died in 1766 she had succeeded, after some intrigue, in adopting as her heir the commander of her household troops, a man called Tukoji Holkar (who was not a blood relative). The two of them came to a working agreement whereby Tukoji commanded the army and managed the Holkar lands in the Deccan and parts of north India, while Ahilyabai ruled in Malwa and concerned herself with questions of justice and revenue.

Ahilyabai's 30-year rule transformed her capital Indore from a small village to a prosperous city. She made a strong impression on those she had to deal with. Sir John Malcolm recorded that "Her first principle of government appears to have been moderate assessment, and an almost sacred respect for the native rights of village officers and proprietors of land. She held every complaint in person; and although she continually referred cases to courts of equity and arbitration, and her ministers, for settlement, she was always accessible; and so strong was her sense of duty, on all points connected with the distribution of justice, that she is represented as not only patient, but unwearied, in the most insignificant causes, when appeals were made to her decision."

The revitalization of Hinduism

There is no doubt that Ahilyabai brought a great measure of peace to the area around Indore, and that she thereby extended the influence of her court. She built roads and forts, and more significantly, was a great patron of Hinduism. Temples, rest-houses, tanks and bathing steps were built or refurbished by her. She sponsored festivals and pilgrimages, and was generous in her donations to other good causes. Her patronage extended to the holy cities of Hinduism beyond Malwa – Varanasi, Dwarka, Rameswaram and Gaya. After her death in 1795, followed by that of Tukoji in 1797, the Holkar patrimony fell victim to a bitter succession dispute. This left the Holkar state much weakened, and placed it at a disadvantage in the feuding that accompanied the Maratha confrontation with the British in the early 19th century.

In the space of little more than 150 years, the Marathas had transformed the political and cultural geography of India. From the most unpromising of

Above During the 1750s, the Marathas, under the leadership of the *peshwa*, had extended their power into northern India and Punjab and made themselves the protectors of the Mughal emperor. The closing years of the decade saw attempts by the Afghan ruler, Ahmad Shah Durani, to take northwestern India in to his own kingdom, and in 1760 a large Afghan army challenged a combined Maratha–Mughal army in the Delhi territories. The

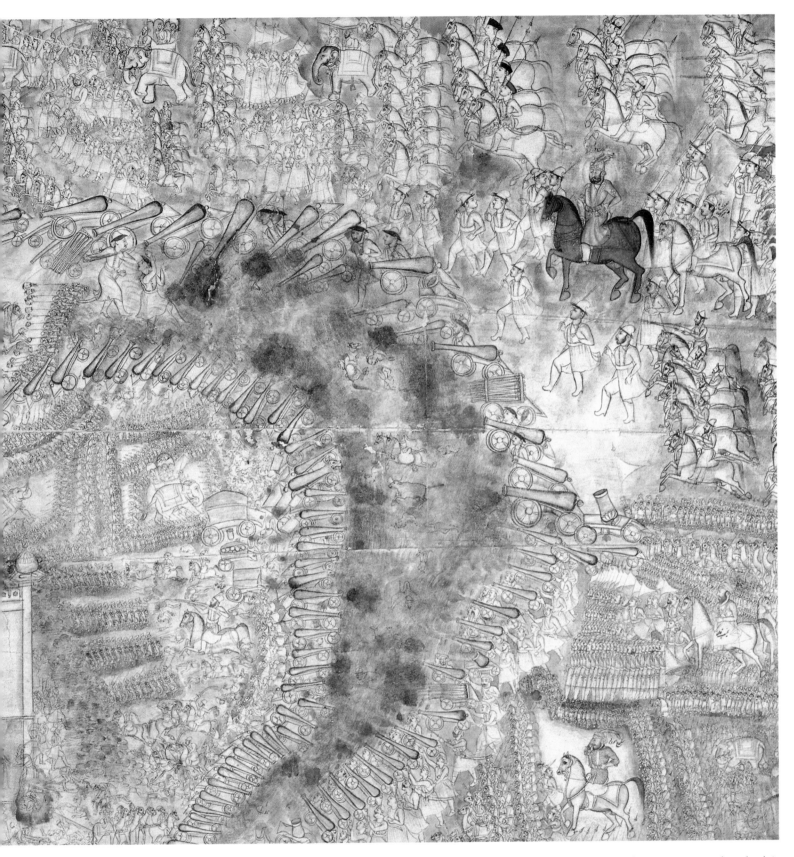

Maratha–Mughal forces dug in for the winter at Panipat. On 14 January 1761 a major engagement took place when the Afghans routed the Maratha–Mughal army, with colossal loss of life. In this drawing, from Faizabad c.1770, Ahmad Shah Durani is shown top right on the brown horse, the wounded Maratha general is being helped away on a horse middle lefthand edge, and the town of Panipat, bottom left, is a scene of rapine and pillage.

terrain they had resisted Mughal penetration of the Deccan and had re-asserted notions of Hindu kingship. Then, with new families rising to power within the Maratha polity, they further reshaped India by capturing parts of the Mughal state and operating from within it. During the 18th century, their military and political prowess gave them influence far beyond Maharashtra and, indeed, outside the districts from which they drew their revenue. One of the most significant features of the century that saw the collapse of Mughal power was the resurgence of the public face

of Hinduism. The Maratha princes (as they had in reality become, however obscure their origins) devoted part, at least, of their public revenues to the support of Hinduism, and they revitalized its public ceremonies. Temples, pilgrimages, and festivals in the northern Deccan and then more widely in India received their official approbation. Hinduism began to show itself on a scale not seen for centuries in the regions where Islam had ruled. Rebuilding in the north, especially in the holy city of Varanasi, began to match that of the Hindu kingdoms of the far south.

THE EUROPEAN IMPACT AND THE RISE OF BENGAL

The first arrival of the Europeans

Contact had long existed between the markets of the Mediterranean and those of Asia, and Indian goods – carried by Arab trading ships to the ports of the Persian Gulf and the Red Sea, or transported along the overland trade routes that linked China and Central Asia to the Black Sea – had been exchanged in southern Europe from earliest times. But it was not until the Portuguese set out on their voyages of exploration and discovery at the end of the 15th century, pioneering the sea route along the west coast of Africa, round the Cape of Good Hope and into the Indian Ocean, that the natural products and manufactures of the subcontinent began to reach the west on any significant scale. The Portuguese, attracted by the prospect of obtaining supplies at source of high value commodities such as spices and reselling them in the expanding European markets of the day, soon established themselves at the ports along the west coast of India; their unscrupulous use of force enabled them to win an advantage over their Arab rivals in the Indian Ocean.

In the following century, other European nations developed navigational and sailing skills to follow the Portuguese into the Indian Ocean – first the Dutch, then the French, the English and the Danes. They soon discovered that there was money to be made not only from the spice trade, but also from the import of other commodities, especially textiles, and even from participating in trade within Asia itself. At first, their enterprises were on an extremely small scale, and limited to areas of the coast. European traders were dependent on gaining access to existing markets, on establishing business contacts with Indian merchants and suppliers, and on being allowed to open warehouses (or factories, as they were called) in which to store their cargoes. The goods that they bought had usually to be paid for with cash, for until the 19th century – when industrialization made cheap manufactured goods available for trade – Europe had very little to offer the Indian consumer.

The effect of this European commerce stimulated economic activity in the coastal regions of the subcontinent quite appreciably. At the same time, the export of Indian goods to other Asian and Middle Eastern markets was growing. In the 1570s, the Mughals – until then entirely a land empire – gained control of the thriving entrepot of Surat in Gujarat. The Portuguese, meanwhile, had established themselves militarily and politically at several places farther down the coast: the port of Goa was captured in 1510, Bombay in 1534, Diu in 1535 and Daman in 1558. Apart from commerce, their chief interest was in the conversion of souls. From the beginning, missionaries were active in their trading enclaves; St Francis Xavier paid two visits to Goa in the 1540s, when many mass conversions were made. As well as erecting huge fortifications, therefore, the Portuguese built massive cathedrals. Nevertheless, European influence was confined to a few minor districts only, and did not penetrate the subcontinent to any great extent before the

Above This fine oil painting by Hendrik van Schuylenberg, 1665, shows the Dutch trading post at Hooghly in lower Bengal. Hooghly was the major port in the region, and from it the Dutch exported silk and fine cottons to Europe and to Batavia in Java, the center of their extensive commercial operations in Southeast Asia. In return they imported silver and copper into Bengal. The picture shows Dutch shipping on the river, and the warehouses and enclosed gardens of the Dutch settlement. Beyond is a camp, perhaps that of a visiting Indian ambassador.

Left This wall-hanging of painted cotton, dating from the middle years of the 17th century, was made in the Madras-Pulicat region of south India especially for the European market. In the lower half of the central panel the Indian artists have included portraits of European traders; the other figures are Indian. The border of cotton dyed with a floral design was added in the 18th century.

Right The Portuguese traders in India were accompanied by missionaries who set about converting souls and founding cathedrals and churches. Their buildings were quite uninfluenced by indigenous architectural styles. The church of the Immaculate Conception at Panaji in Goa would not look at all out of place in Portugal itself.

18th century. Though Akbar summoned Portuguese Jesuits to debate religion with him, and European rulers sent emissaries such as Sir Thomas Roe to the Mughal court, westerners were present in India merely as curiosities and as petitioners for trade.

The growing competition for trade

During the 16th and 17th centuries the European powers trading in the east competed directly with each other for commercial advantage, frequently sending armed fleets into the Indian Ocean to mount raids on each other's ships and trading bases. In the early 1600s the Dutch, French, Danes and English set up East India Companies to enable the merchants of their countries to participate more fully in the trade of Asia, and more particularly to expand their interests at the expense of their competitors, especially the Portuguese. What these companies had in common was that their governments, in return for some sort of financial share of profits, granted the merchants the privilege of being the sole importers of goods from the east to their home country, thus guaranteeing them freedom from competition in the domestic market. In Asia, however, the European merchants had to fend as best they could, adapting to the customs of the places and people they wished to do business with. If they were to succeed commercially, they had to behave politically as any of their Asian competitors.

The English had arrived later in Asia than the other major European trading nations. The Portuguese were already well established in their chain of entrepots that, located at crucial points on the long-distance sea routes, protected by Portuguese arms and linked together by Portuguese interest, straddled the Indian

Christianity in India

According to tradition, Christianity first reached India as early as 52 AD when the Apostle Thomas landed on south India's Malabar coast and proselytized among the local brahmin community. Whatever the historical basis of this legend, Christianity has ancient roots in south India and was certainly established there by the 4th century when the merchant Thomas Cana emigrated from Syria with a group of 400 families and established a branch of what eventually became the Nestorian church in Kerala. This sect, which recites its liturgy in Armenian and has some 30,000 members in the vicinity of Trichur, still recognizes the authority of the patriarch of Baghdad. In south India, several other Eastern Orthodox sects, including Jacobites and Canaanites, maintain formal relations with patriachs in the Near East. Still other sects with eastern origins have largely broken away and established independent leaders. The head of the Malankara Orthodox Syrian church, based in Kottayam, is styled as the successor to the Apostle Thomas in the same way as the Roman Catholic Pope is the successor to the Apostle Peter. With the arrival of Vasco da Gama in 1498 and the establishment of Portuguese ports of trade at places such as Goa, Bassein, Diu and Cochin, the Roman Catholic church gained a small foothold in coastal parts of India. The Anglican church arrived still later with the advent of British rule. However, because the British assumed that the "traditional social fabric" of India was ultimately rooted in religion and would unravel if Christianity were introduced on a large scale, they did not actively encourage conversion. Thus, today, Christians of all denominations only constitute 2.5 percent of India's total population. Despite this small figure, Christianity remains a potent force in parts of the country, particularly Kerala, where a fifth of the population is Christian. It is also strong among India's tribal population, particularly in the northeastern states, such as Nagaland, where it has been seen as a hedge against the growing encroachment of the Hindu-dominated state.

Below left In 1575, the Jesuits sent a mission to Fatehpur Sikri hoping to convert the Mughal emperor Akbar. Though they were unsuccessful, Akbar permitted them to stay in order to debate with learned representatives of India's other religious traditions. The tolerant religious attitude of Akbar and his son Jahangir extended to having Mughal artists copy European engravings of Christian subjects. The Deposition from the Cross was painted under the personal supervision of Jahangir c. 1598, and was inspired by a Raphael composition that reached India via the intermediary of a Flemish print.

Below This photograph, showing an Indian craftsman modeling a clay crucifix, could easily be reproduced in a European setting. However, though much of Indian Christianity is familiar to westerners, Indian Christians have not become insulated from their larger social milieu and often observe Indian practices such as caste customs.

Below Local tradition asserts that the Apostle Thomas was murdered near Madras by a disgruntled brahmin shortly after arriving in India in the year 52. He is still deeply venerated in this part of the country. Here devotees are making a pilgrimage to a shrine dedicated to St Thomas at Malayattur. Other Christian saints with Indian connections also have significant followings. Among them is the great Jesuit missionary St Francis Xavier, who came to India in 1542 and is buried at the church of Bom Jesus in Goa.

Ocean from Mozambique to Ceylon (Sri Lanka) and beyond to Timor and Macao. The Dutch, arriving as independent operators later than the Portuguese, sensed that the best area to establish a base would be the Indonesian archipelago, important not just because it actually produced many of the goods in demand in the European market-place, but also because it lay between the complementary trading zones of China and the Indian subcontinent. The English East India Company, smaller in scale than either of these other two European concerns and lacking their experience and military muscle, found themselves driven from the easiest and most lucrative marts of Asia to the shores of the subcontinent, and had to jostle there for their share of exports in the crowded market-place of Surat and other open trading cities.

Despite this weak and uncertain beginning, the English East India Company found that India held untold potential for trade. It was able to buy spices, either grown in the subcontinent or shipped there from Southeast Asia, together with saltpeter and other Asian goods. But what would make its fortune, and transform it in the course of the 18th century from a minor trading concern to a great political state, was the discovery that India was the world's greatest producer of cottons and silks. These existed in enormous range, from high-priced luxury fabrics to cheap coarse cloth, and the Company was quick to open up markets for Indian textiles in Europe, North America and west Africa as well as at home. In the 17th century fabrics, manufactured either in Gujarat itself or carried there from the cities of the Mughal heartlands by the overland routes across Malwa and Rajputana, were traded mainly in the west coast ports. Others, produced in the weaving districts of the south, were collected together for export from Madras and other ports along the southeast coast (known as the Coromandel Coast), and it was here that the Company operated with greatest commercial success.

In the 1690s, however, Bengal in the east began to rise in importance. Not only were fine fabrics manufactured there, but in the course of the next century, an increasing volume of trade from the interior was carried down the Ganges, turning the towns of the delta into the main outlets for goods from Patna, Allahabad, Varanasi, Lucknow, Delhi and beyond. Thus in the space of a few decades trading settlements along the Hooghly and Bhagirathi rivers grew in size from virtually nothing to major towns. Here the European companies set up their factories (warehouses) and ran their operations, and it was on an area of swampy land by the Hooghly that Job Charnock, a Company agent, acquired three tiny hamlets in 1690 to establish a base for the East India Company. The resulting settlement would become the port of Calcutta.

By 1700, the English Company was operating from autonomous bases at Madras (acquired from the local ruler in 1639), Bombay (given to the English crown by the Portuguese in 1661 as part of the dowry of Catherine of Braganza on her marriage to Charles II) and Calcutta (where by 1700 the English merchants had secured charters from the Mughal emperor entitling them to trade and to collect land revenues). During the first half of the 18th century the Company established itself as one of the most successful multinational traders of its time. It was not exceptionally large – we know of contemporary Arab traders operating out of Surat with more ships and larger turnovers – but it employed about 2 percent of British shipping,

Indian Fabrics

Bottom far left A boy's coat of woven Kashmir wool, late 18th or early 19th century. The famous Kashmir shawl industry is traditionally believed to have been established in the 15th century and was patronized by the Mughal emperors who supported and developed many of India's specialized textile industries. Woven from the wool of a Central Asian mountain goat, the shawls were popular in Europe in the early 19th century, but were unable to compete with jacquard loom imitations after 1870, and the industry collapsed.

The first evidence of textiles in India are madder-dyed fragments of cotton found at Mohenjo-Daro, and there is a long history of overseas trade in textiles. Surviving examples of cloth from the 17th century onward indicate the range of fabrics being produced in India: exquisitely fine muslins and simple, plain cottons; printed, painted and dyed cottons; tie-dyed and woven silks and cottons; embroidered and appliquéd cottons and silks; woven and embroidered wools.

The importance of India's textile industry for world history cannot be overstated. English and Dutch trading companies, investing in Indian textiles in the 16th century as the medium of exchange for Southeast Asian spices, quickly discovered their European market potential. Trade burgeoned in the late 17th and 18th centuries, and by the mid 18th century India was clothing the world. In so doing, it indirectly helped to change fashions and concepts of cleanliness in Europe, altered patterns of agriculture and speeded up the process of industrialization. By the late 19th century British mill-cloth imports were destroying much of the Indian industry. It is not surprising that Gandhi used hand-spun cloth and the spinning wheel as potent symbols of nationalism.

Below left This watercolor of a cotton printer block printing a length of cotton was painted in Punjab c.1890. The rise of the British mill industry decimated the overseas trade with Europe, while the great Mughal centers of textile production in brocaded silks and fine muslins at Ahmadabad, Surat and Dhaka collapsed with the decline of princely patronage. However, medium and low-quality cloths continued to be made in less accessible areas such as Punjab, parts of Gujarat and Sind, and south India still produced woven cloths both for local consumption and for export to Southeast Asia and Africa.

Below A *patola* cloth showing elephants and tigers. *Patola*, the double *ikat* (thread tie-dyed before weaving) silk of Gujarat, was worn for weddings and special occasions by rich Hindus and Jains, who preferred floral, animal and geometric motifs, and Muslim communities, who were restricted to abstract designs.

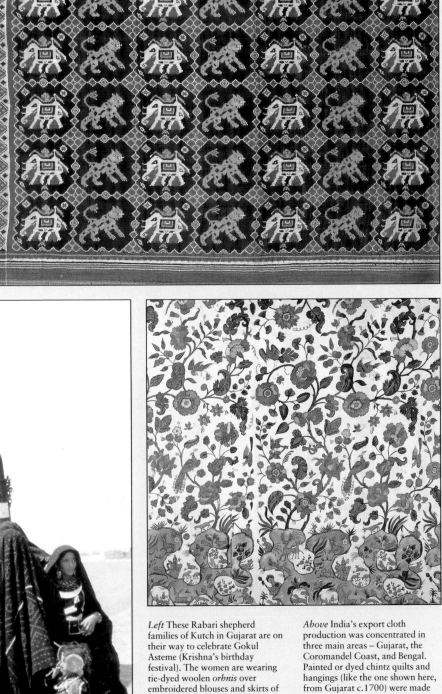

Left These Rabari shepherd families of Kutch in Gujarat are on their way to celebrate Gokul Asteme (Krishna's birthday festival). The women are wearing tie-dyed woolen *orhnis* over embroidered blouses and skirts of cotton and wool. The men wear an embroidered jacket (*keriya*). Cloth has always been produced for domestic consumption as well as export. In western India much of it was embroidered, printed or tie-dyed by local specialists or embroidered by women of the family as part of their dowry.

Above India's export cloth production was concentrated in three main areas – Gujarat, the Coromandel Coast, and Bengal. Painted or dyed chintz quilts and hangings (like the one shown here, from Gujarat c.1700) were made especially for the European market.

accounted for approximately 13 percent of total imports and provided an outlet for between 5 and 6 percent of British exports.

The rise of the East India Company was made possible as much by the economic and social changes that were taking place in India as by its own business enterprise. During the 17th century, and for much of the 18th, its success depended on the deals it was able to make with Indian creditors and suppliers. Its achievement was to distribute in the markets of Europe and North America the goods bought to it by its Indian partners. It had virtually no direct control over the sources of supply, many of which lay far distant from the Company's own factories. Great reliance was therefore placed on Indian entrepreneurs, many of whom laid the foundations for successful business enterprises through this connection.

Until the legal and administrative reforms of the late 18th century brought in by Lord Cornwallis when governor of Bengal (1786–93), employees of the Company were free to seek profits of their own by going into business privately with the Indian merchant communities. Other independent British traders were drawn to India by the prospect of wealth. These men could not import directly to Britain on their own account, so they tended to move into areas of business that did not compete directly with the Company's own interests. By the 1720s there were some 30 or 40 privately run British ships operating out Calcutta specializing in trade with other countries in Asia. Dutch records show that the amount of independent British shipping involved in the Asian trade at their port of Cochin on the southwest Malabar coast of India doubled between 1724 and 1742. The value of private British trade at the inland towns of Patna and Dhaka became very substantial from the 1720s.

These independent merchants, as well as Company servants trading on their own account with Indian partners, extended their interests to the more local trade in goods such as sugar, opium, betelnut and salt. Sometimes they would act as Company suppliers. When they had made their profit – and the scanty evidence suggests that while spectacular successes were to be had, there were also extremely high rates of failure – they would remit it to England, either by lending money to the East India Company, to be repaid in London, or by taking up spare capacity in Company ships, or by despatching it in the form of precious stones. The early fortunes of Robert Clive (1725–74), who was to become governor of Bengal from 1758–60 and 1765–67, were based on the profits he made out of his appointment as commissary for the supply of provisions to the Company's army stationed in Madras. These he then invested in the trade of Bengal.

The dynamism that all this commercial activity represented was reflected in the dramatic rise of Calcutta. By the 1730s it had a population approaching 300,000, and by mid century it was a city of half a million, made up of people of all nationalities and ethnic groups. Though founded to promote the export trade to England, Calcutta had developed as a major force in the economic and social life of Bengal, and soon of the entire subcontinent.

The shift of power to the east

Calcutta's growth reflected the shift in the geographical balance of wealth and power in the subcontinent away from the traditional centers. For centuries overland invasion had come from the northwest and great

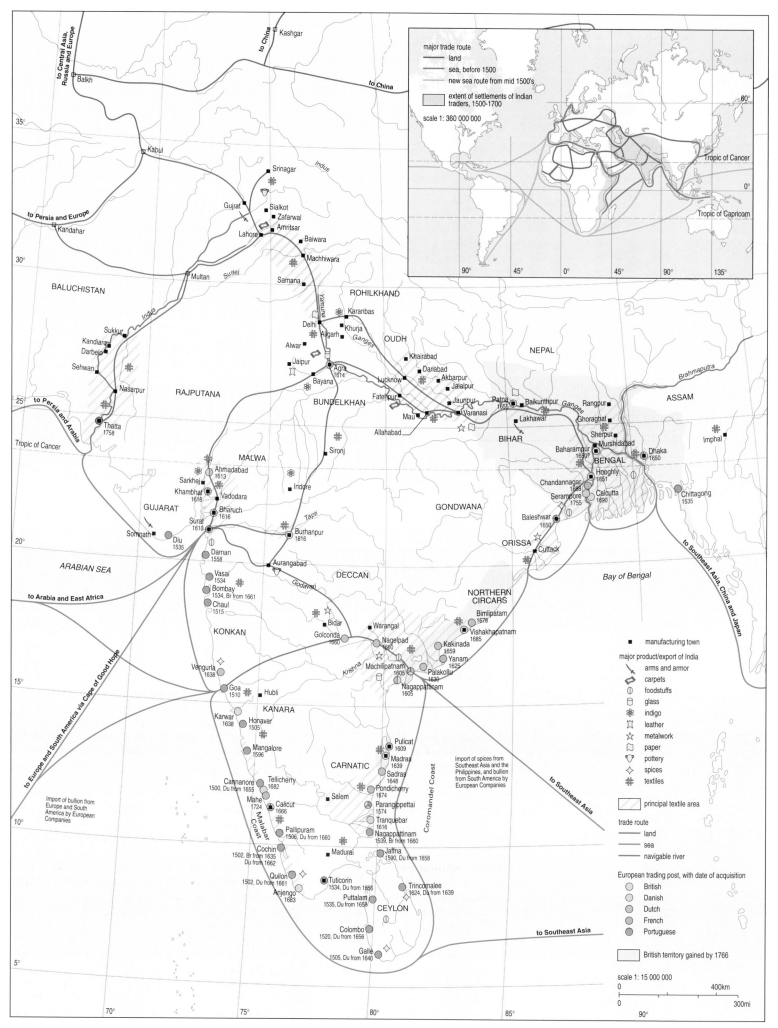

Inset legend:

major trade route
— land
— sea, before 1500
— new sea route from mid 1500's

extent of settlements of Indian traders, 1500–1700

scale 1: 360 000 000

60°
Tropic of Cancer
0°
Tropic of Capricorn

90° 45° 0° 45° 90° 135°

Map labels:

to Central Asia, Russia and Europe
Kashgar
to China
Balkh
Kabul
to Persia and Europe
Kandahar
Srinagar
Gujrat
Sialkot
Zafarwal
Amritsar
Lahore
Baiwara
Machhiwara
Multan
Sutlej
Samana
Indus
BALUCHISTAN
Sukkur
Kandiaro
Darbelo
Sehwan
Nasarpur
Thatta 1758
to Persia and Arabia
RAJPUTANA
ROHILKHAND
Karanbas
Delhi
Khurja
Yamuna
Algarh
OUDH
Alwar
Jaipur
Agra 1614
Bayana
Ganges
Khairabad
Dariabad
Lucknow
Akbarpur
Jalalpur
Fatehpur
BUNDELKHAN
Jaunpur
Mau
Varanasi
Patna 1655
Baikunthpur
Rangpur
Ghoraghat
NEPAL
ASSAM
Brahmaputra
Allahabad
Lakhawar
Sherpur
BIHAR
Baharampur 1690?
Murshidabad
Imphal
Sironj
Dhaka 1650
MALWA
Ahmadabad 1613
Sarkhej
Khambhat 1616
Vadodara
Indore
BENGAL
Chandannagar 1688
Hooghly 1651
Serampore 1755
Calcutta 1690
Chittagong 1535
GONDWANA
Bharuch 1616
GUJARAT
Surat 1610
Somnath
Diu 1535
Burhanpur 1616
Tapti
Baleshwar 1650
Cuttack
ORISSA
to Southeast Asia, China and Japan
ARABIAN SEA
Daman 1558
Aurangabad
DECCAN
Vasai 1534
Bombay 1534, Br from 1661
Chaul 1515
Godavari
Bay of Bengal
to Arabia and East Africa
Bidar
KONKAN
Warangal
Golconda 1650
Nagelpad 1660
NORTHERN CIRCARS
Bimlipatam 1678
Vishakhapatnam 1685
Vengurla 1638
Krishna
Machilipatnam 1605
Kakinada 1659
Yanam 1625
Palakollu 1630
Goa 1510
Hubli
Nagappattinam 1605
KANARA
Karwar 1638
Honavar 1505
Mangalore 1596
to Europe and South America via Cape of Good Hope
Pulicat 1609
Madras 1639
CARNATIC
Sadras 1648
Pondicherry 1674
Salem
Coromandel Coast
Import of spices from Southeast Asia and the Philippines, and bullion from South America by European Companies
to Southeast Asia
Cannanore 1500, Du from 1655
Tellicherry 1682
Mahe 1724
Calicut 1666
Parangippettai 1574
Tranquebar 1616
Nagappattinam 1539, Br from 1660
Pallipuram 1506, Du from 1660
Cochin 1502, Br from 1635, Du from 1662
Madurai
Jaffna 1590, Du from 1658
Quilon 1502, Du from 1661
Anjengo 1683
Tuticorin 1534, Du from 1666
Puttalam 1535, Du from 1658
Trincomalee 1624, Du from 1639
Import of bullion from Europe and South America by European Companies
Malabar Coast
CEYLON
Colombo 1520, Du from 1656
Galle 1505, Du from 1640
to Southeast Asia

Legend (right side):

■ manufacturing town

major product/export of India
⚔ arms and armor
▱ carpets
◍ foodstuffs
▤ glass
✳ indigo
⧓ leather
☆ metalwork
▯ paper
▽ pottery
◇ spices
✚ textiles

▨ principal textile area

trade route
— land
— sea
— navigable river

European trading post, with date of acquisition
○ British
○ Danish
○ Dutch
○ French
○ Portuguese

▢ British territory gained by 1766

scale 1: 15 000 000
0   400km
0   300mi

Above This engraving, after Jan van Ryne and dated 1754, shows Fort William, the English East India Company's headquarters in Calcutta, just before it was captured by Siraj-ud-daula in 1756. Like the Dutch base at Hooghly, Fort William – designed in neo-classical style – consisted of warehouses and offices. It was minimally fortified and depended for its successful operations on maintaining good political relations with the Bengal government.

The European Companies (*left*) The discovery of the sea-route from the Atlantic into the Indian Ocean brought growing numbers of European traders to the subcontinent. The activities of the European trading companies were confined to the coast, and the Europeans were attracted in the first place to ports already of international importance or located near areas producing goods (mainly textiles) that had ready markets in Europe, Africa, the Caribbean and the Americas. These trading ventures depended crucially on partnerships with Indian producers, financiers and traders, the Europeans in effect providing new markets for Indian commodities. Europe had little to export to India in return, and the trade between them was made possible by payment in silver, some of which came from the Americas. A new pattern of international trade was thus established, multiplying India's connections with the outside world.

states had succeeded each other on the fertile plains of Hindustan. But in the 18th century all was turned topsy-turvy. At the same time as the Marathas were extending their empire out of the Deccan at the expense of the Mughals, the British were laying the foundations for a new imperialism based in Bengal – one, moreover, that would come to embrace both the south and the north of India.

The rise in the importance of eastern India in relation to other parts of the subcontinent merits further scrutiny. Despite the marked differences between them, under the Mughal administration Bengal, Bihar and Orissa (which together covered an area greater than that of France) had usually come under the command of a single provincial governor, or *nawab*. These territories, composed of rich alluvial plains and deltas, were generally prosperous, though great wealth might lie cheek by jowl with subsistence poverty within them, and economic growth and movement of population in one part be combined with stagnation and decay in another. In the deltas of east Bengal, new villages would spring up as areas of land created by the deposition of silt were taken over for rice cultivation, while farther west and into Bihar water resources were more difficult to manage. Natural fertility declined, and crop patterns changed. Though potentially rich, the whole region was vulnerable to the vagaries of the rivers and the climate. A failure of the monsoon rains could devastate the agriculture of Bihar and western Bengal, while flood and typhoon might wreak havoc in the east. Famine and disease (malaria and smallpox) were constant threats: epidemics caused major loss of life in 1752, 1761 and 1769–70, when some districts were reckoned to have lost up to a third of their population. Then, as now, eastern India – exposed both to

nature's creative and destructive forces – was an area of high fertility and high mortality.

By the 18th century, Bengal, Bihar and Orissa had gone some way to developing an integrated economy, though one marked by regional specialization. In part, this was because the network of rivers and the coastline made movement by water fairly easy. James Rennell, who compiled the first maps of the region for the Company at the end of the 18th century, commented in his *Memoir of a Map of Hindoostan* that, with the exception of the districts to the west of the Hooghly, "we may safely pronounce, that every part of the country, has, even in the dry season, some navigable stream within 25 miles at farthest; and more commonly, within a third part of that distance." Furthermore, the coastal trade was already sufficiently developed to carry goods to Bengal from manufacturing centers farther south and from the ports on the west coast of India.

There was a flourishing network of markets where the products of the interior were exchanged with those of eastern India, and through them connected them with more distant markets. Rice, pulses and silks were grown in eastern Bengal, wheat and opium in Bihar, salt manufactured at centers along the coast. Major wholesale textile markets were established near Murshidabad and Dhaka, the two Mughal capitals in the region. Some cotton was grown locally, but more was imported by land and sea from the Deccan and other parts of western India to supply weaving communities in Bengal and Orissa; poppyfields near Patna supported the processing of opium in the east. The region was of increasing importance internationally, making and finishing goods to be traded in distant places. Boats took commodities up the Ganges to the Mughal

Anglo-Indian Encounters

Early English traders with India expected to return home loaded with wealth – provided they survived the hazardous expedition. Once the East India Company became a government in Bengal, however, there were opportunities for civil servants, soldiers and diplomats to settle in the country and investigate its customs. As governor, Warren Hastings deployed his patronage in a systematic way to find out about India and its peoples. In part this was genuine curiosity, in part a necessary tool of efficient government. The method of enquiry was to promote study of Indian languages and to ask learned Indians to explain their laws, religion and social customs. As a result, the British came to an understanding of India that was rooted in classical texts with a brahminical perspective. Some employees of the East India Company, like Sir William Jones, revelled in the scholarly potential that India opened up for them. Other officers chose to make their home permanently in the country. A good example is Major William Palmer, a soldier and diplomat, who maintained two wives simultaneously, both of distinguished Muslim families, by whom he had six children. Such establishments came increasingly to be regarded as eccentric and by the mid 19th century were no longer respectable.

Left Captain John Foote (1718–68), a ship's officer, had himself painted in Indian dress by the eminent artist Sir Joshua Reynolds (1723–92). An 18th-century gentleman with service in India would not have considered it peculiar to wear fine apparel in Indian styles.

Above This portrait of William Palmer and his family was painted by Francesco Renaldi in Calcutta in 1786, just before Palmer left to become the East India Company's Resident at Mahadji Shinde's court. Renaldi was one of a number of European artists who found work in India in the late 1700s.

Below Sir William Jones (1746–94) – painted here by A. W. Devis c.1793 – became judge of the Calcutta Supreme Court in 1783. He founded the Asiatic Society of Bengal. His paper "On the Hindus" (1786) argued for connections between Sanskrit, Latin and Greek, fueling interest in the comparative study of languages.

Below Suttee, or *sati* – the Hindu custom of a widow being cremated with her husband as an expression of her devotion – cannot be traced to the most ancient texts and was never common. But it aroused the moral indignation of the English, who publicized its evils in emotive pictures such as this, before outlawing it in 1829.

heartlands; bullocks carried the products of Bengal to Nepal, Tibet and Assam; merchant ships carrying silk and sugar plied the sea routes to Gujarat; textiles were exported to the ports of the Red Sea and the Persian Gulf; there was a large trade in cotton and opium to Southeast Asia.

Some of this trade was masterminded by Bengalis, but the commercial and financial community of the eastern ports was of diverse composition, including people from all parts of the subcontinent, Arabs and other Asians, as well as Europeans. A large number of Gujaratis and Rajasthanis opened up businesses in Bengal that specialized in the export of silk; such men were patrons of the locally established Jain temples. Among the leading Rajasthani businessmen was Manik Chand, who set up the great firm of the Jagat Seths, with offices in all the more important towns of the Gangetic plains. As well as being traders, they were financiers and bankers, and were indispensable to the government as movers of money and credit. Then there were the *gosains* – religious corporations with connections along all the routes across India that supplied armies and groups of pilgrims. Alongside them were representatives from trading groups like the Armenians, and others, all with far-flung connections reaching into Asia and Europe.

When the European trading companies arrived in Bengal in the 17th century they found there a thriving economy, well-developed commerce and long lines of credit and finance. The effect of their coming was to boost Bengal's economy further, promoting in particular trade with Indonesia as well as with Europe and, from there, to other parts of the world. This commercial activity made Bengal a major importer of silver, from the Middle East, Europe and the Philippines. For example, in the first half of the 18th century the English East India Company was importing to Britain every year goods to the value of £2 million, which yielded a profit on overall investment of about £500,000 a year. Though the Company made some attempt to sell British goods such as lightweight woolen materials and metals such as copper, iron and lead to India, they only accounted for around £250,000 a year. The balance had to be made up in bullion; the Company fairly consistently sent upward of £200,000 a year in silver to pay for its imports from India. The Dutch imported bullion at a slightly higher level, the French slightly lower. Furthermore, there were transactions in the hands of Indian and of private European traders. It is now reckoned that much of the wealth carried off by Nadir Shah (1688–1747), the Persian emperor who invaded northern India in 1739, seizing and looting Delhi (and removing the Peacock Throne of the Mughal emperors as well as the Koh-i-noor diamond), found its way back into the subcontinent by way of the trade with the Persian Gulf.

To the central treasury of the declining Mughal empire the Bengal provinces contributed revenues of around 10 million rupees a year. However, by the second decade of the 18th century, Bengal had begun to go its own way. The Mughal center lost control over official appointments and failed to enforce the regular flow of money from Patna, Murshidabad and Dhaka to Delhi. Murshid Kuli Khan, the *nawab* of Bengal between 1716 and 1727, combined in his own person the hitherto quite separate office of *nazim*, responsible for defense and law, and *diwan*, responsible for finance and some aspects of justice. He sought to make both offices hereditary within his own family but con-

trol of them was lost in the succession dispute that followed the death of Shuja Khan in 1739. Alivardi Khan, the Mughal deputy-governor in Bihar, took advantage of the situation to seize Murshidabad by force and had his claim to the office of *nawab* confirmed by the Mughal emperor after remitting money to Delhi by way of the Jagat Seths.

The *nawabs* and the *zamindari* system

Like rulers elsewhere in India, the *nawabs* of Bengal combined force with the conciliation of powerful local interests in order to make their government work. They put into senior military and administrative positions their closest supporters, relatives and kin, drawn from the cadres of Mughal officialdom. Like the *nawabs* themselves, they were not Bengalis, but day to day business at the second and lower tiers of government was in the hands of professional Bengali managers. The huge size of the provinces and the shifting nature of settlement within them created particular problems. There had been no detailed government assessment of revenue demand since 1582. Murshid Kuli Khan undertook a major tax revision in 1722, but rather than base it on inquiry and assessment he hit upon the practical and ingenious scheme of parceling up the revenue demand into large units and contracting out its supervision and collection to holders of revenue-paying rights called *zamindars*.

In simple terms, a *zamindar* was the intermediary responsible for paying revenue from a particular area to the government. However, the amounts for which a particular *zamindar* was responsible could range from a tiny sum representing a part share of one village to a huge sum due from an area covering thousands of square kilometers. In Bihar and some districts of Bengal such as Midnapore and Chittagong the *zamindar* was indeed a villager, representing village interests. But in the early part of the 18th century the government put in place in Bengal a small number of *zamindars*, often belonging to the older chiefdoms of the region, who had virtually the powers of an independent government within the government. Virtually all the functions of the state were passed down to them, including the detailed assessment and collection of revenue as well as policing and judiciary powers. By 1728, a quarter of the revenue of Bengal proper was being administered by the *zamindars* of Burdwan and Rajshahi. The former, the raja of Burdwan, employed over 30,000 militia to help him run his districts, while the territories of Rajshahi covered 33,500 square kilometers. In the north, the raja of Darbhanga was able, by skillful use of the *zamindari* system, to build up for his family an extensive and, to all intents and purposes, independent domain. By the 1760s nearly 60 percent of the revenue of the Bengal provinces was being supplied by just 15 *zamindars*. Nevertheless, the total number of *zamindars* was considerable, and the turnover in actual office-holding very great. The *zamindari* system allowed the wealthy in Bengal to move in and out of revenue-management and of landholding as economic and political conditions dictated. Later in the century, *zamindari* rights became a species of property, heritable, saleable and divisible, leading in the 19th and 20th centuries to the creation of a remarkable urban-based gentry class in Bengal.

The *nawabs* of the early 18th century had to bring into line within Bengal a number of important interests – their own officers, the *zamindars* (especially the very grand ones), the indigenous commercial and banking classes, and the European trading companies (early in the 1730s, Joseph Dupleix, head of the French trading company in Bengal, reckoned that a blockage of the ports and the withholding of silver would force any *nawab* to come to terms). Furthermore, they had the responsibility of bringing about stability in the countryside and protecting cultivators and artisans. These tasks were made all the more difficult by the complex politics that resulted from the collapse of Mughal power. There was Delhi – and whichever faction was in power there – to be reckoned with, while just up the river the Vizier of Oudh, plotting to win independence for an old Mughal province in ways similar to those being pursued by the *nawabs*, was not averse to meddling in the affairs of Bihar and Bengal when it suited him.

Between 1742 and 1751 Alivardi Khan had also to deal with resistance to his rule from the south, and with serious attacks from the Marathas based at Nagpur. The latter presented a formidable challenge. They raided as far as the river Hooghly and, as a famous contemporary Bengali ballad puts it: "They shouted over and over again, 'Give us money', and when they got no money they filled people's nostrils with water, and some they seized and drowned in tanks, and many died of suffocation. In this way they did all manner of foul and evil deeds." Alivardi Khan succeeded in keeping the Marathas out of Bengal, but had to accept the loss of much of his territory in Orissa, which remained under rule from Nagpur until 1803.

Despite this setback, Alivardi Khan kept his provinces in fair order, raising revenue of about £2 million a year from them. On his death in 1756 he was succeeded by his 19-year-old grandson, Siraj-ud-daula. Though the transition seemed smooth enough, within a year Siraj-ud-daula had been overthrown, and in the political revolution that followed a new order was established in Bengal. Siraj-ud-daula brought about his own downfall by a number of political decisions that – though he may have had no choice but to have made them in the short term – succeeded in alienating all sections of support. He began by making new appointments to high offices in Bengal, thereby causing grievance within his extended family and more generally within the Mughal elite of the province. He was heavy-handed with some of the *zamindars* and brutal with important members of the commercial and banking elites. Then he turned on the English in Calcutta. They had foolishly offended him by refusing to desist from fortifying their town; nor would they give up to to Siraj-ud-daula's officers men who had sought refuge there. They would not soothe him with diplomacy or with money, and were as keen as anyone else to take advantage of his political weakness to improve their own position. But this was a reckless course of action. Siraj-ud-daula moved against Calcutta in June 1756 and captured it effortlessly, carrying off at least £540,000 of goods owned by Calcutta's European community alone.

The English in Bengal

What Siraj-ud-daula could not have anticipated was the response of the English East India Company. By the mid 1750s, Bengal had become much the most important of their spheres of operation. Madras, which had been the great success story of the 17th century, appeared to have passed the peak of its commercial development: the Company's servants in the southern Presidency were already offering military and administrative services to the surrounding Indian princes and were becoming deeply involved in local politics and revenue-collection. Moreover, it had been in the south that rivalry with the French had made itself most felt. This came to a head in the Seven Years' War (1756–63) in Europe. The war developed into a conflict for colonial supremacy between England and France and spread into many arenas around the globe, including the subcontinent. As a result, there was a significant build-up of European forces in the region. Money was put into raising an Indian army, which was supplemented by regiments of King's troops, and a squadron from the Royal Navy was permanently posted to the Indian Ocean.

There was no doubting the magnitude of the disaster when news of the loss of Calcutta reached Madras. Put bluntly, the English had no serious commercial future in Asia unless they could regain the port and resume trade in Bengal. In the words of a contemporary French observer, it was a "terrible blow for the English Company. It would have been better for it to lose all its factories on the Coromandel Coast than this colony, so beautiful, so rich, so flourishing." Though distracted by political and military difficulties of their own in the hinterland of Madras, the governor of the southern Presidency and his council concurred in this view. They had to retake Calcutta. Robert Clive was appointed commander of an army made up of troops from the south and entrusted with the task.

The expedition arrived off the Bengal coast in December 1756, and by the following February Calcutta had been regained and provisional agreement reached with the *nawab* about the restoration of the Company's privileges and compensation for damage. But it soon became clear, given the uncertain state of Bengali politics, that the Company was unlikely to gain these objectives without becoming involved in the broader factional struggle for control being waged in the *nawab*'s capital of Murshidabad. An alliance was formed that included prominent bankers such as the Jagat Seths and a number of senior civil and military officers, including Mir Jafar Khan, commander of the Bengal army. The Company moved its army toward Murshidabad and on 23 June defeated Siraj-ud-daula's smaller force at the battle of Plassey. The luckless prince was pursued and killed, and Mir Jafar Khan, who had stood off from the battle, was declared *nawab* by the victorious faction.

For the next 10 years, the Company found itself trapped in the turbulent politics of Bengal. It would have been willing to give firm support to any government able to guarantee its trading privileges, to compensate it for the loss of profit and property, and defray to the full the considerable cost of their military expedition against Siraj-ud-daula, estimated by Robert Clive to be around £3 million. But the treasury at Murshidabad was found to be suspiciously empty. Further negotiations between the allies were carried out, sums were paid on account and men on every side bribed and bought off. The factional maneuvering continued, with the office of *nawab* changing hands several times, without bringing stability to Murshidabad. In 1763–64 the Vizier of Oudh was brought into the picture, and an expensive campaign had to be waged against him.

The decisive battle for English interests in Bengal turned out not to be Plassey but the battle of Buxar, fought on 23 October 1764, when the Company's army and its allies defeated the forces of the Vizier of

Right Alivardi Khan (?1678–1756), who assumed power in 1740, was one of the most successful of the 18th-century *nawabs* of Bengal. He was strong enough to withstand a fierce invasion threat from the Marathas, and also overcame considerable opposition from within the Bengal provinces. Some of the political troubles faced by his successor Siraj-ud-daula may be attributed to a backlash on the part of the ruling elite of Bengal who resented the closer control Alivardi Khan had imposed from Murshidabad, the Bengal capital. This painting, which was made in Murshidabad c.1750, shows Alivardi Khan out hunting.

Below This painting by Francis Hayman shows Robert Clive, commander of the Company's army in Bengal, meeting his ally Mir Jafar Khan just after the battle of Plassey. It is believed to have been the preliminary design for a much larger work that was put on display in 1762 in the annex to the Rotunda at London's Vauxhall Gardens to rally patriotic sentiment during the Seven Years' War.

Oudh and the Bengali factions opposed to it. The victory was followed by diplomatic negotiations that resulted in the treaty of Allahabad of 12 August 1765. Under its terms, the Mughal emperor appointed the East India Company his *diwan* for Bengal, Bihar and Orissa. The Company had become part of the Mughal framework, but as Clive summed it up more bluntly on his way to Allahabad: "We must indeed become the Nabobs [*nawabs*] ourselves."

Economic diversification and political ascendancy

The grant of the *diwani* changed the Company from a relatively simple trading concern to a commercial body that was also a major Indian government. This in itself brought new challenges and new responsibilities, and things did not always run smoothly. But by conciliating the landholders, especially the great *zamindars*, and working out a new relationship with Indian merchants and bankers, the Company was able to improve its trading position. In due course it was to achieve political eminence in Bengal, largely through the efforts of Warren Hastings (1732–1818) who, as governor-general of the province from 1772–85, removed the machinery of central government from the *nawab*'s court at Murshidabad and brought it under direct British control at Calcutta.

The new financial resources now at the disposal of the British allowed them to respond flexibly to the wider political and economic changes that were taking place in the second half of the 18th century. Perhaps the most significant of these was the collapse of the trading pattern that had stood the Company in such good stead for the past 100 years, brought about by the rise of the Lancashire cotton industry in Britain. Drawing its raw materials from North America and the Caribbean, and powered by the new steam engines of the Industrial Revolution, it succeeded in driving Indian-manufactured textiles out of the international market. But while this change was taking place, the Company moved to develop another commercial possibility – the import of tea from China to the west. The soaring fashion for tea-drinking in Europe ensured its success, and the new trade more than compensated for the decline in textiles.

The Chinese at this time had no more need of goods from the west than did the Indians. In order to make the trade work, therefore, the Company encouraged the export of goods – particularly cotton, and later on opium – from India to China. The Company's bilateral trade between India and Britain thus gave way gradually to a more complex triangular trade. The lucrative shipment of tea from China to London was reserved to the Company, but it presided over a massive expansion of private shipping of Indian products to China. At first this benefited mainly Calcutta and its hinterland, but it also provided an opportunity for Bombay, on the west coast, to prosper.

Bombay had been assigned to the East India Company by the English crown in 1668. It began to grow as the fortunes of Surat declined, its good harbor and secure island situation making it an attractive refuge for numbers of skilled artisans, traders and bankers during the turbulent years of the Maratha expansion. Its naval dockyards turned increasingly to the building of large cargo ships capable of working the Asian sea-routes. In 1787 David Cuming, a Company agent, was able to report to London that he had counted as many as 40 privately owned ships from Bombay at anchor in Canton, and that their cargoes, mainly of cotton, were worth £1.25 million. There had been no such trade 20 years before.

Hitherto, Bombay had never been seen by the Company as much of a success, and the costs of maintaining a separate administrative structure there had several times led it to consider reducing the port's status and placing it under the authority of Madras. During the 1780s, however, there was a massive movement of Gujarati – and in particular Parsi – commercial expertise and capital to Bombay. Without this migration, the economic development of the city would have been much slower. Not only did this lead to an expansion of trade with the Middle East as well as with China, but it also put money and skills at the disposal of the young men (the vast majority of them penniless Scots) that the Company shipped out to India to work for it, at the same time allowing them the chance to make their fortunes through private deals. A visiting British dignatory in 1803 not only noted the importance of finding Indian partners to work in the hinterland, but observed the striking fact that there was not a single private British company in the town that was without a Parsi financial backer.

Its increasing involvement in the affairs of the Madras hinterland meant that the East India Company had now become a major player in the politics of India. Revenue from the districts managed by its agents were an important source of funds, affording it a degree of financial self-sufficiency. Because the Company's representatives in India could muster supplies on the spot, they were able to undertake military and political initiatives as local conditions required without first seeking the consent of their commercial or political superiors in London. This gave it a far greater degree of flexibility, and meant that its further territorial expansion in India, largely paid for with Indian resources, was driven by Indian circumstances.

By the end of the 18th century the Company had taken into its direct employ large Indian armies, which were officered by Europeans. These forces were supplemented by King's regiments sent to India to uphold wider British strategic interests, and from the mid 1760s the number of British men recruited to the Company's civilian administration also increased rapidly. By the last decade of the century the Company's directors in London were filling something like 400 jobs a year in India. The offices that had once been the preserve of men from Central Asia, Iran and Afghanistan now belonged to Scotsmen, to Irishmen and to the younger sons of clergy and the lesser squirearchy in the English shires.

The making of the British raj

The territorial expansion of British power at the close of the 18th century was largely the work of three men: Warren Hastings, first governor general of India from 1774 to 1785; Charles, Marquess of Cornwallis (1738–1805), governor general from 1786 to 1793; and Richard, Marquess of Wellesley (1760–1842), governor general from 1797 to 1805. All of them extended British control by making alliances with prominent rulers, if necessary threatening or actually waging war to bring this about. The most important feature of these alliances was that, in return for the East India Company giving him protection, the ruler would pay for, and sometimes house in his own territories, detachments from the Company's army.

By these means the East India Company secured political paramountcy in the Indo-Gangetic plain as well as control of the Indian coastline. At the same time it gradually disarmed (because it came to employ the soldiers of and provided military protection to) all the major Indian states. In turn Oudh, Hyderabad, Mysore and the Marathas gave up an independent

Below The island trading settlement of Bombay came to the English crown from the Portuguese in 1661 as part of the dowry of Catherine of Braganza on her marriage to Charles II. It was considered as something of a make-weight (the usually well-informed English diarist Samuel Pepys thought it was in South America) and Charles II leased it to the East India Company in 1668. Bombay was initially of less value to the Company than its bases in Madras and Bengal, partly owing to the dislocation of trade in western India after the mid 17th century and partly because the port was isolated from the hinterland, but the island offered great security to shipping and was easily defended. Its importance grew during the 18th century as shipping and commerce moved south to Bombay from Surat, and by the end of the century new trading links had been established with the Middle East and China. This painting, by George Lambert and Samuel Scott, was one of six commissioned by the East India Company in 1732 to show its settlements in India. The artists did not visit the places depicted and presumably worked from plans and earlier drawings.

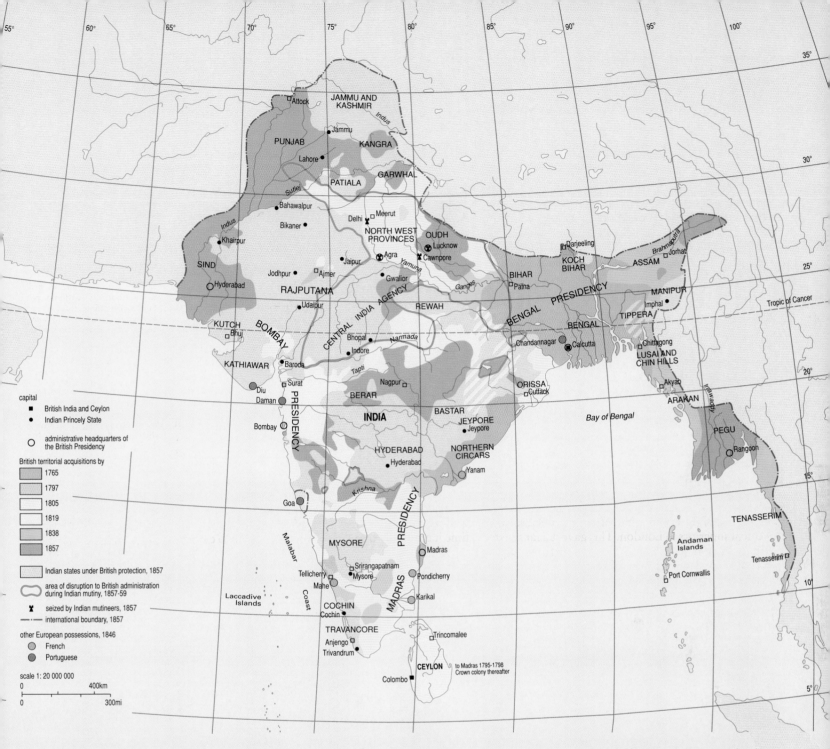

The rise of British power in India The first significant British political gains were made in the mid 18th century in Bengal and in the area around Madras. In both places the East India Company allied itself with local elites, using military and economic muscle to promote its concerns, but once in a position to command the revenues of Bengal it became an Indian government, with the resources to participate in the endgames of the Mughal and Maratha empires. Like its predecessors, the Company matched military prowess with political pragmatism, concentrating on acquiring a strategic hold on the most important of India's core regions. From about 1800 the British explicitly pursued the goal of paramountcy in India and by about 1820 held sufficient territory to overawe the rest. The internal boundaries of their Indian empire, however, were not fixed with certainty before the mid century and, in important respects, the international frontiers remained unclear until much later.

military position to become part of the system of over-lordship the Company was reconstructing on the back of the Mughal empire. Not always was this done willingly or without a struggle. The Marathas resisted the British time and again on the battlefield, and Mysore in the southern Deccan went to war against them several times between 1780 and 1799, led first by Haider Ali Khan (c.1722–82) and then by his son Tipu Sultan (c.1750–99).

In 1793, the Company as a government in India was receiving just over one-fifth of its total revenues from subsidies paid by its allies, or from the management of districts assigned by Indian rulers for that purpose. By 1806–7 the proportion had risen to one-third, from greatly expanded revenues. By the early 19th century, the allied princes were often persuaded to make over districts to the Company to cover the revenue demand for the support of troops. In this way, the British became further involved in the affairs of the Indian rulers and they gained access both to men and to money for use in their political campaigns.

Through its complex intervention in Indian affairs

the Company – with difficulty and incompletely – began to change the nature of empire in the subcontinent. The British had an imperfect grasp of Indian politics. They regarded the subcontinent as consisting of rival states in vigorous competition with each other and considered it to bear some relation to the geographically defined emerging nation-states of Europe. They understood that this analysis was not entirely correct, for they perceived that – despite the growth of major Indian governments that had a territorial core at their center – a striking feature of Indian politics was the way in which states were not defined by territory alone. Interest overlay interest on the same patch of ground, and different lords shared revenues and perquisites in the same village. In many areas, it could be fairly said, there was not one authority but many, and even quite locally-based Muslim and Hindu regimes made grand claims to universality.

Rather than being in control of a definite territory, Indian governments had fluid boundaries, and their rulers placed a premium on acquiring and holding shares in revenue and judicial rights, even if that led to

Tipu Sultan

Tipu Sultan's father, Haidar Ali Khan, was an adventurer who attracted financial backing and adequate mercenary support to overthrow Mysore's Hindu ruling family and soon consolidated the gains he won by the sword. Mysore, with its well-balanced agricultural economy, small population and advantageous position as a trade crossroads for the south, was well placed to became the first modern state in south India. Haidar improved the system of revenue collection and organized a bureaucracy. Both he, and then Tipu, encouraged trade but retained state control of the region's chief resources – sandalwood, cardamoms, betelnuts. Tipu established state pearl fisheries and silk production and developed trade with western Asia. But the heart of Mysore's power, on which its revenues were mainly spent, was its army. Imitating European models, its transportation, munitions, quartermastering and commissariat arrangements were arguably superior to those of the English East India Company. Mysore in the late 18th century was thus the greatest threat to the Company's authority in south India. Caught in the crossfire of Anglo-French rivalry, and in need of more territory to offset the costs of the army, Haidar and Tipu put themselves on the side of the French. Their fortunes fell with those of their European ally, and war with the British followed. A treaty in 1792 entailed the payment of a substantial indemnity and the submission of two of Tipu's sons as hostages to Lord Cornwallis, but war broke out again, ending only with the defeat and death of Tipu Sultan in 1799.

Above right Tipu established his capital at Srirangapatnam, an island in the river Kaveri, 12 kilometers north of Mysore. Tipu's main palace does not survive, but contemporary accounts describe the exquisitely worked ivory doorposts, rich furniture and Persian carpets, together with the muslins, silks and shawls, telescopes and optical glasses, and the extensive library that were found there. Here we see a richly decorated audience hall with an elaborate floorspread held in place by decorative weights, guarded by soldiers in tiger-striped uniforms bearing guns.

Right Tipu's military prowess and his adoption of the tiger as his personal symbol earned him the title "Tiger of Mysore". Tiger motifs adorned most of his possessions, from his throne to his weaponry. This organ in the form of a tiger devouring a man may have been inspired by the gruesome fate that befell the son of an old adversary, General Sir Hector Munro, in Bengal. Taken to London after the fall of Srirangapatnam, the tiger's growls and the man's shrieks made it the most famous object in the East India Company's museum.

uncertainty in the limits of the state. Such a state of affairs, however, did not conform to the Company's view of the subcontinent. From the late 18th century it began to look at it through the eyes of its surveyors and map-makers, and to freeze the political structure in ways that made cartographical sense. The indeterminate and often contested boundaries of the old Mughal provinces became fixed lines on a map; the roving governments of the Marathas were penned, if not into coherent stretches of territory, at least into defined ones; and across western and central India, dozens of territorial governments were created out of the local lords who happened to have dominance in their area at that particular time.

Resistance was never entirely overcome. The British faced chronic disobedience from many quarters, occasionally flaring up into violent clashes. Even as late as 1857, when a mutiny of Indian soldiers at Meerut turned to general revolt and spread from Bengal to the Punjab and into the Deccan, it was possible to conceive of serious British defeat. But the underlying trend was toward the definition and stabilization of geographical limits, both on the northern periphery of the subcontinent and within its bounds. The broad, indefinite zones around its economic and political centers were replaced by clear, if sometimes arbitrary, territorial lines; any subsequent decision to redraw the administrative and political boundaries was usually accompanied by great controversy. At the same time, as the Indian rulers were disarmed and the countryside pacified, settled agriculture was expanded and internal communications improved – developments that all helped to fix the new political order more firmly.

A profitable enterprise

The changes taking place in India were subject to great scrutiny in Britain. Many politicians disliked the way things were going and subjected the Company's affairs, and those of its officers (including, most famously, Warren Hastings), to inquiry and impeachment. A select parliamentary committee at the beginning of the 19th century showed that the accumulated India debt in London had leapt from £10.8 million in 1798 to £32 million in 1806–7 (the period of Wellesley's wars against Mysore and the Marathas), with a similar sharp rise in the annual interest from £740,000 to close on £2.3 million. Further inquiry, however, revealed the tangible economic benefits derived from the Indian connection. Not only did the Company's imports exceed its exports by some £20 million between 1792 and 1807, it brought similar huge sums to Britain through its hiring of British shipping, payment of bills of exchange, imports of bullion and payment of dividends to its stock-holders. In addition, the British government had collected nearly £40 million from the Company in taxation, and had received this revenue (which amounted to nearly a third of its total income at one stage in the 1790s) at virtually no expense to itself in collection.

Though the new political order in India undoubtedly worked to the financial profit of British and Company interests, the benefits were not solely on their side. The Company had to work with Indian associates in every aspect of its activities; its role in the politics and economy of the subcontinent would have been unthinkable if account had not been taken of the quite independent social forces that provided the particular opportunities of the later 18th century. By allying itself with the dynamic, if unstable, elements in

Right When Srirangapatnam fell, the British found an amazing storehouse of military power: four huge arsenals, two foundries for making cannon, armories for small weapons, powder magazines, 99,000 muskets and carbines, 424,000 pieces of shot, gunpowder and abundantly stocked granaries. This steel helmet, taken at the siege, with its band of damascened foliage, sliding nose guard, and protective mail falling to the shoulder, demonstrates the armorer's skills of the time.

Above A portrait of Tipu Sultan by an anonymous Indian artist, Mysore c.1790. Tipu was represented by the British as a cruel tyrant and despot in order to justify their expansion in south India, though professionally they admired him as a warrior-administrator and as a man of culture and learning.

Sikhism

Sikhism is a faith and a community identified particularly with Punjab. Even today, when Sikhs are to be found in cities all over the world, twenty out of twenty-five Sikhs live in Punjab. The founder of the Sikh religion, Guru Nanak (1469–1539), drew inspiration from the vibrant religious life of Punjab, but rejected the teaching of all the major religions. He preached monotheism and strict morality, proclaiming freedom from constant rebirth by meditation on the name of God. Sikhism was not a syncretic religion, but grew from the devotional traditions of Hinduism and Islam alike. Guru Nanak wrote simple hymns of great beauty. His followers, mainly respectable townsfolk and Jat cultivators, became known as "Sikhs" from the Sanskrit *shishya*, meaning disciple.

The Sikhs became a community (the *Panth*). Guru Arjun (1581-1606) built the Golden Temple at Amritsar and compiled the *Adi Granth*, the sacred scriptures, consisting mainly of the hymns of the Gurus and of other holy men. During the 17th century Sikhism became more militant. Gobind Singh (1675–1708) founded the Khalsa order in 1699, infusing the faith with military values. Sikhs were to defend their faith and to carry visible signs of it. They were to leave their hair uncut, wear a comb, steel bangle, breeches, and carry a weapon.

Gobind Singh was the last personal guru, and the Sikhs then accepted the authority of their scriptures (the *Guru Granth*) and their community (the *Guru Panth*). At the end of the 18th century Ranjit Singh (1780–1839) emerged as a ruler in Punjab embodying the Khalsa ideal. The independent Sikh state he created did not survive his death, but military idealism was bolstered by the prominent role the Sikhs played in the modern Indian army, and community values were reinvigorated by reforms in the 20th century.

Left Though Guru Nanak, himself a khatri by caste, rejected caste ideology and placed great emphasis on individual social responsibility in the search for God, this watercolor portrait, originally belonging to William Fraser, a British official at Delhi, is annotated to show the different castes represented among the Sikh community at Patiala in Punjab, c.1815–20. They include a Jat agriculturalist and a Gujar pastoralist as well as a khatri.

Above A Sikh war turban adorned with steel throwing rings and disemboweling claws.

Right Maharaja Ranjit Singh, the son of a Sikh chieftain in Gujranwala, captured Lahore in 1799 and thereafter dominated the politics of Punjab by military force, consolidating his rule over the whole region between the Sutlej and Indus rivers. Here he is depicted as an ideal king with all the traditional trappings of royalty.

India's economy and society, it secured strategic control of certain narrow interests. But the bulk of Indian society, its political, social and economic institutions, were irrelevant to the Company's main concerns. Unless they touched British interests directly, they were left alone.

Because their activities at that time were limited to the quite specific tasks of revenue collection, military organization and trade, the British did not impinge significantly on the position of substantial vested social elites. The latter could afford to ignore the political superstructure the British were putting in place. The new overlords remained distant from the running of the Indian countryside, or from the affairs of religion, social organization and other concerns of daily life; in such matters, they were heavily dependent on the regional rulers who had recently emerged from the Mughal structure, and upon entrenched local and village elites. So long as the British required no more of them than the traditional minimal obedience and tribute, they would to remain quiescent.

In one sense, therefore, the main and most numerous beneficiaries of British rule – and hence the most important – were the princes and local lords who were securely established within definite territories and freed by the *pax Britannica* from interference from neighbors or from above. Beneficiaries too were the host of land-controllers of all sorts, whose rights were recognized and reinforced by the paramount power. For many other significant groups in Indian society, the creation of the Company's raj – in a form that was both traditional and radically new – was at least an irrelevance, and was in many cases advantageous to their local or regional concerns. Of course, there was no uniform pattern in this general process. Nor was it invulnerable to change. But seen in this context, British government in India in the early 19th century is recognizable as being in the mold of earlier Indian states. It is also seen to be a much more fragile construct than might at first be supposed, and one that was limited in its capacity to impose itself on the societies it wished to manage.

Nonetheless, by 1820 the English East India Company had established itself as the dominant ruling power in India. Based in Calcutta, Madras and Bombay, it possessed and directly administered some of the richest and most important parts of the subcontinent – the provinces of Bengal, Bihar and Orissa, large areas of the Indo-Gangetic plains, most of the coastal regions including the Andhra deltas in the east and huge areas farther south around Madras, parts of the Deccan, and valuable districts in Gujarat to the north of Bombay. The Company's paramountcy was established over many other major states: Oudh, Hyderabad and Mysore, for example, were tied by alliances that made them part of the new imperial system controlled by the British, while leaving them technically independent. Other Indian rulers, such as Ranjit Singh (1780–1839), the Sikh leader who created a state in the Punjab, had negotiated more equal alliances, but their territories were marginal to the Company's main concerns at this time and would be more fully incorporated into the raj as the political need arose. For all their attempts to stabilize and define territorial limits, the internal boundaries of the British raj – like those of the Mughals and Marathas before them – were shifting and uncertain. Yet by the second decade of the 19th century the East India Company held enough of India to overawe the rest.

THE MAKING OF MODERN INDIA

The early 19th-century British raj

In the late 18th and early 19th centuries India was subject to tremendous pressures, both domestically and internationally. Natural disasters led to crop shortages, famine and large-scale depopulation. International turmoil and rapidly changing governments marked the politics of the period. At the same time, various parts of the Indian economy were linked in new ways to international markets, providing both opportunity and enhanced exposure to conditions over which Indian producers had no control. The East India Company and the dynamic Indian groups that allied themselves to it began to provide greater political and economic stability, but the benefits of this new state of things were slow in coming and were very unevenly felt, both geographically and socially.

In this fluid situation, the British found it increasingly necessary to hold down government expenditure on the army and on administration, and were forced to pay closer attention to meeting the costs of their rule. Wellesley's wars, first against Tipu Sultan of Mysore and then against the Marathas, coupled with his diplomatic initiatives to bring other Indian states within a British-dominated system of Indian government, proved more costly than the profits of trade could bear. As British rule settled in Bengal and Madras, and then expanded beyond them, taking over more of the Deccan in the wake of the collapse of Maratha power, a prime concern of government came to be the stable collection of land-revenue. This was historically such an important source of public revenue, and so intimately bound up with the structure of local society in the Indian countryside, that the new British rulers found they had little option but to make a pact with those who were able to guarantee some flow of revenue from field to government treasury. In Bengal, for example, this meant dealing with the *zamindars*; in parts of south and western India with the *ryots*, or peasant proprietors. Policies that might have stimulated economic growth or introduced greater equity in the distribution of wealth in the countryside were inevitably sacrificed to those that produced the safest and most regular return.

Even so, by the 1830s the government was faced with falling receipts. There were a number of reasons for this. Revenue systems were difficult to penetrate and manage. The demand for revenue was pitched higher than the economy could comfortably bear and consequently was not paid in full, or fields were deserted. Moreover, the government's financial difficulties were deepened by slumps in international trade, and especially by a further decline in direct trade between India and Britain and the difficulties facing merchants in trading with China. Things were made all the worse by a run of famines within India. The laissez-faire, or free-market, economic policies of Britain at this time worked greatly to the disadvantage of government in India. Lucrative monopolies such as the trade between China and Britain – hitherto held by the East India Company and, by the beginning of the 19th century, its most profitable commercial activity – were thrown open to all-comers.

The late 1820s and early 1830s witnessed a spirited and well-conceived attempt by the British to put their government in India on to a sound footing by inaugurating an era of thorough-going reform. The prime mover was Lord William Bentinck (1774–1839), Governor General from 1828 to 1835. He was ably supported by a number of colleagues, the most famous of whom was Thomas Babington Macaulay (1800–59), sent to India as a member of the recently created Supreme Council in 1834. Enthused by evangelicalism and much influenced by the radical ideas of English political writers such as Jeremy Bentham, James Mill and John Stuart Mill, these men attempted to solve India's problems with a program of reform from above. Reductions were made in overall expenditure by cutting wages and privileges in the army and by employing more Indians at higher levels in the administration. It was argued that an attempt should be made to curb further expansion in order to cut military costs. Plans were laid to improve the economic infrastructure by repairing the Grand Trunk Road that since the days of Ashoka had run from Bihar to the Punjab, and preliminary work was done on renovating and extending the east Jamuna canal. In some provinces (though not in Bengal, where the arrangements made with the *zamindars* in the 1790s had effectively locked the British out of the revenue system) a more scientific approach was adopted toward the assessment of land revenue. Attempts were made to induce more British settlers to India and to encourage private British investment in the country.

Some took a more robust approach to the perceived social problems of India. Christian missionaries, who had won concessions when the East India Company's charter was renewed by the British parliament in 1813, pressed vigorously for reform of Indian social practices. An early success was the outlawing in 1829 of *sati*, the custom whereby Indian widows were burnt on the funeral pyres of their dead husbands. Much thought was given to possible reform of Hindu marriage arrangements, and much ink was spilt on the supposed shortcomings of the caste system. Macaulay took in hand the codification of Indian law, and attempts were made to bring undesirable social and religious customs within the scope of the law. After considerable debate Bentinck's government decided to promote English education in India by providing a subsidy out of public funds; this was followed by a decision to make English the language of all higher administration and of the superior courts. All these reforms were designed to modernize Indian society and to impart to it the useful knowledge of the 19th century. But they were also devices whose purpose was to make government solvent.

The Indian response to western ideas

The reforming government was in part a response to an initiative that came from certain social groups

Chess

There are many ancient myths and modern theories about the origins of chess. As a war-game between two players on a 64-square board, it is generally thought to have first been played in northwest India in the 6th century AD, or even earlier. Its earliest known form was Chaturanga, named after the "four divisions" of an Indian army: infantry, chariots, cavalry and elephants. By the 7th century the game had spread westward to Persia and thence throughout the Islamic world. By 1000 it was well established in Europe.

In India, chess remained popular through the ages. Great artistry was employed in carving elaborate chess sets in ivory and other valuable materials for noble or wealthy patrons, though few early examples survive. The game itself developed relatively little. The more dynamic European game (dating from c. 1475), with an initial pawn move of two squares and a far more powerful Queen, only became widespread in India in the 20th century. In the early 1930s Sultan Khan, the illiterate Punjabi servant of a rich landowner, caused a sensation in Europe by beating the strongest western masters, though he had to learn the European game first. In the early 1990s the highly gifted player Vishwanathan Anand was considered a leading candidate for the next World Championship.

Below A mid 19th-century set of turned and carved ivory chessmen of European type, with one side stained red. The board is of satinwood overlaid with ivory and tortoise-shell. Both are from Vishakhapatnam in Andhra Pradesh. Luxury chess sets were made both for British patrons in India and for export.

Above The chessmen in this picture are from a painted and gilt ivory set made in Rajasthan in the early 19th century. They comprise the red Queen (Vizir or minister, on an elephant), a white Bishop (camel-riding drummer), and a red Pawn (foot-soldier).

Right The battle of Gav and Talhand, from a mid 15th-century Persian manuscript of the *Shahnama* of Firdausi. According to this legend, chess was invented to console a queen whose son had been slain by his brother in a civil war: the game demonstrated the fatal battle between them.

Above Sayyid Ahmad Khan came from a well-established Mughal court family. Having served in the British administration in northern India, he came to play a major role in educational, religious and political reform during the 1860s. He was the driving force behind the movement to make modern secular subjects part of the curriculum for Muslims, and the Muhammadan Anglo-Oriental College he founded at Aligarh is now, as Aligarh University, one of India's leading universities. Sayyid Ahmad Khan also developed the strategy of protecting Muslim interests in India by arguing for separate representation in the political system.

Left Rammohan Roy was a major figure in the intellectual life of early 19th-century Bengal. A civil servant who rose rapidly to the highest position open to an Indian, he studied widely in religion and philosophy, knew Arabic, Persian, Sanskrit and Hebrew, translated the New Testament into Bengali and renewed scholarly interest in the Vedas. Though his role as forming a bridge between Indian and western ideas is often stressed, he was equally important in revitalizing and remaining within indigenous Hindu traditions.

Previous pages Lieutenant-Colonel James Tod, shown here in procession on an elephant in a painting by an Indian artist from Mewar, c.1820, was the first Political Agent to the Western Rajput States (present-day Rajasthan). In 1817–18 he successfully brought the most powerful Rajput rulers of this region into treaty alliance with the British – an alliance that was crucial to the success of the British in finally defeating the Marathas. Tod had great admiration for the Rajputs, as revealed in his classic history *Annals and Antiquities of Rajast'han*, and hoped that mutual respect of each other's sovereignty would rest at the heart of the Anglo-Rajput treaties. But as the British consolidated their position in India the treaties became the cornerstone of an unequal relationship that gradually reduced the Rajput rulers to the status of colonial puppets.

such as *sati*, and stressed the importance of learning about European scientific and mathematical discoveries. But the active membership of the Brahmo Samaj remained very small, and its real importance lay in the fact that it generated debate among the Bengali intelligentsia about a wide range of cultural matters. As the British became politically dominant, Indian society organized itself alongside and against the new foreign culture. Hardly any educated Indian became a Christian, but there was a great interest in the revival of Hinduism and a quest for Indian and Hindu values among English-literate Bengalis. The presence of the British may have presented some sort of a cultural challenge, but the more usual response on the part of the enlightened Indian was to recreate or rediscover an indigenous past.

The same period witnessed a new vigor within Islam. This took a bewildering variety of forms. The loss of political power was keenly felt by many Muslims, and served to stimulate movements for reform among them. Some saw the failure to keep up with modern scientific knowledge as a key element in their political weaknesses and attempted to incorporate into Islamic doctrine the technical and scientific achievements of non-Muslims, at the same time stressing that this in no way undermined fundamentally the Muslim way of life. Across the whole spectrum of Indian Islam a new determination to define and promote the true faith manifested itself at all levels. Shah Valiullah (1703–62) and his son Shah Abdul Aziz (1746–1824) promoted the puritanical and proselytizing Muhammadiya movement that aimed to purge Islam of the contamination of both western and Hindu influences. Even fiercer were the frequent calls to arms issued by Sayyid Ahmad of Bareli (1781–1831), who seemed to conform to the stereotype of the strict and intolerant reformer and died waging *jihad* against the Sikhs. Among Bengali Muslims, the Faraizi movement, led from 1821 by Haji Shariatullah (1781–1840), took the form of a social and religious campaign to persuade villagers to follow the observance of Islam more closely and to give up social and cultural practices shared with their non-Muslim neighbors. At Firangi Mahal, the great Muslim college at Lucknow, impetus was given to the development of the rationalist syllabus within Islamic scholarly tradition, and later Sayyid Ahmad Khan (1817–98), who founded the Muhammadan Anglo-Oriental College at Aligarh in 1875, sought to introduce the study of mathematics, science and modern languages as they were taught at Oxford or Cambridge into a syllabus in which Islam remained in place.

The Indian Mutiny

Despite its virtual monopoly of force from about 1820 onward, the Company's rule in India was never totally secure. There was hardly a year in which its armies were not at war. On its shifting frontiers campaigns were waged against the Burmese in the northeast and the Afghans in the northwest; Sind was annexed in 1843 and the Sikh state of Punjab in 1849. The British faced chronic unrest from their own recalcitrant subjects in the Indian countryside. In this context, the mutiny of part of the Indian army in May 1857 was the last, albeit perhaps the grandest, attempt at resistance to the new social and economic order that had been a century in the making.

The pretext for the rebellion – which began among Indian troops (sepoys) in the barracks at Meerut, 65

within Indian society. The literate classes of Bengal depended heavily upon government employment. They had already seen the benefits of becoming proficient in the language of the new rulers, if only because so few of the latter achieved a real understanding of India and its languages. Education in English enabled many Indians to acquire a technical skill that would secure their employment. It was perfectly possible to attend an English school, even one run by missionaries, yet still to be a good Hindu for whom Christianity was an exotic irrelevance, still prefer Bengali or Tamil literature to the writings of the west, and still live according to the accepted norms of your neighbors.

Nevertheless, some Indians were open to western ideas. Rammohan Roy (1772–1833), a Bengali brahmin hailed as one of the founders of modern India, undertook serious study of western theology and attempted to synthesize Christianity and European Deism with various strands of Hindi monotheism. In 1828 he founded the Brahmo Samaj (Society of God) to promote intellectual and religious exploration. Through it he propounded views that were critical of idol-worship, brahminism and some Indian customs, kilometers north of Delhi – was the issuing of cartridges believed to have been smeared with pig and beef fat, thus offering an insult to both Muslims and Hindus. The mutineers marched on Delhi and proclaimed the aged Mughal emperor Bahadur Shah II (1837–58) restored to full powers. From there the mutiny spread throughout northern India. Order was restored only with great difficulty in the summer of 1858. Though the mutineers had summarily shot their British officers and murdered British women and children, and reprisals against the sepoys were predictably brutal, total loss of life and of property was on a remarkably small scale for modern times. Seen in the long term, the disturbances associated with the mutiny were an uncomfortable reminder of the difficulty of running India and of the inherent tensions in its stratified society. In the short term, its most significant result was the abolition of the East India Company and its replacement by direct British rule.

The mutiny hit British confidence hard not so much because in objective military terms the revolts were impossible to deal with, but because loss of control had been so sudden and the close connection between rural society and the army had been underlined in such a striking way. But in fact there was another side to the coin. Most of India, after all, did not revolt. Punjab, for example, remained firm. Since its recent acquisition it had been the recipient of scarce government investment to develop its economy. Elsewhere, the building of roads, canals, and, most recently, railways, together with an increase in irrigation, were also beginning to have their effect. There had been growth in the number of schools, and the first Indian colleges and universities, were established. The mutiny did not call a halt to this program of public works. But, most importantly, the local elites that had become established in the countryside, partly through the operation of the revenue systems, were now launched on a wave of unprecedented prosperity. The size of the population increased (thus making labor easier to control), the area of cultivated land expanded, and cash crops found new markets. In real terms, the burden of the land revenue demand everywhere began to fall and in some areas the economic gains were very striking indeed.

A significant shift had taken place in the public attitudes of the government. Whereas the Company administrators of the earlier 19th century had trumpeted reform and change to mask their fundamentally conservative activities, in the later Victorian period the prevailing ethos was to hide change under concern for tradition. A virtue was made of protecting undertenants and "poor" peasants, while the legal and economic position of dominant cultivators grew stronger. Religious and social customs were left well alone, unless an established usage, such as child marriage, was flagrantly opposed to British or reforming Indian ideals of right and wrong – whereupon the government stepped briskly forward with legislation, irrespective of the critical outcry. Beneath the policy statements and the laws was the continual quest to find those in India society who could best serve the purposes of the British. Censuses were taken, India was analyzed and classified, and labels placed upon

Below Though the British faced chronic unrest in northern India in the early 19th century and had to contend with major resistance to their rule, the mutiny of troops in the barracks at Meerut on 10 May 1857 marked a turning point in Indo-British history. Failure to deal quickly with the Meerut mutiny meant that before long the British found they had lost control of much of the central Gangetic plain. This, together with the effort that had to be made to restore the British position, caught the imagination of the public and the "mutiny events" were widely reported in the British press. By the standards of the 20th century, the loss of life and level of atrocities were not great, but the killing of British civilians provoked particular outrage, and reprisals were savage. This crude picture shows mutinying Indian soldiers being executed by being blown from guns – a form of capital punishment horrific to us now but believed at the time to be both a deterrent and humane.

Railways

Hindu rulers built temples, Muslims mosques and fortresses, but the British built railways. On 31 October 1850 the first sod was turned to lay the track for the Great Indian Peninsula Railway running out of Bombay, and the first stretch of line between Howrah and Hooghly in Bengal was opened four years later. Railway engineers on both lines faced major hurdles. In the west, ways had to be found of carrying the line from Bombay over the Western Ghats to the Deccan plateau, and in the Gangetic plain track had to be laid across land liable to flood during the wet season.

The trunk system of lines was planned primarily with strategic needs in mind, and even by the late 20th century (despite vigorous efforts from the outset to attract private money) lack of investment in feeder lines inhibited realization of the railways' full economic potential. However, one important early effect was to link the agricultural areas of northern India with Bombay, thereby encouraging a shift of prosperity from the eastern districts of the United Provinces to the west. Punjab, a key frontier province in British eyes, was a principal beneficiary, and the line into the Central Provinces stimulated the production of cotton there. Tourism by rail was promoted early, making feasible otherwise difficult ascents of mountainous areas. Holy cities like Varanasi and Gaya began to serve their devotees in an unprecedentedly efficient fashion – in the 1870s a pandit at Gaya reported that ghosts were much less common since the coming of the railway because funeral rites could be performed so soon after death. Pilgrimage to major festivals became possible on a truly mass scale. In 1950, for example, nearly three-quarters of a million people arrived by train to celebrate the Kumbh Mela at Hardwar.

The line from Bombay to Delhi ran almost entirely through princely states whose rulers took a great interest in the steam engine. The Maharaja of Gwalior even had a model train made for him in silver to circulate port and cigars after dinner. *Right* the luxury express Desert Queen is seen steaming into Jaipur station; *below* smartly liveried waiters pass breakfast trays from the dining car to the first-class compartments.

Left The loop "Agony Point" on the Darjeeling Hill Railway, c. 1890. The line from Siliguri to Darjiling was opened in 1878, engineered by Franklin Prestage of the Eastern Bengal Railway Company. For 82 kilometers the track follows an old cart track, zigzagging over deep ravines and precipices. It rises more than 2,000 meters, taking the passenger from a landscape of sal trees, tea gardens and paddy fields through pine, chestnut and birch to rhododendron and hydrangeas. The need for tunnels is obviated by a system of loops and reverses. In the loop, the railway track circles around and passes over a gradient by a bridge, thereby quickly attaining a higher elevation. In the reverse, the same object is obtained by running the track back diagonally and upwards for a short distance and then using an alignment parallel to the original one, but higher up the mountain.

the social categories that were deemed either reliable or dangerous. The late 19th-century view, held by Indians as much as by the British, divided Indian society into coherent groups that could be used as building blocks in political and cultural games: "peasants", "landowners", "princes", "Muslims", "criminal tribes", "moneylenders", "untouchables". These, and a myriad other social descriptions, whatever their actual basis in fact, took on a life of their own.

India's place in Britain's empire

In the second half of the 19th century India provided an important market for British manufactures, especially cotton textiles and heavy machinery. It was an increasingly important supplier of raw materials – jute, cotton, tea, oilseeds, leather, foodgrains – both directly to Britain and to other markets in Europe and the United States, and proved an excellent place for British investment overseas. British capital was lodged with the government of India, put into Indian railways, and into plantations and business concerns. By the outbreak of World War I, about a fifth of British capital overseas was invested in India. Additionally, the government of India, through the army and its civil service, employed a large number of Britons. Above all, India provided Britain with substantial military resources. It was the Indian taxpayer who provided the money to support units of the British army when stationed in India. The Indian army itself, paid for by Indians and outside parliamentary control, provided the British empire with the wherewithal to promote and defend its interests from the Middle East to China, from South Africa to the Pacific. As the viceroy Lord Curzon (1859–1925) put it in 1900, "We could lose all our dominions and still survive, but if we lost India, our sun would sink to its setting."

These imperial concerns played a large part in determining how India was governed. Under pressure from the government in London to become more efficient for imperial purposes, and forced to assume wider responsibilities by pressures for change within the subcontinent, the government in India ushered in a host of new legislative, consultative and administrative procedures. A single administrative and political system was created, designed to meet British needs for a centralized and coherent system, while at the same time involving Indian society in the process of government: legislative councils, on which Indian opinion was represented, were tentatively introduced in 1861 and expanded in 1892. From the 1880s considerable strides were made in the evolution of representative machinery at local level. District administration was tied more tightly to the provincial structures, while the provinces were made to feel the authority of the government of India. The whole Indian operation was constitutionally subordinate to parliament in London.

The system by and large worked well, though Curzon – as a frustrated reformer – could characterize the government of India as a "mighty and miraculous machine for doing nothing". Unity was given to a state machinery that overlay some of the diversities of the subcontinent, allowing it to grapple with problems inherent in governing such a large and complex area. However, increasing efficiency and better control could only be achieved by decentralizing administrative practices and by incorporating within the state structure those social groups who, being separately and independently of importance within Indian society and its economy, were also likely to be those most

Left Victoria Terminus at Bombay was formally opened in 1887. The railway station is believed to be on the site of a temple of the goddess Mumba Devi (after whom Bombay is named), destroyed by Qutb-ud Din Khalji in 1317, rebuilt and finally demolished by the Portuguese in 1760. VT – as the station is universally known – was designed by F. W. Stevens in the Gothic-Saracenic style, and its series of well-proportioned and delicately ornamented arches give it the look of a grand cathedral. A figure of stone on the top, 5 meters high, symbolizes Progress, while on the principal gables are highly sculptured panels depicting Engineering, Agriculture, Commerce, Science and Trade.

Kalighat Painting

Kalighat painting, a distinctive type of watercolor on paper, originated about 1800 in response to social and economic changes taking place in Calcutta. As the city environs grew, a road was built to an old temple to the goddess Kali, situated in jungly country to the south and previously only accessible by river. The temple's popularity grew. Bengali Hindu artists of the *patua* community responded to the growing pilgrim market by taking advantage of newly available, industrially manufactured paper and watercolor paints. Unlike artists from a courtly background, who were trained by and worked for the British, the Kalighat painters had only indirect access to western techniques and evolved a unique style that drew on both Indian and western traditions. The use of a single theme in abstract and minimal style on a blank background reflects the influence of contemporary western natural history painting but the diluted colors and careful detail of English watercolors soon gave way to more powerful Indian colors and stressed contours. In time, the style became bolder, simpler and more energetic, but eventually even high speed drawing and tinted woodcuts lost the battle with lithography and the printed picture. By 1930 the school was dead.

As well as religious themes, Kalighat artists drew vivid, and – from the 1870s onward – increasingly moralizing and critical pictures of Bengali society, satirically depicting the "westernized" man about town, courtesans, domestic violence and hypocritical priests and holy men.

Below left This subject, which was new to popular Bengali art in the early 19th century, clearly derives from contemporary drawings of fieldsports by British artists. The fashion of the man's dress indicates an 1820–30 date, and the style of the painting – the pale colors and shading that emphasizes contours rather than volume – illustrates the still undigested influence of European watercolor techniques.

Right A permanent temple to the goddess Kali was probably first built in the late 16th century but was destroyed in the 18th century. The present temple (completed c. 1809) was built by the family of *zamindars* who had earlier sold the East India Company the three villages that formed the nucleus of Calcutta. This depiction by the Flemish artist Balthazar Solvyns shows the typical Bengali *athachala* (eight-roofed) structure of the temple with an adjacent hall.

Above Rani Lakshmi Bai, widow of Raja Gangadhar Rao of Jhansi, whose state had been annexed by the British when he died without a male heir, was proclaimed ruler of Jhansi in 1857 in the course of the Mutiny. She led her troops in resistance to the British wearing male clothes, and died in action in 1858. Her fame was legendary and she came to be revered almost as a popular goddess.

Left Kali (meaning "black") personifies death and destruction and in Bengal she typically wears only a skirt of severed arms and garland of severed heads. Her left hands hold the head of a demon and a sword; her right hands reflect her benign qualities. She is often shown trampling on the prostrate body of Shiva, her husband, and her tongue protrudes, according to folklore, from shame at this act.

Right Apparently a natural history subject, this large, bold painting, which is un-Indian in style, in fact illustrates a proverb satirizing false ascetics. In some versions the cat's forehead carries the distinctive markings of a worshiper of the god Vishnu. Vaishnava holy men, supposedly vegetarians, were often known to eat fish in private.

critical of its control by a foreign power. Such groups would seek to use the political system to deny the British a clear run in extracting benefits from India for non-Indian purposes, and would seek to enhance their own standing within Indian society.

The rise of nationalism

As the government impinged more directly on Indian society, so it brought more Indians into the business of making and implementing policies. As the years went by, general principles were increasingly formulated on a national basis, and then adapted to, and imposed on, the various provinces and regions of the subcontinent. With the emergence of this new style of government connections were forged across the districts and provinces, and it was no longer enough for Indians to secure political benefits in the localities alone; it became increasingly important to be heard at the centers of government, both at provincial and national level, where so many potentially important strategic decisions were made. In the countryside, where wealth, property, or inherited ritual or social status still held sway, the vigor of village, district and small-town politics continued unabated. But in the newly forming arenas of provincial and national politics, a different sort of political association led by a new type of politician was required – one who had to know English and the way the organs of government functioned, be familiar with the law codes and the administrative handbooks, expert in the most recent theories of taxation and political economy, and capable of mediating between several interests and of arranging broad alliances between them.

After the 1870s the most prominent Indian politicians were rarely the powerful *zamindars*, merchant princes or caste-bosses, though it would be very wrong to imply that such important local figures lost real political authority in their neighborhoods. Typically, the new breed of politicians were town-based, literate in English and employed in occupations that brought them into contact with the day-to-day working of government – usually the law, teaching or journalism. Whether you were from Bombay or Calcutta, Madras or Allahabad, whether you spoke Tamil or Bengali, Marathi or Hindi, Gujarati or Telugu, whether you were Hindu or Muslim, Sikh or Parsi – if you were educated in English, lived in one of the great towns and belonged to one of the professions, you had sufficient in common to unite you on some issues (namely those in which the government had a hand) with other Indians of similar standing.

In the late 19th century in the main centers of British rule in Bengal, Bombay and Madras, men like these began to form political associations to press for reform in government. Institutions such as the Indian Association of Calcutta, the Bombay Presidency Association, the Pune Sarvajanik Sabha and the Madras Mahajana Sabha heralded a new development in India politics. They grouped people together according to shared interests in public affairs and drafted resolutions, petitions and memorials for submission to government. These societies exploited to the full the changing constitution of the government of India and thereby created new grounds for unity in India society. Since they were open groups, their members might belong to all castes and communities; since they commented on matters of concern to all, they claimed to stand for interests wider than those of their members. Such broad-based associations, founded for particular

ends and built up out of compromise and alliance, were indispensable for dealing with the government at a provincial or national level and, within limits, were capable of maintaining continued cooperation among their members.

Finding the government in India unreceptive to their demands, it was soon realized that what was wanted was Indian representation in Britain. Indian politicians could seek to influence government decision-making by taking their case to Britain, lobbying Members of Parliament and securing the support of influential interest groups within British metropolitan society. But, in order to influence English political parties, it was essential to draw up a single all-India political program.

The Indian National Congress

On 28 December 1885 a gathering took place in Bombay of "certain well-known men". The advertized object of the meeting was to make all the "most earnest labourers in the cause of national progress" personally known to each other. Close on 100 people, from nearly every corner of the subcontinent, attended this inaugural meeting of the Indian National Congress, the first and by far the most important and long-lived all-India political association. Before 1915, the Congress drew its most regular support from the coastal provinces of Bombay, Madras and Bengal. Through its annual meeting, held in the Christmas week when the lawcourts and government offices were closed, it provided Indians with a continental platform to put forward the demands they had already been making through the provincial associations. Among these were proposals to make the legislative councils

Above The magnificent High Court in Bombay, built 1871–79, was designed by Colonel James Fuller. The dominating central tower is flanked by smaller octagonal spire-capped towers crowned by statues of Justice and Mercy. The High Court stands in a row of self-confident public buildings, including the Secretariat, University and Post Office, put up after the 1860s when the city was transformed by new wealth and by the vigorous activity of both municipal and private benefactors. Though British architects such as Fuller, Henry Wilkins and George Gilbert Scott designed in the Gothic style then at the height of its popularity in Britain, what makes their Bombay buildings so interesting is the creative use of local materials and the incorporation of indigenous architectural features. Not only do they function well for their respective purposes, but taken together they form an extraordinarily impressive skyline.

Right George V and his consort Queen Mary were the only reigning British monarchs to visit their Indian domain. The ceremonies accompanying their arrival and departure in 1911 took place at the Apollo Bunder, Bombay, where an arch designed in 16th-century western Indian style was specially erected. It became known as the Gateway of India and achieved permanent form in honey-colored basalt. Symbolically, the last British troops to leave India in 1948 departed through the gate.

in India more powerful and to include more Indians, to allow more Indians easier access to the highest ranks of the civil service, to bring judicial administration and legal procedure into line with British practices, to end discriminatory racial legislation (notably the acts that forbade Indians to carry firearms on the same terms as Europeans), and to change methods of levying taxes. In part these demands, though general in tenor, represented the specific interests of the particular groups that provided the leadership of the Congress during its first 40 years. But what is most remarkable about them is that they could genuinely be presented as a national demand.

Given the size and complexity of India, the obstacles to creating a common political platform that incorporated all the diverse concerns of every interest group – regional, religious, cultural and social – were considerable, and without a cautious and pragmatic approach the Congress would never have established itself as the mainstream vehicle for the nationalist agenda. Early on, the Congress developed a central organization that encompassed secular national political aspirations. A party grew up that combined openness of membership with a quite fierce managerial committee structure. From the very earliest days of the nationalist movement, the benefits were realized of taking a pragmatic approach to politics, one that stressed the need for alliance and cooperation, eschewed regional, class, ethnic and religious differences and formed the basis for a party organization designed to hold together as many groups as possible. As more and more Indians began to participate in the struggles for political power, either locally or regionally, the Congress continually reshaped itself to

accommodate them, and so was able to hold on to its central dominating role.

Other attempts to create national organizations were less successful. The most significant of these was the All-India Muslim League, founded in 1906. Though the Muslim population was most densely concentrated in the northwest and the northeast, large numbers were scattered throughout the subcontinent, and they were, moreover, divided theologically, linguistically, racially, and by class. In the Punjab, and to some extent in Bengal, where they were the majority population, Muslims found their political aspirations were met by concentrating on provincial politics. For these reasons, the League found difficulty in framing policies that represented the interests of all Muslims in every region.

Decline of the imperial interest

The half-century before the outbreak of World War I was indeed the highpoint of the imperial connection between Britain and India. On 12 December 1911 this was symbolized by the holding of a great coronation *durbar* in Delhi. The King-Emperor George V, with his consort the Queen-Empress Mary, appeared before his Indian subjects and received the homage of India and her princes in person – the only reigning British Emperor of India so to do. In grand ceremony, which combined re-invented English medieval ritual with Mughal splendor – a royal pavilion draped in velvet of crimson and gold was surmounted by "a bulbous dome, which is typical of late Mohammedan architecture" – the King-Emperor made a short speech proclaiming the fact of his coronation. He also announced that the capital of British India would be

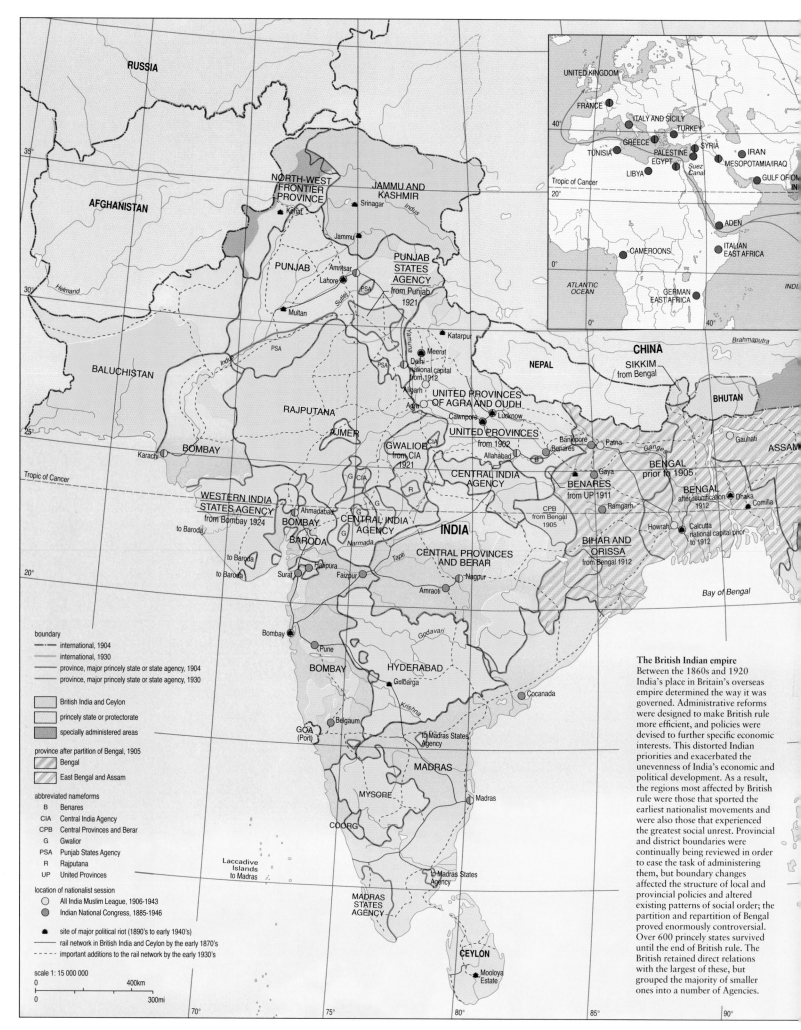

RUSSIA

AFGHANISTAN

NORTH-WEST
FRONTIER
PROVINCE
Kohat

JAMMU AND
KASHMIR
Srinagar
Indus

Jammu

PUNJAB
Amritsar
Lahore
Multan
Sutlej
PSA

PUNJAB
STATES
AGENCY
from Punjab
1921

BALUCHISTAN

Indus
PSA

Helmand

Karachi

BOMBAY

RAJPUTANA

AJMER

Katarpur
Yamuna
Meerut
Delhi
national capital
from 1912
Aligarh
Agra

UNITED PROVINCES
OF AGRA AND OUDH
Cawnpore Lucknow

UNITED PROVINCES
from 1962

CHINA

SIKKIM
from Bengal

Brahmaputra

NEPAL

BHUTAN

GWALIOR
from CIA
1921

CIA

Allahabad

CENTRAL INDIA
AGENCY

CENTRAL INDIA
AGENCY

G CIA

G
R

INDIA

Bankipore Patna
Benares
B
CPB
from Bengal
1905

Gauhati

ASSAM

BENARES
from UP 1911

Gaya
BENARES

Ramgarh

BENGAL
prior to 1905

BENGAL
after reunification
1912
Dhaka
Comilla

WESTERN INDIA
STATES AGENCY
from Bombay 1924

Ahmadabad
G

to Baroda

BOMBAY
BARODA

Narmada

Tapti

CENTRAL PROVINCES
AND BERAR

BIHAR AND
ORISSA
from Bengal 1912

Howrah Calcutta
national capital prior
to 1912

to Baroda

to Baroda

Surat
Halipura
Faizour

Amraoti

Nagpur

Bay of Bengal

Bombay

Pune

BOMBAY

HYDERABAD

Gulbarga

Godavari

Krishna

Cocanada

Belgaum

GOA
(Port)

to Madras States
Agency

MADRAS

MYSORE

Madras

COORG

Laccadive
Islands
to Madras

to Madras States
Agency

MADRAS
STATES
AGENCY

CEYLON

Mooloya
Estate

boundary

— international, 1904

— international, 1930

— province, major princely state or state agency, 1904

— province, major princely state or state agency, 1930

British India and Ceylon

princely state or protectorate

specially administered areas

province after partition of Bengal, 1905

Bengal

East Bengal and Assam

abbreviated nameforms

B   Benares
CIA   Central India Agency
CPB   Central Provinces and Berar
G   Gwalior
PSA   Punjab States Agency
R   Rajputana
UP   United Provinces

location of nationalist session

All India Muslim League, 1906-1943

Indian National Congress, 1885-1946

site of major political riot (1890's to early 1940's)

—— rail network in British India and Ceylon by the early 1870's

---- important additions to the rail network by the early 1930's

scale 1: 15 000 000

0 ———— 400km

0 ———— 300mi

UNITED KINGDOM
FRANCE
ITALY AND SICILY
TURKEY
GREECE
TUNISIA SYRIA IRAN
PALESTINE
EGYPT MESOPOTAMIA/IRAQ
Suez
Canal
LIBYA GULF OF OM

Tropic of Cancer

ADEN

CAMEROONS
ITALIAN
EAST AFRICA

ATLANTIC
OCEAN

INDI

GERMAN
EAST AFRICA

The British Indian empire
Between the 1860s and 1920
India's place in Britain's overseas
empire determined the way it was
governed. Administrative reforms
were designed to make British rule
more efficient, and policies were
devised to further specific economic
interests. This distorted Indian
priorities and exacerbated the
unevenness of India's economic and
political development. As a result,
the regions most affected by British
rule were those that sported the
earliest nationalist movements and
were also those that experienced
the greatest social unrest. Provincial
and district boundaries were
continually being reviewed in order
to ease the task of administering
them, but boundary changes
affected the structure of local and
provincial policies and altered
existing patterns of social order; the
partition and repartition of Bengal
proved enormously controversial.
Over 600 princely states survived
until the end of British rule. The
British retained direct relations
with the largest of these, but
grouped the majority of smaller
ones into a number of Agencies.

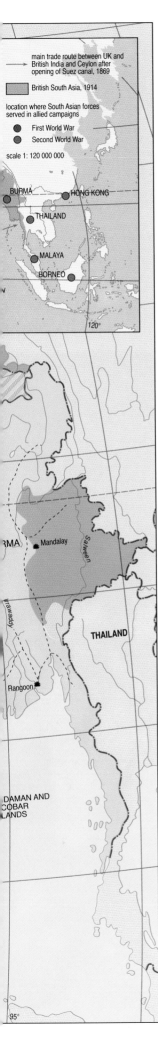

transferred from Calcutta to the traditional seat of Indian empire at Delhi. Furthermore, Bengal – which had been divided into two by Curzon in 1905 in the interests of administrative efficiency – would be reconstituted as a single province with its own governor, a concession to Bengali nationalists who had bitterly opposed the partition. Their cause had been taken up by Congress leaders, who in the fervor of the moment adopted as their anthem the Bengali poem *"Bande Mataram"* ("Hail to the Mother"), set to music by Rabindranath Tagore (1861–1941), the great Bengali poet and social reformer.

To some degree, however, the *durbar* was already a hollow gesture. For by the end of World War I, India's position in relation to Britain and within the British empire had altered. In the economic sphere, shifts in the pattern of international trade meant that India began to decline in importance as a market for British goods. By the late 1930s it was exporting more to Britain than it imported. British investment in India fell, and more and more British firms began to take Indian managers on board or be amalgamated with Indian enterprises. Indian-owned concerns such as the massive Tata Iron and Steel Company now outstripped them in economic importance. The growing disengagement of the British and the Indian economies was reflected in the establishment of the Reserve Bank of India in 1935, which gave Delhi a greater voice in determining the value of the rupee against the pound.

The people of India had made a major contribution to the conflict in Europe: over 1,200,000 men had fought in the Indian army, which had been deployed as far away as Mesopotamia and the western front. In the age of the tank and the airplane, however, the pride of the Indian army was still its cavalry regiments. As a fighting force it was ill-equipped for modern warfare. The point was clearly made by successive viceroys that if the Indian army was to continue to have an imperial role, it had to be reorganized and re-equipped, but Delhi was insistent that it should be the empire, and not India, that paid for any such improvements. The continuing failure to invest in new technology restricted the effectiveness of the Indian army to an order-keeping force. The ties of empire were loosening in other ways as well. India was no longer seen as a place of advancement by young Britons in search of employment. By the mid 1920s the government was expressing its concern over the dearth of British candidates for entry into the Indian civil service, and by 1945 fewer than 500 British senior civil servants and 200 British police remained in service in the entire subcontinent.

A widening of opposition

Indian political interests were also becoming more formidable. Half a century of economic growth in places like Punjab, Gujarat, the Andhra deltas (where the area planted for rice multiplied), the western districts of the United Provinces and parts of Tamil Nadu had thrown up classes of farmers engaged in cash-cropping and participating in the market place. Industrial development, though slow and patchy, was not negligible as Indian bankers and industrialists responded to new market demands from inside and outside the subcontinent. Local enterprise and the skilled deployment of indigenous capital helped to make Bombay city one of the leading textile producers of the world. The economy overheated during the war years and social dislocation and disorder followed. There were new

demands for reform, and political agitation grew better organized and more widespread. Much of this was easily contained, but in Punjab matters got badly out of hand and government forces reacted violently to demonstrations in the cities. Particularly appalling were excesses committed in 1919 in Amritsar where, during a period of martial law, soldiers opened fire on a protest gathering of unarmed civilians in the Jallianalala Bagh. At least 400 were killed and many more wounded. Political leaders of every persuasion used the massacre to undermine the legitimacy of British rule.

In the tradition of Indian government, however, alongside violent repression the British also turned to the path of reform, as much to strengthen their political position as to make concessions to Indians. The Montagu-Chelmsford reforms contained in the Government of India Act of 1919 sought to meet pressing demands for government action by increasing the autonomy of the provincial legislative councils and opening them to wider Indian representation. Enfranchisement continued to be based on property and education, but the number of people entitled to vote in provincial elections was increased to 5 million. As always, the thinking behind the government's constitutional reforms was that Indians could not be trusted to have views on imperial matters or on internal security. Instead, their political energies were to be diverted into policy-making decisions on such matters as irrigation, education, or the provision of clean drinking water and street-lighting. However, the groups that involved themselves in government tended to represent the most powerful and dynamic Indian social and economic interests. Such people were able to turn the situation to their own advantage, pressing for further reform and greater influence in serious decision-making as the price for giving their support to the maintenance of effective government.

Economic growth in the years after World War I continued to be dismally low and patchy. Inadequate though it was, however, it nevertheless led to a marked rise in literacy, particularly in Indian languages, and fostered a heightened cultural and political awareness. Though the Indian National Congress and the Muslim League came to dominate the Indian political debate, a number of smaller parties had extensive influence among particular sections of the population. These included the Hindu Mahasabha, representing a new conservative Hindu communal interest, a plethora of socialist parties, and the Communist Party of India. Some political parties such as the Unionist Party in Punjab or the Justice Party in Madras represented pragmatic alliances of regional elites anxious to capture and possess provincial power. Outside the scope of the larger parties were working-class organizations that found their support in Bombay's textile mills and Calcutta's jute factories. In many cases, the desire for major political reform was mixed with passionate religious and cultural beliefs, often of a narrow kind. Movements of social uplift and of caste organization also flourished. Though many of these organizations brought sections of the population together on a new and wider basis and gave support and hope to many in the manifold struggles for existence, their social, religious or cultural exclusivity sometimes had the effect of sharpening communal antipathies. Intolerant of any apparent willingness to compromise ideals and interests, they did not fit easily into the pragmatic broader alliances of the main parties.

THE PAST

Mohandas Karamchand Gandhi (1869–1948)

The Indian National Congress undoubtedly owed much of its success after 1920 to the brilliant leadership provided by Mohandas Karamchand Gandhi, and to his ability to bring and keep together the diversity of interests demanding a say in Indian politics. Born in Porbander, in the Kathiawar peninsula in Gujarat, Gandhi came from a devout, well-to-do business-caste family: for three generations the menfolk had been in public service and had provided several of the Kathiawar states with prime ministers. This part of Gujarat had long been the center of reforming and synthesizing movements within the Hindu and Jain traditions, and mutual tolerance existed between its communities, including Muslims. The region had experienced considerable economic growth in the 19th century, with the result that standards of living and literacy had increased, fostering a revival of Gujarati religion and culture. British rule was very distant and western culture had made little impact.

Gandhi was the youngest of four children. He seems to have been greatly indulged by his parents, and much was expected of him. In 1887 his family sent him to England to study law. On his return to India in 1890, Gandhi had difficulty in settling down. He mishandled his first court appearance in Bombay, and retired to a provincial backwater. Even this did not work out well, and so in 1894 he accepted an assignment in South Africa, where he remained for 20 years – a period of time that established him as a social reformer and politician of the first rank. It was while he was in South Africa that Gandhi set up his first experiments in communal living and began to work out a complex set of beliefs and practices relating to self-control, suffering, and non-violence.

What threw Gandhi into active politics was the racialist, anti-Indian policies of the South African authorities. Despairing at the way in which his compatriots seemed willing to lie down under the insults offered to them by the government, he campaigned vigorously to change things. He wrote letters and articles and carried the campaign abroad to England and

India: the Indian National Congress took up the plight of Indians in South Africa as one of its permanent causes. When, in 1908, the authorities passed a law requiring Indians to carry passes, Gandhi organized a demonstration in a mosque in Johannesburg when 2,000 people made a communal bonfire out of their registration cards. Later, in 1913, he conducted a mass walk of men, women and children from Transvaal to Natal, thus breaking the law that banned Indians from traveling between states. In both these cases the authorities were informed well in advance of what was going to happen. However they responded, they were bound to put themselves in the wrong: if ignored, the demonstrators would have carried their point; if force were used to break up a non-violent demonstration, the government's moral authority would have been severely undermined. It was a tactic that Gandhi was to use on more than one occasion in India, with devastating effect.

In 1914 Gandhi, now nearly 45 years old, returned to India. Though his early political experience was in South Africa, the distinctive ideology he had developed was firmly rooted in his Gujarati background: his guiding ideas about non-violence and social responsibility came from a radical reworking of the Hindu and Jain traditions of his homeland. He approached the problems of creating unity from the rich diversity of India partly from the position of one whose own background drew upon a range of Indian traditions, and partly as an outsider. Both his childhood in Gujarat and his experience in South Africa persuaded him that Islam could be assimilated within Indian civilization. Gandhi was particularly adept at promoting general ideas that were non-divisive because they could be read with many meanings, and he was skillful in creating a vocabulary and symbols for the nationalist movement that could rally the masses. In this way, he broadened support for the Congress and gave what was in essence a secular political movement a distinctive Indian character.

Gandhi and the Congress

Gandhi proved himself no less adept at practical organization. The main problem facing Congress was how to unify its many disparate voices in order to confront and defeat the British. It was Gandhi who drew up the new constitution that was adopted by the Congress at its annual meeting in December 1920. This succeeded in setting up a clear chain of command within the organization while allowing it to remain open and receptive to as wide a representation of Indian interests as possible. Anyone over 21 years of age who agreed to the aims of the Congress could be a member of it. These aims were expressed in a simple formula devised by Gandhi that gave *swaraj* (independence) as its first objective: the form of words used was ambiguous enough to be assented to by the most cautious constitutionalist as by the most extreme radical.

But the genius of the 1920 constitution was the way it created a hierarchy of committees to provide the means of control over what could otherwise have become a diverse and anarchical movement. This ascended from village to district to the provincial committees that were established in each of the main linguistic regions of India, thus providing equal opportunities for groups that had previously found it hard to work together locally in Congress affairs. The provincial committees were represented on, and were subordinate to, an All-India Congress committee – a

Left Bengali literature and art boasts a rich tradition of satirizing the Indian intellectual caught between east and west. Gaganendranath Tagore (1867–1938), along with his distinguished brothers Abanindranath and Samarendranath, nephews of Rabindranath Tagore, was one of the most individual and influential members of the New School of Indian painting that came to prominence after the 1890s. Gaganendranath experimented creatively with various forms of Indian and Japanese art and, most strikingly, in the early 1920s with prisms, cubes and refracted planes of light. From 1915 he worked on a lively set of caricatures, of which this "Confusion of Ideas" is one. They bitingly satirized the hypocrisies and dissipation of his own society.

body of some 350 people. All policy-making initiatives and day-to-day executive powers were conceded to an inner cabinet, the Congress Working Committee. Though Gandhi was not for most of the time a member of this committee, he greatly influenced its workings. It gradually took charge of Congress affairs and handled its political negotiations with the British and with other Indian parties. The Congress drew its strength from the fact that it was an alliance of the most dynamic of India's regional, social and cultural groupings. Its greatest support and most of its resources were drawn from the most economically advanced provinces: Gujarat, Bombay, the United Provinces and Bihar, some groupings within Bengal and Calcutta, Madras and the Andhra deltas. In terms of social support, it was an alliance of industrialists, merchants and bankers, some land-owners, upper tenants and prosperous cultivators, lawyers, teachers and students. In cultural terms, it embraced those whose Gandhian nationalism was inspired by love of the vernacular literatures and cultures, and by worship of the gods through *bhakti* cults or through broad-based reforming and synthesizing movements. As such, it was also acceptable to those influenced by English education and by the broader international currents of secular intellectual movements. It appealed to ritually respectable people who idealized the simple life and were vegetarian by conviction as well as by habit. This cultural synthesis found ample room for the large numbers of Muslims who did not feel that their allegiance to Islam was threatened by the allegiance they gave to India.

To begin with, those most closely associated with Gandhi in the Congress included some of those who had been fighting longest for Indian nationalism, such as Motilal Nehru (1861–1931) and Madan Mohan Malaviya (1861–1946) from the United Provinces and Chittaranjan Das (1870–1925) from Bengal. As death took its toll of the old political establishment, a new generation of leaders arose who – however acute their differences – were content to accept Gandhi's lead. Prominent among this group was Jawaharlal Nehru (1889-1964) who became Congress President in 1936; later, as the statesman best able to maintain unity

Below To bring the government to the negotiating table in the late 1920s, Congress determined to organize a campaign of civil disobedience, to be led by Gandhi. In 1930 he announced that he would defy the salt monopoly laws by walking from his ashram at Ahmadabad to Dandi, where he would illegally make salt by evaporating seawater on the shore. Gandhi's every move was given great publicity, and at first the government ignored the march. But once the scale of support for it became clear, the government lost its nerve and the peaceful demonstration ended in violence and arrests. Gandhi is seen here leaving the Sabarmati ashram at the start of his march to the sea.

within Indian nationalism, he assumed the role of Gandhi's heir-apparent. Also influential were Chakravarti Rajagopalachari (1879–1972), a lawyer from Madras; Rajendra Prasad (1884–1963), a lawyer from Bihar; Abul Kalam Azad (1883–1958), an Islamic scholar from Bengal; and Sardar Vallabhbhai Patel (1875–1950), a lawyer with farming connections from Gujarat. All these men went on to hold high office in independent India. Gandhi's influence was greater at some times than at others, and toward the end of his life he seemed to be becoming increasingly isolated from the main stream of things.

The Congress's foremost aim in the 1920s was to force concessions from the British. Gandhi chose the issues on which he was prepared to fight carefully; his campaigns were designed to point up the fundamental injustice and immorality of foreign imperial rule. As an instance of this, he embraced the pan-Islamic Khilafat movement that had grown up among Indian Muslims angry at the dismemberment of the Ottoman empire under the terms of the Treaty of Sèvres (1920). He hoped that championship of the Khilafat cause would forge bonds between Hindus and Muslims, and it was one of the issues that occasioned Congress's policy of non-cooperation with the government in 1920. The campaign included non-participation in elections, withdrawal from government law courts and schools, and a boycott of British-made goods, but it spiralled out of control and in 1922 Gandhi called for it to end, following a violent attack against a police station. Though unsuccessful in its declared aim to achieve *swaraj* within a year, non-cooperation marked a new milestone in India's political development.

In 1927 the British decided to review the working of the government of India and appointed a commission under the chairmanship of Sir John Simon (1873–1954). To the outrage of the Congress, no Indian was appointed to serve on it. Under the guidance of Motilal Nehru, Congress devised a new Indian constitution for India, and demanded from the British full Dominion status – that is, constitutional equality within the empire with Canada, Australia, New Zealand and South Africa, amounting in effect to self-rule – by December 1929. Failure to reach agreement on these issues with the viceroy, Lord Irwin (1881–1959) caused Gandhi to launch the Congress on a new campaign of civil disobedience. In March 1930 he led a well-publicized march from Ahmadabad in Gujarat to Dandi on the coast, where he symbolically broke the law by making a pan of salt from the sea. The government broke up the march by using violence against unarmed men and women – a fact the nationalist press turned to great advantage.

For the next four and a half years the Congress and the government were locked in conflict and negotiation as the terms of what became the 1935 Government of India Act were hammered out. At the center of the debate was the question of the relationship between central government and the provinces in a future constitution, and whether, and to what extent, communal safeguards should be extended to significant minorities – Muslims in particular, but also such groups as Sikhs, the aboriginal tribes, Anglo-Indians and so-called untouchables. The Congress and the British were both agreed that India should be governed as a unitary state. Sheer size, however, dictated that it should have some form of federal structure. But there were strongly felt differences on where power should ultimately lie.

Left Though he was born of a mercantile family in Karachi, Muhammad Ali Jinnah moved to Bombay where he became one of the most brilliant members of the bar in the early years of the century. A great liberal and constitutionalist, he supported the early Indian National Congress and then the All-India Muslim League. He came into his own as a political leader in the late 1930s when he gave coherence and purpose to the Muslim League and made articulate the demand for Pakistan. The Pakistan movement was seen by some as representing a religious interest, but for Jinnah what mattered was the adequate protection of minorities. By displaying consummate skill in negotiations in 1946 and 1947, Jinnah earned for himself the title "Qaid-i-Azam" or Founder of the Nation, and became the first Governor-General of the independent state of Pakistan.

The position of the quasi-independent Indian princes (who numbered nearly 600, all standing in separate and varying legal relationship to the British government) was also coming to be seen as a serious problem in the creation of a new India. Their scattered territories covered some two-fifths of the subcontinent and included between a fifth and a quarter of the total population. Though a few had steered their states toward some form of representative government, the vast majority still ruled as autocrats. The 1935 Government of India Act handed government in the provinces over to ministries and envisaged the creation of a future federation (the introduction of which, however, would be dependent on the willing accession of one-half of the princely states). Congress condemned it, but nevertheless took part in the elections held in the winter of 1936–7 under the new constitution, winning convincing victories and forming ministries in eight of the eleven provinces.

Wartime politics

By 1939, no British politician seriously questioned that India should become more independent. A new realism about Britain's economic and political strength, coupled with demands from the British electorate for a greater part of public resources to be allocated to healthcare and education, had caused a reassessment of imperial policy. Within the subcontinent, Indians held key offices in the administration, and Indian politicians effectively determined government policies in the provinces. But the outbreak of war ended for the time being further discussions about what form independence should take, how it was to be achieved, and within what timescale.

In some respects, British rule in India during World War II was outstandingly successful. Despite opposi-

Above From 1946 onward, as relations between Hindus and Muslims deteriorated, Gandhi devoted himself to the cause of communal harmony, but seemed increasingly ineffective. He argued strongly against partition and was greatly distressed by the violence that accompanied it. As part of his attempt to bring an end to intercommunal hatred he moved to Delhi where he held daily prayer meetings. On 30 January 1948, as he was walking to his daily prayer meeting, he was shot and killed by Nathuram Godse, a young member of the militant Hindu Rashtyia Sewak Sangh, who believed that Gandhi was too conciliatory toward Muslims. Gandhi is seen here with his supporters shortly before his death.

tion by some Indian politicians, India was brought fully into the war effort. Over 2 million Indians were recruited into the army, many of them from the south and other areas that had not traditionally supplied soldiers, and massive resources were devoted to their support. In an attempt to deal with the social and economic repercussions of mobilizing for war, there was government intervention on an unprecedented scale. Some areas of the economy boomed, but there were also serious shortages, and clumsy intervention may have exacerbated rather than helped to alleviate the effects of terrible famine in Bengal in 1943.

By May 1942 the Japanese advance had reached the Assam-Burma border. Following the collapse of political negotiations between the British and the Congress leadership, Gandhi launched the "Quit India" campaign, demanding Britain's immediate withdrawal so that Indians could be left to deal with the threat of Japanese invasion by non-violent means. After calling for a mass movement of non-cooperation, Gandhi and other Congress leaders were arrested. The government had little difficulty in quelling further resistance, and it was able to find political allies to keep the machinery going, or to do without the participation of politicians at all. Lord Linlithgow (1887–1952), retiring as viceroy in 1943 after seven years of masterly political inactivity, thought that British rule could last for another 30 years: most observers knew, however, that a handover of central power could not be long deferred beyond the end of the war. But if central government was to remain a strong and effective body capable of holding India together, it mattered vitally who succeeded the British.

As the main vehicle of the nationalist movement, the Congress – particularly after its election victories of 1936-7 – appeared to have the strongest claim to

national power. But it would be strongly challenged. It did not command much support in the northwest, northeast and south. For some people it was too Hindu in its leanings, for others it was not Hindu enough. For some it was too much a party of the socially and economically privileged, for others it was too radical and socially subversive. There was concern on the British side that the untouchables, poor laborers and cultivators would be vulnerable to oppression and exploitation by the classes who imparted such vigor to Congress politics. It was not at all clear how the princely states could be integrated into an independent India against their will, but it could not survive without them. But all the other divisions of Indian society paled into insignificance beside the differences between Hindus and Muslims. It was the failure to overcome these that led to the subcontinent's partition between Muslims and non-Muslims once the British granted independence.

Jinnah and the Muslim League
Though there was a well-established separatist strand in Muslim politics, it was by no means inevitable that it should have led to partition in 1947. In the late 19th century, the call for separate Muslim political representation had been strongest in the heartland regions of the old Mughal empire – particularly the United Provinces – where Muslims were in a minority. Urban, landholding and literate Muslim groups had benefited from fighting for a protected and privileged political position in local and provincial government. But more recently it had become clear that a new constitution for India that gave special consideration to minorities would benefit Hindus and Sikhs in those regions, Punjab and Bengal, where Muslims constituted a majority of the population. Until the mid 1930s, what most Muslim politicians in Punjab and Bengal wanted was provincial self-rule with a compliant central government, allowing them to dominate virtually autonomous regions. In other parts of the subcontinent where Muslims were a tiny minority, self-interest dictated that they worked together with their neighbors and did not stress too stridently their distinctive identity or relative importance.

What brought about a change in Muslim politics was the leadership of Muhammad Ali Jinnah (1876–1948), a Karachi-born lawyer based in Bombay. He had begun his political career as an ardent Congressman, but during the 1920s and 1930s had moved across to the Muslim League. His greatest achievement was his ability to tread carefully between the conflicting opinions of Muslim politicians and to act as broker between different Muslim groups. Under his leadership from the late 1930s the Muslim League became the acknowledged representative of a particular brand of Muslim aspiration. It articulated a set of policies designed to safeguard the position of Indian Muslims. What came first was a demand that Muslims must be represented in political institutions only by Muslims. Next arose the demand that, if their concerns were to get proper attention, Muslims should be allowed additional representation beyond their mere numbers. The culmination of this line of argument was that, in order to protect their community properly, Muslims should be given an equal share of power with everyone else put together. Muslims made up only a fifth of the population, and with the development of representative and democratic institutions, the danger arose that they would become subordinate

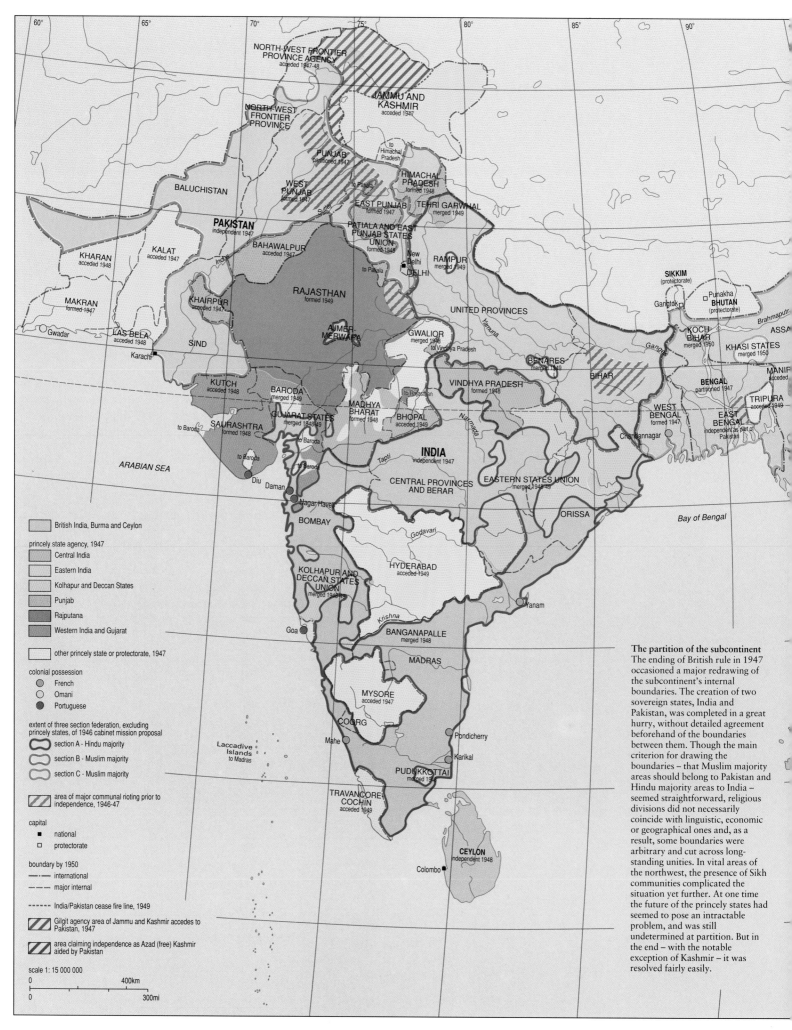

The partition of the subcontinent
The ending of British rule in 1947 occasioned a major redrawing of the subcontinent's internal boundaries. The creation of two sovereign states, India and Pakistan, was completed in a great hurry, without detailed agreement beforehand of the boundaries between them. Though the main criterion for drawing the boundaries – that Muslim majority areas should belong to Pakistan and Hindu majority areas to India – seemed straightforward, religious divisions did not necessarily coincide with linguistic, economic or geographical ones and, as a result, some boundaries were arbitrary and cut across long-standing unities. In vital areas of the northwest, the presence of Sikh communities complicated the situation yet further. At one time the future of the princely states had seemed to pose an intractable problem, and was still undetermined at partition. But in the end – with the notable exception of Kashmir – it was resolved fairly easily.

to the non-Muslim majority and be lost in Indian society at large. The logical outcome of this was the demand for a separate Muslim state.

Following the success of the Congress in the elections in 1936–7, Muslim leaders were determined to restrict any political advance nationally that might allow the Congress to consolidate its already strong hold on the government. In this, they found ready allies in the princes, other regionally based political groups, and the British. In September 1939 the Muslim League declared itself "irrevocably opposed" to any federal objective. In March 1940, meeting at Lahore, it demanded the partition of India and the grouping of those regions in which Muslims were the numerical majority into "Independent States". This became the charter for the creation of Pakistan.

The Lahore resolution did not envisage an exclusively Muslim state, but rather called for a separation of existing provinces in which Muslims were a majority, and perhaps only a scant majority at that. The question of the relationship between this new state and the rest of India was left open, and it was clear that the resolution was intended as a bargaining counter in future negotiations with the British and the Congress. But it was also a device to bring Muslim leaders in Punjab and other provinces where Muslims were a majority – areas where support for the League had never been strong – into line. Unlike the Congress, the activities of the League were not curtailed during the war, and it was able to hammer home its message that provincial autonomy would not protect the Muslim position if Congress were allowed to become the central power in national government.

Partition and its aftermath

When, with the ending of the war, the British began in earnest to work out a new political deal, it was clear that only the Congress and the League counted in their discussions: the princes, Sikhs and other special interest groups were pushed into second place. Partition was now firmly on the agenda – though the League's insistence that Muslims would not be ruled by Congress overlooked the fact that many Muslims supported the Congress. In the North Western Frontier Province, for example, it had almost unanimous backing from Muslims, and the Congress president, A. K. Azad, was himself a Muslim.

As the League continued to push its demands that Pakistan should include all those provinces and princely states where Muslims made up a sizable population, communal tempers flared. Each new outbreak of violence made it more difficult to look for a compromise, and by 1946 – when the League's case was strengthened by electoral success in winning seats in the Muslim majority provinces – some form of partition seemed inevitable. The British were clear that large numbers of Hindus and Sikhs could not be included in Pakistan against their will. This would mean excluding western Bengal, including Calcutta, and at least two-fifths of the eastern Punjab. Jinnah greeted the proposal with incredulity.

As political deadlock hardened, parts of the country lapsed into anarchy. In Punjab the presence of large numbers of well-armed demobilized soldiers contributed to the communal violence. Muslim villagers were murdered in rural Bihar, Hindus in eastern Bengal. Calcutta was subject to communal frenzy as mobs from rival neighborhoods outdid each other in the shedding of blood. The terrible upheaval at the grassroots of Indian society caught all the politicians off-balance and no longer sure of how to moderate and control their supporters.

Then, early in 1947, the British Labor prime minister Clement Attlee (1883–1967) announced to the House of Commons the government's intention to hand over power in India by "a date not later than June 1948". Britain at this stage still believed that its own best interests would be served by handing over power to a single government. However, shortly after arriving in India as viceroy in March 1947 to oversee the transfer of power, Lord Mountbatten (1900-79) concluded that the British had lost so much political control that the date set for the handover must be brought forward; furthermore, it would only be possible for the British to leave if power were transferred to two independent governments. The boundaries of their states would be determined by the religious composition of the population by district. Mountbatten made it clear to Jinnah that the League's arguments for the partition of the subcontinent as a whole had to be applied to Punjab and Bengal as well, forcing the League to accept, in Jinnah's words, a "truncated" and "motheaten" but independent Muslim state.

India and Pakistan accordingly came into being as separate and sovereign nations at midnight on 12 August 1947. The boundaries of the new states were established in the following months, often at the cost of geographic, economic or linguistic integrity. The partition of Bengal, for example, placed the eastern, largely Muslim, sector in East Pakistan, while the predominantly Hindu areas in the west, including Calcutta, became the Indian province of West Bengal. This arrangement overrode the cultural frontiers of the Bengali language. Moreover, the jute-growing lands of east Bengal were detached from the industry's manufacturing and exporting centers located in and around Calcutta, causing severe disruption and loss of trade for a number of years until the east developed new processing facilities and the west began to grow jute for itself. The division of Punjab cut across a delicately integrated economy that straddled the whole of the northwest; it left long-lasting differences about water management of the rivers that cross from one country to the other.

It is impossible to determine the exact number of those who lost their lives in the political upheaval and communal violence of the years between 1946 and 1948, but it was certainly very large, perhaps well in excess of 500,000. Between 12 and 14 million were made homeless, about half of this number fleeing as refugees from Pakistan to India, the rest making the journey the other way. Other groups, not immediately part of the Hindu-Muslim divide, were caught up in the turmoil: the Sikhs, clustered in riot-torn districts in central Punjab, fared particularly badly.

The great majority of the princes were persuaded to merge their states with India, though a number of Muslim states in the northwest naturally adhered to Pakistan. In Kashmir, over 90 percent of the population was Muslim though the ruler was Hindu. After a failed bid for independence, he agreed to link his state with India. A similar situation existed in the large central state of Hyderabad, where the Muslim Nizam ruled a predominantly Hindu population of 16 million. He attempted to hold out against India, but in 1948 was forced to accede on the same terms as the other princely states. His state was later divided up among its neighbors.

The British legacy

In many ways, the British left a more ambivalent and ambiguous imprint on the peoples of the Indian subcontinent than earlier rulers had done. Certainly, in broad cultural terms their legacy was weaker – there was virtually no increase in the proportion of the population subscribing to their religion, and only a tiny minority were literate in their language. Ironically, the proportion of Indians knowing English has more than doubled in the half century since the ending of British rule – testifying more to the international importance of English as the medium of science, technology and American culture than to its being the language of the British overlord.

Nonetheless, promotion by the British of education in English, with its emphasis on liberal rather than vocational values, gave a particular twist to the general development of literacy in India. Lack of inclination, coupled with shortage of funds, meant a relative neglect of primary education and of education for both boys and girls in modern Indian languages. Tech-

nical schools also had to fight hard for recognition and resources. Consequently, India developed an educational system that could boast some of the best universities and research institutions in the world but which had made little impact on general levels of literacy. It was a system that prized English-language knowledge above others, and that produced graduates mainly suited for employment in government service or the professions, rather than men and women equipped with basic literacy skills for the needs of everyday life.

A further consequence was the way in which Indians increasingly considered their cultures, languages, literatures, religions and arts in relation to those of the politically and economically dominant West. There was some eagerness to take advantage of new scientific and technical knowledge, or to give superior place to western fashions. Inevitably, familiarity with western intellectual trends, particularly in social and political theory, had an effect on Indian thinking. But for the main part it prompted a self-conscious search for

Above This striking image of a refugee camp at Kurukshetra in northern India was taken by the French photographer Henri Cartier-Bresson. He has captured both the distress and the inherent human dignity of the millions of people deprived of home and livelihood by the upheaval of partition.

indigenous values. A discovery began of Indian religion, philosophy, literature, folk-tale and history, spread first through the publishing press and then more forcefully and effectively by means of cinema, radio and television. Indian writers invested modern literary forms with indigenous content. Painters and architects defined a new aesthetic by injecting local forms into international movements, or by explicitly rejecting foreign values in favor of native ones. Such developments, however, were not uniquely Indian: similar debates about what was new and what was old, what was indigenous and what was foreign in the arts and literature were taking place across the world.

Undoubtedly, the colonial experience decisively shaped the economy and politics of the subcontinent, setting it on a course that has proved difficult to change and is only now, half a century later, beginning to be altered. While some of these changes might have occurred whether or not India had been governed by the British, the fact remains that it was under British rule that they took place. The British found the subcontinent, as it remains today, an overwhelmingly agrarian society. By and large, its rural peoples lived remote from each other – until fairly recently virtually nine-tenths of the population stayed put in the district in which they were born and had only the vaguest ideas about the other inhabitants of the subcontinent. It is true that in previous centuries and under previous rulers there had been interconnections of trade, belief

and pilgrimage – even sometimes of administration and political order – but the British acted as if India were a single place, something their predecessors had never done.

Across India, there were countless variations in the way local societies were structured and the land was worked. Nevertheless, the overwhelming pattern was one of small-scale peasant production. In the last century and a half the trend toward intensive cultivation and the fragmentation of properties has seen many of the oldest and richest agrarian regions of the subcontinent, whose wealth underpinned the glories of past empires – parts of the central Gangetic plains, Bihar and some of Bengal, for example – transformed into distressed and impoverished districts. Population growth since the later 19th century, and especially from the 1920s onward, led to a rapid expansion of settlement in these areas, disrupting the often delicate balances between areas of jungle, mountain and plain, between nomadic pastoralist, hunter and settled villager, between countryside and town, without always providing new agrarian wealth in compensation.

In other regions – parts of Punjab, some of the coastal regions and some areas of the Gangetic plain – investment in agriculture intensified and cropping became more specialized. This brought into being a new type of farmer who, responding to commercial forces, was able to operate at higher levels of prosperity than mere subsistence. But these developments,

Right This girls' school in Calcutta was photographed by the British designer and photographer Cecil Beaton (1904–80) who worked as an official photographer in India and China for seven months in 1944. These girls, daughters of the urbanized Bengali middle class, were exceptional in receiving an education. Under British rule, the education syllabus concentrated on the humanities, with the aim of producing civil servants and clerks, and excessive emphasis was given to the passing of examinations. Boys were much more likely to benefit than girls and schools were concentrated in the towns, especially Calcutta, Bombay and Madras. Despite the enormous increase in education at all levels since the 1950s, there is still great disparity between urban and rural areas, and lower priority is given to the education of girls, particularly in rural areas.

Indian Dress

In general terms, the subcontinent's eastern and southern regions have tended to retain the classical styles of indigenous draped costume, while the north and west have adopted the tailored garments of a succession of invading rulers from the Kushans to the Muslim dynasties. Tailored clothing extended its influence in the region after the consolidation of Muslim power in the north. Initially the sewn clothing of the Muslim rulers contrasted with the bare-chested, bare-headed Hindus who wore a single wrapped waist garment (*dhoti*) and scarf (*uttariya*). Gradually the two traditions influenced each other, particularly at the higher levels of society, but religion, occupation and context of use continued to affect styles of dress. In the later period of British rule (19th to early 20th centuries) western styles began to influence men's dress. Local rulers, emulating the British, incorporated features of military costume in their dress and adopted tight, front-buttoning coats, riding breeches and western-style shoes but reverted to "traditional" courtly dress for ceremonial. By the mid 20th century the collared, rather than the round-necked (*kurta*) or side-fastening short coat (*angarkhi*), was increasingly worn by urban men with the wrapped lower garment (*dhoti* or *lungi*). In the towns and cities of India today most children and middle-class men wear western dress, though women continue to wear the wrapped *sari*, or the long shirt (*qamiz*) or dress over trousers. Tribal communities remained outside the mainstream of Hindu, Muslim or western influence until recently, and religious ascetics maintained their own traditions of clothing and bodily decoration.

Below Headwear may indicate a man's home town, district, occupation or community. This man, possibly from the Maratha clan who ruled in Tanjore (Thanjavur) in the 17th and 18th centuries, wears a variation of the Maratha turban, and a short *angarkhi* with *dhoti* and shawl.

Left The early Mughal emperors, particularly Akbar, encouraged Hindu-Muslim synthesis in all its forms. Akbar, having drawn the powerful Rajput princes into his empire by alliance or conquest, adopted some of their fashions, notably the flat Rajput turban (*pag*), worn here by the emperor Jahangir. The quintessentially Mughal garment, the *jama* (Persian: garment, robe, vest, gown, coat, wrapper) – a side-fastening coat with tight body, high waist and flared skirt reaching to the knees or below – worn with the tight *churidar pajama*, gathered at the ankles, became the required fashion for both Muslims and Hindus at the Mughal court.

Below left Women's dress in the paintings of the early Muslim period, and in this early 18th-century painting from Kulu in the Punjab hills, is close to present-day western Indian usage: a short bodice, a large, light cloth that covers the head and falls down the back (*orhni*), and a skirt-like garment wrapped around the waist and pleated at the front. By the 18th century the dress of the ruling classes in northern India, both Muslim and Hindu, was a mixture of the sewn and the wrapped – draped shawls, turbans and sashes accompanied the sleeved coat worn by men.

Below These Hindu priests are wearing their *dhotis* and *uttariya* in styles similar to those on sculptures dating from the 1st century AD, which show both men and women in single draped garments tied around the hips. Hindu texts exhort the male householder to wear clean white clothes, and an upper and lower garment – though, if poor, the sacred thread on his upper body will suffice. Knowledge of sewing was present in India from an early date, but climate together with Hindu beliefs and prescriptions reinforced the preference for the unsewn garment.

Above The *sari* – a single large cloth covering both the upper and lower body – was being worn in eastern India by the 10th century: before then women wore separate upper garments. Today the sari is worn, usually with a bodice, in the Gangetic plain, eastern, central and southern India, and in Sri Lanka. The style of tying often varies between districts and from community to community within a region, as in Madhya Pradesh, where the styles shown *center* and *right* are worn. A standardized style now predominates in the cities (*left*).

once set in train, were not encouraged – and indeed were often held in check – by the short-term needs of the British raj to maintain its authority. Though the British continually sought ways of attracting investment and of developing the Indian economy, they shrank from promoting too much change. British policy kept India a land of smallholders, and a pernicious effect of this – though doubtless one that was not intended – was to place a dead hand on economic initiative. As a result, India entered the second half of the 20th century with a relatively stagnant rural economy, trapped in proverty and without sufficient resilience either to respond to market opportunities or to withstand the shocks delivered to too rigid an economic and social structure.

The same was true of industry. The middle years of the 19th century were full of promise as Indian entrepreneurs developed textile manufacturing and the great port cities opened up as centers of diversifying and expanding economic opportunity. But India's emerging industrialists were forced to concentrate their efforts on supplying the domestic market, which lacked long-term potential to support growth. Commercial, industrial and financial interests became overly dependent on government intervention and regulation to protect British manufactures and services. By the first decade of the 20th century, exports – other than a few selected primary products – did not come high on India's economic agenda, and its domestic economy failed to fuel significant growth. The rapid increase in urban populations from the mid 20th century onward has more to do with the strength of economic pressures driving people away from the land than with the drawing power of new opportunities for wealth in the cities.

The political legacy of the British was greater still. The subcontinent – brought, however lightly, under one government beneath their rule – was divided into two states on their departure, and these, because of the very circumstances of their coming into being, were ranged in hostility toward each other, with very great consequences for the political and economic development of both. Furthermore, the British raj had been at heart a despotism, albeit one massively constrained in practice, in which the executive powers of government and the authority of its bureaucracy had always outweighed the popular constitutional checks upon them. Its operations encouraged sectarianism.

British policies were predicated on the existence within India of innumerable but definite social or communal interests, which were represented within the political system. Though some of these interests may not have had a clear-cut existence in reality, once they became part of the government's thinking people responded to them as if they did, and banded together for political reasons on grounds of region, kin, caste, language or religion, either to support the government's policies or to force it to change its mind. The government, then perceiving that it sat on a heaving mass of confused and competing groups, increased the trend toward the communal organization of politics by attempting to balance interests and promote social justice. Groups seen as becoming too powerful would be reined back, particularly if they were in receipt of public patronage or occupied key positions within the governmental structure. At other times, deliberate attempts would be made to advance the backward. Bankers would be prevented from possessing the fields of indebted farmers, places would be reserved in

Music, Dance and Drama

The Bombay film industry's inclusion of music and dance in all its popular films is in keeping with India's performing traditions and with an aesthetic philosophy that asserts the unity of all artistic forms. The *Natyasastra*, believed to have been written before the 3rd century AD, deals with the theory and practice of music as part of a study of drama. Speech was the source of everything, and distinctive systems of chanting in set musical patterns were elaborated to ensure the correct oral transmission of religious texts. All instruments imitated the human voice, and a sophisticated system of modal music developed. The importance of rhythmic sound, the other element in Indian music, is reflected in the myth of Shiva as Nataraj, the lord of the dance, who plays the drum (*damru*) and then performs his dance of creation. Over time a variety of stringed, wind and percussion instruments and a considerable range of musical practice came into being. The music of north and the south grew distinct, but both traditions were sustained by a system of family-based aural transmission passed from master to disciple, from father to son.

Indian drama has traditionally dealt with themes from Hindu mythology. Classical dramatists of the Gupta period created historical plays, and folk drama continues to incorporate incidents of local history and contemporary issues. But since drama, like the other arts, was intended to blend the audience's emotions harmoniously, forms of tragedy never developed. Temples, princes and lesser landowners all patronized music, dance and drama. Night-long performances of regional and traditional dramas were given to local audiences by itinerant performers at festival times. Cinema and television still draw on these familiar themes and styles of performance today.

Left The *sitar*, the best-known Indian instrument abroad, is also the most popular stringed instrument among north Indian musicians. Originating in the 13th century, its development reflects the influence of western and central Asian music on India. "*Seh-tar*" means "three-stringed" in Persian, but it now has six or seven main strings, four of which are played with a plectrum, while two or three act as drone or rhythm. A seasoned gourd serves as the *sitar*'s resonating chamber.

Right Life-cycle rites are celebrated with music throughout the subcontinent. Here the emperor Akbar's musicians mark the birth of his first son Salim (later the emperor Jahangir) in 1569. Akbar, like other Muslim and Hindu rulers of the time, patronized musicians of different traditions. The most famous was the singer Miyan Tansen, a brahmin from Gwalior adopted by a Muslim fakir who trained under a famous Hindu in Brindaban. Tansen's music spanned the two religious traditions, a pattern followed by subsequent Muslim musicians.

Right The *Natyasastra* associated melody archetypes with particular emotional states, and these were subsequently elaborated into complex categorizations of *ragas* – combinations of notes and melody motifs – which form the basis of a number of compositions. They later gave rise to specific pictorial motifs. The earliest known *ragamala* (garlands of melodies) illustrations date to c.1500. Miniatures representing the musical modes were popular in the Punjab hill states from the late 17th century onward. This *ragamala* painting, from Kulu c.1710, of a prince feeding pigeons, illustrates the musical mode *Kuntala raga*.

Above Ram Gopal was the first performer to bring classical dance to the west. Photographed by Cecil Beaton in the 1940s, he dances *Bharata Natyam*, originally a temple dance of Tamil Nadu. Reformist zeal against "prostitution" had abolished the tradition of female temple dancers, but the male members of traditional dance communities helped revive this and other temple dances, thereby giving them "classical" status and respectability. Indian dance distinguishes between pure dance (*nrtta*), based on melody and meter, and mimetic dance (*nritya* or *abhinaya*), where the sung poetic line is interpreted through mime using hand gestures.

government service for those seen to be particularly disadvantaged in society. At one level British rule had united the peoples of the subcontinent as never before, but it had also divided them as never before into antagonistic groups competing for survival.

Sri Lanka: western impact and modern development

When the British assumed control of Sri Lanka's trading ports at the end of the 18th century European influence in the island (then known as Ceylon) did not extend beyond the Jaffna peninsula in the north and the coastal regions. However, following the conquest of the kingdom of Kandy (1817–18), the British established a complete hold on the island, and the interior was opened up for the growing of coffee. By World War I, Sri Lanka's economy had come to be dominated by plantations, though tea, rubber and coconuts had replaced coffee as the main crops. The plantations (particularly tea and rubber) were managed by British interests who also controlled the processing, shipping and international marketing of the crops. The earlier coffee plantations had attracted migrant labor, mainly from south India, to harvest the crop, but the tea and rubber plantations required year-round cultivators. A new wave of Tamil workers settled permanently in Sri Lanka, adding to those already long established in the north of the island.

By the 20th century Tamils had come to be seen as having disproportionate advantages, both in respect of English-language education and of their prominence in entrepreneurial activity. As elsewhere in the subcontinent, the British at first encouraged change, but later came to be more solicitous of the interests of conservative elite groups and of quiescent majorities who could be balanced against vocal minorities pressing for further reform. While maintaining the notion of the strict religious neutrality of the state, they began to afford judicious patronage to the Sinhalese and Buddhist majority. By the 1920s, Tamil politicians were already arguing for the need to protect their minority community.

Sri Lanka was not, however, part of the Indian empire, but was a Crown Colony, separately administered by the Colonial Office. Political change took a very different route here than on the mainland. Though local demands for reform were moderate, Sri Lanka also had an active trades union movement and there were growing demands for a fair share of the island's wealth. A new constitution introduced in 1931 anticipated nationalist demands by allowing for the election of political representatives on the basis of universal suffrage. Combined with the strengthening Buddhist revival, this reform had the effect of promoting the politicization of Sri Lankan society. Throughout the 1930s and 1940s development funds were directed at extending irrigation in the island's dry zone – once the heart of Sri Lanka's agricultural wealth – and at providing other benefits (education, the provision of health care, food subsidies) for the mass of people who could now vote.

The transfer of power in Sri Lanka was consequently much more straightforward and peaceful than in the mainland. Formal independence came on 4 February 1948. Don Stephen Senanayake (1884–1952), the island's former minister for agriculture, became prime minister, and his United National Party was committed to strengthening the welfare program. But despite relative prosperity and high levels of literacy (by comparison with other Asian countries), ethnic and religious tensions existed not far below the surface. Though Senanayake tried to spread the benefits to the island's Tamil and Hindu minorities, he could not disguise the fact that 70 percent of the population were Sinhalese and 67 percent Buddhist.

The dependence of the island's economy on plantation crops made it vulnerable to fluctuations in international demand and market prices. It could not withstand inflationary pressure, which began to build up in the 1950s. Moreover, government control of the economy made it difficult to impose major structural changes. Massive unemployment exacerbated the friction between the island's religious and ethnic groupings. Dudley Shelton Senanayake (1911–71), who succeeded his father as prime minister in 1952, was unable to keep the United National Party together, and it fell victim to internal squabbling and to attacks from Leftist groups without. In 1956 a political alliance put together by Solomon Bandaranaike (1889-1959) swept to electoral victory. Bandaranaike tapped into a populist Buddhist and Sinhalese vein, and injected it with a dose of Leftist policies. Sinhalese was made the official language of the country, and the new government's unabashed pro-Sinhalese stance increased Tamil opposition. Failure, through economic restraints, to implement fully his social program led to disillusionment among his own followers. Bandaranaike was assassinated on 26 September 1959 and was succeeded by his widow Sirimavo Bandaranaike, who pursued broadly similar policies so far as language and religion were concerned, but managed to contain Tamil resistance.

The government, however, could not solve the island's economic problems. In 1964 Mrs Bandaranaike signaled a significant shift in direction when she brought the major Marxist party into her government. This did not satisfy the electorate, and in 1965 Dudley Senanayake was returned to power. He was unable to reverse government control of the economy; nor did he have much room for maneuver on ethnic and religious matters. Inflation got out of hand, and continuing unemployment drove the young educated to despair. Mrs Bandaranaike regained office in 1970 and used her Left-wing support to push though a number of socialist measures, including the nationalization of the plantations and some of the island's large commercial and industrial concerns.

The decade saw the Tamil separatist movement gain ground in its demand for an independent state in the north of the island. While the Sri Lankan authorities were willing to concede greater local autonomy to the country's existing provinces, they refused to contemplate the breakaway of the Northern and Eastern provinces. The Tamil movement soon acquired a violent edge. Serious ethnic riots broke out in 1977, 1981 and 1983, and the campaign spawned an active terrorist wing – the Tamil Tigers.

Elections in 1977 brought a further shift in Sri Lankan politics. Junius Richard Jayawardene, who had succeeded Senanayake in 1973, revitalized the United National Party and moved to more explicitly free-market economic policies and a more pro-western stance in foreign affairs. The constitution was amended in 1978 to bring in a presidential structure, with safeguards for minorities. Jayawardene set about reducing state control of the economy and set up a Free Trade Zone in Colombo. This began to attract investment and create new jobs, though the bulk of these were for unskilled workers. Nonetheless, his

Above Tamil guerrillas undergoing basic training in south India, March 1986. In order to appease Tamil sentiment during the early 1980s the Indian government turned a blind eye to the existence of Tamil guerrilla training camps in south India. As the political situation in Sri Lanka deteriorated, however, the government reversed its policy and intervened in support of the Sri Lankan government against the Tamil separatist movement on the island. A direct consequence of this policy was the assassination of Rajiv Gandhi by a Tamil separatist at an election meeting in May 1991.

creating enormous problems of organization, but the regions hurriedly thrown together in 1947 had very little in common with each other except a long history of fierce provincial particularism. East Bengal, a mass of inland waterways and dispersed hamlets and villages, had always been hard to control beyond the local level, but it was part of the economy and culture of eastern India. Its peoples, though mainly Muslim, spoke Bengali. The Eastern Wing was the most populous component of the new state and – through its export of primary products – the principal earner of Pakistan's foreign exchange. Yet East Pakistanis seemed to have less than their fair share of central development funds, or of senior positions in the civil service and the armed forces. As time went on and politicians failed to reach agreement over a federal constitution for Pakistan, pressures would build up for the East to cut loose from the Western Wing.

The regions that composed West Pakistan also sat somewhat uneasily together. Under the British, the undeveloped and sparsely populated Baluchi-speaking districts of Baluchistan had consistently resisted any central government. The North-West Frontier Province, where Pushtu was spoken, had been fervently supportive of the Indian National Congress. Sind, where the inhabitants spoke mainly Sindhi with a significant Urdu-speaking minority, had long boasted a distinctive culture and history and was wary of its neighbors. All three of the smaller provinces of West Pakistan were suspicious of the relatively populous and prosperous Punjabi-speaking agriculturalists of Punjab. Significantly, Punjabis also bulked large in the civil service and the army. In addition, the new state had to absorb more than 7 million Muslims from India – it was calculated that as many as one in six of the population of West Pakistan was a refugee.

Jinnah died in September 1948, only 13 months after independence. Without a dominating political party – for those in Bengal and Punjab who had rallied behind the Muslim League in 1946–7 to ensure continuing autonomy for their regions soon abandoned it for the politics of the locality – Jinnah's successors found it hard to agree upon a constitution, to devise policies that united the component parts of the country, and to implement decisions. This was all the more serious since solution of the problems facing Pakistan – the need to cope with the influx of refugees, to build up a new economic infrastructure, to encourage investment in industry and commerce, to promote agricultural productivity while attempting to extract revenues from the countryside – could only come through state intervention on a large scale.

The new state also faced expensive problems of security. It needed to defend its boundaries with India, some of which remained in dispute. It was difficult to protect adequately East Pakistan, and in the northwest Afghanistan revived claim to territory: the 20th century had seen no final resolution to age-old disputes about control of mountain passes through which the routes ran from Central Asia to the subcontinent. More serious was the immediate dispute with India over Kashmir, itself a fragile political construct held together since 1846 by the skills of its rulers and the acceptance by the British of its usefulness as a buffer state. Following the Maharaja's decision to opt for union with India, Pathan forces, backed by the Pakistani army, invaded the state. The Indian government threw its forces into the field to defend the territory, which rapidly assumed a symbolic importance as the

economic policies began to bear fruit as the Sri Lankan economy showed signs of moving from a position of stagnation to one of growth, and in 1982 Jayawardene became the first Sri Lankan leader to be returned to office in a general election. Sri Lanka, however, continued to be troubled by high levels of unemployment, and Sinhalese-Tamil relations showed very few signs of improvement.

Pakistan: problems of nationhood

As Jinnah had foreseen, in the rush to bring about the transfer of power a barely viable state had been created in Pakistan. Partition had set p two states of unequal size, with Pakistan inheriting 17.5 percent of the assets of undivided India and a third of the armed forces. But it did not occupy contiguous territory. Not only were its two provinces, located on the northwest and the northeast of the subcontinent, separated from each other by 1,600 kilometers of hostile territory, mark of India's true secularism in politics. Military stalemate followed and a ceasefire line was brokered in 1949, giving rise to one of the most intractable problems in modern international affairs.

The financial costs for Pakistan of this first war with India were enormous; so, too, were the political repercussions. Whatever Pakistan's domestic problems, they began to take second place to the need to secure its very existence. Politicians engaged in fierce debate over such matters as the choice of a national language, the shape of the constitution, or the development of the economy, while the day-to-day affairs of government were managed by bureaucrats and, increasingly, by soldiers: the center of political power began to move toward the military headquarters at Rawalpindi. Given the vital task of defending Pakistan's frontiers, and increasingly anxious to obtain modern armaments, the Pakistani high-command became desirous of committing the country to broader post-World War II security arrangements in return for supplies and military aid. Pakistan's politicians at first fought shy of entering external alliances, but political and economic necessity dictated that by 1955 Pakistan was a member of both the Southeast Asian Treaty Organization and the Central Treaty Organization – western alliances designed to contain Soviet expansion in Southeast Asia and the Middle East. As a result Pakistan became the recipient of western, particularly American, military and economic aid.

A constitution was finally agreed in 1956, but did not last long. Continuing political instability provided the justification for a military coup. The seizure of power by General Muhammad Ayub Khan (1907–74) in October 1958 ushered in a decade or more of relative calm. Parliamentary forms of government were replaced with a new system of "basic democracy", formalized in the 1962 constitution, which attempted to create an effective central government by establishing directs links, by means of government patronage, with local councillors, who in turn served as the electorate for a presidential form of government. The experiment was not without success, particularly on the economic front. But development in the countryside exacerbated inequalities, and wealth created in the industrial and commercial sectors also tended to be concentrated in few hands. Disparity between East and West Pakistan, failure to improve Pakistan's position during the second war with India in 1965, and simmering unrest in the towns undermined Ayub's position. In March 1969 he gave way to a government head by General Agha Muhammad Yahya Khan (1917–80) in preparation for a return to civilian rule.

The breakup of Pakistan

The results of the general elections held in 1970 showed how divided Pakistan was. The Awami League, led by Sheikh Mujibur Rahman (1921–75), campaigning on a program for provincial autonomy, captured nearly every seat in East Pakistan and won an absolute majority in the National Assembly. In West Pakistan, the picture was more complicated, but the largest single group was formed by the Pakistan People's Party, led by the flamboyant populist Zulfiqar Ali Bhutto (1928–79), born into a land-owning family in Sind and educated at Berkeley and Oxford universities. It was unthinkable to the politicians, soldiers and civil servants of West Pakistan that the Awami League should form the national government. Political stalemate precipitated an uprising in East

Pakistan, and attempts to suppress it led to the third war with India as its government weighed in to support the breakaway movement. East Pakistan was established as the independent state of Bangladesh and Sheikh Mujibur, who had been jailed by the West Pakistan authorities in March 1971, was released and returned to Dhaka as prime minister in January 1972.

The breakup of Pakistan temporarily discredited the rule of soldiers and civil servants. But even in these favorable political circumstances, the Pakistan People's Party found it difficult to wield real power. Its support came overwhelmingly from Sind and Punjab (and even there it lacked solid grassroots organization). Consequently, Bhutto remained dependent on the tacit support of the military and the bureaucracy if his government was to be respected in the North-West Frontier Province and Baluchistan. He worked hard to devise a new constitution, finally promulgated in 1973, which made major concessions to the non-Punjabi provinces, but failed to implement the federal provisions of that constitution at all fully. His government resorted more and more to coercive measures to deal with mounting opposition, and his economic reforms were sweeping enough to provide him with a firm social base. Following a second electoral victory in 1977, Bhutto was accused of vote-rigging by a coalition of opposition groups. Outbreaks of violence in the towns provided the pretext for another military coup. On 5 July 1977 General Muhammad Zia-ul Haq (1924–88) imposed martial law; he became president the following year. Political parties were banned, and Bhutto was imprisoned. He was executed on murder charges on 4 April 1979.

The search for stability

The position of Zia's government was at first weak. But Pakistan's key role in Cold War power politics in western Asia meant that support for his regime was likely to come from the West, and the Soviet invasion and occupation of Afghanistan in December 1979 strengthened his hand. Zia also attempted to give legitimacy and popularity to his government by emphasizing the Islamic nature of Pakistani society, believing that a program of Islamicization, in step with his Middle East neighbors, would help forge national unity. In 1984 Zia won support for his reforms and gained another five years in office by means of a referendum. But his program was not without ambiguity and controversy. A wide range of opinion emerged about what was meant by Islamicization: the committee of scholars, jurists and *ulema* set up to look for ways to bring it into being disagreed with each other, and genuine popular support never followed the stricter interpretations of orthodoxy. Much publicity was given in 1979 to a redrawn schedule of "Islamic" punishments to be meted out for various crimes, and some changes were made in civil law. But it is debatable how rigorously the new laws were applied.

At the end of 1985, Zia announced the lifting of martial law and a return to civilian rule. Political parties were revived and Benazir Bhutto, daughter of the former premier, returned to Pakistan in April 1986 to campaign for the overthrow of the Zia government. While drawing large crowds to her rallies, she could not immediately turn her popularity to real political advantage. Serious riots in Karachi in December 1986 played again to Zia's advantage, but in May 1988 the military-political alliance that had been in place for the past three years broke down. Zia dismissed his

Above A contemporary shop sign from the tobacco bazaar in Jodhpur, Rajasthan, advertizing "King's Brand *Naswar*", an Indian snuff. Despite half a century of independence and an ancient indigenous tradition of kingship, the image of kingship chosen for this sign is the last British king of India, George VI. This is all the more remarkable in view of the fact that during the colonial period the British perpetuated the authority of the local Indian prince in Jodhpur, controlling only his external relations. This sign, from a relatively remote part of India, shows the impact of British imperialism in some ways to have been more enduring than might be expected.

State boundary changes in India since 1948 (*right*)
Having lived through the trauma of partition, the Indian government was at first reluctant to contemplate further changes to state boundaries for fear of encouraging a break-up of the new Union. By the mid 1950s, however, it was clear that some reorganization was called for on grounds of administrative convenience and to meet political demand. As far back as 1920 Gandhi had proposed a provincial alignment for Congress purposes that coincided with linguistic frontiers rather than with the administrative divisions of British rule, and this was the principle finally adopted by the republic of India for its own internal organization. The multilingual presidencies of Madras and Bombay gave way to states based on their linguistic components, and subsequently a number of other new states have been formed.

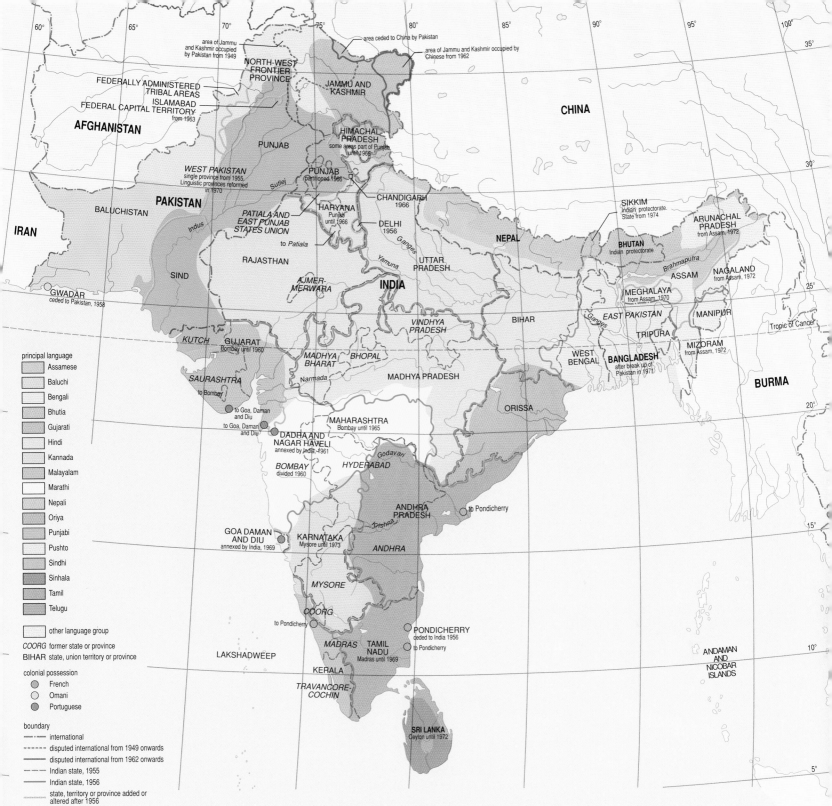

60°   65°   70°   75°   80°   85°   90°   95°   100°

area of Jammu
and Kashmir occupied
by Pakistan from 1949

area ceded to China by Pakistan

area of Jammu and Kashmir occupied by
Chinese from 1962

35°

NORTH-WEST
FRONTIER
PROVINCE

FEDERALLY ADMINISTERED
TRIBAL AREAS

ISLAMABAD
FEDERAL CAPITAL TERRITORY
from 1963

JAMMU AND
KASHMIR

CHINA

AFGHANISTAN

PUNJAB

HIMACHAL
PRADESH
some areas part of Punjab
until 1966

30°

WEST PAKISTAN
single province from 1955.
Linguistic provinces reformed
in 1970

Sutlej

PUNJAB
(partitioned 1966)

CHANDIGARH
1966

SIKKIM
Indian protectorate.
State from 1974

ARUNACHAL
PRADESH
from Assam, 1972

PAKISTAN

BALUCHISTAN

Indus

PATIALA AND
EAST PUNJAB
STATES UNION
to Patiala

HARYANA
Punjab
until 1966

DELHI
1956

BHUTAN
Indian protectorate

Brahmaputra

NAGALAND
from Assam, 1972

IRAN

NEPAL

ASSAM

SIND

RAJASTHAN

Ganges

UTTAR
PRADESH

Yamuna

MEGHALAYA
from Assam, 1970

EAST PAKISTAN

MANIPUR

GWADAR
ceded to Pakistan, 1958

AJMER-
MERWARA

INDIA

25°

KUTCH

GUJARAT
Bombay until 1960

VINDHYA
PRADESH

BIHAR

Ganges

WEST
BENGAL

TRIPURA

MIZORAM
from Assam, 1972

Tropic of Cancer

SAURASHTRA
to Bombay

to Goa, Daman
and Diu

MADHYA
BHARAT

BHOPAL

BANGLADESH
after break up of
Pakistan in 1971

BURMA

Narmada

MADHYA PRADESH

to Goa, Daman
and Diu

DADRA AND
NAGAR HAVELI
annexed by India, 1961

MAHARASHTRA
Bombay until 1965

ORISSA

20°

BOMBAY
divided 1960

HYDERABAD

Godavari

GOA DAMAN
AND DIU
annexed by India, 1969

KARNATAKA
Mysore until 1973

ANDHRA
PRADESH

to Pondicherry

Krishna

ANDHRA

15°

MYSORE

COORG

to Pondicherry

MADRAS

PONDICHERRY
ceded to India 1956

to Pondicherry

LAKSHADWEEP

TAMIL
NADU
Madras until 1969

ANDAMAN
AND
NICOBAR
ISLANDS

10°

KERALA

TRAVANCORE-
COCHIN

SRI LANKA
Ceylon until 1972

5°

principal language

- Assamese
- Baluchi
- Bengali
- Bhutia
- Gujarati
- Hindi
- Kannada
- Malayalam
- Marathi
- Nepali
- Oriya
- Punjabi
- Pushto
- Sindhi
- Sinhala
- Tamil
- Telugu

☐ other language group

COORG former state or province

BIHAR state, union territory or province

colonial possession

- ⬤ French
- ◯ Omani
- ⬤ Portuguese

boundary

- ·—·— international
- - - - - disputed international from 1949 onwards
- ———— disputed international from 1962 onwards
- — — — Indian state, 1955
- ———— Indian state, 1956
- · · · · · state, territory or province added or altered after 1956

scale 1: 17 500 000

0   400km

0   300mi

cabinet, dissolved the national and provincial assemblies, and announced new elections later in the year. These were held, despite Zia's death in a plane crash on 17 August. The Pakistan People's Party emerged as the largest group in the assembly, giving Benazir Bhutto the premiership at the age of 35.

Despite further changes of government since 1988, both at national and provincial level, Pakistani politics remained volatile. All politicians faced formidable challenges and restraints. The population had reached 114 million by 1991, and the considerable economic growth that occurred in the 1980s and early 1990s pointed up the unevenness of Pakistan's development and the diversity between its constituent units. It was difficult to set or hold national priorities that also met the particular needs of Punjab (around 56 percent of the population), Sind (23 percent), the North-West Frontier Province (13 percent) and Baluchistan (8 per-

cent). Whether military or civilian, religious or secular in form, the government still struggled to find ways of promoting sustainable and manageable economic and social development, of achieving unthreatening integration, and of providing for national security at reasonable political and economic cost.

Independent India

India inherited the bulk of the land and of the population in 1947, as well as a well-established machinery of government. This underlying geopolitical fact has meant that India is the dominant power in the region. The Indian National Congress, which had done so much to bring about the end of British imperial rule, took charge of the government and continued in power for the next two decades without serious challenge. With Jawaharlal Nehru as prime minister (an office he retained until his death in 1964), Congress set about restoring order. By 1950 a new constitution had been put in place, establishing India as a republic with a strong central government and a federal form. Elections to the national parliament (Lok Sabha; House of the People) and state legislatures were by universal suffrage.

The framework of government and the electoral dominance of the Congress Party within it ensured a high degree of political stability. But India was a huge multi-ethnic and multicultural society, and tensions were bound to arise between different parts of the country and between social and religious groups. As in earlier periods, a precarious balance was often struck between keeping India together and recognizing the strength of centrifugal forces. It was not always easy to see when central authority should be fiercely asserted in the national interest and when more accommodating, pluralist and pragmatic agreements should be encouraged. Major redrawing of state boundaries to bring them into line with the main linguistic regions was achieved without the breakup of the Indian Union that many feared would follow from making concessions to "linguistic nationalism". Early Congress governments had some success in juggling other regional and minority conflicts, usually by stressing the importance of creating "unity from diversity". But by the beginning of the 1960s it had become clear that the Congress could no longer be all things to all men. There was a sharpening of debate and factionalism within the party, and growing opposition outside it was particularly effective in capturing power both at local and at regional level.

Nehru's death in 1964 brought these underlying problems to the fore. None of his colleagues who had powerful regional bases were able to win acceptance, for that reason, as national leader. They therefore chose to succeed him Lal Bahadur Shastri (1904–66) who had served in all Nehru's cabinets since 1952 and had great experience as a political negotiator. On his death of a heart attack in Tashkent (having successfully agreed a peace treaty to end the second Indo-Pakistan war), the Congress leaders turned to Nehru's daughter, Indira Gandhi (1917–84). At a time when Indian politics were experiencing major and uncertain change, there was symbolic value in marking continuity in this way. It was also believed that, as a woman and as someone without an independent political base, she would be amenable to control by the party bosses until a more suitable leader could be found once the pending elections were out of the way.

The old guard were to be proved wrong. The Congress performed disastrously, both at national and state level, in the 1967 elections, though Indira Gandhi just held on as prime minister. Many key politicians failed to retain their seats. With her former patrons now out of parliament and with Congress out of power in many of the states, Indira Gandhi used her position as prime minister to create a new political alliance and a new base for herself. The Congress party was split and only partially reconstituted under her direct control. Over the next five years Indira Gandhi used central ministerial authority to interfere in the states and to intervene in other social disputes, attempting to create new stability within the system as a whole.

The early 1970s saw rapid fluctuations in the fortunes of state governments, and constant switches in loyalty by politicians at every level. For a while, Indira Gandhi was borne up by the popularity that followed

her successful intervention in the Bangladesh war. She introduced economic policies that, though socialist in rhetoric, actually tried to reach out to the aspiring small farmer and industrial entrepreneur by increasing subsidies and making credit cheaper. But in 1973–4 there were recurring food crises, and inflation ran out of control. There were serious disturbances in Bihar and Gujarat. The charismatic Jayaprakash Narayan (1902–79), universally respected as a true successor of Mahatma Gandhi in the field of social work, voiced criticism of government policy and gave moral authority to the various groups now seeking to bring down the government. In 1975 a petition lodged in the Allahabad High Court alleging electoral malpractice by Indira Gandhi during the 1971 election campaign found against her.

Indira Gandhi's response to this setback was swift. Believing that the opposition consisted of reactionary and unprincipled elements, she used reserve powers in the constitution to declare an Emergency; regular government was suspended and direct rule from Delhi

Above The transfer of power in India was eased to a degree by the good relationship that Lord Mountbatten, the last viceroy of India (seen on the left in this photograph by Cartier-Bresson) established with Jawaharlal Nehru (third from left), India's first prime minister. Nehru dominated the politics of the country after independence, shaping its early economic and social policies. He won wide respect for his moral approach to international relations and in the 1950s and 1960s worked to promote nonalignment (a term he originally coined), which sought to create an alternative voice in world politics free of dependence on either the western or the Communist bloc.

imposed throughout the country as was deemed necessary. Opposition politicians were imprisoned and normal political debate stifled. The press experienced unprecedented censorship, programs of sterilization were announced and enforced, especially among poorer government employees, the slums of Delhi were bulldozed, and public-sector wages frozen.

By 1977 Indira Gandhi believed her vigorous action had kept order and maintained national unity, and she felt secure enough to hold elections in March. But she had underestimated the unpopularity of her actions. Despite the short time they had to prepare and run their campaign, her opponents from both Left and Right formed a coalition, the Janata Party, that defeated her. Moraji Desai, an old and respected Gandhian politician from Gujarat, became prime minister. But though India's democratic freedoms were restored, the Janata coalition did not succeed in holding on to power – it consisted of too many diverse elements for common policies to be hammered out. Indira Gandhi achieved electoral success again in 1979, holding office until her assassination on 31 October 1984 at the hands of her Sikh bodyguards. She was succeeded by her son Rajiv (1944–91) who remained prime minister until his electoral defeat in 1989. The National Front government of V. P. Singh was unable to hold on to power for long, and elections were called in 1991. Rajiv Gandhi was assassinated by a Tamil separatist guerrilla while campaigning for office, and Congress, now led by P. V. Narasimha Rao, was returned to power. Many of these changes represented not so much the alternation of different parties as shifting alliances between the leading politicians.

Ethnic and cultural conflicts

Much of the drama and rapid changes in fortune in national politics in India stems from the fact that the government presides over a huge and diverse multicultural society. Central government policies have done little in nearly half a century to rectify imbalances between the 24 states that now compose the India Union. Reorganization of state boundaries in the 1950s and 1960s went some way toward meeting regional aspirations, but in many regions major domestic problems have arisen. In the northeast states, the use of linguistic criteria in determining boundaries has been complicated by the continuing resistance of the hill peoples to the intrusion of the outside world, and the migration of large numbers of other Indians, especially from West Bengal, into the Assam valley and Tripura.

In Punjab, the aspirations of the Sikhs, who constitute a religious as well as a linguistic group, have not been fully met, despite its reorganization into three states: Punjab, Haryana and Himachal Pradesh. The problem remains a complex one: the majority Sikh community in Punjab has not been able to establish political dominance in the state, while the tremendous economic development of the region has led to an influx of non-Punjabi-speaking, non-Sikh Indians. Between 1980 and 1984 various extremist and terrorist Sikh organizations flourished virtually unchecked, with disastrous consequences for law and order, and for Sikh-Hindu relations. The Sikh extremists occupied the Golden Temple at Amritsar, making it their operations base. Indira Gandhi's use of the army to clear them out in June 1984 not only led to great loss

Below In the 1970s Indira Gandhi's promotion of her eldest son Sanjay gave rise to much popular talk of the establishment of a "Nehru dynasty", though this took little account of the complexity of contemporary Indian politics. In June 1979 Sanjay was killed in a flying accident. Mrs Gandhi is pictured here at a political meeting held not long afterwards holding her grandson, Sanjay's son. With her (second from the left) is her younger son Rajiv, who was to succeed her as prime minister in 1989, and his children.

of life (including her own) and destruction of property, but has left behind a bitter legacy that makes the political problems the more difficult to negotiate. In Kashmir, the pressures of economic development and migration into the state, combined with a large army presence, have jeopardized the balance between communities and interests that had been maintained, albeit precariously, in the previous 100 years.

Communal and caste differences have taken on new leases of life since independence. The founding fathers of the Indian republic were determined to have equality before the law and to eschew the divisive social categories that they believed to have been played up by the British. But Hindu-Muslim communal differences, especially in the towns of northern India, persisted and from time to time resulted in rioting and death. A recent development has been the attempt of a number of politicians to mobilize support on the basis of being Hindu. They argue that successive governments, at both national and state levels, have been over-protective of minority groups and have failed to represent the interests of the Hindu majority. Certain symbolic issues have been fixed on to try to raise political consciousness, the most notable being the campaign (which has run in one form or another for over a century) to remove the mosque built in Babur's time at the sacred birthplace of Rama at Ayodhya.

Tensions between Hindus and Muslims increased significantly in the mid 1980s. In 1984 the Vishwa Hindu Parishad was formed to "liberate Lord Ram from his Muslim jail", and the following year a court order gave Hindus the right to worship in the disputed building, leading to widespread agitation across India.

During the general election campaign in November 1989 the Vishwa Hindu Parishad attempted to build a new temple for Rama on the site of the Ayodhya mosque, using bricks that were, amid great publicity, brought by Hindu pilgrims from all over India. Government intervention to stop the building provoked Hindu-Muslim riots in many parts of the country: the loss of life was particularly great in Bihar. The flames of communal hatred were fanned by politicians for electoral gain, and the Ayodhya crisis was a major factor in the Congress's defeat at the polls. In 1992 the Hindu extremists had their way, and the mosque was dismantled by an angry crowd, precipitating further widespread communal violence.

Such incidents have done much to promote particularist Hindu communal politics in India, making more difficult political arrangements with others, such as Muslims and Sikhs. The Bharatiya Janata Party, explicitly representing Hindu interests, has become a significant force in Uttar Pradesh, Delhi, Rajasthan and Gujarat. But it would be wrong to suggest that a new Hindu fundamentalism is sweeping all before it. Where the BJP has achieved electoral success, it has found it difficult to hold power without taking account of the cultural diversity of Indian society. Moreover, modern Hindu revivalist movements gain the greatest support from those who belong to the higher castes, or are town-dwellers seeking to discover their roots and traditions. Populist Hindu rhetoric may seize the imagination in the heat of the moment, but it cannot necessarily prevail against the divisions and discriminations practiced among Hindus themselves over the centuries.

Above Ironically, New Delhi, today the seat of the federal government of the Republic of India, was laid out as a vast imperial city in the dying years of the British raj. Its architecture was conceived on a grand scale, combining European monumentalism with a self-conscious echoing of Indian, especially Mughal, imperial traditions. At the center of the plan drawn up by the British architects Edwin Lutyens (1869–1944) and Herbert Baker (1862–1946) was a broad avenue named King's Way that ran from the war memorial to the viceroy's palace: crossing it at rightangles was the Queen's Way. This view looks down from the old viceregal palace (now the residence of the president of the Republic) along King's Way (now Rajpath), across Queen's Way (now democratically renamed Janpath – People's Way) to the canopy beneath which a statue of Gandhi has replaced that of the King Emperor George V.

Contemporary Hindu fundamentalism, which seeks to bring all Hindus together under a single umbrella, has also been checked by the rise of intercaste conflict. Though the constitution of independent India gave no recognition to caste, some effort was made to address problems of social backwardness and provision was made to allow for policies of positive discrimination to help the disadvantaged. A "schedule" was drawn up, consisting primarily of those categories hitherto regarded as "untouchables" – or "Harijans" ("children of God") as Gandhi had redesignated them, but who prefer today to call themselves Dalits – and other "backward" castes of low intermediate status, to whom special privileges would be given in matters of government employment and educational benefits.

The deployment of state patronage in this way has been controversial and provocative. In a number of areas where the intermediate and backward castes have bulked large in number, they have often been among the principal agricultural and landowning communities, though lagging behind the traditionally literate elite castes in matters of education and civil service employment. The adoption of a range of policies by state governments giving them preferential treatment has led to resentment on the part of the elite castes, for whom literacy and the prospect of government employment is often the only way of life. In 1985, there were serious riots in Gujarat after the Congress government there announced an increase in backward class reservations in universities and government employment from 10 to 28 percent. There have been further violent outbreaks since over new proposals put forward to distribute public patronage more widely.

A planned economy

In the early years of independence, the prime aim of the government was the eradication of poverty and the vigorous promotion of a secular democratic society.

Nehru, who had played a vital role in the final stages of negotiations with the British, had a clear view of history and an understanding of India's destiny, believing that the end of colonialism and the development of a state-planned economy would clear the way for a secular, liberal and humanist society. Under his leadership, with enormous courage India set about planning for social change. The model it looked to, in line with the best beliefs of the European socialists of the 1930s and 1940s, was that of the Soviet Union. There, it was believed, a backward, inegalitarian, agrarian empire had transformed itself into a secular, classless, industrial state. In 20 years, a peasant society had become a world power, strong enough to defeat the forces of Nazi Germany, achieved through policies of state-planning, with a belief in the efficacy of education and science.

Above right Ganesha, or Ganpati, is one of the most popular of Indian gods, the son of Shiva and Parvati. He is the "Remover of Obstacles" and the god who is worshipped at the beginning of any venture or at the start of a series of rituals. This splendid representation of Ganesha, c.1965, is by the Bombay artist Badri Narayan, noted for his work as a mosaicist and a painter on ceramic tile (as in this case), as well as for his watercolors.

Right After more than a century of dispute, a number of Hindu militants finally stormed the mosque-temple compound at Ayodhya on 6 December 1992, destroying the ruined mosque built in the early 16th century, in preparation for the erection of a new temple on what was claimed to be the site of the birthplace of Krishna. The violence of the event, and what it symbolized, provoked vigorous debate about the cultural identity of civil society in India.

Cinema

The cinema has been an important influence on Indian culture in the 20th century. The industry was established very early and by the mid century operated on a scale equivalent to the motion picture industry of the United States. Moreover, the Indian cinema not only became truly popular, reaching out to mass audiences, but it also made its mark internationally with art movies (such as those made by the Bengali director Satyajit Ray) that appealed to an elite cosmopolitan audience. The first cinematographic film was shown in India in Bombay on 7 July 1896, just seven months after the Lumière brothers opened their cinematograph in a Paris restaurant. Bombay quickly established itself as the headquarters of the Indian movie industry, producing short documentaries. In 1909 came the first feature film proper, a performance of a popular Marathi play. In 1913, D.G. Phalke (who set up an early distribution network, touring movie shows around by bullock cart) set a distinctive trend by filming a 50-minute epic about a Hindu king – *Raja Harischandra*. Indian movies still typically draw on stories from the Indian classics and from Indian folk-stories for their themes. The coming of the talkies posed potential problems for an industry that depended on a subcontinental market. Other production centers were established, the most important of them at Bangalore in the south and at Calcutta, and a distinctive style of Hindi movie was developed, in which long musical interludes were cut into a familiar story. In this way the Indian movie industry has remained essentially national in appeal and has encouraged a sense of national identity. Today the cinema industry of India is one of the largest in the world, employing more than 2 million people. Movies are exported to many countries including China, where their romantic plots and musical accompaniments make them especially popular.

Below A movie theater in Bangalore, which has become the second center of India's movie industry, producing films in the Dravidian languages. The industry in the south has developed close connections with state politics, especially in Karnataka and Tamil Nadu, where leading movie actors and actresses have been elected to power on an anti-Hindi and anti-northern ticket.

Above One of the first stars to translate movie fame into political power was India's leading dramatic actress, Nargis, who was elected to the federal parliament in the 1950s. She is seen here in her most famous starring role, as Radha in Mehboob Khan's *Mother India* (1957), a story about a village girl who fights a valiant battle for the survival of her land and her sons, and is an allegory for India itself.

Below Posters advertizing Indian movies are among the most prominent and dramatic forms of street art. Here a painter puts finishing touches to a giant movie poster in Bombay. Movies achieve enormous box office success, and are sometimes accused of pandering to escapist fantasy, thereby reinforcing the fatalism and conservatism of the Indian masses.

Above An actress, Tina Minum, is directed in a movie being made at Bombay's production studios. Movie stars play a prominent part in the life of the city, and many live in luxurious homes at Pali Hill in Bandra, north of Mahim Creek. This district is regarded as the Beverly Hills of Bombay, and the whole Bombay movie industry is popularly referred to as "Bollywood".

Left Indian movies have been noted for their fairy-tale morality and for their almost inevitable happy ending, once the hero and heroine have undergone a requisite degree of suffering. Since the early 1970s, however, Indian film-makers, influenced by international trends, have turned to more realistic and often more violent stories. This English-language poster advertizes a gangster movie – an increasingly popular genre.

During the years of British rule, the Indian economy had been run for the benefit of British interests, exploited merely as a supplier of primary products and raw materials for British industry. Since India had been kept as an agrarian society, and a poor one at that, the way forward must be by planned industrialization. On the Soviet model, a Five Year Plan (1951–56) proposed some corrective measures: detailed central planning concentrated on building up India's capacity to produce capital goods, but left the rest of the economy to run itself. Its targets were mostly achieved.

A second Five Year Plan (1956–61), masterminded by Nehru and Professor P. C. Mahalanobis, chairman of the Planning Commission, went much further. It proclaimed a policy for development that blended Fabian socialism with the anti-materialism of Gandhi. There was disdain for consumer goods and a distaste for luxuries of any kind. Imports were to be turned away by high tariffs and quotas, or by straightforward bans on entry. There was to be no encouragement for exports, since domestic needs must be met first. Individual saving would be encouraged to provide the resources for investment. There would be no need for foreign capital, the effect of which in the past had been to take profits out of the country.

The government nationalized leading industries. A regime of licences and political controls was ushered in. Firms were told where they had to set up business (often in "backward areas") and what they had to produce. A manufacturer of cotton cloth geared to a high fashion market, for example, might be required as the price for procuring necessary licences and permissions to produce a certain amount of cheap textiles for the lower end of the market, even if his factory was unsuited to their production. To hold down unemployment, businesses were not allowed to close. As in the Soviet Union and Eastern Europe, the long-term effect of handing large sections of the economy over to bureaucrats and of protecting indigenous producers from the effects of international competition was inevitable inefficiency. Some 250,000 Indian workers produced the same amount of steel as 8,000 Japanese workers.

In the 1960s, the government turned its attention to the relief of the country's agrarian majority. Investment packages were put together to increase agricultural productivity. As part of the "green revolution" high-cropping varieties of wheat and rice were introduced to increase yields, the use of fertilizers and machinery was encouraged, and irrigation extended. But the social and economic effects were not evenly felt. Some districts pulled far ahead of others, and some farmers were better placed to benefit than others. Regional and social economic inequalities became even more marked. This might not have mattered had the general level of wealth risen substantially. But this was not the case, and after 1971 Indira Gandhi's government floated a raft of policies designed to help the poor directly. Government aid was directed at small companies rather than big ones and at labor-intensive projects rather than capital-intensive ones. Subsidies for hand-loomers were preferred to investment in more power looms.

Such strategies were not without success. During the 1960s industrial production went up by about 5.5 percent, sufficient to a doubling of output every 12 years. But other developing Asian countries did better – Pakistan, Thailand, Taiwan and South Korea all grew

As a successful and rapidly growing city, Ahmadabad in Gujarat has its share of street-dwellers (*left*), but it is also the home of the National Institute of Design and has for long been at the forefront of modern architectural development and town planning. Besides fine old buildings, Ahmadabad boasts some of the best 20th-century domestic architecture in India. The influence of the architect Le Corbusier, who designed the new Punjabi capital of Chandigarh, and his Indian followers can be seen (*below*) in a new housing complex for office-workers.

faster. Agricultural improvement showed the same patterns. Until the 1960s, India had had to import food grains, but by the 1980s it had become self-sufficient and was even producing surpluses, in spite of a sharp increase in the numbers of people requiring to be fed. Still, other countries outpaced India. Between 1970 and 1989, for example, Malaysia's agricultural output doubled, while that of India went up by 40 percent. Moreover, success in the countryside was related to a narrow range of crops (particularly wheat and rice) and was dependent on other factors such as improvements in levels of literacy and the availability of good irrigation, roads, and markets. Thus Punjab and parts of the northwest prospered, while growth in potentially rich agricultural areas in the eastern and central states was much slower.

The government tended to undervalue policies that might have significantly improved the physical infra-structure and boosted the economy by investing more heavily in the country's vast human resources. It omitted to improve roads, railways and other services, had not devised appropriate policies for cheap mass education and healthcare, and had discounted the contribution that could have been made to India's greater prosperity by expanding overseas trade and encouraging foreign investment.

A third of the world's poorest people live in India. In 1970, it was reckoned that 50 percent of the population (300 million people) fell below the poverty line; by 1980, because of population increase, the percentage had dropped to 40 percent, but the actual figure living at subsistence level remained at 300 million. In 1985, figures from the World Bank classified some 420 million Indians as "poor" (living on less than $30 a month) and of these, around 250 million fell into the category of "extremely poor" (living on less that $23 a month). Yet – despite such statistics – quite significant changes have taken place. Those below the poverty line are not so low as once they were, while there has been a striking increase in the number of those – put at between 100 and 200 million in the early 1990s – who are able to afford, and are demanding, a better and more secure material life.

PART THREE

THE REGIONS
OF THE
SUBCONTINENT

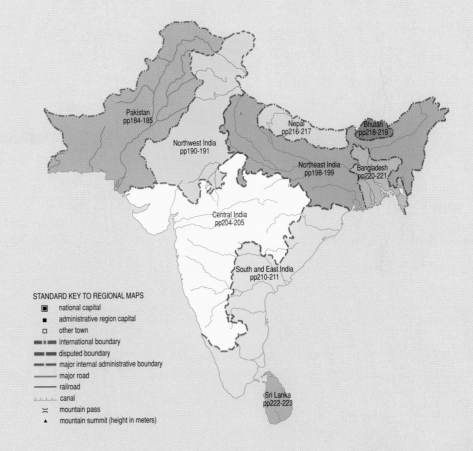

Pakistan
pp184-185

Nepal
pp216-217

Bhutan
pp218-219

Northwest India
pp190-191

Northeast India
pp198-199

Bangladesh
pp220-221

Central India
pp204-205

South and East India
pp210-211

Sri Lanka
pp222-223

STANDARD KEY TO REGIONAL MAPS

- ▣ national capital
- ■ administrative region capital
- ▫ other town
- ▅▃▅▃ international boundary
- ▅▅▅▅ disputed boundary
- ▅▅▅ major internal administrative boundary
- ——— major road
- ——— railroad
- ┴┴┴┴ canal
- ⊐⊏ mountain pass
- ▲ mountain summit (height in meters)

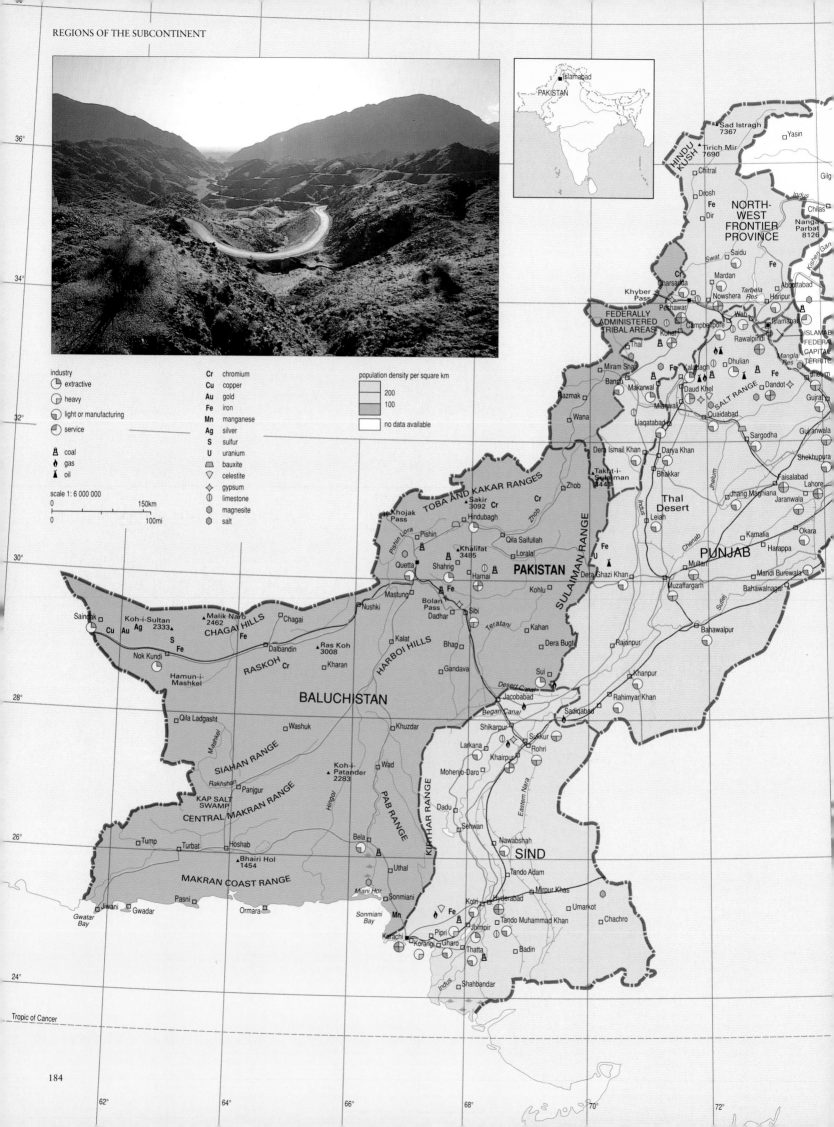

REGIONS OF THE SUBCONTINENT

PAKISTAN

Area (sq km)	796,095
Population	114 million
Capital	Islamabad
Official/first Language	Urdu

Pakistan came into being in 1947, when British India was divided into two independent states to create a separate homeland for India's Muslims. The areas of the subcontinent where Muslims were in a majority, the northwest and East Bengal, united to become the provinces of West and East Pakistan, separated by 1,600 kilometers of Indian territory. Of the former provinces of British India, only the North-West Frontier Province, Baluchistan and Sind in West Pakistan passed to the new state intact. Punjab and Bengal were divided between Pakistan and India, and Kashmir became disputed property. In 1965 the dispute with India over Kashmir erupted into war. In 1971, East Pakistan seceded from West Pakistan to become the independent state of Bangladesh.

Pakistan has experienced military government on several occasions, most recently between 1978 and 1985. The Constitution of 1973 provides for a federal parliamentary system of two legislative bodies, the national assembly and the senate. The national assembly, elected by popular vote, is headed by the prime minister. Members of the senate are chosen by the four provincial assemblies. The president, selected by an electoral college, has wide-ranging powers. He is both head of government and commander of the army. Since the 1980s there have been several attempts to make the *sharia* the foundation of Pakistan's legal system. There is considerable regional tension between Sind – the area where support for the Pakistan People's Party (PPP) led by the Bhutto family is strongest – and the other provinces.

Pakistan is divided physically between the mountains of the north and west, and the plains of the Indus valley in the south and east. The highest ranges in the far north – the Himalayas, the Karakoram Range and the Hindu Kush – include many mountains over 7,400 meters, among them K2 (Godwin Austen), at 8,611 meters the second highest mountain in the world. The melting snows from these mountains feed the headwaters of the Indus and its tributaries. The few routes through the high mountains are extremely difficult, and the region is sparsely populated. To the south of the mountains are ranges of lower hills. Over the whole region, winters are cold but, more significantly, a rainshadow effect means that the south-facing wooded slopes contrast sharply with the bare, dry, north-facing hills.

The mountains of the North-West Frontier Province, between 1,500 and 4,600 meters high and crossed by the Khyber Pass into Afghanistan, are also arid and bare of vegetation. However, river valleys – including that of the Kabul which forms the Vale of Peshawar – are fertile oases of irrigated land, where wheat, maize, sugar and tobacco are commercially grown. Farther south, the Baluchistan Plateau has an average height of more than 500 meters, broken by higher ridges running north–south.

As the Indus and its four main tributaries emerge from their deep mountain valleys and gorges onto the Punjab plains, the flow of water slows down. The tributaries turn southward and converge before joining the Indus to form a wide, slow-moving body of water that enters the Arabian Sea south of Karachi. The volume of water carried in the Indus river system is enormous. At peak seasons of flow, in the snowmelt or the rainy season, there is frequent severe flooding when new channels may be formed.

The Punjab and Sind plains are made up of fertile alluvial soils deposited by the rivers. However, the paucity of rainfall (which falls only in the summer monsoon season and decreases in amount southward from about 900 mm in the Islamabad region to 250 mm or less around Karachi) means that their potential for agriculture can be released only by irrigation, for example, from canals fed from schemes such as the Sukkur Barrage or the Tarbela or Mangla Dams. However, summer temperatures range from 26°C to over 32°C, resulting in the evaporation of water which causes widespread salinization of irrigated land. Government-sponsored schemes are now focusing on ways of alleviating the problem and prolonging the life of irrigated soils.

Aridity, difficult terrain and salinization mean that even after great investment still less than one third of Pakistan's land area is cultivable. Around one half of the workforce is engaged in agriculture. The "Green Revolution" of the 1970s introduced higher-yielding

Top left The Khyber Pass crosses tribal territory. Both road and railway snake through bare arid mountains from Peshawar to Torkhum on the Afghan frontier. The border has been periodically challenged by Afghanistan since it was established by Britain in 1893, necessitating the defense of the Pass. Today opium and hashish are grown in this region and drug-trafficking is rife.

Right Dusk in Rawalpindi's Sadr Bazaar. All kinds of local crafts and produce are sold; spices and incense scent the air and vehicles jostle for space. The meeting of cultures is vividly illustrated by the different scripts seen on shop signs.

Left In parts of Pakistan, especially in the north, painted trucks are a common sight. These highly personalized and extravagantly decorated vehicles are completely transformed by local artists and metal workers, often disguising the original style and shape.

Above left Thatta, an ancient town in the Indus delta, has had varied fortunes. A prosperous period in the 16th and 17th centuries was followed by prolonged decline. Shah Jahan, who built the Taj Mahal and laid out the Shalimar gardens in Lahore, built this mosque in the 16th century. It has over 900 domes and an impressive tiled interior with glazed red brickwork.

Above right A typical view of the river Indus near Thatta during the rainy season. Vast quantities of silt are carried to the delta, some of which is deposited en route, adding to the fertility of the land. The rest extends the delta seawards at the river's mouth.

Right This beautifully symmetrical and architecturally satisfying building is only one of the many mosques in Karachi where more than 95 percent of the population is Muslim (including many of Pakistan's Shiite Muslims). Before 1947 Karachi had a Hindu majority.

varieties of grain, as well as new techniques and mechanization. As a result, Pakistan is now self-sufficient in wheat, rice and sugar cane, producing surpluses for export. Maize and pulses are also grown, and cotton production is increasing. Baluchistan is an important fruit-growing region. Cattle and buffalo provide meat, milk and motive power, and sheep and goats are kept in the highlands. In Baluchistan up to 80 percent of the population are pastoral farmers. At present only about 4 percent of the land is forested, but there are plans to increase this.

The most important industries are concerned with the processing of food and other agricultural products. Karachi, Faisalabad and Hyderabad are major centers of cotton production, with many other smaller centers in Sind and Punjab. Imported raw jute is processed in several centers including Karachi, and more plants are being established. Sugar-processing factories are widely distributed, especially in eastern Punjab and Sind.

Pakistan has some poor-quality coal and oil, and extensive reserves of natural gas, which now supply almost half the country's power needs. Other industrially exploited mineral deposits include rock salt, gypsum and chrome. Cement manufacture, iron and steel production (using imported raw materials) and engineering are important industries. Hydroelectricity is generated as part of the major irrigation projects at Tarbela on the Indus, Mangla on the Jhelum and Warsak on the Kabul, but current policy is for the development of small-scale hydroelectric schemes that have less damaging environmental impact. There are nuclear generating stations at Karachi and Chashma, near Liaqatabad, and solar power projects are being developed in remote areas.

With a history of settled occupation stretching back more than 5,000 years, the Indus plain is rich in sites of historic or architectural interest. Among these are Harappa and Mohenjo-Daro, the excavated cities of the Indus valley civilization that flourished about 2,500 BC. Thatta, about 100 kilometers east of Karachi on the Indus delta, contains many fine architectural relics of the Mughals, including the Jami mosque built by Shah Jahan in 1647. Lahore, capital of Punjab, is one of the finest Mughal cities of the subcontinent. It was here that Akbar held his court from 1584 to 1598, and he began the great fort, with its palaces, tombs and gardens, later extended by Jahangir and Shah Jahan. Farther north, especially in the area between Rawalpindi and Peshawar, are many stupas and monasteries from the Gandharan and Ashokan periods. Peshawar, guarding the Khyber Pass, is the gateway to Central Asia, and the bazaar within the walls of the old city is still a bustling and exotic market-place. Outside the city large camps were set up to house many of the 3 million refugees who fled into Pakistan after the Soviet invasion of Afghanistan in 1979.

The mountain areas of northern Pakistan are especially attractive to tourists. The green and fertile Swat valley is popular with trekkers and sportsmen, and contains many archaeological sites. Gilgit and Hunza in Kashmir lie on the Karakoram Highway that twists for 1,284 kilometers through magnificent mountain scenery, following the line of one of the ancient silk roads, and connects Pakistan with China. Kashmir's forests, mountains, lakes and alpine meadows of wild flowers provide unequaled opportunities for fishing, walking and observing wild life.

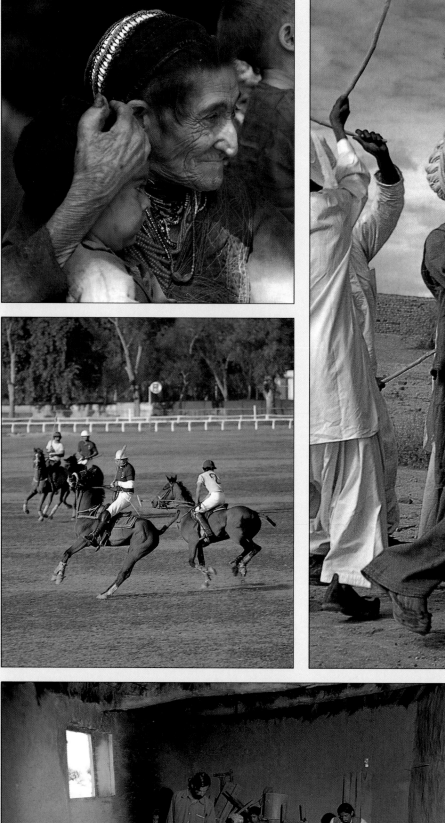

Top left A heavy head-dress and black robes worn with multicolored beads form the traditional dress of all Kalash women, including older girls. The many social and dietary taboos and strict customs of this hill tribe are still strong, though gradually being infiltrated by Islamic culture.

Center left Polo, played here at the Lahore Club, originated in the Indian subcontinent and is a highly popular national sport played with fierce competitiveness. Lahore, one of Pakistan's most important Mughal centers, contains the Shalimar gardens and the enormous Badshahi mosque.

Bottom left Literacy levels are still low in rural Pakistan. In Baluchistan these boys are at school but this region contains many nomadic people whose traditional local culture is orientated towards physical and oral rather than literary skills.

Above Dancing is an important strand in traditional culture in many tribal regions of Pakistan. Here a group of men perform a stick dance accompanied by a traditional instrument. Dance is believed to aid the defeat of evil and please the gods.

Left The devout Muslim prays several times a day. Here the Pakistan navy observes a higher command as the men face toward Mecca to pray. Government policy has encouraged an increasing awareness of Islam at every level of life in Pakistan.

NORTHWEST INDIA

Haryana

The state of Haryana was created in 1966 when the former state of Punjab was divided into Hindi-speaking Haryana in the south and Punjabi-speaking Punjab in the north. Most of Haryana lies on the Indo-Gangetic plain, while in the northeast is part of the Terai – a narrow and formerly malarial tract of forest on the southern edge of the Himalayas. The southwest lies on the edge of the Thar Desert and is very arid. Rainfall is scanty in most areas and, with the exception of the Yamuna, rivers are seasonal. Well over half the area of cultivable land is irrigated. Water is transported from dam projects in neighboring states, but increasing efforts are being made to tap subsoil water through pumps and tube wells. More than 80 percent of the population work on the land. The chief crops are rice, wheat, pulses, cotton and oilseeds. There is a center for improving cattle breeds at Karnal. Textiles including carpets are the main industry, but engineering is growing in importance.

Haryana was the birthplace of Hinduism, and it contains many archaeological sites, temples and places of pilgrimage including Kurukshetra, the site of the battlefield where Krishna delivered the teachings contained in the *Bhagavadgita* to the warrior Arjuna. Haryana lies on the route into the subcontinent from the northwest, protecting the way to Delhi, and has been fought over many times: Panipat on the Yamuna river was the scene of no less than three decisive battles, in 1526, 1556 and 1761.

Himachal Pradesh

The snow-covered mountains of Himachal Pradesh, in the western Himalayas, rise to about 6,700 meters, and its wooded valleys, cascading streams, waterfalls and lakes make it a place of great scenic beauty. Created first a substate and then a Union Territory after 1948, it was enlarged by the addition of the district of Bilaspur in 1954 and parts of Punjab in 1966. It became a full state of the Union of India in 1971.

Himachal Pradesh is sparsely populated with few towns. Most of the population, which includes a number of hill tribes, are engaged in agriculture. Buffalo, cattle, sheep and goats are raised; wheat, maize and barley are the cereal crops. It is an important fruit-growing region and tea, mushrooms, ginger and potatoes are also commercially grown. About 40 percent of the land area is covered by coniferous forest, which is being actively conserved. Large- and small-scale hydroelectric schemes, exploiting the fast-flowing mountain rivers, supply electricity to the whole state, and power is exported to neighboring states. Industrial enterprises include resin and turpentine manufacture, brewing and some light engineering.

Tourism is increasingly important. There is skiing in Narkanda and Kufni and hang-gliding in the Kangra valley, while the natural scenery and wild life of the Kulu, Kangra and Ravi valleys attract large numbers of backpackers and other visitors. The capital Shimla, more than 2,000 meters above sea-level, is a popular

Right Shimla, high in the western Himalayas, is a much-favored holiday resort. Above the town, with its narrow streets and crowded bazaars, larger, more affluent houses and apartment blocks spread over the pine and cedar-covered slopes.

Below The Leh valley, in the Ladakh region of Kashmir, is some 3,500 meters above sea-level. The river here has formed an alluvial fan, the thin soils of which are intensely cultivated. There is little or no rain, and the tiny, stone-walled fields are irrigated by the spring meltwater. Barley, buckwheat and sown grass (for fodder) are the main crops.

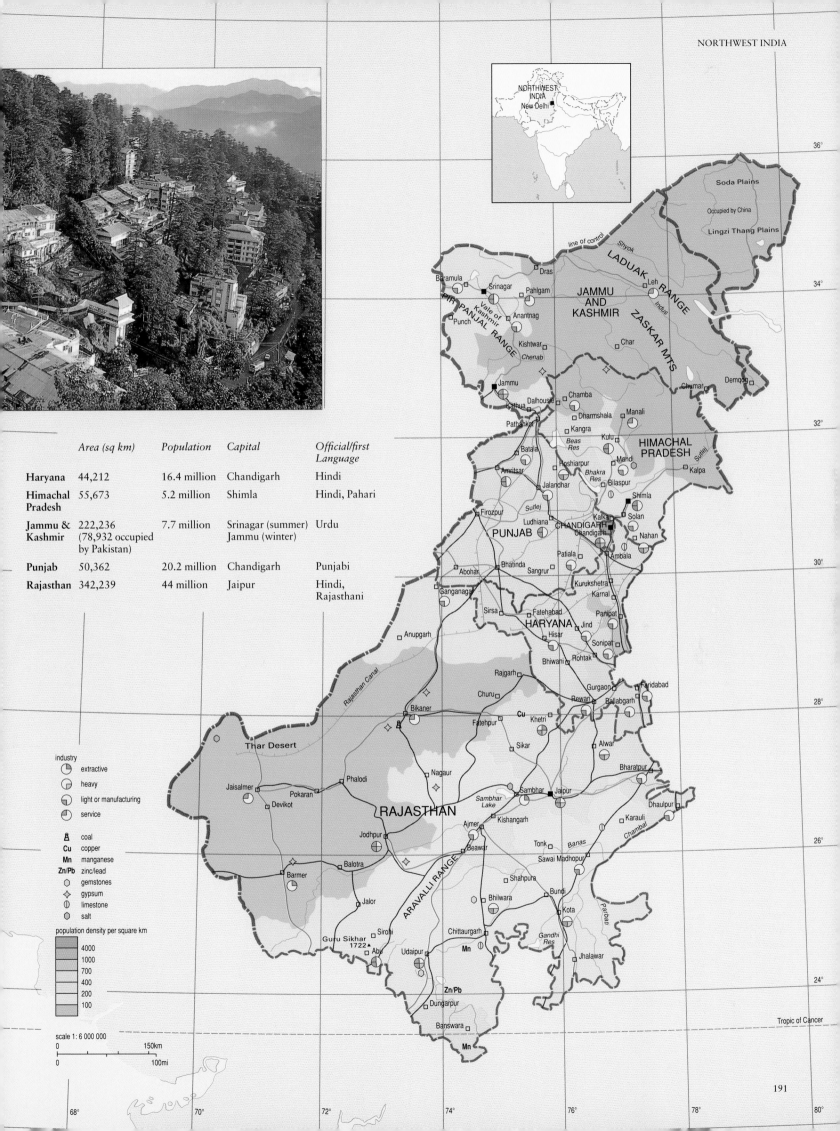

NORTHWEST
INDIA
New Delhi

Soda Plains
Occupied by China
Lingzi Thang Plains

line of control

Shyok

LADUAK
RANGE

Leh

JAMMU
AND
KASHMIR

ZASKAR MTS

Indus

Char

Chumar

Demoog

Baramula
Srinagar
Pahlgam
Vale of
Kashmir
PIR
PANJAL
RANGE
Punch
Anantnag
Kishtwar
Chenab

Jammu
Kathua
Dalhousie
Pathankot
Chamba
Dharmshala
Manali
Kangra
Kulu
HIMACHAL
PRADESH
Beas
Res

Batala
Amritsar
Hoshiarpur
Mandi
Bhakra
Res
Bilaspur
Sutlej
Kalpa

Jalandhar
Shimla
Solan

Firozpur
Sutlej
Ludhiana
Kalka
Nahan

PUNJAB
CHANDIGARH
Chandigarh
Ambala

Abohar
Bhatinda
Sangrur
Patiala

Ganganagar
Sirsa
Fatehabad
Kurukshetra
Karnal

Anupgarh
Hisar
Jind
Panipat
HARYANA
Sonipat

Rajgarh
Bhiwani
Rohtak

Rajasthan Canal
Churu
Gurgaon
Rewari
Faridabad
Ballabgarh

Bikaner
Fatehpur
Cu
Khetri

Thar Desert
Sikar
Alwar

Phalodi
Nagaur
Bharatpur

Jaisalmer
Pokaran
Devikot
Sambhar
Jaipur
Dhaulpur

Sambhar
Lake
RAJASTHAN
Ajmer
Kishangarh
Karauli

Jodhpur
Beawar
Tonk
Banas
Chambal

Balotra
Shahpura
Sawai Madhopur

Barmer
Bhilwara
Bundi

Jalor
Kota
Parbati

ARAVALLI RANGE
Chittaurgarh
Gandhi
Res

Guru Sikhar
1722
Siroli
Jhalawar
Abu
Udaipur
Mn

Zn/Pb
Dungarpur

Banswara

Mn

	Area (sq km)	Population	Capital	Official/first Language
Haryana	44,212	16.4 million	Chandigarh	Hindi
Himachal Pradesh	55,673	5.2 million	Shimla	Hindi, Pahari
Jammu & Kashmir	222,236 (78,932 occupied by Pakistan)	7.7 million	Srinagar (summer) Jammu (winter)	Urdu
Punjab	50,362	20.2 million	Chandigarh	Punjabi
Rajasthan	342,239	44 million	Jaipur	Hindi, Rajasthani

industry
◑ extractive
◔ heavy
◑ light or manufacturing
◕ service

Ä coal
Cu copper
Mn manganese
Zn/Pb zinc/lead
⬡ gemstones
✧ gypsum
◧ limestone
⬡ salt

population density per square km
4000
1000
700
400
200
100

scale 1 : 6 000 000
0   150km
0   100mi

68°   70°   72°   74°   76°   78°   80°

36°
34°
32°
30°
28°
26°
24°
Tropic of Cancer

hill resort and trekking-center. It was the summer headquarters of the British administration and its architecture reflects this era.

Jammu and Kashmir

The borders of Jammu and Kashmir have been in dispute since 1947. The north and west are claimed and occupied by Pakistan. Though a "line of control" was agreed by India and Pakistan in 1971, disputes continue and there is frequent unrest. In the northeast, part of Ladakh has been occupied by the Chinese since the Sino-Indian war of 1962. The Buddhist Ladakhs are of Tibetan stock and speak a Tibetan-related language. The summer capital of Jammu and Kashmir is at Srinagar, in the Kashmir valley, and in winter at Jammu, in the foothills of the Himalayas. The population here are predominantly Hindu, with cultural links to the Punjab state of India.

Communications are very difficult in this region of high mountain ranges divided by deep valleys, and many roads are impassable for much of the year. Winters are very cold, and the climate is dry. More than 80 percent of the population are farmers. The high mountain meadows provide summer grazing for yaks and sheep, and rice, wheat and maize are grown on terraced slopes. Apart from the arid Ladakh region, almost half the land is covered by forest. The most fertile area is the Vale of Kashmir, where there are extensive orchards, but the average size of agricultural holdings is very small, and incomes are low. Food processing is almost the only industry. Traditional crafts such as silk-weaving, carpet-making and wood-carving are the main non-farming occupations. Hydroelectric stations supply power to towns and a majority of villages.

Leh, the capital of the Ladakh district, is an ancient town on the traditional caravan route through the Himalayas: there are many Buddhist monasteries and monuments in the area. Jammu's Hindu temples are among the largest in northern India and the town, which was the seat of a Rajput dynasty, has an ancient fort that later became the raja's palace.

Punjab

Since the 15th century, the history of Punjab has been closely tied to the rise of Sikhism, which has its birthplace in the region. In the 18th century the Sikhs became the dominant power in Punjab, and Ranjit Singh (1780–1839) created an effective independent kingdom, part of which was absorbed into British India after his death. After independence in 1947, Punjab was divided between Pakistan and India, the smaller, eastern part becoming the Indian state of Punjab. In 1966 it was divided further on linguistic lines to form the present state of Punjab and the Hindi-speaking state of Haryana. There are recurrent periods of tension between the Sikh and Hindu communities. Demands for an autonomous Sikh state (Khalistan) was the cause of communal violence in the 1980s. This came to a head in 1984 when an assault was made by the Indian army on the Sikhs' Golden Temple at Amritsar.

Most of Punjab is flat, except for the Siwalik Hills, rising to 900 meters, in the northeast. About four-fifths of the land is cultivated, and 75 percent of the population are engaged in farming. Punjab accounts for a high proportion of India's wheat and rice production. Other food grains, pulses, cotton, oilseeds, tobacco, sugar and potatoes are also grown. Livestock

Above A train of camels passes in front of the walled town of Jaisalmer in Rajasthan. Founded in 1156 on the caravan route across the Thar Desert, Jaisalmer was an important trading center. In the 15th and 16th centuries its Rajput rulers permitted the wealthy Jain merchants of the town to build a group of sanctuaries close to the fort and palace within its walls.

Left The Golden Temple at Amritsar in Punjab is the Sikhs' most holy place. Its white marble walls and domes are decorated with gold filigree work. In 1984 it was the scene of an assault and three-day siege by the Indian army during the Sikh militant campaign for an independent homeland: 576 people were killed in the fighting.

Previous page In Leh, colorful prayer flags spread out against the sky, send prayers heavenward. The Ladakh region is steeped in Buddhist culture and religion, and monasteries and sacred walls with prayer wheels and flags abound.

Above The annual fair at Pushkar in Rajasthan is the largest in India. More than 200,000 people and many thousands of cattle and camels arrive for the ten days of trading. Camel racing, music, dancing, entertainments and a huge bazaar accompany the fair. Tented villages house the visitors, many of whom are pilgrims who bathe in the sacred lake and worship at the many temples.

Right The 18th-century palace at Mandawa, north of Jaipur, is now an hotel where visitors can experience the surroundings and ambience of a Rajput court. Turbaned servants add to the atmosphere. Each room is named after a member of the former princely family.

Left The people of Ladakh are of Tibetan stock and language. This old man is wearing the typical hat of the region, with stiffened brim and distinctive stitching.

Chandigarh

Chandigarh is situated 240 kilometers north of Delhi at the foot of the Himalayas. This city came into being after the chaos of Indian partition in 1947 when Lahore, the capital of the former province of Punjab, was placed within Pakistan, leaving Indian Punjab without a state capital. The desire to assert India's independence and strength influenced the decision to construct a new city. "Let this be a new town," declared Nehru, "symbolic of the freedom of India, unfettered by the traditions of the past . . . an expression of the nation's faith in the future."

In 1951 the state government of Punjab secured the services of the celebrated and controversial Swiss architect Charles-Edouard Jeanneret (1887–1956), better known by the soubriquet Le Corbusier, to supervise the design of the new city, assisted by his cousin Pierre Jeanneret and the British architects Maxwell Fry and Jane Drew. Le Corbusier seized the opportunity to apply his theories of the ideal city, incorporating the "Modulor" concept, to an actual situation. Chandigarh was divided into a number of rectangular sectors, each of which came to include its own school, health facilities and community center. Though Nehru was later to eulogize Chandigarh as a "temple of new India", the city has not received universal approval. In particular, the residential areas have been seen as dull and depressing, the wide roads giving the city an impersonal feel. Since 1966, the city of Chandigarh has served as the joint capital of Punjab and Haryana. With an area of surrounding countryside, it constitutes a Union Territory of 114 square kilometers and has a population of 642,000.

Right The Secretariat building lies at the heart of the administrative district, the Capitol complex. Le Corbusier was the exclusive designer of the complex. Though he was later to confide that "As architect I had a free hand but very little money", the scale of the project allowed him to realize previously unfulfilled ambitions. Situated on the northern fringe of the city, the Capitol complex consists of a number of buildings, including the High Court, the Palace of Assembly and the Secretariat. Completed in 1958, the latter consists of ministerial offices grouped in the center, with offices for 3,000 employees arranged on either side. As a means of coping with the Indian climate, Le Corbusier created a continuous screen of *brises-soleil* that keep out the sun when it is high, but allow it in when it is low in the sky and the temperature is cooler.

Right Before partition, the various colleges and institutions of the University of East Punjab were dispersed through a number of cities. Under the initial proposals for Chandigarh, a rationalization of the university and its concentration within the new capital was envisaged, and this suggestion was eventually incorporated into the final plans. While Le Corbusier enjoyed the position of chief architectural consultant for the city as a whole, his cousin Pierre Jeanneret (who eventually rose to be chief architect, a position he held until 1965) was responsible for the designs of the new Punjab University, now widely regarded as one of the disappointments of Chandigarh. A common complaint has been that as an institution, the university is too isolated from the rest of the city, a particularly serious criticism in view of the social and political need to stress the unity, cohesion and common purpose of the new capital.

Left The K.C. Theater reflects the grand scale and architectural symmetry that characterize many of the buildings of Chandigarh.

farming includes buffalo, cattle, sheep, goats and horses. Agricultural methods have been substantially mechanized and modernized in recent years, and there is widespread irrigation, for example, from the Bhakra Dam project in neighboring Himachal Pradesh.

Craftwork and small-scale industry form an important part of the economy. Punjab is responsible for most of India's woolen textile manufacture. Food processing, fertilizer production, light engineering and shoe manufacture are also important. Amritsar, a walled city with many religious and historic buildings, manufactures textiles, silk and carpets. It is an important commercial center for the entire region. Ludhiana has a thriving cereal market.

Rajasthan

Rajasthan – known as Rajputana ("the country of the Rajputs") until the integration of the princely states into independent India in 1950 – lies in the arid west of northern India. Its present boundaries date from 1956, when Ajmer, Abu Taluka and Sunel Tappa were added to it and Sironj transferred to Madhya Pradesh. With the exception of the southwest part of state, which benefits from both the Arabian Sea and Bay of Bengal summer monsoons, rainfall is sparse and unreliable: less than 100 mm a year falls in the Thar Desert, which straddles the western border with Pakistan.

Rajput dynasties dominated the region from the 11th century and built many palaces, fortresses and market towns. Most of the ancient towns and forts lie in and east of the Aravalli Range, which bisect the state from northeast to southwest. Jaipur, the capital, is noted for its pink-colored buildings and palaces, dating from the 18th century, including the famous outdoor observatories built by the Maharaja Sawai Jai Singh II. Jodhpur's rich architectural heritage dates back to the 15th century. Bikaner, another 15th-century city, was established on the caravan route across the desert, and camels are still an important part of the local economy. Ajmer is an ancient walled city of much architectural and historic interest, and Udaipur, lying among hills in the southernmost part of the state, has several palaces including one that is set on an island in the middle of a lake.

Population density is among the lowest in India but the urban population is growing fast. Nevertheless, agriculture remains the most important part of the economy. The main crops range from wheat and millet in the drier areas to sorghum, cotton, maize, oilseeds, sugar cane, tobacco, rice and potatoes. Pastoralism predominates in arid areas, and Rajasthan is a major producer of wool. Recent years of drought have severely affected agriculture throughout the state, exacerbating problems of desertification. Less than 20 percent of the cultivated land is irrigated, but large-scale projects have come into operation in recent years, and more – both large and small – are either planned or under construction.

Rajasthan has rich reserves of minerals. It is either India's sole or leading contributor of lead, zinc, emeralds, garnets, gypsum and asbestos. There is varied industry, including textiles, cement, sugar refining, chemicals, zinc and copper smelting. There are both nuclear and hydroelectric power stations at Kota, which is now the industrial capital of the state. Traditional crafts (leatherwork, jewelry, pottery, embossed brasswork) are carried out throughout the state. The state's desert scenery, ancient cities and nature reserves attract tourists.

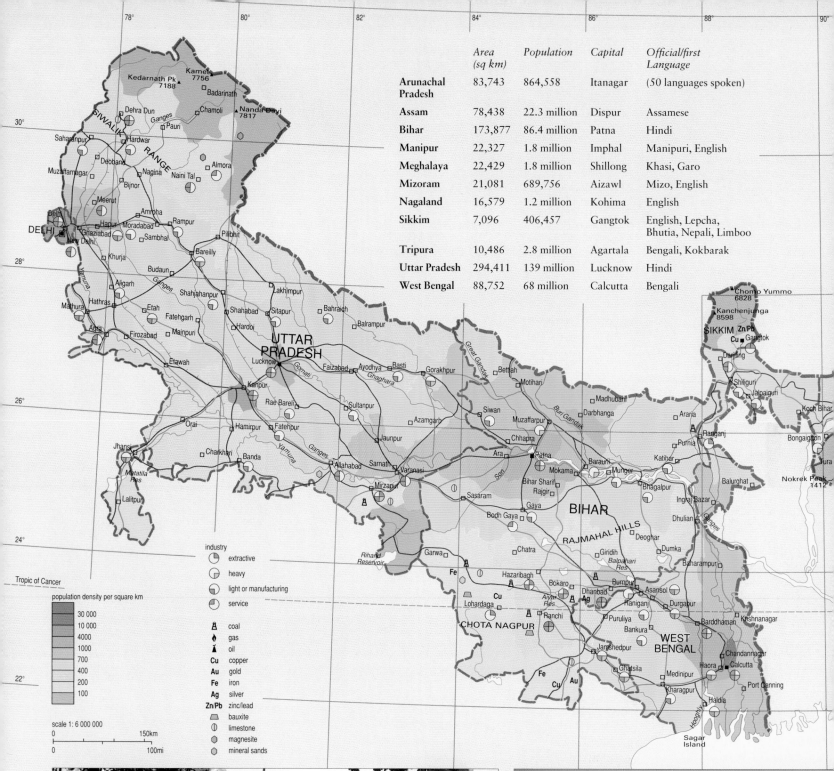

	Area (sq km)	Population	Capital	Official/first Language
Arunachal Pradesh	83,743	864,558	Itanagar	(50 languages spoken)
Assam	78,438	22.3 million	Dispur	Assamese
Bihar	173,877	86.4 million	Patna	Hindi
Manipur	22,327	1.8 million	Imphal	Manipuri, English
Meghalaya	22,429	1.8 million	Shillong	Khasi, Garo
Mizoram	21,081	689,756	Aizawl	Mizo, English
Nagaland	16,579	1.2 million	Kohima	English
Sikkim	7,096	406,457	Gangtok	English, Lepcha, Bhutia, Nepali, Limboo
Tripura	10,486	2.8 million	Agartala	Bengali, Kokbarak
Uttar Pradesh	294,411	139 million	Lucknow	Hindi
West Bengal	88,752	68 million	Calcutta	Bengali

industry

⊙ extractive
⊙ heavy
◑ light or manufacturing
◔ service

coal
gas
oil
Cu copper
Au gold
Fe iron
Ag silver
Zn/Pb zinc/lead
bauxite
limestone
magnesite
mineral sands

Tropic of Cancer

population density per square km

30 000
10 000
4000
1000
700
400
200
100

scale 1: 6 000 000

0   150km
0   100mi

NORTHEAST INDIA

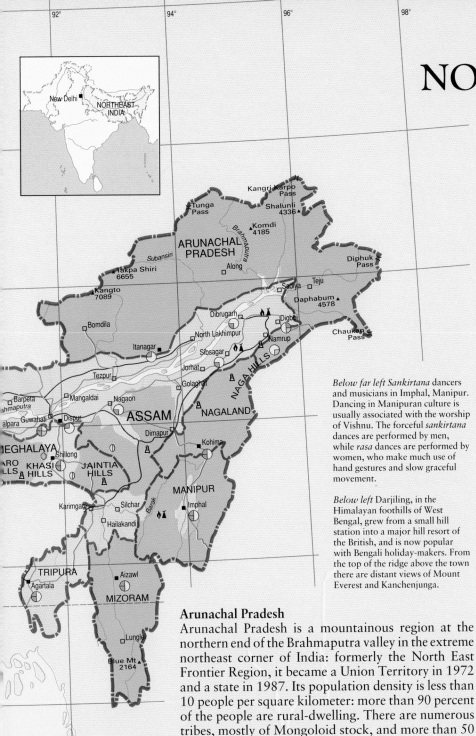

Below far left Sankirtana dancers and musicians in Imphal, Manipur. Dancing in Manipuran culture is usually associated with the worship of Vishnu. The forceful *sankirtana* dances are performed by men, while *rasa* dances are performed by women, who make much use of hand gestures and slow graceful movement.

Below left Darjiling, in the Himalayan foothills of West Bengal, grew from a small hill station into a major hill resort of the British, and is now popular with Bengali holiday-makers. From the top of the ridge above the town there are distant views of Mount Everest and Kanchenjunga.

Arunachal Pradesh

Arunachal Pradesh is a mountainous region at the northern end of the Brahmaputra valley in the extreme northeast corner of India: formerly the North East Frontier Region, it became a Union Territory in 1972 and a state in 1987. Its population density is less than 10 people per square kilometer: more than 90 percent of the people are rural-dwelling. There are numerous tribes, mostly of Mongoloid stock, and more than 50 distinct languages and dialects are spoken.

About 60 percent of the state is forested. Traditionally farmers practice shifting cultivation, cutting and burning the trees to clear an area of land that they cultivate for a few years until the soil fertility is exhausted, when they move on to a new patch, leaving the old one to regenerate. This causes erosion on slopes stripped of vegetation, without tree roots to hold the soil. Rice, millet, maize, wheat, potatoes and mustard are the main crops, together with orchard fruits. Traditional crafts include carpet and basket-making and textile weaving: silk production is increasing in importance. Small industries include fruit processing and the production of plywoods and veneers. Hydroelectricity is being developed, with increasing emphasis on small-scale schemes. Potential mineral resources include coal and oil.

Assam

Assam occupies almost the entire floor of the upper Brahmaputra valley with some higher land in the southeast. Together with the other extreme northeast-

ern states, it is virtually separated from the rest of India by Bangladesh except in the northwest where it is joined to a narrow corridor of land running through West Bengal. Rainfall is among the highest in the world, averaging between 1,778 and 3,048 mm a year, most of it falling from June to September. Rivers are liable to flood, and can cause widespread damage to crops at the height of the growing season; a number of dams have consequently been built to control the flow.

About 65 percent of the population are engaged in agriculture, 10 percent of them in the tea industry: almost half of India's total tea production is grown on plantations around Dibrugarh in Upper Assam. Rice is the principal food crop, and jute, cotton, oilseeds, sugar cane, pulses, fruit and potatoes are also grown. The forests that cover about 20 percent of the land area are commercially exploited, but part are reserved as national parks and wildlife sanctuaries, including the Kaziranga National Park, established in 1926 to protect the rare Indian one-horned rhinoceros. There are valuable mineral reserves in Upper Assam including oil, gas and coal. There is a growing petrochemical industry.

Most Assamese are Hindu, but around a quarter are Muslim, many of them recent settlers from Bangladesh. Many of the tribal hill people are of Mongoloid stock. Festivals are important social and cultural occasions, particularly the Majh Bihu in January, the Bohag or Rongali Bihu in April and the Kati or Kangali Bihu held in October.

Bihar

The state of Bihar lies mostly on the middle Gangetic plain, extending southward into a region of higher land, the Chota Nagpur plateau. It is one of the poorest and most populous states of India, with the highest densities concentrated on the plains. Though there are several large industrial cities, Bihar is a predominantly rural state, and by far the greater number of people live in villages. Hindus form about 85 percent of the population and Muslims more than 10 percent. Most people speak Hindi or its dialects; a small proportion speak Urdu.

More than 50 percent of the cultivated land is devoted to the production of rice. Wheat, pulses, maize and oilseeds are grown where conditions are more arid. Commercial crops include jute, tobacco, sugar cane, fruit and vegetables. There is a developing industrial economy based on the rich deposits of minerals in the crystalline rocks of the Chota Nagpur plateau. Bihar is India's leading supplier of coal and mica, and it also has large deposits of copper, china clay, iron ore, bauxite and uranium. Industries range from iron and steel, heavy engineering, metallurgy and chemicals to electronics and food processing.

Bihar contains many places of religious importance. The temple complex of Gaya attracts several thousands of Hindu pilgrims every year, and nearby is the temple at Bodh Gaya, commemorating the place where the Buddha attained enlightenment. Nalanda,

199

south, is the site of a celebrated Buddhist monastic university, and the hills around Rajgir, in the south area, are pitted with Buddhist and Jain caves.

Manipur

Manipur occupies the upper Manipur valley that runs between the north–south mountain ranges on India's border with Burma (Myanmar). About two-thirds of the population live in the central valley: they are Meithei and are largely Hindu. Hockey and polo are popular pastimes, and Manipuri dance dramas form an important part of religious life. The rest of the population belong to hill tribes of either the Naga or Kaki clans who speak Tibeto-Burman languages. Many of the tribal peoples are now Christian.

The hills are densely forested with bamboo, teak, oak, magnolia and rhododendron. They contain many rare plants, including the shiroy lily, and animals such as elephants, tigers and leopards. The brow-antlered deer is in danger of extinction. Forestry provides a main source of income. Hillsides are terraced for farming to prevent soil being washed away. Rice, wheat, maize and pulses are grown and fruit production is increasing in importance. Cottage craft production includes silk-making, textile weaving, bamboo and canework and leatherwork.

Meghalaya

The territory of Meghalaya, formerly part of Assam, was created in 1970, becoming a state in 1972. It occupies a tableland that runs from west to east within a broad curve of the Brahmaputra river, and rises to heights of between 1,350 and 1,800 meters, declining toward the east. One of the wettest places in the world, it is densely forested with pine, bamboo, sal and magnolia. Meghalaya's rich animal life includes elephants, tigers, bears, leopards, wild boar, flying squirrels and langurs, and among its abundant birds are species of partridge, pheasant, teal, quail and hornbill.

Culturally Meghalaya is very diverse. Hinduism, animism and Christianity are practiced. Garo, a Tibetan-Burman language, and Khasi, belonging to the Mon-Khmer group that includes Cambodian, are the main languages. The folkdances and music of the tribal peoples of the area are rich and colorful. Shifting slash and burn agriculture is still practiced. Rice, maize, millet, potatoes and commercial crops such as cotton, tea, spices, fruit and mushrooms are grown. The state is potentially rich in minerals, including coal. Wood products and cement are the main industries.

Mizoram

Mizoram was created out of the state of Assam as a Union Territory in 1972 and made a full state in 1987. Bordered on the east by the Chin Hills of Burma (Myanmar), it consists of a series of parallel ridges running north–south that rise to heights of 2,000 meters and are covered with thick evergreen forest; there is a small lowland area in the northwest. The state has a wide variety of wildlife and is especially rich in tropical plants. The population is composed of numerous tribal groups who speak a variety of Tibeto-Burman languages, of which Miso is the most common. The people are predominantly Christian and have a very high literacy level of 84 percent for men and 78 percent for women. Shifting agriculture is still widespread. Maize, rice, oilseeds, vegetables, spices and fruit are the main crops. Industry is mainly craft-based, though schemes to manufacture modern con-

sumer goods such as television sets, lamps, and vehicle parts have been introduced. The provision of electricity is being extended by investment in small-scale hydro-electric plants.

Nagaland

Nagaland occupies a region of forested hills and mountains between Burma (Myanmar) and the Brahmaputra river. It is populated by a number of tribal groups and subgroups, many of whom live in isolated villages. Local traditions and customs are very strong; some groups are ruled by powerful hereditary chiefs, others by village councils. More than 60 Sino-Tibetan dialects are spoken. Nagaland entered the Indian Union in 1963 against the wishes of a sizable minority who sought separate sovereign status for the region. This led to several years of dissident fighting.

About 90 percent of the population are farmers. Many still practice shifting agriculture and attempts are being made to increase the area of cultivation on terraces as a soil conservation measure. Rice, millets, pulses, potatoes and tobacco are the principal crops. Mineral resources are undeveloped and industry is limited to food processing and wood products. Forestry is important. Traditional crafts include richly decorated textiles, basketry, woodwork and pottery.

Sikkim

The small Himalayan state of Sikkim is bordered by Tibet to the north, Nepal to the west and Bhutan to the east. Kanchenjunga, the third highest mountain in the world and regarded as a god and the abode of gods by the Sikkimese, lies on its border. An independent kingdom under the rule of a *chogyal* (temporal and spiritual king), Sikkim was made a British protectorate in 1886. In 1947 India assumed responsibility for its external relations and defense, and in 1952 it elected for integration with India as a Union Territory, becoming a full state in 1975.

Right In contrast to the seething turmoil of Calcutta's streets, the white marble Victoria Memorial stands serenely beside the water among ornamental gardens. The building, which opened in 1921, is a synthesis of Mughal and European design. Today it houses exhibits of the British raj and the history of Calcutta.

Below Tea became a major commercial crop in India only in the second half of the 19th century. Today teas from the plantations of Assam are exported worldwide. Tea pickers, mainly women and girls, wear shady hats as they pluck the tender green shoots and toss them into their baskets.

Below right The squatter settlements of Delhi shelter up to 30 percent of the city's population. Many of the people struggling to survive here are migrants, attracted to the capital from all parts of rural India.

There are three main ethnic groups: the indigenous Lepcha; the Bhutia, Tibetan-speaking migrants who moved in from the 13th century onward; and the Nepalese. Hinduism is followed today by about two thirds of the population, but cultural life remains strongly influenced by Tibetan Buddhism. Terraced farming was introduced by the Nepalese. The main food crops are rice, maize, wheat, millet and barley. Fruit, potatoes, flowers, ginger and cardamom are grown for export. Sikkim is known to possess rich mineral deposits, including gold, silver and garnets, but only copper, lead and zinc are mined in any quantity. Industry is small in scale. Sikkim's greatest resource is its forests, which cover a third of its land area and are carefully controlled. They range from subtropical to temperate and alpine forest and contain more than 4,000 species of plants, including 600 species of orchid, and a great variety of animal life.

Tripura

The small state of Tripura projects into Bangladesh from northeastern India. In the north and east it is divided into four parallel valleys running north–south separated by low forested hills; the west and south consists of a lowland plain that extends into Bangladesh. Tripura – once the seat of a dynasty whose rule extended over Bengal, Assam and Burma and which became a tributary state of the Mughals in the 17th century – was ceded to the Indian Union by the last ruling maharaja in 1947. It became a Union Territory in 1956 and a state in 1972. A high proportion of the population is tribal and almost 90 percent are Hindu. Bengali is spoken by more than half the population. Agriculture is the principal activity. About half of the total land area is wooded, but less than 10 percent of the original forest remains, and planting schemes (often of rubber trees) have been started in deforested areas as a conservation measure to prevent soil loss and degradation. There is some small-scale industry.

Uttar Pradesh

By far the largest part of Uttar Pradesh (known as the United Provinces until 1950) lies on the upper Gangetic plain. On its northern edge rise the Siwalik Hills and, in the far northeast, the Himalayas; between the plain and the mountains is the marshy tract of jungle and tall grass known as the Terai. In the south are the northern ranges of the Deccan plateau. The fourth largest in land area, Uttar Pradesh is the largest state in population. Hindi is the largest mother tongue, with Urdu the next most important language. Hindus are about 85 percent of the population and Muslims (mostly living in the cities) about 15 percent.

More than 75 percent of people work on the land. Uttar Pradesh is a major producer of food grains, sugar cane and oilseeds. Agriculture in much of the state is dependent on irrigation, which now extends to more than 60 percent of the cultivated area. In addition to major schemes such as the Eastern Ganges Canal, pumps and tube wells powered by electricity have extended irrigation. The planting of quick-growing trees is being undertaken to replenish vanishing woodlands, now only about 17 percent of the land area, and to conserve soils and wildlife. The state is a major producer of limestone and silica: cement and glass are leading industries. Textiles, food processing and sugar refining are important, and there is some heavy industry. There are many thriving centers of

Above The Maharaja of Benares, Vidhati Narain Singh, and his granddaughter, splendid in their jewelry and traditional robes. The kingdom of Benares (Varanasi), centered on the holy city (today in Uttar Pradesh), came into being under the Marathas who restored the city as a center of Hindu learning and culture after a long period of decline.

Right More than three-quarters of the population of West Bengal live in villages. Here, as throughout rural India, traditional crafts remain important, serving the needs of local communities. This pottery turns out vessels of all kinds for domestic use.

Right This cow, wearing a brightly colored halter, has been brought to the great Sonepur Fair near Patna in Bihar, which is held at the same time as the Kartik Purnina festival, attended by large numbers of pilgrims. Thousands of cattle are traded, while dancing, competitions, bazaars and other diversions entertain the crowds.

Below The deep alluvial soils of the Gangetic plain north of Calcutta have been cultivated for centuries. Many varieties of rice are grown, and traditional methods of farming are still employed. Here baskets are used to transfer the rice grains by hand to sacks made from jute, which is also grown and processed locally.

Bottom right Agra, in Uttar Pradesh, is one of the great cities of Mughal India. Rickshaw drivers compete with local taxis to convey visitors to view the sights, the most famous of which are the Red Fort, built by Akbar and later extended by Shah Jahan and Aurangzeb, and the Taj Mahal.

handicrafts; for example, embroidery at Lucknow, brassware at Varanasi and ebony work at Nagina.

Uttar Pradesh has occupied a central place in Indian history and culture from earliest times. Four of the sacred cities of Hinduism are here: Ayodhya, the birthplace of Rama; Mathura, the birthplace of Krishna; Hardwar, site of Vishnu's footprint; and Varanasi, where pilgrims bathe in the sacred waters of the Ganges. The place where Buddha preached his first sermon at Sarnath is commemorated by a great stupa and numerous temples. Every 12 years Allahabad is the site of perhaps the largest festival gathering in the world, the Kumbh Mela. During the Muslim period this part of northern India was known as Hindustan; it contains many monuments from the period of Mughal rule, including the fort and Taj Mahal at Agra and the Aurangzeb mosque at Varanasi.

West Bengal

West Bengal was created in 1947 when Bengal was partitioned between India and East Pakistan (later Bangladesh). Its territory was enlarged in 1950 by the addition of the princely state of Koch Bihar and again in 1953 when the former French enclave of Chandannagar was added. In 1956 a narrow corridor of land, in places as little as 16 kilometers wide, was transferred from the state of Bihar; this united the northern and southern parts of the state, which had previously been separated. Most of West Bengal lies on the lower Ganges plain and delta. In the north is part of the Terai lowland, once malarial but now drained and cultivated. The district of Darjiling, where more than 20 percent of India's tea is produced, lies in the foothills of the Himalayas. Trees cover about 13 percent of the land area, and include the mangrove forests of the delta, the sal and reed jungle of the Terai and the oak, chestnut and magnolia woods on the lower slopes of the Himalayas.

West Bengal is densely populated and highly industrialized, accounting for about one-sixth of India's domestic product. With over 10 million inhabitants, the capital, Calcutta, is India's largest urban agglomeration and most important port, despite silting up of the waterways of the Hooghly delta on which it lies. Extensive coal reserves in the west of the state helped to establish West Bengal as a major center of steel production and heavy engineering, including shipbuilding. Jute processing, textiles, oil refining, chemicals and food processing are also important. Despite its concentration of industry, about 75 percent of West Bengal's population are rural-dwelling, and agriculture generates about half the state's income. Rice is the most important crop, followed by jute and tea. Pulses, oilseeds, jute, tobacco, potatoes, sugar cane and some wheat are also grown. Fishing, both inland and marine, is also important here.

Union territory
Delhi
(Area 1,483 sq km, population 9.4 million)
Delhi was created a Union Territory in 1956: it consists of New Delhi (the national capital), the crowded streets of Old Delhi clustered around the main bazaar of Chandni Chowk and the Red Fort, and a surrounding area of countryside. The population has grown staggeringly since 1947, when it numbered only around 700,000. The territory is administered directly by Parliament through the home ministry. The chief administrator is the lieutenant governor.

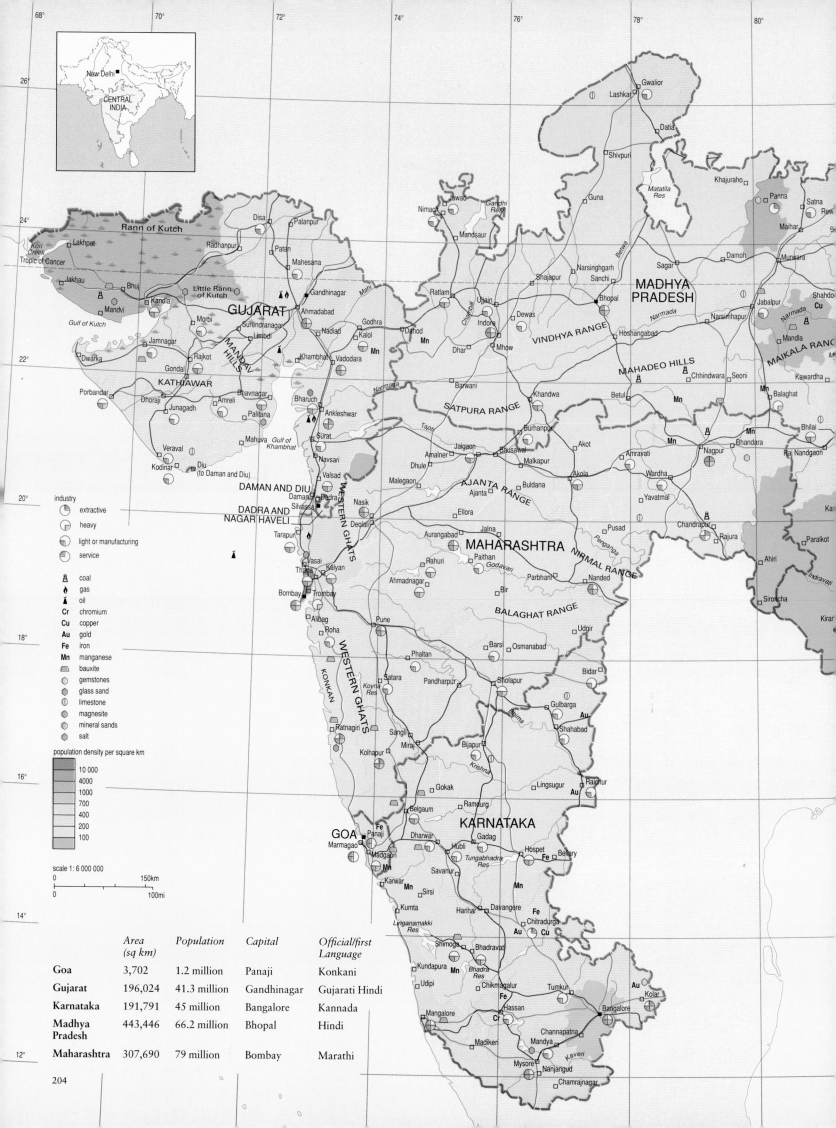

CENTRAL INDIA

New Delhi

68° 70° 72° 74° 76° 78° 80°

26°

Gwalior
Lashkar
Datia
Shivpuri
Guna
Khajuraho
Panna
Satna
Rewa
Maihar
Shahdol

24°
Rann of Kutch
Disa
Palanpur
Radhanpur
Patan
Mahesana
Jawad
Nimach
Gandhi Res.
Matatila Res.
Tropic of Cancer
Lakhpat
Kori Creek
Mandsaur
Guna
Damoh
Murwara
Jakhau
Bhuj
Kandla
Little Rann of Kutch
Gandhinagar
Narsinghgarh
Sanchi
Sagar
Shahdol
Cu
Mandvi
Morbi
MANDAV HILLS
Ahmadabad
Shajapur
Bhopal
MADHYA PRADESH
Jabalpur
Narmada
Gulf of Kutch
Surendranagar
Limbdi
Nadiad
Godhra
Dahod
Ratlam
Ujjain
Dewas
Hoshangabad
VINDHYA RANGE
Narsimhapur
MAHADEO HILLS
Chhindwara
Seoni
Mandla
MAIKALA RANGE
Kawardha

22°
Dwarka
Rajkot
Gondal
KATHIAWAR
Khambhat
Vadodara
Mn
Indore
Mhow
Dhar
Barwani
Narmada
Khandwa
SATPURA RANGE
Betul
Mn
Chhindwara
Mn
Balaghat
Porbandar
Dhoraji
Junagadh
Amreli
Bhavnagar
Palitana
Bharuch
Ankleshwar
Narmada
Taptı
Burhanpur
Akot
Amravati
Mn
Nagpur
Mn
Bhandara
Raj Nandgaon
Bhilai

20°
Veraval
Diu
Kodinar
Mahuva
Gulf of Khambhat
Surat
Navsari
Valsad
DAMAN AND DIU
Daman
Silvassa
DADRA AND NAGAR HAVELI
Jalgaon
Bhusawal
Malkapur
Akola
AJANTA RANGE
Ajanta
Ellora
Amalner
Dhule
Malegaon
Buldana
Wardha
Yavatmal
Chandrapur
Rajura
Ahiri
Sironcha
Indravati
Kirar

Tarapur
Nasik
Deolali
Aurangabad
Jalna
Pusad
Penganga
NIRMAL RANGE
Paralkot

18°
Vasai
Thana
Kalyan
Bombay
Trombay
Alibag
Roha
WESTERN GHATS
Rahuri
Paithan
Godavari
Parbhani
MAHARASHTRA
Ahmadnagar
Bir
Nanded
BALAGHAT RANGE
Udgir
Pune
Barsi
Osmanabad

16°
Phaltan
Satara
Koyna Res.
Pandharpur
KONKAN
WESTERN GHATS
Ratnagiri
Sangli
Miraj
Kolhapur
Bijapur
Sholapur
Bidar
Bhima
Gulbarga
Au
Shahabad
Krishna
Lingsugur
Raichur
Au

14°
Belgaum
Ramaur
Dharwar
Gadag
Hospet
Bellary
Fe
GOA
Panaji
Marmagao
Madgaon
Mn
Karwar
Mn
Sirsi
Hubli
Tungabhadra Res.
Savanur
Mn
Fe
Kumta
Hariar
Davangere
Chitradurga
Cr
Au
Cu
Shimoga
Bhadravati
KARNATAKA
Kundapura
Bhadra Res.
Mn
Udipi
Chikmagalur
Tumkur
Au
Kolar
Fe
Hassan
Bangalore
Mangalore
Cr
Channapatna
Mandya
Madikeri
Mysore
Nanjangud
Kaveri
Chamrajnagar

12°

industry
⊘ extractive
◐ heavy
◑ light or manufacturing
◔ service

⛏ coal
♦ gas
⚒ oil
Cr chromium
Cu copper
Au gold
Fe iron
Mn manganese
⬣ bauxite
⬡ gemstones
⬡ glass sand
⊘ limestone
⬢ magnesite
⬡ mineral sands
⬡ salt

population density per square km
10 000
4000
1000
700
400
200
100

scale 1: 6 000 000
0   150km
0   100mi

	Area (sq km)	Population	Capital	Official/first Language
Goa	3,702	1.2 million	Panaji	Konkani
Gujarat	196,024	41.3 million	Gandhinagar	Gujarati Hindi
Karnataka	191,791	45 million	Bangalore	Kannada
Madhya Pradesh	443,446	66.2 million	Bhopal	Hindi
Maharashtra	307,690	79 million	Bombay	Marathi

CENTRAL INDIA

Goa

The smallest state of the Union of India and a former Portuguese colony, Goa became a full state in 1987. The fusion of Indian and European culture is still evident here, and almost 30 percent of the population are Christian. The first language is Konkani, but Marathi, Hindi and English are also commonly used. More than 85 percent of men and 68 percent of women are literate. Goa lies between the Western Ghats and the sea and is less than 100 kilometers long. The ancient trading city of Goa, on a rocky promontory between the Mandavi and Juari rivers, was captured by the Portuguese in 1510. It became the capital of the Portuguese empire in the east but was abandoned in the 18th century and the seat of government moved to Panaji, which remains the capital today. The largest city and main port, however, is Marmagao, with over 90,000 inhabitants.

The majority of the population are employed in agriculture and fishing. Seafood is a staple item in the local diet, and fish is processed for export. Agricultural exports include fruit, coconuts, cashew nuts and spices: high-yielding varieties of rice and other food grains are also cultivated. Mineral exports include manganese and iron ores and bauxite, and manufactures range from shipbuilding, electronics, fertilizers and pharmaceuticals to clothing and footwear. Goa is a popular destination for tourists, attracted to its sandy beaches and coastal resorts.

Gujarat

No part of Gujarat, the westernmost state of India, is more than 240 kilometers from the sea, and its coastline extends more than 1,500 kilometers. The sparsely populated Rann of Kutch, an arid saltmarsh covering approximately 20,000 square kilometers and part of the Thar Desert, borders Pakistan. The only surviving wild asses in India are found here. South of the Kutch, the low-lying peninsula of Kathiawar is also generally arid. Farther south, rainfall increases and the silts deposited by the Narmada and Tapti rivers are fertile. The coastal plains give way to hilly country in the northeast and east. Gujarat's variety of habitats preserve a rich wildlife. The Gir National Park in Kathiawar contains the only remaining Asiatic lions anywhere in the wild, and the bird sanctuary at Lake Nal Sarovar near Ahmadabad attracts over 140 species of native and migratory birds, including bustards, pelicans, ibises, flamingoes and geese.

Gujarat's coastal towns have a long history of trade with Persia and the Middle East and later with Europe. Gujarati, an Indo-Aryan language, is spoken by the majority of the population. The predominant religion is Hinduism, with significant Muslim and Jain minorities. The temple at Dwarka is one the most important Hindu sites of pilgrimage: this and other temples and monuments preserve the architectural style for which Gujarat is famous. Mahatma Gandhi was born at Porbandar, a trading port on the Kathiawar peninsula.

Gujarat is one of India's main producers of tobacco, cotton and groundnuts, the latter grown in the Kathiawar peninsula. Wheat and millets are the staple food crops, with rice in wetter areas. Sugar cane, spices and fruit are also grown. About one quarter of the cultivated land (about one half of the total land area) is irrigated. Gujarat has a highly developed urban and industrial base: the largest city is Ahmadabad, with over 3 million inhabitants, followed by Vadodara and Surat. Gujarat is a major petroleum producing state, and has a growing petrochemical industry. The cement, synthetic fibers and cotton textile industries are also important, and it is the leading producer of salt. Crafts include gold and silver embroidery, toymaking, perfumery and decorative woodwork.

Above right Cattle are grazed on the sparse pasture of an arid, sunbaked hillside in Gujarat. In the background stands the imposing palace built in the late 19th century for the ruler of Wankaner.

Karnataka

Karnataka consists of the former princely state of Mysore. Boundary changes in 1953 and 1956 united the Kannada-speaking peoples and extended its territory, giving it access to the sea. It took its present name in 1973. The Western Ghats, rising to 900 meters, form a watershed from which some rivers flow west through forest-covered valleys and across the narrow coastal plain to the Arabian Sea and others east across the Deccan plateau to the Bay of Bengal. The rich wildlife of the state can be seen in a variety of habitats ranging from monsoon forests and swamps to dry scrubland; for example, at the sanctuaries of Daudeli, Ranchpur, Nagarhole and in the National Park at Baudihur near Mysore.

Kannada is spoken by two-thirds of the population. Other languages include Telugu, Marathi, Urdu and Tamil. Karnataka is a mainly rural state. The main crops are food grains, pulses, sugar cane, groundnuts, coffee, mulberries (for silk) and cotton, which is grown in the black volcanic "regur" soils of the northwest. On the dry Deccan, irrigation is essential, provided by damming the eastward-flowing streams, which include the upper waters of the Kaveri and Krishna rivers: these are also exploited for hydroelectricity. Teak, rosewood, bamboo and sandalwood are extracted from the forests, and fishing is also important. The ancient rocks of the Deccan plateau are rich in minerals. Gold is mined at the Kolar Gold Fields, and the state is a major producer of chromite and manganese. Its high-quality iron ore reserves supply the iron and steel industry at Bhadravati and the heavy engineering works at Bangalore.

The markets, fort and palaces of the old town of Bangalore, dating from the 16th century, contrast with the modern city, which is the state capital and the center of India's aerospace and hi-tech electronics industry. At Mysore, the former capital, are splendid palaces and gardens. Nearby is the fort of Srirangapatnam where Tipu Sultan fell to the British in 1799. There is an important Hindu temple at Somnathpur and a number of Jain sites, including giant carved stone figures peculiar to the Kannada culture.

Madhya Pradesh

Madhya Pradesh lies in the heart of the subcontinent, bordered by seven other states and with no coastline. Its forested hills, extensive plateaus and river valleys occupy the northern ranges of the Deccan. About 80 percent of the population are engaged in agriculture. Less than one third of the land is irrigated, mainly by means of canals, village tanks or ponds, and tube wells. The chief crops include rice (principally in the east, where rainfall is higher), wheat, sorghum, pulses, soybeans, oil seeds, cotton and sugar cane. Timber is extracted from the forests.

Mineral resources include coal, diamonds, tin, asbestos, copper, iron and manganese. There is aluminum processing at Korba, steel at Bhilai, heavy electrical engineering at Bhopal and vehicle and armament manufacture at Jabalpur. Other centers are at Indore, Gwalior, Ujjain and Raipur, and industries include cement, paper, textiles, ceramics, sugar refining and food processing. Traditional crafts include silk, embroidery and gold and silver wirework.

There is great cultural diversity within the state. Hindi, the most widely spoken language, is present in a number of dialects, and many other languages are spoken. Almost one quarter of the population are clas-

sified as belonging to scheduled tribes. Most people are Hindus, but there are sizable minorities of all the other religions of the subcontinent. Among the state's most important religious monuments are the Buddhist stupa at Sanchi and the exuberantly carved temples at Khajuraho. Notable also are the temples at Gwalior, an ancient city containing many Mughal remains, which is overlooked by a walled fort high on a sandstone cliff. Orchha, to the southeast, also contains a number of well-preserved palaces and temples. The natural attractions of Madhya Pradesh include the Marble Rocks and Dhuandhar Falls near Jabalpur. Kanhar National Park is famous for its swamp deer and the Bondhogarh National Park for its white tigers. The palaces, gardens and lakes at Shivpuri, a summer retreat for the Maratha Shinde dynasty who were the rulers of Ujjain and Gwalior in the 18th century, lie within another national park.

Maharashtra

The state of Maharashtra was created in 1960 when Bombay state was divided between Marathi-speakers in the south and Gujarati-speakers in the north. But the name Maharashtra has been applied to the upland area of the northwest Deccan since at least the 7th century, and it forms a distinct cultural region. It was here

Above One of the most impressive relics of princely rule in India is the palace at Mysore, Karnataka, built a century ago to replace an earlier building destroyed by fire. During festivals, its many domes are lit up by the glitter of thousands of lights, emphasizing the extravagance of its design.

Right A Bora household in Gujarat. The Boras are a Gujarati Muslim sect, descendants of Hindus who were converted to Shia Islam in the 11th century. The name means pedlar, and the Boras have always been traders. Prominent in the business communities of Gujarat and Bombay, many of them adhere to their traditional lifestyle.

Far right There are still around 20,000 *dhobi*s, traditional washermen, operating in the city of Bombay. They collect and deliver laundry, often by bicycle, and use the tubs provided by the municipal corporation. Those shown here are at Jacob's Circle.

Left This strikingly decorated tribal hut is in the Kutch region of northwestern Gujarat – a remote area that is partly semidesert and partly saltmarsh.

Below A woman makes her way with a container of water to her house on the bank of the Narmada river near Mandla in Madhya Pradesh. The river at Mandla is regarded as sacred and the banks are lined with temples and ghats to accommodate the needs of the many pilgrims. Away from the teeming crowds rural life proceeds in the traditional way.

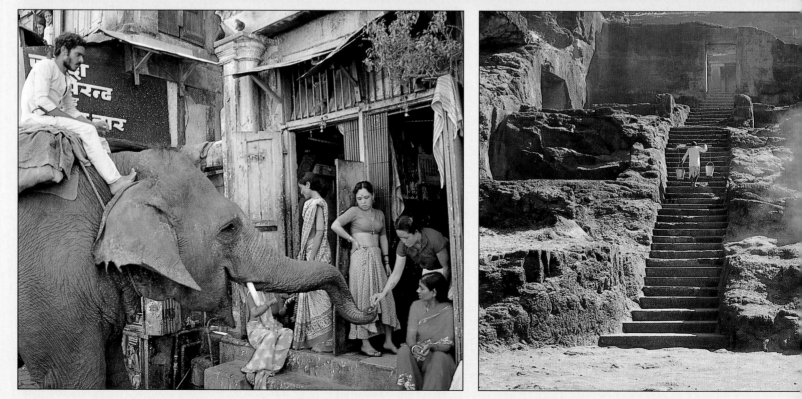

that the Marathas emerged to challenge the power of the Mughals in the 17th and 18th centuries. The state forms three distinct physical areas from west to east: the narrow coastal plain (the Konkan), the Western Ghats, and the Deccan uplands (the Desh), which are drained to the east by a number of rivers including the Godavari and Krishna. The region is known for the extensive lava outpourings ("traps") that have been eroded over time, resulting in its characteristic table-top landscape.

Maharashtra is responsible for one-fifth of India's industrial production, yet approximately 70 percent of the population are engaged in agriculture. Only millets and pulses can be grown in the most arid parts of the interior plateau, which lies in the rainshadow of the Western Ghats, but wheat, cotton, tobacco, oilseeds and rice are cultivated where rainfall allows. The area given to sugar cane and fruit has expanded as the result of irrigation.

The island city of Bombay, with a population of nearly 10 million, dominates Maharashtra's industry and commerce, but Pune, Thane, Aurangabad and Nagpur (the center of a coal-mining region) and other smaller centers are also important. The oldest and largest industry is cotton textiles. A recent development, following the discovery of offshore oil in the Bombay area, has been the growth of the petrochemical industry. Engineering ranges from armaments to electronics and food processing includes fish canning and sugar refining. The Indian motion-picture industry is based in Bombay.

Maharashtra contains many Buddhist cave temples and monasteries. Particularly famous are those at Ajanta, Ellora, Kanheri and Aurangabad. In the vicinity of Bombay is Elephanta Island, where a Hindu temple has been carved into a cliff high above the water. Nasik, set on the banks of the Godavari river, is one of the holy cities of Hinduism, where Rama is believed to have spent part of his exile. The Mughal remains at Aurangabad have recently been restored, including the citadel and Jami Masjid mosque built by the Mughal emperor Aurangzeb. The old walled town at Vasai (Bassein), a Portuguese possession for 200 years from the mid 16th century, contains a ruined cathedral, churches and convents.

Union Territories

Daman and Diu

(Area 112 sq km, population 101,586)
The tiny enclave of Daman, with an area of 72 square kilometers, lies on the Gujarat coast 160 kilometers north of Bombay; Diu (38 square kilometers) is an island off the southeast coast of Kathiawar. Former Portuguese forts that guarded the entrance to the Gulf of Khambhat, they were occupied by Indian troops in 1961 and incorporated, with Goa, into the Indian Union. After Goa was granted statehood in 1987 they remained as a Union Territory.

Dadra and Nagar Haveli

(Area 481 sq km, population 138,401)
The centrally administered Union Territory of Dadra and Nagar Haveli forms an enclave at the southernmost point of the border between Gujarat and Maharashtra. The two Portuguese-controlled territories were seized by Indian nationalists in 1954. The new pro-India administration made a formal request for incorporation into the Union of India, which was granted in 1961.

Top left A shop in Mysore displays colored powders, joss-sticks and fairy-lights in readiness for a major holiday season, perhaps Holi. Though Karnataka is largely Hindu, the salesman (who is reading an Urdu newspaper) is Muslim – a reminder of the Deccan's complex cultural mix.

Far left Exotic or performing animals are part of Indian street-life. Their owners walk them in public to receive small payments or gifts of food. Here in Falkland Road, Bombay (originally the location of European theaters and since the early part of the 20th century at the heart of the city's red-light district) an elephant is handed choice tid-bits.

Left At the Ellora caves in Maharashtra – one of the most celebrated architectural sites in India – a water-carrier climbs a flight of steps leading to one of the many temples carved into the volcanic rock of the hillside.

Top A young woman in Diu steadies the bundle of wood she is carrying on her head. In rural India the collection of wood for fuel is a never-ending daily task.

Above A team of oxen at work in rice fields on the Deccan plateau of Karnataka, where irrigation is essential for crop cultivation. Though traditional labor-intensive farming methods are still widely employed, efforts have been made to increase agricultural production by introducing higher-yielding crop varieties.

SOUTH AND EAST INDIA

Andhra Pradesh

The state of Andhra Pradesh was created in 1953 out of part of the former state of Madras to meet the demand by speakers of Telugu (one of the main Dravidian languages) for a state of their own; in 1956 Telugu-speaking areas of Hyderabad were added to it. Physically, the state is divided between the coastal plain in the east (including the fertile deltas of the Godavari and Krishna rivers), the mountain ranges of the Eastern Ghats, broken by many river valleys, and the central plateau of the Deccan still farther to the west. About 70 percent of the population are engaged in farming. Irrigation schemes have extended both the area of land under cultivation and the range of crops grown. Rice is the major crop, especially in the delta regions. Pulses, tobacco, sugar cane, cotton, chillies and fruit are also cultivated. The state has substantial forests, from which teak, eucalyptus, cashew and bamboo are extracted on a commercial basis. Freshwater and sea fishing are both important.

Andhra Pradesh has commercially exploited reserves of asbestos, barite, quartz and coal, and diamond mining has recently started up again close to where the Koh-i-Noor diamond was found in the 17th century. Rapid industrial development is encouraging migration to the cities, particularly to the three main centers of Hyderabad, Vishakhapatnam and Vijayawada. Manufacturing includes steel and shipbuilding (at Vishakhapatnam, where an oil refinery is located), and heavy engineering. There has been a rapid increase in hydroelectric power, and natural gas is also a source of energy.

Silk-making is important in the state, particularly at Dhamavaran, which is noted for its saris. Other traditional crafts include gold and silver embroidery and filigree work. The old walled city of Hyderabad, the state capital, is famous for its mosques and palaces. Also impressive are the ruins of the nearly 2,000-year-old Buddhist university at Nagarjunakonda, despite being only partially saved from flooding when the Nagarjunasagar Dam was constructed. Warangal, the capital of an important 12th-century dynasty, has lakes and wildlife sanctuaries nearby.

Kerala

One of the smallest states in the Republic of India, Kerala lies in the extreme southwest of the peninsula, sandwiched between the Arabian Sea and the mountains of the Western Ghats. The mountains, which include Anai Mudi (2,695 meters), the highest peak in peninsular India, receive heavy rainfall during the monsoon and are well forested. With nearly 600 kilometers of the Malabar Coast lying within the state, Kerala was for centuries an important center of trade across the Arabian Sea, and has a rich and diverse culture. The form of Hinduism observed by about 58 percent of the population has absorbed elements of Buddhism and Jainism. There is a small Jewish and larger Christian and Muslim communities (each of the latter accounting for more than 20 percent of the

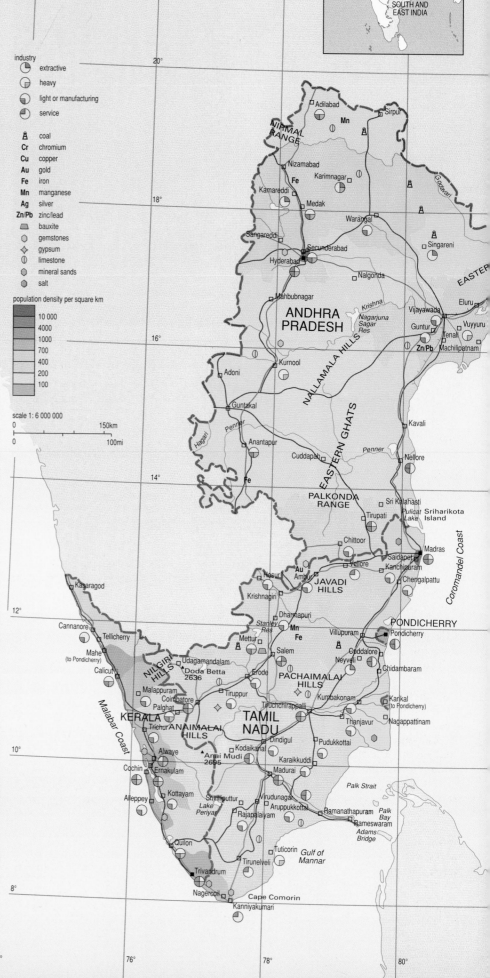

	Area (sq km)	Population	Capital	Official/first Language
Andhra Pradesh	275,068	66.5 million	Hyderabad	Telugu
Kerala	38,863	29 million	Trivandrum	Malayalam
Orissa	155,707	31.6 million	Bhubaneswar	Oriya
Tamil Nadu	130,058	55.8 million	Madras	Tamil

Above A Kathakali dancer in Kerala. The Kathakali dance tradition dates back almost 2,000 years, and the dances were originally performed in a temple setting. The dancers enact scenes from the *Mahabharata* and *Ramayana*, using a number of specific gestures to convey exact meaning. The eyes express various emotions. Elaborate costumes, wigs, head-dresses and masks in vivid colors are traditionally worn, and the face is painted to heighten dramatic impact.

Below For devout Hindus, Bhubaneswar in Orissa is second only to Varanasi as a holy place devoted to Shiva. There are several groups of temples in the environs of the city. The most dominating is the 11th-century Lingaraja temple, shown here; its tall curved tower, resembling a giant beehive, rises about 36.5 meters high and is visible at a great distance.

population). All were introduced from the Middle East, Christianity perhaps as early as the 1st century AD and Islam in about the 8th century. All the festivals of the main religions are celebrated, but the major occasion in Kerala is Onam, the harvest festival.

The present state was created in 1956 to accommodate Malayalam speakers. Its literacy rates, approaching 100 percent, are the highest in India. Kerala is one of the most densely populated states. Though most people live in villages, fewer than half the workforce are engaged in farming. Nevertheless agriculture is the main economic activity: rubber, cardamom, pepper, coconut, cashew nuts, sugar cane, tea and coffee are all grown as plantation crops for export. The staple food crops are rice, pulses and sorghum. Fishing is very important, both for domestic consumption and for export. Most industry is small in scale and of a traditional nature, such as weaving, carpet manufacture and the processing of coir (coconut fiber) and cashew nuts. A range of modern industries such as electrical engineering, ceramics, chemicals, and synthetic textiles has been established.

The forests supply rare timbers such as teak and

Left The slim towers of a mosque on the shore at Vizhinjam in Kerala proclaim the presence of Islam, brought to the region centuries ago by traders from the Middle East. In front of the mosque fish are being laid out on the ground to dry.

Right A woman carries a basketful of freshly caught fish from the beach to a village on the coast near Puri in Orissa. In many parts of India marketing fish is the woman's task and – in a society where male dominance is assumed – this places a degree of power in female hands.

Below The Konarak Sun Temple at Puri stands on an isolated coastal site and has been a navigational aid to sailors for centuries. It is a magnificent example of temple architecture. Designed as a giant chariot, 12 pairs of intricately carved wheels dominate the lower faces. The quality of decoration is outstanding. At the base of the platform, under the great wheels, are carved more than 1,500 elephants and other animals in various poses.

rosewood. Their wildlife is protected in reserves such as the Thekhady Wildlife Sanctuary on Lake Periyar. Particularly attractive is the hill country on the western edge of the Ghats, set with plantations of tea, cardamom and pepper. The numerous rivers that cross the coastal plain are an important means of transport. Along the coast, shallow lagoons are sheltered by long lines of sand dunes.

Orissa

Orissa, in the northeastern corner of peninsular India, was the seat of the Ganga dynasty, who held power over a large area of central India in the 11th and 12th centuries. In the 16th century Orissa lost its independence to the Afghan rulers of Bengal and was later absorbed into the Mughal empire as part of the province of Bengal, which came under British rule in the 18th century. Orissa was constituted a separate province by the British in 1936: after independence a number of princely states were taken into its territory.

Much of Orissa consists of undulating plateaus and uplands cut by several rivers including the Mahanadi, whose wide valley divides the state in two. The rivers deposit their fertile silt across the coastal plain before entering the Bay of Bengal. Orissa lies in the path of the summer monsoon. It receives on average 1,524 mm of rain a year and forests still cover about 35 percent of its land area. There are numerous nature reserves and sanctuaries throughout the state. Chilka Lake – the largest saltwater lagoon in India – is a haven for bird life.

More than 80 percent of the population live in villages. Not all are engaged in farming – many families depend on rural crafts such as handloom weaving, appliqué, basketry, woodwork, silver and brass work. Land shortage and rural unemployment are encouraging migration to the cities. About one-tenth of India's total rice crop is produced in Orissa, especially on the Mahanadi delta. Pulses, oilseeds and sugar cane are also grown, and turmeric is a significant crop in upland regions. Fishing is also important. Chromite, graphite, dolomite, manganese and diamonds are all mined in the state. Large-scale industries include the production of steel, ferro-chrome and aluminum, fertilizers and cement, but despite the growth of electronics and computer-based industries, especially in the vicinity of the capital, Bhubaneswar, industry involves fewer than 3 percent of the population.

Orissa is rich in architectural and archaeological sites such as carved rocks at Dhauli and Jaugarh, the remains of a fortified city at Shishupalgarh, ruins of Buddhist monasteries at Lalitgiri, Udaigiri and Ratnagiri, and Jain caves at Udayaguru and Khandgur. The 13th-century Sun Temple at Konarak and the Jagannatha temple at Puri (where hundreds of thousands of pilgrims from all over India gather each year for the Rath Yatna, or Chariot Festival) are among the most important examples of Hindu architecture in India.

Tamil Nadu

Tamil Nadu lies in the extreme southeast of the peninsula. It was created in 1956 out of the former state of Madras to accommodate Tamil-speakers, and was given its present name in 1968. Dravidian culture is deep-rooted in this part of India, and Tamils have fiercely resisted attempts by the union government to make Hindi the national language. About 90 percent of the population are Hindus. There are more than 9,300 temples, and the cycle of temple festivals – for example, those at Kanchipuram (one of the seven most sacred places in India), Thanjavur (Tanjore), Rameswaram, Kanniyakumari (on the southernmost tip of the peninsula) and Madurai – attract large numbers. Hindu classical dance is widely practiced, and there are numerous dance and music festivals.

Tamil Nadu divides naturally into an extensive fertile coastal plain in the east and uplands in the west (the southernmost hills of the Eastern Ghats in the center and north and the mountains of the Western Ghats). Rainfall in the Nilgiri Hills in the northwest reaches 1,900 mm but is scarce over much of the rest of the state, which lies in the rainshadow of the Western Ghats, and falls as low as 440 mm in the southeast. The rivers that cross the plain – of which the Kaveri, the Palar and the Tambraparani are the most important – have long been used for irrigation; water is stored in reservoirs or tanks. Tamil Nadu is self-sufficient in food grains (rice, maize, pulses and millets). Sugar cane, oilseeds, groundnuts, cotton, tobacco, coffee, tea, rubber and pepper are grown as commercial crops. Timber from the well-forested mountains is commercially exploited.

Tamil Nadu is one of the most highly industrialized states of India, especially around the capital, Madras. Other major centers are Coimbatore, Madurai, Salem and Tiruchchirappalli. Cotton processing and weaving continue to be the main industries, but the production of automobiles, motorcycles, cycles, fertilizers, chemicals and paper is also important. There is an oil refinery at Madras. Craft industries include leatherwork, handloomed silk, hand-painted fabrics, copper and bronze wares, canework and woodcarving.

Union Territories
Andaman and Nicobar Islands
(Area 8,429 sq km, population 280,661)
The Andaman Islands lie in the Bay of Bengal about 1,400 kilometers off the coast from Madras. There are four main islands in the group and more than 200 smaller ones. South of them are the 19 Nicobar Islands, 12 of which are inhabited. Together they form a Union Territory that is administered from Port Blair on South Andaman. Forestry, coconuts and fishing are the mainstays of the economy.

Lakshadweep
(Area 32 sq km, population 51,707)
The Union Territory of Lakshadweep consists of the Laccadive, Minicoy and Amandivi Islands – 20 coral reefs and 14 islands (none longer than 1.5 kilometers) that lie scattered over 77,700 square kilometers of sea about 480 kilometers off the coast of Kerala. Only 10 of the islands are inhabited. The people – of mixed Indian and Arab descent – are Muslim, and the Arabic script is used. The administrative center is Kavaratti in the Laccadive group.

Pondicherry
(Area 492 sq km, population 807,758)
Pondicherry became a Union Territory in 1962. It consists of four widely separated areas on the coast of south and east India – Yanam on the Godavari delta, Pondicherry and Karikal south of Madras, and Mahé on the Malabar coast. These tiny enclaves were French until 1954, and a great variety of languages are spoken: Tamil is predominant in Pondicherry and Karikal, Telugu in Yanam and Malayalam in Mahé.

Above left A group of women and girls stand by the wattle fence that surrounds their thatched dwelling in a forest clearing in the Eastern Ghats of Andhra Pradesh; their nose rings and simple necklaces are worn as an indication of the wealth and standing of the family.

Above The Blue Mountain narrow gauge railway pulled by a steam engine crosses more than 250 bridges over rivers and ravines as it winds its way through pine and eucalyptus-covered hills, tea and coffee plantations and wonderful mountain scenery between Mettapalayam and Ootacamund in Tamil Nadu.

Above right A Toda man in the Nilgiri Hills. The Todas – one of several groups of tribal people in the remote hill regions of Tamil Nadu – are pastoral farmers who graze herds of buffalo. Both men and women wear patterned shawls that they wrap tightly round their bodies.

Left Vegetarianism is common in southern India. Vegetables are grown in garden plots and fields around the villages wherever climate and soils permit. Here a large load of onions is being offloaded at a vegetable market at Cochin in Kerala, where they will be bagged ready for sale.

Right Water provides an important means of communication in Kerala, especially in the Alleppey region where there is an extensive canal network. Backwater cruises along the quiet waterways, shaded by palm trees, are now popular with tourists.

NEPAL

The small kingdom of Nepal, bordered by Tibet (now occupied by China) to the north and India on all other sides, possesses some of the most rugged mountain terrain in the world. In the north the Great Himalayas contain seven peaks of more than 8,000 meters, including Everest, the world's highest mountain at 8,848 meters. They descend southward to the Mahabharat mountains, ranging between 600 and 9,100 meters, and then to the Siwalik and Churia Hills. Still farther south, on the edge of the Gangetic plain, are the subtropical Terai lowlands, only 100 meters or less above sea-level. The summer brings heavy monsoon rains, and flooding is a serious problem in low-lying areas of the Terai. More than one-third of the country is forested. The tropical deciduous forests of the south, which shelter tigers, leopards, deer, monkeys and a few Indian rhinos, give way on the hills to mixed deciduous and evergreen trees (oak, maple, magnolia, rhododendron) and then at higher altitudes to conifers, with alpine tundra above the treeline.

The ancient Vedic texts contain the earliest references to Nepal, which stands on the cultural borders between India and Tibet. Its people show a number of different ethnic and cultural characteristics. The official language is Nepali, a derivative of Sanskrit, but more than 30 other languages or dialects are spoken, many of them by the various tribal groups of the hill regions. The most densely populated area is the Kathmandu valley, which lies at about 1,400 meters between the Himalayas and Mahabharats. A distinct group of people, the Newars, are found here, highly skilled in agriculture and craftwork and with rich and influential cultural and economic traditions. Most Nepalese are Hindu, but in the more sparsely populated north the people are Buddhist and speak a variant of the Tibetan language. The Sherpas of the high Himalayas are yak farmers who practice transhumance during the short summer season. Sherpa porters, using mules, have provided the means of transporting goods over the rough tracks of the Himalayan passes for centuries, and still do so today.

The modern history of Nepal dates from the 18th century when the Gurkha principality, ruled by the Shah family, became preeminent throughout the country and the capital was established at Kathmandu. During the 19th century the Shahs became reduced to the status of puppet rulers, and real power lay with the Rana family. In 1860 an accommodation was reached with the British government in India that allowed it to exercise a guiding role in Nepal's external affairs and to recruit Nepalese soldiers into Gurkha units in the British army – as still happens today. A revolution in 1950 ousted power from the Rana family, restoring the royal family to full sovereignty. The constitution of 1959 provided for parliamentary elections, but a ban was placed on political parties in 1961. This was lifted in 1990, following pro-democracy demonstrations, and a new constitution was enacted that transferred power from the monarchy to the elected government.

Above Bodhnath, near Kathmandu, is on the ancient route linking the capital with Lhasa in Tibet. The stupa, with its massive dome topped by a square tower on which are painted the "all-seeing eyes of supreme buddha-hood", in turn supports a 13-stepped structure representing the path to enlightenment. This is one of the most important Buddhist shrines in Nepal and attracts pilgrims from neighboring countries.

Left Bhaktapur is the third largest city in the Kathmandu valley. In spite of earthquake damage in 1934, it has retained much of its medieval atmosphere. Cottage industries and the growing of fruit, vegetables and oilseeds are important here. Some of the most impressive of Nepal's medieval palaces and temples are found in Bhaktapur.

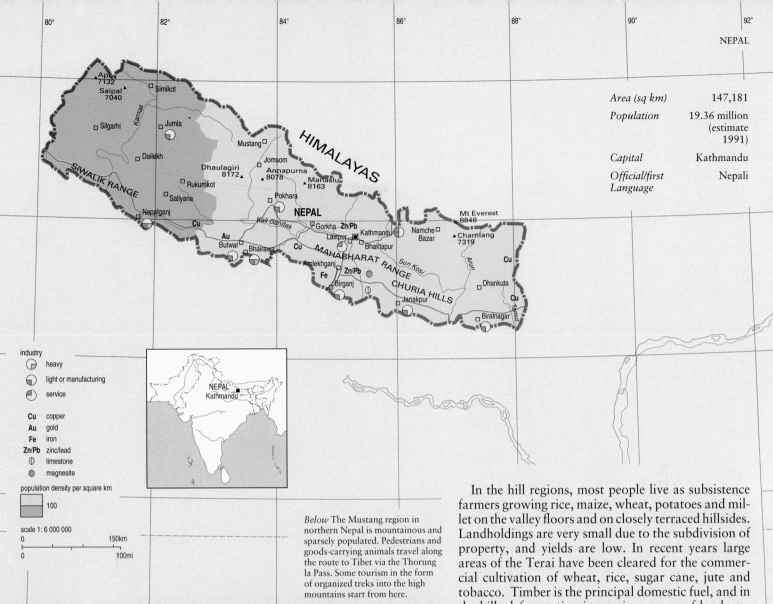

Area (sq km)	147,181
Population	19.36 million (estimate 1991)
Capital	Kathmandu
Official/first Language	Nepali

industry

🝪 heavy

🝪 light or manufacturing

🝪 service

Cu copper
Au gold
Fe iron
Zn/Pb zinc/lead
Ⓛ limestone
🞄 magnesite

population density per square km

☐ 100

scale 1: 6 000 000

0 ——— 150km
0 ——— 100mi

Below The Mustang region in northern Nepal is mountainous and sparsely populated. Pedestrians and goods-carrying animals travel along the route to Tibet via the Thorung la Pass. Some tourism in the form of organized treks into the high mountains start from here.

In the hill regions, most people live as subsistence farmers growing rice, maize, wheat, potatoes and millet on the valley floors and on closely terraced hillsides. Landholdings are very small due to the subdivision of property, and yields are low. In recent years large areas of the Terai have been cleared for the commercial cultivation of wheat, rice, sugar cane, jute and tobacco. Timber is the principal domestic fuel, and in the hills deforestation is a serious cause of land erosion. There has been little development of hydroelectricity, though the potential for it is great. There is a small amount of food-processing industry, most of it in the Kathmandu valley. In recent years, some manufacturing industry has been developed in the growing towns of the southern lowlands. Some craft goods are exported, but the economy remains dependent on foreign aid, tourism and remittances from Gurkha soldiers. Though Nepal remains a poor country, health standards and life expectancy are improving. Migration has always been the traditional escape route from poverty – more than 6 million Nepalese live in India, with substantial numbers in Bhutan and Malaysia.

Nepal's varied wildlife is protected in numerous national parks and reserves. The Royal Chitwan National Park in the Terai shelters around 35 species of large mammals, including endangered sloth bears, tigers, gaurs and Ganges river dolphins, as well as 489 species of birds. Visitors ride on elephants to view the wild life. The Royal Botanical Gardens near Godavari contain a wide variety of plants, especially orchids. Since the 1960s Kathmandu, with its tall, elaborately carved wooden houses and narrow streets, apparently remote from the 20th century, has been a magnet for western tourists. In the mountains organized treks can be made through stupendous scenery with panoramic views of the Himalayas, remote villages, yak-grazing grasslands, rhododendron forests and past monasteries and lakes. The village of Namche Bazar, a Sherpa center, is the starting point for treks up to the Everest Base Camp.

Below The Swayanburath Temple, near Kathmandu, on the site where the "Self-existent One" emerged from a lotus flower, is the major center of Buddhism in Nepal. From the eastern entrance more than 300 steps flanked by carvings and statues lead to the ancient white-domed chaitya.

Bottom left The elephant provides transport and motive power in the jungle-covered Terai region of Nepal. The Terai is a complete contrast to the mountainous north. Tropical plants and trees grow here but, in a region of increasing population and development, forests are now being cleared.

Below Dancing, often extending over several days and accompanied by traditional instruments, is part of Bhutanese festivals. Its role is steeped in the nation's religion and culture. Masked dancers, wearing elaborate head-dresses and traditional costume, enact ancient rituals.

Bottom right Takstang Dzong (the Tiger's Nest) is Bhutan's holiest place. Perched in a spectacular setting on a ledge near the top of a precipitous 1,000-meter high cliff, it marks the place where Guru Rippoche (who introduced Buddhism to this region) arrived by flying tiger in 747 AD.

Below right Archery is Bhutan's national sport. Local festivals often include archery contests. Competition is fierce and accompanied by traditional chanting, loud vocal support and, perhaps, dancing. Rival competitors gather round the targets – confirmation of the archers' skill and accuracy.

BHUTAN

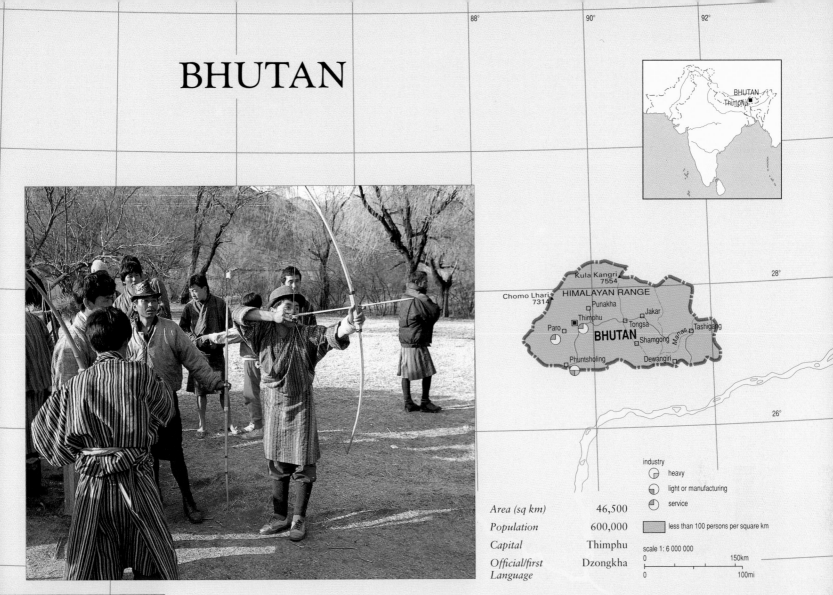

Area (sq km)	46,500
Population	600,000
Capital	Thimphu
Official/first Language	Dzongkha

industry
- heavy
- light or manufacturing
- service

less than 100 persons per square km

scale 1: 6 000 000

The tiny kingdom of Bhutan in the eastern Himalayas is a country of high mountains and deep valleys. Along its southern border with India is the Duars, a narrow, lowland plain, between 12 and 16 kilometers wide, that receives heavy seasonal rainfall of 5,000–7,500 mm a year. Until recently the prevalence of malaria restricted settlement here but this is now eradicated, and the bamboo forests are being cleared for farming. To the north, the mountains of the Inner Himalayas are cut by broad, fertile valleys suitable for arable farming: rice, wheat and potatoes are the principal crops, and there is commercial fruit-growing. Shifting agriculture is still practiced in more remote areas. In the far north the Great Himalayas rise to heights of over 7,000 meters; they are inhabited only by yak-herders who graze their animals on the high alpine meadows in the summer months.

Little is known of Bhutan's early history. Tibetan Buddhism was introduced in the 7th century AD. Bhutan became a unified state in the 17th century under Ngawang Namgyel, a Tibetan monk who gave it a system of law and established it as a theocracy under separate spiritual and secular leaders. Each spiritual leader, or Dharma Raja, was regarded as the reincarnation of his predecessor. On the death of the last Dharma Raja at the beginning of the 20th century no reincarnation was found, and the office ceased.

In 1775 a treaty was concluded between Bhutan and the East India Company, and British influence grew throughout the 19th century. Britain had responsibility for the country's external affairs until 1949, when it passed by treaty to India. In 1907 the installation of a hereditary monarch brought an end to the system whereby regional military governors fought each other to become the secular leader. Today the king enjoys supreme authority, but rules with a council of ministers and shares administrative responsibility. There are no recognized political parties.

The Bhutanese people are of Tibetan origin and are Buddhist. They speak Dzongkha, a form of Tibetan. In the last 150 years large numbers of Hindu Nepalese have settled in the south and west. They are restricted from moving into the center of Bhutan, and attempts have been made to suppress their language and customs: tensions with the indigenous Bhutanese have flared into unrest on occasion in recent years.

Reminders of Buddhism are to be seen everywhere, in the form of fluttering white prayer flags, prayer wheels turned by mountain streams, and the distinctive Bhutanese *chortens* (stupas). Bhutan has frequent colorful festivals (*tsechus*) that are based on the numerous *dzongs*, or fortified monasteries. They are accompanied by music and dancing, and traditional costumes are worn. The men drape themselves with large colored scarves (*kabne*) that denote rank according to their color. The massive sloping walls of the *dzongs*, decorated with richly detailed woodwork, combine solidity and elegance. Simpler in form are the smaller *lhakhangs*, or temples, some dating back more than 1,000 years. Many of these buildings cling precipitously to cliffsides. Tourism operates under strict government controls to protect Bhutan's unique natural and cultural environment. Trekking is permitted over recognized routes in the high mountains.

BANGLADESH
Dhaka

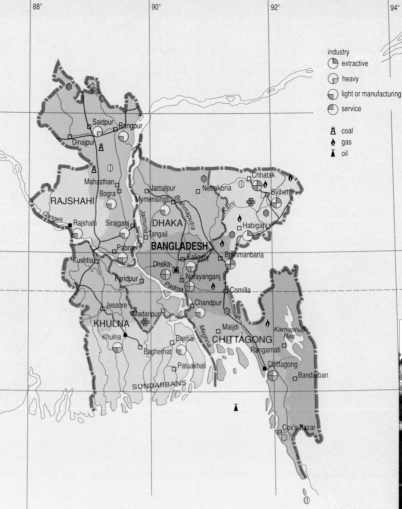

industry
- extractive
- heavy
- light or manufacturing
- service

- coal
- gas
- oil

glass sand
gravel
limestone
mineral sands
peat

population density per square km
1000
700
400
200
100

scale 1: 6 000 000
0   150km
0   100mi

BANGLADESH

RAJSHAHI

Saidpur
Rangpur
Dinajpur
Mahasthan
Bogra
Jamalpur
Mymensingh
Nettrakona
Chhatak
Sylhet
Rajshahi
Sirajganj
Tangail
Habiganj
DHAKA
Kushtia
Pabna
Kaliganj
Brahmanbaria
Faridpur
Dhaka
Narayanganj
Comilla
Jessore
Chandpur
Madaripur
Maijdi
Karnaphuli
Res
KHULNA
Khulna
Barisal
Meghna
CHITTAGONG
Rangamati
Bagherhat
Chittagong
Patuakhali
Bandarban
SUNDARBANS

Ganges
Jamuna
Brahmaputra
Kalni
Padma

Cox's Bazar

Below A father and son take their crop of vegetables to market. They are wearing the traditional *dhoti* with western-style shirts. Bangladesh suffers from both floods and drought, adding to the difficulties of the small subsistence farmer in this crowded land.

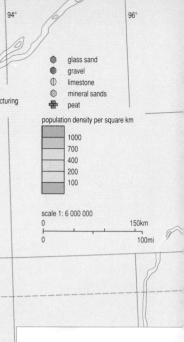

Below Sugar cane is an important cash crop in Bangladesh. This peaceful dawn scene in wooded countryside near Paharpur is close to the site of an immense Buddhist monastery, excavated in the last hundred years.

Right This train, north of Dhaka, is overflowing with people, many of whom occupy the roof of the carriage. The railways were mostly built by the British. Much transportation is carried on the country's many inland waterways.

BANGLADESH

Area (sq km)	143,998
Population	122 million
Capital	Dhaka
Official/first Language	Bengali

Bangladesh occupies the eastern two-thirds of the Ganges delta. There are hilly areas in the east and some higher land in the north and west, but 90 percent consists of low alluvial plain crossed by over 200 rivers that drain into the Bay of Bengal. The constant deposition of silts makes Bangladesh a fertile land, but cyclones sweep in from the sea with regular frequency, bringing devastating floods to coastal areas. The climate is dominated by the summer monsoon when most of the annual rainfall, ranging between 1,250 mm in the west and 5,000 mm in the northeast, occurs. Temperatures reach 34°C and there is high humidity.

Under British rule, Bangladesh belonged to the province of Bengal. Partition in 1947 left the western part of the province in India; the eastern, predominantly Muslim, part joined the new state of Pakistan. The relationship between West and East Pakistan was always unbalanced. The east had the greater population, but the military and civil government was centered in the west. Growing resentment of West Pakistan led to a demand for independence. In March 1971 civil war broke out between the two halves of the country, only ended when India (which had been forced to absorb 10 million refugees fleeing from the fighting) invaded East Pakistan and captured Dhaka, the capital. In December 1971 the new state of Bangladesh ("Bengal nation") was proclaimed. The 1972 constitution provides for a parliamentary form of government, headed by a president, directly elected by parliament every five years. He appoints the prime minister. In the difficult political circumstances of building a new state the army has played a major role in securing national stability, and the constitution has been suspended on more than one occasion.

Bangladesh is one of the most densely populated countries in the world with more than 740 people per square kilometer. About 80 percent of the population are peasant farmers and landless laborers. Life expectancy is about 52 years, less than 30 percent of adults are literate and there is rapid population increase. Nevertheless, despite enormous problems of wealth generation and national debt, progress is being made in improving living standards and raising agricultural and industrial productivity.

Principal crops are jute, rice, sugar cane, wheat, tobacco, pulses, tea and potatoes. Fishing is an important part of the economy, both for home demand and for export. There are few mineral resources. Jute processing, sugar refining and papermaking (from bamboo harvested in the Chittagong Hill Tracts and softwood trees that grow in the Sundarbans) use local raw materials; textiles and garment manufacture, steel, shipbreaking and shiprepairing, light engineering, cement and fertilizer production are all reliant on imported raw materials. Most industrial cargoes are transported by river. Natural gas reserves at Sylhet in the northeast provide thermal power, and oil beneath the Bay of Bengal is piped to a refinery at Chittagong. The main source of hydroelectricity is the Kaptai dam on the Kharnaphuli river in the Chittagong Hill Tracts. Dhaka was founded by the Mughals and the old town contains many interesting buildings and monuments. Rajshahi, on the Ganges in the west of the country, the seat of the 8th-century kings of Bengal, is today the center of a silk-weaving industry. Mahasthan, in the same region, is an important site with Buddhist, Hindu and Muslim connections. Paharpur has an impressive concentration of Buddhist shrines and buildings.

Tribal people still live in the forests of the Chittagong Hill Tracts, parts of which are now being cleared for plantation farming. There are long stretches of sandy beach at Cox's Bazar in the east of the country. At the mouth of the Ganges lie the Sundarbans, one of the most extensive mangrove forests in the world, which extend westward into India. In Bangladesh, more than 323 square kilometers of this unique ecosystem are protected in three separate sanctuaries. Bengal tigers survive in these forests and there are more than 300 species of plants. However, large parts of the Sundarbans are threatened by salinization. Water-sharing agreements with India broke down in 1989, and the waters of the Ganges are diverted by the Farruka barrage dam on the Indian side of the border. This reduces the flow in the river channels downstream in Bangladesh during the dry season and allows seawater to penetrate long distances inland from the Bay of Bengal, killing vegetation.

Below Two months of monsoon rains have brought flooding to the Ganges delta, making an island of this tiny farming hamlet. Despite such natural hazards, progress is being made in raising Bangladesh's agricultural productivity, largely by adopting multiple cropping patterns.

SRI LANKA

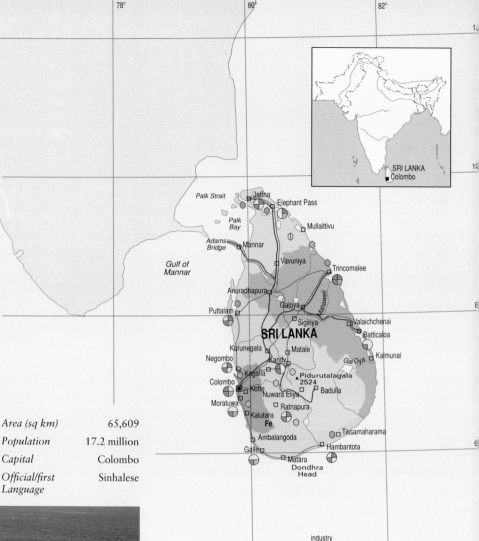

Lying off the southeast coast at the tip of the subcontinent, the island of Sri Lanka (known as Ceylon until 1972) rises from palm-fringed sandy beaches to the forested central highlands, the highest peak of which, Pidurutalagala, reaches a height of 2,524 meters. The climate is equatorial, modified by the southwestern (summer) and northeastern (winter) monsoons. Sri Lanka is widely held to be one of the most beautiful islands in the world. Rice paddies interspersed with groves of spice and nut trees cover the lowland plains, the hillsides are clothed with tea and coconut plantations, and the central highlands are drained by numerous fast-flowing streams that cascade down the forested slopes. The island has more than 400 species of butterflies and 250 species of non-migratory birds. Animal life has been much depleted by agricultural activity, but national parks such as those at Yala in the southeast and Gal Oya in the east afford visitors opportunities to see elephants, leopards, sloth bears, crocodiles and other species in their natural habitat.

Plantation crops – rubber, tea and coconuts – are grown for export. Rice is the principal food crop;

Area (sq km)	65,609
Population	17.2 million
Capital	Colombo
Official/first Language	Sinhalese

industry
- extractive
- heavy
- light or manufacturing
- service

Fe iron
- gemstones
- limestone
- mineral sands
- salt

population density per square km
- 1000
- 700
- 400
- 200
- 100

scale 1: 6 000 000

0 ———— 150km

0 ———— 100mi

Left Mihintale, a rugged 300-meter peak in North Central Province, is a holy site commemorating the introduction of Buddhism to Sri Lanka by Mahinda. More than 1,800 steps lead to the monastery. Here, also, is the "couch of Mahinda" carved in the rock and the Ambasthata dagoba, marking the place where Mahinda met the king and converted him in 243 BC. Views toward Anuradhapura from the summit are impressive.

Right Elephants are essential to the economy in rural Sri Lanka, used to haul timber in the forests. They are bathed twice daily in the river by their mahouts. Abandoned young elephants are reared in elephant orphanages, for example, at Katugastola.

Below Anuradhapura, "the lost city", is an ancient capital and regarded as sacred. It flourished 2,000 years ago but fell into ruin and disappeared. Excavation and restoration have been in progress for more than a century. Many temples, palaces and monastic buildings have been found, together with imposing statues and carvings. This recumbent Buddha is in one of the restored temples.

Right Hikkadura beach, backed by waving palms, is typical of the southwestern coast and tourist resorts have been developed here. Miles of unspoilt natural shores are flanked by coconut groves and banana, tea, rubber and spice plantations. Tropical fish abound in the clear waters.

Left The traditional ten-day festival, the Perera, at Kandy, celebrates the annual renewal of "cosmic power" descending to the faithful. Elephants kept at Kandy for ceremonial duties are clothed in richly decorated and jeweled drapery for the processions; first within the temple precincts, later parading the Tooth relic, reputed to have belonged to the Buddha, throughout the city by torch and lamplight.

breadfruit, cacao, coffee and spices are also grown. Some of the artificial lakes and tanks that are used for irrigation are very ancient. Sri Lanka has extensive mineral deposits, including graphite, ilmenite (iron titanate) and gemstones (sapphires, rubies, garnets and topaz), quartz and limestone. Salt is evaporated from seawater in shallow coastal lagoons. Food-processing, papermaking, leather, textiles, cement production, ceramics and some light engineering are the most important manufacturing industries. Tourism is now being actively developed.

The island has been settled for more than two millennia. Its people belong to two main linguistic groups. The Sinhalese (approximately 74 percent of the population today) appear to have migrated from India about the 5th century BC; the Tamils (18 percent) moved into the north of the island after 1200 AD. About 70 percent of the population (predominantly Sinhalese) are Buddhist, and 15 percent (predominantly Tamils) are Hindu. Muslims (Tamil-speakers, perhaps descended from Arab traders), and Christians account for less than 8 percent each. Sri Lanka has long been a meeting place for traders from east and west. The Portuguese arrived in the 16th century, the Dutch in the 17th century, and from the late 18th century the island came under British control. It achieved independence in 1948. It is a republic, headed by a president who is elected by the people every six years. Long-standing tensions between the Sinhalese majority and the Tamil minority – who demand an independent homeland in the north and east of the island – escalated into violence in the 1980s.

There are many signs of Sri Lanka's religious and cultural history. At Sigiriya, the ancient royal palace built as a fortress at the summit of a rock, a vast staircase mounts up between two gigantic carved lion's paws. The ruined cities of Anuradhapura and Habarana include monastery buildings, temples and statues. The Golden Buddha, the Temple of the Tooth and other shrines at Kandy, capital of the island's last kingdom until it fell to the British in 1817, testify to its lasting importance as the religious center of Sri Lanka.

GLOSSARY

amir A commander, chief, or lord; governor or official of high rank.

Aryans Ancient peoples speaking a group of Indo-European related languages, presumed to have originated in Central Asia. They colonized the territories from Iran to northwestern India in the 2nd millennium BC, bringing the SANSKRIT language and worship of BRAHMA to the subcontinent.

ashram A hermitage or place where any group with shared religious or social aims live together.

Awami League "Peoples' League" – a Bengali political party that, under the charismatic leadership of Sheikh Mujibur Rahman, transformed East Pakistan into Bangladesh in the 1970s.

bhaga A share, a basic form of land tax that was a fixed proportion of the crop.

bhakti In HINDUISM, religious devotion or piety as a means of salvation, as opposed to the performance of rituals or the quest for knowledge; devotion to a personal god, especially KRISHNA.

Brahma The creator god; in both HINDUISM and BUDDHISM, the highest god.

brahmin A member of the highest of the original four VARNAS, or divisions of Hindu society, endowed with specialist religious knowledge and potency; a specially trained priestly CASTE.

Buddhism A religious and philosophical system founded in the 5th century BC, based on the teachings of Siddartha Gautama.

caste A term derived from Portuguese meaning race, breed, kind, that is used to describe Indian social structure as composed of ranked and closed corporate groups formed through descent and marriage, often associated with specific occupations; it is now used interchangeably with *jati*.

Chagatai A political and ethnic term derived from Chaghatai (d.1242), a son of the Mongol emperor Chengis Khan, whose territories included Transoxiana, parts of Kazakhstan, eastern Turkestan and northern and eastern Afghanistan; the 15th century saw a great flourishing of Chaghatai literature under the patronage of the TIMURID courts at Samarkand, Shiraz and Herat.

chaitya A shrine; in BUDDHISM a place or object of reverence.

Chandella A dynasty that ruled the Bhudelkhand plateau in central India, based on the city of Khajuraho, from the mid-9th to the early 14th century.

chattri An umbrella or parasol; in architecture, a domed pavilion or kiosk, often used as a crowning decorative feature.

chauth A tax claimed by the MARATHAS, amounting to one quarter of the revenue.

Chisti A SUFI order of northern India, which had its center at Ajmer. It traced its spiritual genealogy back to Hasan al-Basra (d.728) and derived its name from a village near Herat, the birthplace of Khwajah Abu Ishaq (d.940) another early saint of the order.

Chola A south Indian dynasty based in the Kaveri valley and delta, which ruled an extensive territory from its capital at Thanjavur from the mid 9th to the late 13th century.

Congress See INDIAN NATIONAL CONGRESS.

Dalit The term (meaning "downtrodden" or "oppressed") currently favored by politicized ex-UNTOUCHABLES to describe themselves and their political and social movements.

Deccan The southern part of India, the peninsula, the country south of the river Narmada.

Dehastha A term used to describe those claiming to be the original BRAHMINS of Maharashtra.

Desmukh A revenue collector.

dharma The established, proper order; justice or duty; universal truth.

dhoti A length of cotton or silk cloth that a man wraps round his body, the end being passed between the legs and tucked into the waist so that a festoon hangs down to the knees.

Divali The Hindu festival, held at the end of the lunar month of Asvin and the beginning of Karttika (October-November) to celebrate the new season following the MONSOON, when lights are lit, various divinities worshiped and presents exchanged.

diwan The chief financial minister in many Muslim governments; the prime minister of an Indian state; the chief official in charge of certain government establishments such as a mint; an official in charge of confidential business.

Dravidian Used to describe a group of languages spoken chiefly in south India and distinct in origin from the Indo-European family of languages; it also describes the ethnic groups in south India and Sri Lanka that speak such languages.

durbar A court or levee.

Gandhara In ancient times, an area of northwestern India, Pakistan and Afghanistan where an Indo-Hellenistic school of art, especially BUDDHIST, flourished between the 1st and 5th centuries.

Ganesha Elephant-headed god, the son of PARVATI and SHIVA, whose principal attribute is that of removing obstacles.

gopuram Tower over the gate of a south Indian temple.

Gupta A dynasty that ruled northern India from the early 4th to the late 5th century AD, under whose patronage the arts, literature, science and technology blossomed.

guru A spiritual teacher.

hadith A reported saying or deed of the Prophet Muhammad, which collectively form one of the principal sources of the SHARIA.

Hanuman Monkey-god of HINDUISM, a beneficent guardian spirit.

Harijan The name, meaning "children of God", given by Gandhi to the out-castes, since 1935 known officially as SCHEDULED CASTES. See also DALIT.

Hinduism A system of religious beliefs and social customs prevalent in India, the word being derived from the Persian word used by the Muslim conquerors of the subcontinent to describe those of Indian religion and race.

Hindusthan Originally the country of the Hindus, more specifically the subcontinent north of the river Narmada exclusive of Bengal and Bihar, but also used loosely (even by the emperor Babur) to describe the whole subcontinent.

Holi The Hindu spring festival accompanied by much merry-making and the throwing of colored powders and liquids, a time when social conventions are inverted.

imam Leader of mosque prayers, or the leader of the Muslim community.

Indian National Congress A broad-based political alliance that crosses regional, sectional, communal, CASTE and class interests. It first met in Bombay in December 1885 and gave focus to the Indian nationalist movement; despite a schism in 1969, it continues to dominate Indian politics long after Independence.

Indra The greatest god of the ARYAN warriors, the god of war and of the weather, combining many of the characteristics of the Greek god Zeus and the Germanic god Thor.

Islam The religion established by the Prophet Muhammad, based on his teaching in the QU'RAN and on the SHARIA, a collection of customary laws, the religion of Muslims; also the body of Muslims, the world-wide Muslim community.

jagir The grant of public revenues or produce of a district to an individual or group for some specific purpose – e.g. for the maintenance of troops or the upkeep of a temple, or as a form of salary.

Jainism Non-brahminical religion founded in

India by the 6th century BC that lays stress on non-violence and strict asceticism as the means to salvation.

jati See CASTE above.

jihad Sacred war of Muslims against non-Muslims, hence the notion of a vigorous campaign or crusade in some cause; also a spiritual struggle against one's baser instincts.

jiziya A poll-tax levied by Muslim governments on their non-Muslim subjects.

Kali Manifestation of Durga, the Mother Goddess, wife of SHIVA, particularly popular in Bengal.

karma Fate; the effect of former deeds, performed either in this life or in a previous one, on the present and future condition of the soul.

khatri A north Indian mercantile CASTE of high social status.

Krishna The eighth and most popular incarnation of VISHNU.

kshatriya The kingly or warrior *VARNA* of the original four-fold division of Hindu society.

Kumbh Mela A Hindu festival in the sign of Aquarius held in a 12-year cycle at four sacred sites, when pilgrims bathe in the holy river to wash away their sins. The most important takes place at Allahabad.

Kushan A powerful dynasty, of which Kanishka was the most notable ruler, in northern India in the 1st to 3rd centuries AD. The Kushans traced their origins to the clans of the Yuezhi, a Tokharian-speaking tribe from Gansu, China; they came to occupy territory north of the river Oxus and then conquered Bactria and Sogdiana, from where they moved into the northwest of the subcontinent.

linga Sacred object constituting the symbol of the god SHIVA, specifically a phallic emblem.

Lodi An Afghan dynasty of the Delhi sultanate, established in 1451 and ousted by the MUGHAL emperor Babur in 1526.

Maharaja Title of an Indian prince, meaning "great king".

mahdi "He who is rightly guided", the restorer of religion and justice who will rule before the end of the world, the title of a messianic leader, the awaited descendant of the Prophet Muhammad who will purify ISLAM.

mandala A symbolic circular figure, usually with symmetrical divisions and figures of deities in the center, used to represent the universe.

mansabdar An official in MUGHAL military or civil service, graded according to rank.

Maratha A member of the Marathi-speaking

agricultural castes of Maharashtra; collectively, the families and clans who, through land-control and military service, established the Maratha kingdoms from the mid-17th century.

Maurya A dynasty that established control over much of northern India from about 324–187 BC, of whom Ashoka (ruled 268/7–233) was the most celebrated.

monsoon The name given to the periodical winds, and to the seasons they affect, that blow from the southwest in summer (the rainy season, or "the rains") and from the northeast in winter (the "dry monsoon").

Mughal A dynasty claiming descent from Timur (Tamerlane) that ruled in India from the 16th century; its real authority declined in the 18th century but it survived in formal terms until 1857 when the last Mughal emperor, Bahadur Shah, was deposed by the British.

Muslim League The main specifically Muslim party in British India, founded in 1906.

Naqshbandi SUFI order originating in Central Asia that derived its name from the master Bahauddin an-Naqshband (d.1389). Its teachings were influential in India from the early 17th century, particularly those of Ahmad Sirhindi (d.1624), who emphasized a scripturalist approach to ISLAM and put the Naqshbandis at the center of the Islamic revivalist movement. In the 18th century it was important in initiating many Indonesians and Central Asians into ISLAM. Unlike some other *sufi* orders the Naqshbandis favored private meditation and rejected the use of music as a spiritual aid.

Nawab Originally a deputy in the sense of a viceroy or chief governor under the MUGHAL emperor, as in the Nawab of Bengal, but then used more widely as a title of respect.

nirvana Literally "blown out" like a candle, a state of enlightenment, when the soul is liberated from the effects of *KARMA* and from bodily existence; blissful annihilation.

Nizam Abbreviation of *nizam ul-mulk*, "administrator of a realm", the title of the ruler of the MUGHAL province of Hyderabad in south India.

Pallava A dynasty tracing its origins to a north Indian BRAHMIN family that emerged in the 2nd century AD as rulers of parts of the south and east peninsula; it reached its greatest height in the later 6th century but continued to be of major importance until the end of the 9th century. Its capital was at Kanchipuram.

Pandya A dynasty ruling territory in the Tamil-speaking districts of south India with its center at Madurai.

pargana Administrative subdivision of a district.

Parsis Indian ZOROASTRIANS of Iranian descent

who fled to India mainly in the 10th century to escape religious persecution in Iran, settled in Gujarat and moved into trade and ship-building. From the 18th century they migrated to Bombay city where they formed an elite.

Parvati Goddess of the Mountain, consort of SHIVA. She rides a lion.

patel The headman of a village, who has general control of village affairs and forms the channel of communication with government officials.

peshwa The chief or prime minister in MARATHA government. From the early 18th century, the office became hereditary in the family of Ballaji Vishvanath Bhat; subsequently the *peshwa* was the *de facto* leader of MARATHA expansion.

puja Hindu ceremonies; offering and worship before the image of a deity.

Puranas Collections of Hindu myths and legends.

Qu'ran The sacred scripture of ISLAM containing the revelations received from God by the Prophet Muhammad; the actual word of God.

raga A series of notes on which a melody is based.

raj Sovereignty, rule, kingdom, applied particularly in recent times to the period of British rule in India – the Raj, or the British Raj.

Raja A Hindu king; more generally applied after the 18th century as an honorific title to clan heads, petty chiefs, important ZAMINDARS and humbler dignitaries.

Rajput "King's son", a term embracing a number of CASTES and clans in northwestern India belonging to landed and military families claiming descent from four or five original KSHATRIYAS who sprang into existence from the sacred fire on the summit of Mount Abu.

rupee Standard monetary unit of the subcontinent, still in use in India, Pakistan, Nepal, Bhutan, Sri Lanka and the Seychelles. Once a silver coin, the rupee was subdivided into 16 *annas* which in turn were made up of four *paise*, but the Indian rupee has now been decimalized by being divided into 100 *paise*.

ryot A tenant of the soil, an individual occupying land as a farmer or cultivator.

sadhu Hindu holy man.

Safavid The dynasty that effectively ruled Iran from 1501 to 1722.

Sanskrit The ancient Indo-ARYAN language of the subcontinent and the principal language of religious writing and scholarship; it carries the meaning of "purified" or "perfected", as opposed to the Prakrit languages of everyday use. Sanskrit is related to other classical languages of the Indo-European group, such as

Greek and Latin. An important source, since the 18th century, of enrichment of the modern vernacular languages in India.

sardesmukhi A tenth of the revenues of a province demanded by the MARATHAS from the territories they tried to control.

sari A seamless cloth that constitutes the main part of a woman's dress in much of India, wrapped round the body and then thrown over the head.

sati Pure, chaste, a virtuous woman, especially a widow who immolates herself on her husband's funeral pyre – a practice outlawed by the British in the 19th century.

scheduled castes Social groups who are placed on a schedule or list and receive thereby special consideration in matters of public policy – the basis for programs of affirmative action to help the depressed and poor.

sepoy An Indian soldier, used particularly to describe those of the East India Company's (and subsequently the British) army, who were disciplined and uniformed in European military style.

serai Originally a royal residence, but in the Indian context a building for the accommodation of travelers with their pack animals, consisting of an enclosed yard with chambers round it.

sharia The revealed law of ISLAM relating to human conduct as distinct from religious belief. The law is contained in the QU'RAN and in the HADITHS, and other rules for social behavior are inferred through analogy.

Shia The branch of ISLAM that believes that the correct interpretation of the teaching of the Prophet Muhammad was entrusted exclusively to Ali ibn Abi Talib, the Prophet's cousin and son-in-law, and then to a line of divinely inspired IMAMS, all descended from Ali. Shi'ism itself subsequently divided into three main groups each accepting the legitimacy of a different line of IMAMS.

Shiva Hindu god characterized by his cosmic energy manifested in many creative and destructive forms. The genius of fertility, Shiva is commonly worshipped in the form of a standing phallic pillar or LINGA.

shudra The lowest of the four original VARNAS or classes that compose Hindu society, to which belonged the servant and laboring CASTES.

Sikhism Religion and community founded by Guru Nanak (d.1538) and particularly associated with Punjab.

stupa A circular dome, surmounted by an umbrella (CHATTRI) to enshrine the remains or relics of the Buddha or of a BUDDHIST saint. A stupa may be a small portable object or a massive building.

suba A province of the MUGHAL empire.

sufi A Muslim mystic and ascetic; a mystical tradition within ISLAM that dates from the 8th and 9th centuries and arises from towns in the province of Khurasan, in Iraq and in Egypt. The term is thought to come from the Arabic word for wool since the early Muslim ascetics wore coarse woolen garments.

sultan Prince or monarch.

Sunni A short form of the Arabic phrase *ahl al-sunna wa-al-jama'a*, "the people of custom and community", used to describe the majority religious group of Muslims, commonly referred to as orthodox, who hold as authoritative the QU'RAN and a body of traditions attributed to Muhammad; they reject the claim of Ali, the Prophet's son-in-law, to be the first true and exclusive successor and interpreter of the Prophet.

suwar An Indian cavalry soldier, also numerical ranking denoting the number of armed heavy cavalrymen each MUGHAL officer was required to bring to muster.

swaraj Self-government or home-rule; agitation in favor of independence for India.

Timurid The last great Turco-Mongolian dynasty controlling most of Iran and Central Asia from about 1385 to 1507. Founded by Timur (Tamerlane) who rose to power in Transoxiana around 1370 and embarked on a major scheme of conquest in the Middle East.

Tirthankara One of the 24 teachers of JAINISM who appear in each age of the world.

Tughluq Dynasty of the Delhi sultanate, in power from 1320—1414.

ulema (plural form of *'alim*) Muslim jurist-theologians.

untouchables Individuals falling outside the framework of CASTE and regarded as being polluted and polluting, either because of their ethnic origin, or because of the nature of the work they did. See also DALIT and HARIJAN.

Upanishads A group of SANSKRIT texts, composed between c.800 BC and 300 AD, containing religious and philosophical treatises and instructions about ritual.

Urdu Language allied to Hindi but with Persianized vocabulary and written in the Persian script, the official language of Pakistan.

vahana Vehicle, usually a bird or beast, traditionally ridden by a Hindu god.

vaishnava A devotee of VISHNU.

vaishya One of the four original divisions of Hindu society, traditionally the category to which landowners, merchants and bankers belong.

varna Literally appearance, aspect, color; Hindu society was divided into four *varnas* : BRAHMINS, KSHATRIYAS, VAISHYAS and SHUDRAS.

Vedas/Vedic Derived from the SANSKRIT word meaning "knowledge", Vedas are the collections of Hindu sacred knowledge composed from around 1800 BC onward in an archaic form of SANSKRIT; Vedic, relating to the Vedas or, more loosely, to the historical period in India from c.1800–600 BC.

Vishnu Together with BRAHMA and SHIVA one of the great gods of HINDUISM, Vishnu is regarded as the preserver and maintainer of the established order, the god of accepted behavior and the home, and of love and emotion; he appears in a number of incarnations of which the seventh and eighth, as Rama and as KRISHNA, are the most widely worshipped. His favored wife is Lakshmi, the goddess of wealth and fortune, and his VAHANA is the mythical hawk, Garuda.

yogi A practitioner of asceticism and meditation designed to achieve union of self with the supreme being.

zamindar One holding land on which he pays revenue direct to the government and not to any intermediary; loosely, and technically incorrectly, used to mean a large landowner or landlord.

zat Personal numerical rank held by a MUGHAL officer.

Zoroastrianism Religious system of ancient Iran as expounded by Zoroaster, which became the official religion of the Achaemenid, Parthian and Sassanid empires. Zoroastrianism proposes a cosmic dualism based on conflict between spirits of light and dark, good and evil, and has a special reverence for fire. It is the religion of the PARSIS in modern India.

BIBLIOGRAPHY

A great deal has been written about India and what follows is designed simply to introduce the general reader to a further range of literature on the subject. This is by no means a comprehensive list of important or interesting books about India, and it is ruthlessly selective. In compiling it I have, on the whole, restricted myself to works which I have found particularly interesting or helpful and which should be fairly easy to find: this means that there is a bias towards books published in Europe and North America, but the reader should be aware that the last twenty years have seen a vast expansion of excellent research and publication in the subcontinent itself, which deserves wider exposure than is at present the case. Also I have given priority to works that themselves have good bibliographies. Lack of specialist knowledge should not deter the reader from the more specialist studies: much of the best and most illuminating writing about India is to be found in the detailed monograph or article.

General

Joseph E. Schwartzberg (ed), *A Historical Atlas of South Asia* (Chicago University Press, Chicago and London, 1978; 2nd edn, with significant revision of parts of the text, Oxford University Press, New York, 1992) is a key work of reference and an outstanding contribution to 20th-century scholarship. Professor Schwartzberg is also the author of "South Asian Cartography" in J.B. Harley and David Woodward (eds), *The History of Cartography Volume Two, Book One, Cartography in the Traditional Islamic and South Asian Societies*, pp. 293–509 (University of Chicago Press, Chicago and London, 1992). Ainslee T. Embree (ed), *Encyclopedia of Asian History* (4 vols, Charles Scribner's Sons, New York and Collier Macmillan, London, 1988) sets quite new standards for this sort of reference work; the coverage of India is excellent. Francis Robinson (ed), *The Cambridge Encyclopedia of India, Pakistan, Bangladesh, Sri Lanka, Nepal, Bhutan and the Maldives* (Cambridge University Press, Cambridge, 1989) is scholarly, comprehensive and easily accessible. A major, though now dated, bibliography is Maureen L.P. Patterson and Ronald B. Inden (eds), *South Asia: An Introductory Bibliography* (Chicago University Press, Chicago, 1962). *The Cambridge Economic History of India* (vol 1, Tapan Raychaudhuri and Irfan Habib (eds), vol 2, Dharma Kumar (ed), Cambridge University Press, Cambridge, 1982 and 1983) broke new ground in bringing together modern scholarship on India's economic and social development. Gordon Johnson, Christopher Bayly and John F. Richards (eds), *The New Cambridge History of India* (Cambridge University Press, Cambridge, 1987 onwards, 14 vols published so far) covers in short individual volumes, each with a detailed bibliographical essay, key themes in India's modern history. Volumes in the *New Cambridge History of India* [*NCHI*] are listed below under their individual authors. The best concise history of modern India is Sumit Sarkar, *Modern India 1885–1947* (Macmillan, Madras, 1983 and subsequent reprints). K.M. de Silva, *A History of Sri Lanka* (Oxford University Press, Delhi, 1981) is a model of historical analysis and literary skill. Three journals that regularly carry important new research on India are: *The Indian Economic and Social History Review*, *The Journal of Asian Studies*, and *Modern Asian Studies*.

Geography

The current trend in geographical studies is to treat the subject thematically, so much of importance about India is to be found volumes such as those included in *The Illustrated Encyclopedia of World Geography*, 11 vols (Oxford University Press, New York, 1990–93). But among the books devoted exclusively to the subcontinent, O.H.K. Spate and A.T.A Learmonth, *India and Pakistan: A General and Regional Geography* (Methuen, London, 1954, 3rd edn 1967) is notable for its detailed coverage and for its literary quality. More recent volumes in the same vein have been those by B. C. L. Johnson: *India, Resources and Development* (Heinemann Educational Books, London and Barnes and Noble, New York, 1979); *Pakistan* (Heinemann, London and Exeter, New Hampshire, 1979); *South Asia* (Heinemann, London and Exeter, New Hampshire, 1969, 2nd edn 1981); and, with M. Le M. Scrivenor, *Sri Lanka, Land, People and Economy* (Heinemann, London and Exeter, New Hampshire, 1981). B. H. Farmer, *An Introduction to South Asia* (Methuen, London and New York, 1983; 2nd revised edn, Routledge, London and New York, 1993) covers an amazing amount of ground within a short compass. Important new scientific work is reported in, for example, R.M. Shackleton and others (eds), *Tectonic Evolution of the Himalayas and Tibet* (The Royal Society, London, 1988); K. J. Miller (ed), *The International Karakoram Project* (2 vols, Cambridge University Press, Cambridge, 1984); J. S. Lall (ed), *The Himalaya: Aspects of Change* (Oxford University Press, New Delhi, 1981); James Lighthill and Robert Pearce (eds), *Monsoon Dynamics* (Cambridge University Press, Cambridge, 1981). A popular account of the monsoon is Alexander Frater, *Chasing the Monsoon* (Viking, London and New York, 1990).

Art and Architecture

Books on Indian art and architecture, both general and specific studies, are particularly numerous and particularly rich. A good way into the subject is J.C. Harle, *The Art and Architecture of the Indian Subcontinent* (Penguin Books, London, 1986 and subsequent reprints). Excellent guides are George Michell, *The Penguin Guide to the Monuments of India, volume I: Buddhist, Jain, Hindu* (Penguin Books, London, 1989 and subsequent reprints) and Philip Davies, *The Penguin Guide to the Monuments of India, volume II: Islamic, Rajput, European* (Penguin Books, London, 1989 and subsequent reprints). Susan L. Huntington, *The Art of Ancient India* (Weatherhill, New York and Tokyo, 1985) is a particularly impressive and well-illustrated general study. Madanjeet Singh, *Ajanta: Painting of the Sacred and the Secular* (Macmillan, New York, 1965) remains a key work for understanding the art of the Ajanta caves; George Michell, *The Vijayanagara Courtly Style* (Manohar, for the American Institute of Indian Studies, New Delhi, 1992) and John M. Fritz and George Michell, *City of Victory: Vijayanagara* (Aperture, New York, 1991) have done much to rescue the remains of the Vijayanagara capital from obscurity.

Catherine B. Asher, *NHCI, The Architecture of Mughal India* (Cambridge University Press, Cambridge, 1992), now provides the best introduction to the subject, while Milo Cleveland Beach, performs the same function for *Mughal and Rajput Painting* (*NCHI*, Cambridge University Press, 1992). A study of individual Mughal painters is Amina Okada, *Imperial Mughal Painters: Indian Miniatures from the Sixteenth and Seventeenth Centuries* (Flammarion, Paris, 1992). George Michell's contribution to the *NCHI*, *Architecture and Art of Southern India: Vijayanagara and the Successor States, 1350–1750* (Cambridge University Press, Cambridge,1995) deals with the Deccan. G.H.R. Tillotson has covered Rajasthan in *The Rajput Palaces: The Development of an Architectural Style, 1450–1750* (Yale University Press, New Haven and London, 1987).

Every museum with a significant Indian collection has its own publications, usually of very high standard. Recent examples include: Robert Knox, *Amaravati: Buddhist Sculpture from the Great Stupa* (British Museum Press, London, 1992); J.C. Harle and Andrew Topsfield, *Indian Art in the Ashmolean Museum* (Ashmolean Museum, Oxford, 1987); T.Richard Blurton, *Hindu Art* (British Museum Press, London, 1992 and subsequent reprints); John Guy and Deborah Swallow (ed), *Arts of India 1550–1900* (Victoria and Albert Museum, London, 1990).

Exhibition catalogs often have a life far beyond the event they commemorate. Such examples include: *In the Image of Man: The Indian Perception of the Universe through 2000 years of Painting and Sculpture* (Arts Council of Great Britain, Weidenfeld & Nicolson, London 1982); Elizabeth Errington and Joe Cibb, with Maggie Claringbull, *The Crossroads of Asia: Transformation in Image and Symbol in the Art of Ancient Afghanistan and Pakistan* (The Ancient India and Iran Trust, Cambridge, 1992); Vishakha N. Desai and Darielle Mason (eds), *Gods, Guardians, and Lovers: Temple Sculptures from North India AD 700–1200* (The Asia Society Galleries, New York in association with Mapin Publishing Pvt. Ltd., Ahmadabad, 1993); Milo Cleveland Beach, *The Imperial Image: Paintings for the Mughal Court* (Freer Gallery of Art, Smithsonian Institute, Washington, D.C., 1981); J. Bautze, *Indian Miniature Paintings c.1590–c.1850* (Galerie Saundarya Lahari, Amsterdam, 1987); Howard Hodgkin and Terence McInerney, *Indian Drawing* (Arts Council of Great Britain, London, 1983); Stuart Carey Welch, *India: Art and Culture 1300–1900* (The Metropolitan Museum of Art, New York, 1985); Christopher Bayly (ed), *The Raj: India and the British 1600–1947* (The National Portrait Gallery, London, 1990). An important collection of essays is Robert Skelton, Andrew Topsfield, Susan Strong and Rosemary Crill (eds), *Facets of Indian Art* (Victoria and Albert Museum, London, 1986), which contains a particularly interesting essay by Elinor W. Gadon, "Dara Shikuh's mystical vision of Hindu–Muslim synthesis", about the miniature picture *A gathering of mystics* reproduced above on p. 92.

Writing about the art of the late 18th and early 19th centuries is dominated by the numerous monographs and catalogs of W.G. Archer and Mildred Archer; a token representation of their vast output includes: W.G. Archer, *Paintings of the Sikhs* (Victoria and Albert Museum, London, 1966); W.G. Archer, *Kalighat Paintings* (Victoria and Albert Museum, London, 1971); W.G. Archer, *Visions of Courtly India : The Archer Collection of Pahari Miniatures* (Sotheby Parke Bernet, 1976); Mildred Archer, *Natural History Drawings in the India Office Library* (HMSO, London, 1962); Mildred Archer, *India and British Portraiture 1770–1825* (Sotheby Parke Bernet, London and New York, 1979). Important recent monographs on aspects of modern Indian art and architecture are Tapati Guha-Thakurta, *The Making of a New "Indian" Art: Artists, Aesthetics and Nationalism in Bengal, c.1850–1920* (Cambridge University Press, Cambridge, 1992); Partha Mitter, *Much Maligned Monsters: European Reactions to Indian Art* (Oxford University Press, Oxford, 1977); the same author, *Occidental Orientations: Art and Nationalism in Colonial India, 1850–1922* (Cambridge University Press, Cambridge, 1995).

Modern architecture has been well served by, for example: Sten Nilsson, *European Architecture in India 1750–1850* (Faber & Faber, London, 1968); Robert Grant Irving, *Indian Summer: Lutyens, Baker and Imperial Delhi* (Yale University Press, New Haven and London, 1981); Thomas R. Metcalf, *An Imperial Vision: Indian Architecture and Britain's Raj* (Faber & Faber, London and Boston, 1989); G.H.R. Tillotson, *The Tradition of Indian Architecture* (Yale University Press, New Haven and London, 1989); Norma Evenson, *The Indian Metropolis: A View Toward the West* (Yale University Press, New Haven and London, 1989). Marg Publications of Bombay has a distinguished list of cultural studies, recent examples being George Michell and Snehal Singh (eds), *Ahmedabad* (1988); Pratapaditya Pal (ed), *Changing Visions, Lasting Images: Calcutta through 300 years* (1990); the same editor, *Master Artists of the Imperial Mughal Court* (1991); Shehbaz H. Safrani (ed), *Golconda and Hyderabad* (1992); Christopher W. London (ed), *Architecture in Victorian and Edwardian India* (1994).

Religion and Society

Editions and translations of Indian religious texts exist in abundance. Perhaps the easiest introduction to them is by way of popular anthologies such as Edward Conze (selected and translated), *Buddhist Scriptures* (Penguin Books, London, 1959, reprinted); R.C. Zaehner, *Hindu Scriptures* (J.M. Dent, London and Charles E. Tuttle, Rutland, Vermont, 1938, 1966 and subsequent reprints); Wendy Doniger O'Flaherty, *Hindu Myths: A Sourcebook Translated from the Sanskrit* (Penguin Books, London, 1975); William Buck, *Ramayana* (University of California Press, Berkeley, Los Angeles and London, 1976 and subsequent reprints); Juan Mascaro, *The Bhagavad Gita* (Penguin Books, London 1962 and subsequent reprints); Juan Mascaro, *The Upanishads* (Penguin Books, London, 1965 and subsequent reprints); J. E. B. Gray, *Indian Tales and Legends* (Oxford University Press, Oxford, 1961); Brenda E.F. Beck, Peter J. Claus, Praphulladatta Goswami and Jawaharlal Handoo (eds), *Folktales of India* (University of Chicago Press, Chicago and London, 1987); R.K. Narayan, *Gods, Demons and Others*, (Heinemann, London, 1965); Shahrukh Husain and Durga Prasad Das, *Demons, Gods and Holy Men from Indian Myths and Legends* (Peter Lowe, London, 1987); Lakshmi Lal, with illustrations by Badri Narayan, *The Ramayana* (Orient Longman, Bombay, 1988); Shanta Rameshwar Rao, with illustrations by Badri Narayan, *The Mahabharata* (Orient Longman, Bombay,1985); the same author and illustrator, *In Worship of Shiva* (Orient Longman, Bombay, 1986). An influential anthology, particularly for North American readers, is William Theodore De Bary (ed), *Sources of Indian Tradition: Muslim India and Pakistan included* (Columbia University Press, New York, 1958 and subsequent reprints).

A critical edition of the *Mahabharata* in English, edited by J.A.B. van Buitenen, has been in the course of publication by Chicago University Press since 1973, and one of the *Ramayana*, edited by R.P. Goldman, from Princeton University Press since 1984. An unusual and illuminating work dealing with an oral tradition is J.D. Smith, *The Epic of Pabuji: A Study, Transcription and Translation* (Cambridge University Press, Cambridge, 1991). Other influential studies drawing on both textual and sociological materials include: Milton Singer (ed), *Krishna: Myths, Rites and Attitudes* (Chicago University Press, Chicago, 1968); Barbara S. Miller, *Love Song of the Dark Lord: Jayadeva's Gitagovinda* (Columbia University Press, New York, 1977); J.C. Heesterman, *The Inner Conflict of Tradition: Essays in Indian Ritual, Kingship and Society* (Chicago University Press, Chicago, 1985); T.N. Madan, *Non-renunciation: Themes and Interpretations of Hindu Culture* (Oxford University Press, New Delhi, 1987); Richard Gombrich and Gananath Obeyesekere, *Buddhism Transformed: Religious Change in Sri Lanka* (Princeton University Press, Princeton, 1988).

Among short general intoductions to Hinduism, S. Radhakrishnan, *The Hindu View of Life* (Allen & Unwin, London, 1927 and subsequent reprints) and R. C. Zaehner, *Hinduism* (Oxford University Press, Oxford and New York, 1962) continue to hold their own. A more recent attempt at a general study is Julius Lipner, *Hindus: Their Religious Beliefs and Practices* (Routledge, London and New York, 1994). Wendy Doniger O'Flaherty is an important contemporary interpreter of Hinduism, see especially: *Karma and Rebirth in Classical Indian Traditions* (University of California Press, Berkeley, 1980); *The Origins of Evil in Hindu Mythology* (University of California Press, Berkeley, 1976 and subsequent reprints); *Asceticism and Eroticism in the Mythology of Shiva* (Oxford University Press, Oxford, 1973). Diana L. Eck, *Banaras: City of Light* (Routledge, London, 1983) is a fascinating study of one of Hinduism's most sacred places, and her *Darsan: Seeing the Divine Image in India* (Anima, Chambersburg, 1981) deserves wide readership.

Literature on Indian social organization knows no bounds. By far the best book for the reader to turn to for stimulation and guidance is C.J. Fuller, *The Camphor Flame: Popular Hinduism and Society in India* (Princeton University Press, Princeton and Oxford, 1992), which is accessible to the nonspecialist and has excellent notes and bibilography. Classic writing on Indian society includes James Tod, *Annals and antiquities of Rajast'han or the Central and Western Rajpoot States of India* (2 vols, Smith Elder & Co, London, 1829, 1832, and subsequent reprints); Alfred C. Lyall, *Asiatic Studies: Religious and Social* (2 vols, John Murray, London, 1899); Denzil Ibbetson, *Panjab Castes: Races Castes and Tribes of the People of Panjab* (Superintendent of Government Printing, Lahore, 1916; reprinted Cosmo, New Delhi, 1981); and a series of ethnographic studies, of which H.H. Risley's *Castes and Tribes of Bengal – Ethnographic Glossary* (Government Press, Calcutta, 1891) was the first to be published, and Edgar Thurston and K. Rangachari, *Castes and Tribes of Southern India* (8 vols, Government Press, Madras,

1909) has a special claim to distinction. Max Weber, *The Religion of India: The Sociology of Hinduism and Buddhism* (first published 1917, reprinted Free Press, New York, 1958 and subsequently) has been a point of departure for many later sociological and anthropological works.

Modern anthropological studies, in chronological order, that claim the attention of the nonprofessional student include: M.N. Srinivas, *Religion and Society among the Coorgs of South India* (Asia Publishing House, London, 1952); G.M. Carstairs, *The Twiceborn: A Study of a Community of High Caste Hindus* (Hogarth Press, London, 1957); Adrian C. Mayer, *Caste and Kinship in Central India: A Village and its Region* (Routledge & Kegan Paul, London, 1960); Edmund Leach, *Pul Eliya: A Village in Ceylon. A Study of Land Tenure and Kinship* (Cambridge University Press, Cambridge, 1961); G.D. Berreman, *Hindus of the Himalayas* (University of California Press, Berkeley, 1963); Andre Beteille, *Caste, Class and Power: Changing Patterns of Social Stratification in a Tanjore Village* (University of California Press, Berkeley, 1965); Louis Dumont, *Homo Hierarchicus* (Editions Gallimard, Paris, 1966; English trans, Weidenfeld and Nicolson, London, 1970); M.N. Srinivas, *Social Change in Modern India* (University of California Press, Berkeley, 1966); G. Obeyesekere, *Land Tenure in Village Ceylon: A Sociological and Historical Survey* (Cambridge University Press, Cambridge, 1967); E. R. Leach (ed), *Aspects of Caste in South India, Ceylon and North-West Pakistan* (Cambridge University Press, Cambridge, 1969); David G. Mandelbaum, *Society in India* (2 vols, University of California Press, Berkeley, 1970); Milton Singer, *When a Great Tradition Modernizes* (Pall Mall, London, 1972); Surinder M. Bhardwaj, *Hindu Places of Pilgrimage in India: A Study in Cultural Geography* (University of California Press, Berkeley, 1973); Ronald B. Inden and McKim Marriott, "Caste Systems" in *The New Encyclopaedia Britannica* (15th edn, Chicago, 1974); Madeleine Biardeau, *L'Hindouisme: Anthropologie d'une Civilisation* (Flammarion, Paris, 1981; English trans, Oxford University Press, Delhi, 1989); Akbar S. Ahmed, *Pukhtun Economy and Society: Traditional Structure and Economic Development in a Tribal Society* (Routledge & Kegan Paul, London, 1980); Arjun Appadurai, *Worship and Conflict under Colonial Rule: A South Indian Case* (Cambridge University Press, Cambridge, 1981); C.J. Fuller, *Servants of the Goddess: The Priests of a South Indian Temple* (Cambridge University Press, Cambridge, 1984); Nicholas B. Dirks, *The Hollow Crown: Ethnohistory of an Indian Kingdom* (Cambridge University Press, Cambridge, 1987); Susan Bayly, *Saints, Goddesses and Kings: Muslims and Christians in South Indian Society 1700–1900* (Cambridge University Press, Cambridge, 1989); Jonathan Parry, *Death in Benaras* (Cambridge University Press, Cambridge, 1994); Norbert Peabody, *Hindu Kingship and Polity in India: The Kota Sarkar 1719–1990* (Cambridge University Press, Cambridge, 1996).

History and Politics
The best general surveys of ancient India are by Hermann Kulke in H. Kulke and Dietmar Rothermund, *A History of India* (Croom Helm, Beckenham, 1986) and Romila Thapar, *A History of India*, vol 1 (Penguin Books, Harmondsworth, 1966 and subsequent reprints). A.L. Baham, *The Wonder that was India: A Survey of the History and Culture of the Indian Subcontinent before the coming of the Muslims* (Sidgwick & Jackson, London, 1954, 3rd revised edn, 1967 and subsequent reprints) is a classic of its type. The prehistoric period is excellently surveyed in Bridget and Raymond Allchin, *The Birth of Indian Civilization: India and Pakistan before 500 BC* (Penguin Books, Harmondsworth, 1968, 2nd edn 1994) and *The Rise of Civilization in India and Pakistan* (Cambridge University Press, Cambridge, 1982). Important new work on the Indus Valley is contained in Gregory L. Possehl (ed), *Harappan Civilization: A Recent Perspective* (Oxford and IBH Publishing Co., for the American Institute of Indian Studies, New Delhi, 1982, 2nd edn 1993). Asko Parpola, *Deciphering the Indus Script* (Cambridge Uni-

versity Press, Cambridge, 1994) covers wider matter than the title might suggest. A splendidly controversial book is Colin Renfrew, *Archaeology and Language: The Puzzle of Indo-European Origins* (Jonathan Cape, London, 1987; Cambridge University Press, New York, 1988). Picking up on an argument first proposed by P.T. Srinivas Iyengar in 1914, Edmund Leach wrote a much needed sceptical polemic about the Aryan invasions: "Aryan Invasions over Four Millenia", in Emiko Ohnuki-Tierney (ed), *Culture through Time: Anthropological Approaches* (Stanford University Press, Stanford, 1990). The social and political development of the Vedic period is well covered in Romila Thapar, *From Lineage to State. Social Formations in the Mid-first Millenium BC in the Ganga Valley* (Oxford University Press, Bombay, 1984), and political theory in J. C. Heesterman, *The Ancient Indian Royal Consecration: The Rajasuya described according to the Yajus Texts* (Mouton, S'Grafenhage, 1957).

Early Indian history still awaits its historians, and the most reliable accounts of the rise and fall of dynasties and of economic, social and cultural development, are those painstakingly put together by Professor Schwartzberg in *A Historical Atlas of South Asia* and A.L. Baham's *The Wonder that was India*, cited above. The following can also be read with profit: R.C. Majumdar (ed), *The Age of Imperial Unity* (Bharatiya Vidya Bhavan, Bombay 1951); Romila Thapar, *Asoka and the Decline of the Mauryas* (Oxford University Press, Oxford, 1961); the same author, *The Mauryas Revisited* (K.P. Bagchi, Calcutta, 1987); K.A. Nilakanta Sastri, *A History of South India from Prehistoric Times to the Fall of Vijayanagara* (3rd edn, Oxford University Press, Madras, 1966); G. Yazdani (ed), *The Early History of the Deccan* (2 vols, Oxford University Press, London, 1960); Burton Stein (ed), *Essays on South India* (University Press of Hawaii, Honolulu, 1975); R.C. Majumdar (ed), *The Age of Imperial Kanauj 750–1000 AD* (Bharatiya Vidya Bhavan, Bombay, 1955); D. Devahuti, *Harsha: A Political Study* (Clarendon Press, Oxford, 1970; 2nd edn Oxford University Press, Delhi, 1983); B.M. Morrison, *Political Centers and Cultural Regions in Early Bengal* (University of Arizona Press, Tucson, 1970); Burton Stein, *Peasant State and Society in Medieval South India* (Oxford University Press, Delhi, 1980); A.Eschmann, H.Kulke, G.C. Tripathi (eds), *The Cult of Jagannath and the Regional Tradition of Orissa* (Manohar, New Delhi, 1978); D.D. Shulman, *Tamil Temple Myths* (Princeton University Press, Princeton, 1980).

A comprehensive survey of the Delhi sultanate is M. Habib and K.A. Nizami (eds), *The Delhi Sultanate AD 1206–1526* (Peoples' Publishing House, Delhi, 1970) and R.C. Majumdar (ed), *The Delhi Sultanate* (Bharatiya Vidya Bhavan, Bombay, 1960). The Mughals and their contemporaries are now most easily approached through the relevant volumes in *NCHI*: John F. Richards, *The Mughal Empire* (Cambridge University Press, Cambridge, 1993); Burton Stein, *Vijayanagara* (Cambridge University Press, Cambridge, 1989); J.S. Grewal, *The Sikhs of the Punjab* (Cambridge University Press, Cambridge, 1990); Stewart Gordon, *The Marathas 1600–1818* (Cambridge University Press, Cambridge, 1993). Everyone should be aware of the emperor Babur's Memoirs and fall to its charm: A.S. Berveridge (trans. and ed) *Babur-Nama (Memoirs of Babur)* (2 vols, London, 1922, reprinted in 1 vol, Oriental Books Reprint Corporation, New Delhi, 1970). An outstanding study of the Mughal period, which has influenced all subsequent work, is Irfan Habib, *The Agrarian System of Mughal India* (Asia Publishing House, London, 1963), and the same author, *An Atlas of the Mughal Empire* (Oxford University Press, Delhi, 1982) is also highly commended. Other key studies of the period include M. Athar Ali, *The Mughal Nobility under Aurangzeb* (Asia Publishing House, London 1968); the same author, *The Apparatus of Empire: Awards of Ranks, Offices and Titles to the Mughal Nobility (1574–1658)* (Oxford University Press, Oxford, 1985); Satish Chandra, *Parties and Politics at the Mughal Court* (2nd edn, Peoples' Publishing House, New Delhi, 1972); M.N. Pearson, *Merchants and Rulers in Gujarat: The Response to the Portuguese in the Sixteenth Century* (California University Press, Berkeley, 1976); Sanjay Subrahmanyam, *The Political Economy of Commerce: Southern India, 1500–1650* (Cambridge University Press, Cambridge, 1990); A.R. Kulkarni, *Maharashtra in the Age of Shivaji* (Deshmikh & Co, Pune, 1969); Hiroshi Fukazawa, *The Medieval Deccan: Peasants, Social Systems and States, 16th to 18th Centuries* (Oxford University Press, Oxford, 1991); Dirk H.A. Kolff, *Naukar, Rajput and Sepoy: the Ethnohistory of the Military Labour Market in Hindustan, 1450–1850* (Cambridge University Press, Cambridge, 1990); John F. Richards, *Mughal Adminstration in Golconda* (Clarendon Press, Oxford, 1975).

The 18th century has produced impressive monographs in recent years, for example: Andre Wink, *Land and Sovereignty in India: Agrarian Society and Politics under the 18th-century Maratha Svarajya* (Cambridge University Press, Cambridge, 1986); Stewart Gordon, *Marathas, Marauders and State Formation in 18th-century India* (Oxford University Press, Delhi, 1994); Muzaffar Alam, *The Crisis of Empire in Mughal North India: Awadh and the Punjab 1707–1748* (Oxford University Press, Delhi, 1986); K. P. Mishra, *Banaras in Transition 1738–1795: A Socio-economic Study* (Munshiram Manoharlal, New Delhi, 1975); B.G. Gokhale, *Poona in the 18th Century: An Urban History* (Oxford University Press, Delhi, 1988); Richard B. Barnett, *North India between Empires: Awadh, the Mughals, and the British, 1720–1801* (University of California Press, Berkeley, 1980); M.H. Gopal, *Tipu Sultan's Mysore: An Economic Study* (Popular Prakashan, Bombay, 1971); J.R. McLane, *Land and Local Kingship in 18th-century Bengal* (Cambridge University Press, Cambridge, 1993). The transition to British rule is covered in the *NCHI* volumes: P.J. Marshall, *Bengal, the British Bridgehead: Eastern India 1740–1828* (Cambridge University Press, Cambridge, 1987) and C.A. Bayly, *Indian Society and the Making of the British Empire* (Cambridge University Press, Cambridge, 1988). An excellent short book that sets British expansion in a wider context is C.A. Bayly, *Imperial Meridian: The British Empire and the World, 1780–1830* (Longman, London and New York, 1989).

The early 19th century is still relatively neglected, though key monographs include: Ravinder Kumar, *Western India in the Nineteenth Century: A Study in the Social History of Maharashtra* (Routledge & Kegan Paul, London, 1968); David Kopf, *British Orientalism and the Bengal Renaissance: The Dynamics of Indian Modernization, 1773–1835* (California University Press, Berkeley, 1969); C.A. Bayly, *Rulers, Townsmen and Bazaars: North Indian Society in the Age of British Expansion, 1770–1870* (Cambridge University Press, Cambridge, 1983); R.E. Frykenberg (ed), *Land Control and Social Structure in Indian History* (University of Wisconsin Press, Madison, 1969); the same author's seminal study, *Guntur District, 1788–1848: A History of Local Influence and Central Authority in South India* (Oxford University Press, London, 1965); Eric Stokes, *The Peasant and the Raj: Studies in Agrarian Society and Peasant Rebellion in Colonial India* (Cambridge University Press, Cambridge, 1978); the same author, *The Peasant Armed: the Indian Rebellion of 1857* (Clarendon Press, Oxford, 1986). Tapan Raychaudhri has explored new worlds with *Europe Reconsidered: Perceptions of the West in Nineteenth-century Bengal* (Oxford University Press, Delhi,1988).

Many have been introduced to 20th-century India through the autobiographies of Gandhi and Nehru: M.K. Gandhi, *An Autobiography or The Story of My Experiments with Truth* (2nd edn, Navajivan Press, Ahmadabad, 1940, and countless others since); Jawaharlal Nehru, *An Autobiography With Musings on Recent Events in India* (Bodley Head, London, 1936 and subsequent reprints). Gandhi has defied those who would write his life within one volume: the best attempts are B.R. Nanda, *Mahatma Gandhi: A Biography* (Oxford University Press, Delhi, 1958, reprinted) and J.M. Brown, *Gandhi: Prisoner of Hope* (Yale University Press, New Haven, 1989), but a work of great insight is N.K. Bose, *My Days with Gandhi* (Nishana, Calcutta, 1953). Nehru has been more fortunate: Sarvepalli Gopal's official biography is a work of distinction, and is available in a sensitively abridged edition: *Jawarhalal Nehru A Biography* (Oxford University Press, Delhi, 1989). Another memoir that caught the imagination on publication was Nirad C. Chaudhuri, *The Autobiography of an Unknown Indian* (Macmillan, London, 1951).

The academic study of modern Indian politics has been transformed since the later 1960s by such works as: Anil Seal, *The Emergence of Indian Nationalism: Competition and Collaboration in the later 19th Century* (Cambridge University Press, Cambridge, 1968); J.H.Broomfield, *Elite Conflict in a Plural Society: 20th-century Bengal* (California University Press, Berkeley, 1968); Judith M. Brown, *Gandhi's Rise to Power: Indian Politics 1915–1922* (Cambridge University Press, Cambridge, 1972); Gordon Johnson, *Provincial Politics and Indian Nationalism: Bombay and the Indian National Congress 1880–1915* (Cambridge University Press, Cambridge 1973); Francis Robinson, *Separatism among Indian Muslims: the Politics of the United Provinces' Muslims 1860–1923* (Cambridge University Press, Cambridge, 1974); Leonard H. Gordon, *Bengal: the Nationalist Movement 1876–1940* (Columbia University Press, New York, 1974); C. A. Bayly, *The Local Roots of Indian Politics: Allahabad 1880-1920* (Clarendon Press, Oxford, 1975); B.R. Tomlinson, *The Indian National Congress and the Raj 1929–1942* (Macmillan, London, 1976); D.A. Washbrook, *The Emergence of Provincial Politics: the Madras Presidency 1870–1920* (Cambridge University Press, Cambridge, 1976); C.J. Baker, *The Politics of South India 1920–1937* (Cambridge University Press, Cambridge, 1976); Kenneth W. Jones, *Arya Dharm: Hindu Consciousness in 19th-century Punjab* (California University Press, Berkeley, 1976); D.A. Low (ed), *Congress and the Raj: Facets of the Indian Struggle 1917–47* (Heinemann, London, 1977); J.R. McLane, *Indian Nationalism and the Early Congress* (Princeton University Press, Princeton, 1977); David Lelyveld, *Aligarh's First Generation: Muslim Solidarity in British India* (Princeton University Press, Princeton, 1978); G. Pandey, *The Ascendancy of the Congress in Uttar Pradesh 1926–34* (Oxford University Press, Delhi, 1978); the same author, *The Construction of Communalism in North India* (Oxford University Press, Delhi, 1990). Ranajit Guha and others, *Subaltern Studies: Writings on South Asian History and Society (*7 vols so far, Oxford University Press, Delhi, 1982 continuing) attacks almost all existing South Asian historical work; it made a flamboyant entry in North America as Ranajit Guha and Gayatri Chakravorty Spivak (eds), with a Foreword by Edward W. Said, *Selected Subaltern Studies* (Oxford University Press, New York, 1988). Other important recent studies are: Dilip M. Menon, *Caste, Nationalism and Communism in South India: Malabar, 1900–1948* (Cambridge University Press, Cambridge, 1994); Milton Israel, *Communications and Power: Propaganda and the Press in the Indian Nationalist Struggle, 1920–1947* (Cambridge University Press, Cambridge, 1994); Rajnarayan Chandavarkar, *The Origins of Industrial Capitalism in India: Business Strategies and the Working Classes in Bombay, 1900–1940* (Cambridge University Press, Cambridge, 1994), which gives new meaning and depth to Indian historical scholarship.

The transfer of power has been well narrated in V.P. Menon, *The Transfer of Power in India* (Princeton University Press, Princeton, 1957) and H.V. Hodson, *The Great Divide: Britain, India, Pakistan* (London, 1969). Good personal accounts are P. Moon, *Divide and Quit* (Chatto & Windus, London, 1961) and P.Moon (ed), *Wavell: the Viceroy's Diary* (Oxford University Press, 1973). The historical background is well covered in David Page, *Prelude to Partition: The Indian Muslims and the Imperial System of Control 1920–1932* (Oxford University Press, Delhi, 1982); R.J. Moore, *Escape from Empire: the Attlee Government and the Indian Problem* (Clarendon Press, Oxford, 1983; the same author, *Endgames of Empire: Studies in Britain's Indian Problem* (Oxford University Press, Delhi, 1988); Amit Kumar Gupta (ed), *Myth and Reality: The Struggle for Freedom in India, 1945–47* (Manohar, Delhi, 1987). However, two outstanding monographs significantly alter the perspective on events: Ayesha Jalal, *The Sole Spokesman: Jinnah, the Muslim League and the Demand for Pakistan* (Cambridge University Press, Cambridge, 1985) and Joya Chatterji, *Bengal Divided: Hindu Communalism and Partition, 1932-1947* (Cambridge University Press, Cambridge, 1994).

There is no shortage of material on post-independence South Asia, but much of the best is in the form of articles. Two periodicals have outstanding coverage of current affairs: *The Economic and Political Weekly* and *India Today*. While not everyone would agree with his approach, P.R. Brass provides an excellent guide to current academic and journalistic literature in *NCHI*: *The Politics of India since Independence* (2nd edn, Cambridge University Press, Cambridge, 1994). Other standard texts include: W.H. Morris Jones, *The Government and Politics of India* (Hutchinson, London, 1964 and subsequent edns); Kusum Nair, *Blossoms in the Dust: The Human Factor in Indian Development* (Praegar, New York, 1961); Francine R. Frankel, *India's Green Revolution: Economic Gains and Political Costs* (Princeton University Press, Princeton, 1971; the same author, *India's Political Economy, 1947–1977* (Princeton University Press, Princeton, 1978); Robert L. Hardgrave Jnr. and Stanley A. Kochanek, *India: Government and Politics in a Developing Nation* (4th edn, Harcourt Brace Jovanovich, San Diego, 1986); Prem Shankar Jha, *India: A Political Economy of Stagnation* (Oxford University Press, Delhi, 1980); Atul Kohli, *The State and Poverty in India: The Politics of Reform* (Cambridge University Press, Cambridge, 1987); the same author, *Democracy and Discontent: India's Growing Crisis of Governability* (Cambridge University Press, Cambridge, 1990); Lloyd I. Rudolph and Suzanne H. Rudolph, *The Modernity of Tradition: Political Development in India* (Chicago University Press, Chicago, 1967); the same authors, *In Pursuit of Lakshmi: the Political Economy of the Indian State* (Chicago University Press, Chicago, 1987); Myron Weiner, *Sons of the Soil: Migration and Ethnic Conflict in India* (Princeton University Press, Princeton, 1978). Michael Brecher, *Succession in India: A Study in Decision Making* (Oxford University Press, Oxford, 1966) is a fascinating account of elite politics in the 1960s. The Ayodhya mosque affair resulted in the publication of two passionate but well-researched pamphlets: Sarvepalli Gopal (ed), *Anatomy of a Confrontation: Ayodhya and the Rise of Communal Politics in India* (1st edn, Penguin Books, Delhi, 1991; Zed Books, London and Atlantic Highlands, 1993) and D. Mandal, *Ayodhya: Archaeology after Demolition: A Critique of the "New" and "Fresh" Discoveries* (Sangam Books, London, 1993). A significant work of political theory is Rajni Kothari, *State Against Democracy: In Search of Humane Governance* (Ajanta Publishers, Delhi, 1989). The outstanding general book of recent years, that introduces modern India to a non-Indian readership, is V.S. Naipaul, *India: A Million Mutinies Now* (William Heinemann, London, 1990).

On Pakistan: L. Binder, *Religion and Politics in Pakistan* (University of California Press, Berkeley, 1961); L.F. Rushbrook Williams, *The State of Pakistan* (Faber & Faber, London, 1962); E.A. Schuler and K.R.Schuler, *Public Opinion and Constitution Making in Pakistan 1958–1962* (Michigan State University Press, Michigan, 1967); M. Ayub Khan, *Friends Not Masters: A Political Autobiography* (Oxford University Press, London, 1967); K.B. Syeed, *Pakistan: The Formative Phase 1857–1948* (Oxford University Press, London, 1968); Shahid Javed Burki, *Pakistan under Bhutto 1971–77* (St Martin's Press, New York, 1980); the same author, *Pakistan: the Continuing Search for Nationhood* (2nd edn, Westview Press, Boulder, 1991); Akbar S. Ahmed, *Religion and Politics in Muslim Society: Order and Conflict in Pakistan* (Cambridge University Press, Cambridge, 1983); S.P. Cohen, *The Pakistan Army* (University of California Press, Berkeley, 1984); Ayesha Jalal, *The State of Martial Rule: The Origins of Pakistan's Political Economy of Defence* (Cambridge University Press, Cambridge, 1990).

LIST OF ILLUSTRATIONS

CONTRIBUTORS TO SPECIAL FEATURES

Professor Michael Jansen, Institute for the History of Urban Planning, Aachen, Germany:
Mohenjo-Daro

Dr George Michell, London:
Sanchi; *Rock-cut Monuments*; *Khajuraho*; *Vijayanagara*

Dr Norbert Peabody, Centre of South Asian Studies, University of Cambridge:
Astronomy; *Madurai*; *Rajput Courts*; *Natural History Painting*; *Mughal Gardens*; *Christianity in India*

Linda Proud, Oxford:
The Story of Buddha

Dr Margaret Shepherd, Wolfson College, Cambridge:
Regions of the Subcontinent

Dr John D. Smith, Faculty of Oriental Studies, University of Cambridge:
Shiva; *Vishnu*; *Festivals*; *The Mahabharata*; *The Ramayana*

Simon C. Smith, Royal Holloway and Bedford New College, University of London:
Weather; *Chandigarh*

Dr D. A. Swallow, Victoria and Albert Museum, London:
Indian Fabrics; *Tipu Sultan*; *Kalighat Painting*; *Indian Dress*; *Music, Dance and Drama*

Andrew Topsfield, Ashmolean Museum, Oxford:
Chess

All other features by Gordon Johnson

GAZETTEER

An entry includes a descriptive term if it is a physical feature and the modern country name eg Doda Betta (*mt*), (*India*). An entry followed by an asterisk* indicates a territorial unit eg a province, kingdom or region.

Abbottabad (*Pakistan*), 34°09′N 73°13′E, 184
Abohar (*India*), 30°08′N 74°12′E, 191
Abu (*India*), 24°41′N 72°50′E, 191
Adilabad (*India*), 19°40′N 78°32′E, 210
Adoni (*India*), 15°38′N 77°16′E, 210
Adulis (*Eritrea*), 15°16′N 39°23′E, 74
Aelana (*Jordan*), 29°36′N 35°00′E, 74
Agartala (*India*), 23°49′N 91°15′E, 199
Agra (*India*), 27°09′N 78°00′E, 94, 111, 134, 141, 158, 198
Agra*, 94, 111
Ahar (*India*), 24°33′N 73°48′E, 59
Ahichhattra (*India*), 28°21′N 79°08′E, 73
Ahinposh (*Afghanistan*), 34°04′N 70°41′E, 72
Ahiri (*India*), 19°26′N 80°04′E, 204
Ahmadabad (*India*), 23°03′N 72°40′E, 12, 80, 94, 111, 134, 158, 204
Ahmadnagar (*India*), 19°08′N 74°48′E, 111, 121, 204
Ahmadnagar*, 80, 94, 111
Aihole (*India*), 18°14′N 75°35′E, 77
Aiyar (*res*), (*India*), 23°37′N 85°44′E, 198
Aizawl (*India*), 23°45′N 92°45′E, 199
Ajanta (*India*), 20°30′N 75°48′E, 75, 77, 204
Ajanta Range (*mts*), (*India*), 204
Ajayameru (*India*), 27°16′N 74°00′E, 75
Ajmer (*India*), 26°29′N 74°40′E, 94, 111, 141, 191
Ajmer* (Rajputana), 94, 111, 158
Ajmer-Merwara*, 164, 175
Akbarpur (*India*), 26°25′N 82°32′E, 134
Akola (*India*), 20°40′N 77°05′E, 204
Akot (*India*), 21°06′N 77°08′E, 204
Akyab (*Burma*), 20°09′N 92°55′E, 141
Alamgirpur (*India*), 29°15′N 77°31′E, 59
Alexandria (*Afghanistan*), 33°33′N 68°26′E, 70
Alexandria (*Egypt*), 31°13′N 29°55′E, 74
Alexandria *see* Ghazni
Alexandria *see* Herat
Alexandria *see* Kandahar
Alexandria *see* Kokand
Alexandria Prophthasia (*Afghanistan*), 31°32′N 65°30′E, 70
Alibag (*India*), 18°38′N 72°55′E, 204
Aligarh (*India*), 27°54′N 78°04′E, 134, 158, 198
Allahabad (*India*), 25°27′N 81°50′E, 12, 94, 111, 121, 134, 158, 198
Allahabad*, 94, 111, 121
Allahdino (*Pakistan*), 23°00′N 66°56′E, 59
Alleppey (*India*), 9°30′N 76°22′E, 210
Almora (*India*), 29°36′N 79°40′E, 198
Along (*India*), 28°10′N 94°46′E, 199
Alor (*Pakistan*), 27°32′N 69°17′E, 75
Alwar (*India*), 27°32′N 76°35′E, 134, 191
Alwaye (*India*), 10°06′N 76°23′E, 210
Amalner (*India*), 21°01′N 75°09′E, 204
Amaravati (*India*), 16°35′N 80°20′E, 75
Ambala (*India*), 30°19′N 76°49′E, 191
Ambalangoda (*Sri Lanka*), 6°14′N 80°03′E, 222
Ambikapur (*India*), 23°09′N 83°12′E, 205
Ambur (*India*), 12°48′N 78°44′E, 210
Amlekhganj (*Nepal*), 27°17′N 85°00′E, 217
Amra (*India*), 25°20′N 83°27′E, 59
Amraoti *see* Amravati
Amravati (Amraoti), (*India*), 20°58′N 77°50′E, 158, 204
Amreli (*India*), 21°36′N 71°20′E, 204
Amri (*Pakistan*), 26°09′N 68°02′E, 59
Amritsar (*India*), 31°35′N 74°56′E, 12, 134, 158, 191
Amroha (*India*), 28°54′N 78°29′E, 198
Amu Darya (*r*), 59, 70
Anaimalai Hills (*mts*), (*India*), 210
Anai Mudi (*mt*), (*India*), 10°14′N 77°07′E, 12, 210
Anakapalle (*India*), 17°42′N 83°06′E, 211
Anantapur (*India*), 14°42′N 77°05′E, 121, 210
Anantnag (*India*), 33°44′N 75°11′E, 191
Andaman and Nicobar Islands*, 159, 165, 175
Andaman Islands (*India*), 11°00′N 93°00′E, 13, 141
Andhra*, 72, 175
Andhra Pradesh*, 175, 210
Andijan (*Afghanistan*), 41°10′N 72°23′E, 94
Anga*, 70
Angkor (*Cambodia*), 13°26′N 103°50′E, 75
Angkor Borei (*Cambodia*), 13°26′N 103°50′E, 75
Anjengo (*India*), 8°40′N 76°47′E, 111, 134, 141
Ankleshwar (*India*), 21°38′N 73°02′E, 204
Annapurna (*mt*), (*Nepal*), 28°34′N 83°50′E, 217
Anupgarh (*India*), 29°10′N 73°14′E, 191
Anuradhapura (*Sri Lanka*), 8°20′N 80°25′E, 70, 72, 75, 222
Api (*mt*), (*Nepal*), 30°00′N 80°56′E, 217
Ara (*India*), 25°34′N 84°40′E, 198
Arachosia*, 72
Arakan*, 141
Arani (*India*), 12°41′N 79°17′E, 111
Araria (*India*), 26°09′N 87°31′E, 198
Aravalli Range (*mts*), (*India*), 12, 191
Aria*, 72
Armenia*, 72
Arun (*r*), 217
Arunachal Pradesh*, 175, 199
Aruppukkottai (*India*), 9°31′N 78°03′E, 210
Asaka*, 72
Asansol (*India*), 23°40′N 86°59′E, 198
Asika*, 72
Asmaka*, 70
Assam*, 134, 141, 158, 164, 175, 199
Attock (*Pakistan*), 35°52′N 72°20′E, 94, 141
Aurangabad (*India*), 19°52′N 75°22′E, 77, 80, 111, 134, 204
Avanti*, 70
Awadh* *see* Oudh*
Ayodhya (*India*), 26°47′N 82°12′E, 94, 111, 198
Azamgarh (*India*), 26°03′N 83°10′E, 198

Bactra *see* Balkh
Bactria*, 72
Badami (*India*), 15°58′N 75°45′E, 77
Badarinath (*India*), 30°44′N 79°29′E, 198
Badayun*, 80
Badin (*Pakistan*), 24°38′N 68°53′E, 184
Badulla (*Sri Lanka*), 6°59′N 81°03′E, 222
Bagh (*India*), 22°22′N 74°49′E, 77
Bagherhat (*Bangladesh*), 22°40′N 89°48′E, 220
Baglana*, 94
Baharampur (*India*), 24°06′N 88°15′E, 111, 134, 198
Bahawalnagar (*Pakistan*), 29°59′N 73°16′E, 184
Bahawalpur (*Pakistan*), 29°24′N 71°41′E, 141, 184
Bahawalpur*, 164
Bahmani Kingdom*, 80
Bahraich (*India*), 27°35′N 81°36′E, 198
Baikunthpur (*India*), 24°34′N 81°25′E, 134
Baiwara (*India*), 31°13′N 75°47′E, 134
Balaghat (*India*), 21°48′N 80°16′E, 204
Balaghat Range (*mts*), (*India*), 204
Balakot (*Pakistan*), 25°35′N 66°50′E, 59
Balangir (*India*), 20°43′N 83°29′E, 211
Baleshwar (*India*), 21°31′N 86°59′E, 111, 134, 211
Balimila (*res*), (*India*), 18°10′N 82°00′E, 211
Balkh (Bactra), (*Afghanistan*), 36°18′N 67°19′E, 70, 72, 75, 134
Ballabgarh (*India*), 28°20′N 77°19′E, 191
Balotra (*India*), 22°50′N 72°21′E, 191
Balpahari (*res*), (*India*), 24°10′N 86°18′E, 198
Balrampur (*India*), 27°25′N 82°10′E, 198
Baluchistan*, 134, 158, 164, 175, 184
Balurghat (*India*), 25°12′N 88°50′E, 198
Bampur (*Afghanistan*), 27°13′N 60°28′E, 59
Banas (*r*), 191
Banavali (*India*), 29°35′N 75°31′E, 59
Banda (*India*), 25°28′N 80°20′E, 198
Bandarban (*Bangladesh*), 22°13′N 92°13′E, 220
Bangalore (*India*), 12°58′N 77°35′E, 12, 204
Banganapalle*, 164
Bankipore (*India*), 25°36′N 86°07′E, 158
Bankura (*India*), 23°14′N 87°05′E, 198
Bannu (*Pakistan*), 33°00′N 70°40′E, 184
Banswara (*India*), 23°32′N 74°28′E, 191
Barak (*r*), 199
Baramula (*India*), 34°12′N 74°24′E, 191
Barauni (*India*), 25°28′N 85°59′E, 198
Barbaricum (*Pakistan*), 24°00′N 67°40′E, 72, 75
Barddhaman (*India*), 23°14′N 87°54′E, 198
Bareilly (*India*), 28°20′N 79°24′E, 198
Baripada (*India*), 21°52′N 86°48′E, 211
Barisal (*Bangladesh*), 22°41′N 90°20′E, 220
Barmer (*India*), 25°43′N 71°25′E, 191
Baroda *see* Vadodara
Baroda*, 158, 164
Barpeta (*India*), 26°20′N 91°02′E, 199
Barsi (*India*), 18°14′N 75°48′E, 204
Barwani (*India*), 22°02′N 74°56′E, 204
Barygaza *see* Bharuch
Bastar*, 141
Basti (*India*), 26°48′N 82°44′E, 198
Batala (*India*), 31°48′N 75°17′E, 191
Batticaloa (*Sri Lanka*), 7°43′N 81°42′E, 222
Bayana (*India*), 26°55′N 77°18′E, 134
Beas (*res*), (*India*), 31°57′N 76°00′E, 191
Beawar (*India*), 26°02′N 74°20′E, 191
Bela (*Pakistan*), 26°12′N 66°20′E, 184
Belgaum (*India*), 15°54′N 74°36′E, 158, 204
Bellary (*India*), 15°11′N 76°54′E, 204
Benares *see* Varanasi
Benares*, 158, 164
Bengal*, 80, 94, 111, 121, 134, 141, 158, 164
Bengal Presidency*, 141
Berar*, 80, 94, 111, 141
Bettiah (*India*), 26°49′N 84°30′E, 198
Betul (*India*), 21°50′N 77°59′E, 204
Betwa (*r*), 204
Bhadra (*res*), (*India*), 13°42′N 75°08′E, 204
Bhadrakh (*India*), 21°05′N 86°36′E, 211
Bhadravati (*India*), 13°54′N 75°38′E, 204
Bhag (*Pakistan*), 29°02′N 67°52′E, 184
Bhagalpur (*India*), 25°14′N 86°59′E, 198
Bhagatrav (*India*), 21°38′N 72°59′E, 59
Bhairavakonda (*India*), 15°32′N 78°17′E, 77
Bhairawa (*Nepal*), 27°32′N 83°23′E, 217
Bhairi Hol (*mt*), (*Pakistan*), 25°52′N 64°10′E, 184
Bhaja (*India*), 18°18′N 73°19′E, 77
Bhakkar (*Pakistan*), 31°40′N 71°08′E, 94, 184
Bhakra (*res*), (*India*), 31°24′N 76°28′E, 191
Bhaktapur (*Nepal*), 27°42′N 85°27′E, 217
Bhalki (*India*), 18°04′N 77°10′E, 121
Bhandara (*India*), 21°10′N 79°41′E, 204
Bharatpur (*India*), 27°14′N 77°29′E, 191
Bharhut (*India*), 24°15′N 80°24′E, 72
Bharuch (Barygaza), (*India*), 21°40′N 73°02′E, 72, 75, 111, 134, 204
Bhatinda (*India*), 30°10′N 74°58′E, 191
Bhatnair (*India*), 29°33′N 74°21′E, 80
Bhavnagar (*India*), 21°46′N 72°14′E, 204
Bhawanipatna (*India*), 19°57′N 83°10′E, 211
Bhilai (*India*), 21°12′N 81°26′E, 204
Bhilwara (*India*), 25°23′N 74°39′E, 191
Bhima (*r*), 204
Bhiwani (*India*), 28°50′N 76°10′E, 191
Bhonsle*, 121
Bhopal (*India*), 23°17′N 77°28′E, 121, 141, 204
Bhopal*, 164, 175
Bhota*, 72
Bhubaneswar (*India*), 20°13′N 85°50′E, 211
Bhuj (*India*), 23°12′N 69°54′E, 141, 204
Bhusawal (*India*), 21°01′N 75°50′E, 204
Bidar (*India*), 17°56′N 77°35′E, 134, 204
Bidar*, 80, 111
Bihar Sharif (*India*), 25°13′N 85°31′E, 198
Bihar (*India*), 25°13′N 85°31′E, 94
Bihar*, 80, 94, 111, 121, 134, 141, 164, 175, 198
Bihar and Orissa*, 158
Bijapur (*India*), 16°47′N 75°48′E, 111, 121, 204
Bijapur*, 80, 94, 111
Bijnor (*India*), 29°22′N 78°09′E, 198
Bikaner (*India*), 28°01′N 73°22′E, 94, 141, 191
Bilaspur (*India*), 31°18′N 76°48′E, 191, 205
Bimaran (*Afghanistan*), 34°15′N 70°20′E, 72
Bimlipatam (*India*) , 17°54′N 83°31′E, 111, 134
Bir (*India*), 18°59′N 75°50′E, 204
Biratnagar (*Nepal*), 26°27′N 87°17′E, 217
Birganj (*Nepal*), 27°01′N 84°54′E, 217
Blue Mt, (*India*), 22°35′N 93°02′E, 199
Bodh Gaya (*India*), 24°42′N 84°59′E, 73, 75, 198
Bogra (*Bangladesh*), 24°52′N 89°28′E, 220
Bokaro (*India*), 23°46′N 85°55′E, 198
Bolan (*pass*), (*Pakistan*), 29°41′N 67°34′E, 12, 184
Bombay (*India*), 18°56′N 72°51′E, 12, 111, 121, 134, 141, 158, 204
Bombay*, 158, 164, 175
Bombay Presidency*, 141
Bomdila (*India*), 27°20′N 92°20′E, 199
Bongaigaon (*India*), 26°28′N 90°34′E, 198
Brahmanbaria (*Bangladesh*), 23°58′N 91°04′E, 220
Brahmapur (*India*), 19°19′N 84°47′E, 211
Brahmaputra (*r*), 12, 72, 73, 75, 80, 94, 141, 158, 164, 175, 199, 220
Bravasti (*India*), 27°43′N 82°14′E, 73
Bucephala (*India*), 33°18′N 73°42′E, 70
Budaun (*India*), 28°02′N 79°07′E, 198
Bukhara (*Uzbekistan*), 39°47′N 64°26′E, 72, 94
Buldana (*India*), 20°31′N 76°18′E, 204
Bundelkhan*, 134
Bundi (*India*), 25°28′N 75°42′E, 191
Burhanpur (*India*), 21°18′N 76°08′E, 80, 94, 111, 134, 204
Buri Gandak (*r*), 198
Burma*, 159
Burnpur (*India*), 23°47′N 86°55′E, 198
Butwal (*Nepal*), 27°43′N 83°27′E, 217

Calcutta (*India*), 22°30′N 88°20′E, 12, 111, 134, 141, 158, 198
Calicut (*India*), 11°15′N 75°45′E, 111, 134, 210
Campbellpore (*Pakistan*), 33°46′N 72°26′E, 184
Canda (*India*), 19°58′N 79°21′E, 80
Cane (*Yemen*), 13°38′N 44°10′E, 75
Cannanore (*India*), 11°53′N 75°23′E, 111, 134, 210
Carmakhandika*, 72
Carmania (*Iran*), 30°10′N 56°50′E, 72
Carmania*, 72
Carnatic*, 134
Cawnpore see Kanpur
Central India Agency*, 141, 158
Central Makran Range (*mts*), (*Pakistan*), 184
Central Provinces and Berar*, 158, 164
Ceylon*, 111, 134, 141
Chachro (*Pakistan*), 25°07′N 70°15′E, 184
Chagai (*Pakistan*), 29°18′N 64°42′E, 184
Chagai Hills (*mts*), (*Pakistan*), 184
Chaiya (*Thailand*), 9°25′N 99°13′E, 75
Chamba (*India*), 32°33′N 76°10′E, 191
Chambal (*r*), 191, 204
Chamlang (*mt*), (*Nepal*), 27°47′N 86°59′E, 217
Chamoli (*India*), 30°22′N 79°19′E, 198
Chamrajnagar (*India*), 11°58′N 76°54′E, 204
Chandannagar (*India*), 22°49′N 88°20′E, 111, 134, 141, 164, 198
Chanderi (*India*), 24°43′N 78°08′E, 94
Chandigarh (*India*), 30°44′N 76°54′E, 191
Chandigarh*, 175
Chandpur (*Bangladesh*), 23°15′N 90°40′E, 220
Chandrapur (*India*), 19°58′N 79°21′E, 204
Chang (*r*), 75
Chanhu-Daro (*Pakistan*), 26°12′N 68°13′E, 59
Channapatna (*India*), 12°43′N 77°14′E, 204
Char (*India*), 33°15′N 77°10′E, 191
Charax (*Iraq*), 30°16′N 47°58′E, 75
Charkhari (*India*), 25°24′N 79°45′E, 198
Charsadda (*Pakistan*), 34°12′N 71°46′E, 184
Chatra (*India*), 24°14′N 84°57′E, 198
Chaukan (*pass*), (*Burma/India*), 27°07′N 97°10′E, 199
Chaul (*India*), 18°35′N 72°57′E, 111, 134
Chedi*, 70
Chenab (*r*), 184, 191
Chengalpattu (*India*), 12°42′N 79°58′E, 210
Chhani Sahnpal (*Pakistan*), 31°48′N 73°18′E, 80
Chhapra (*India*), 25°48′N 85°43′E, 198
Chhatak (*Bangladesh*), 25°02′N 91°39′E, 220
Chhindwara (*India*), 22°04′N 78°58′E, 204
Chidambaram (*India*), 11°25′N 79°42′E, 210
Chikmagalur (*India*), 13°20′N 75°46′E, 204
Chilas (*Pakistan*), 35°24′N 74°11′E, 184
Chilka (*l*), (*India*), 19°46′N 85°20′E, 210
Chiniot (*Pakistan*), 31°43′N 72°59′E, 80
Chitradurga (*India*), 14°16′N 76°23′E, 111, 204
Chitral (*Pakistan*), 35°52′N 71°58′E, 184
Chittagong (*Bangladesh*), 22°20′N 91°48′E, 12, 134, 141, 220
Chittagong*, 220
Chittaurgarh (*India*), 24°54′N 74°42′E, 94, 191
Chittoor (*India*), 13°13′N 79°06′E, 210
Chomo Lhari (*mt*), (*Bhutan*), 27°53′N 89°16′E, 219
Chomo Yummo (*mt*), (*India*), 28°02′N 88°34′E, 198
Chorasmia*, 72
Chota Nagpur (*plat*), (*India*), 198
Chumar (*India*), 32°38′N 78°36′E, 191
Churia Hills (*mts*), (*Nepal*), 217
Churu (*India*), 28°18′N 75°00′E, 191
Cocanada see Kakinada
Cochin (*India*), 9°56′N 76°15′E, 111, 134, 141, 210
Cochin*, 141
Coimbatore (*India*), 11°00′N 76°57′E, 210
Colombo (*Sri Lanka*), 6°55′N 79°52′E, 12, 111, 134, 141, 164, 222
Comilla (*Bangladesh*), 23°28′N 91°10′E, 158, 220
Comorin, Cape (*pen*), (*India*), 8°04′N 77°35′E, 210
Constantinople (*Turkey*), 41°02′N 28°58′E, 74
Coondapoor *see* Kundapura
Coorg*, 158, 164, 175
Coromandel Coast (*India*), 134, 210
Cox's Bazar (*Bangladesh*), 21°25′N 91°59′E, 220
Ctesiphon (*Iraq*), 33°06′N 44°36′E, 72, 75
Cuddalore (*India*), 11°43′N 79°46′E, 210
Cuddapah (*India*), 14°30′N 78°50′E, 210
Cuttack (*India*), 20°26′N 85°56′E, 134, 141, 211

Dabar Kot (*Pakistan*), 29°42′N 69°14′E, 59
Dadhar (*Pakistan*), 29°28′N 67°41′E, 184
Dadra (*India*), 20°22′N 73°00′E, 204
Dadra and Nagar Haveli*, 175, 204
Dadu (*Pakistan*), 26°42′N 67°48′E, 184
Dahala*, 72
Dahod (*India*), 22°48′N 74°18′E, 204
Dailekh (*Nepal*), 28°50′N 81°42′E, 217
Dakshinapatha*, 70
Daksina Kosala*, 72
Dalbandin (*Pakistan*), 28°56′N 64°30′E, 184
Dalhousie (*India*), 32°32′N 76°01′E, 191
Daman (*India*), 20°25′N 72°58′E, 111, 134, 141, 164, 204
Daman and Diu*, 204
Damascus (*Syria*), 33°30′N 36°19′E, 74
Damb Sadaat (*Pakistan*), 30°17′N 67°10′E, 59
Damoh (*India*), 23°50′N 79°30′E, 204
Dandot (*Pakistan*), 32°43′N 73°00′E, 184
Daphabum (*mt*), (*India*), 27°40′N 96°40′E, 199
Dara (*Iran*), 35°56′N 59°32′E, 72
Darbelo (*Pakistan*), 26°33′N 69°08′E, 134
Darbhanga (*India*), 26°10′N 85°54′E, 198
Dariabad (*India*), 27°00′N 81°28′E, 134
Darjeeling *see* Darjiling
Darjiling (Darjeeling), (*India*), 27°02′N 88°20′E, 141, 198
Darya Khan (*Pakistan*), 31°47′N 71°10′E, 184
Datia (*India*), 25°41′N 78°28′E, 204
Daud Khel (*Pakistan*), 32°52′N 71°35′E, 184
Daulatabad (*India*), 19°57′N 75°18′E, 80, 121
Davangere (*India*), 14°30′N 75°52′E, 204
Debal (*Pakistan*), 25°00′N 67°24′E, 75
Deccan (*plat*), (*India*), 12, 121
Deccan*, 134
Dehra Dun (*India*), 30°19′N 78°03′E, 198
Delhi (Shajahanabad), (*India*), 28°40′N 77°14′E, 12, 80, 94, 111, 121, 141, 134, 158, 198
Delhi*, 80, 94, 111, 164, 175, 198
Demqog (*India*), 32°42′N 79°24′E, 191

Quetta (*Pakistan*), 30°15′N 67°00′E, 12, 184
Quilon (Kollam), (*India*), 8°53′N 76°38′E, 75, 111, 134, 210

Radhanpur (*India*), 23°52′N 71°49′E, 204
Rae Bareli (*India*), 26°14′N 81°14′E, 198
Rahimyar Khan (*Pakistan*), 28°22′N 70°20′E, 184
Rahuri (*India*), 19°26′N 74°42′E, 204
Raichur (*India*), 16°15′N 77°20′E, 204
Raigarh (*India*), 21°53′N 83°28′E, 205
Raipur (*India*), 21°16′N 81°42′E, 205
Rajahmundry (*India*), 17°01′N 81°52′E, 211
Rajanpur (*Pakistan*), 29°05′N 70°25′E, 184
Rajapalaiyam (*India*), 9°26′N 77°36′E, 210
Rajasthan*, 164, 175, 191
Rajgarh (*India*), 28°38′N 75°21′E, 191
Rajgir (*India*), 25°01′N 85°26′E, 198
Rajkot (*India*), 22°18′N 70°53′E, 204
Rajmahal Hills (*mts*), (*India*), 198
Raj Nandgaon (*India*), 21°06′N 81°08′E, 204
Rajputana*, 121, 134, 141, 158
Rajshahi (*Bangladesh*), 24°24′N 88°40′E, 220
Rajshahi*, 220
Rajura (*India*), 19°48′N 79°25′E, 204
Rakhshan (*r*), 184
Ramanathapuram (*India*), 9°23′N 78°53′E, 210
Ramdurg (*India*), 15°57′N 75°24′E, 204
Rameswaram (*India*), 9°18′N 79°19′E, 121, 210
Ramgarh (*India*), 23°37′N 85°32′E, 94, 158
Rampur (*India*), 28°48′N 79°03′E, 198
Rampur*, 164
Rana Ghundai (*Pakistan*), 30°15′N 69°11′E, 59
Ranchi (*India*), 23°22′N 85°20′E, 198
Rangamati (*Bangladesh*), 22°40′N 92°10′E, 220
Ranganj (*India*), 25°58′N 87°59′E, 198
Rangoon (*Burma*), 16°47′N 96°10′E, 13, 75, 141, 159, 165
Rangpur (*Bangladesh*), 25°45′N 89°21′E, 134, 220
Rangpur (*India*), 22°25′N 72°05′E, 59
Raniganj (*India*), 23°35′N 87°07′E, 198
Rann of Kutch (*flood area*), (*India*), 12, 59, 204
Rann of Kutch, Little (*flood area*), (*India*), 204
Ras Koh (*mt*), (*Pakistan*), 28°50′N 65°12′E, 184
Raskoh (*mts*), (*Pakistan*), 184
Ratanpur (*India*), 22°18′N 82°12′E, 80
Ratlam (*India*), 23°18′N 75°06′E, 204
Ratnagiri (*India*), 17°00′N 73°20′E, 204
Ratnapura (*Sri Lanka*), 6°41′N 80°25′E, 222
Raurkela (*India*), 22°16′N 85°01′E, 211
Rawalpindi (*Pakistan*), 33°40′N 73°08′E, 184
Rayigama (*Sri Lanka*), 6°21′N 80°00′E, 80
Razmak (*Pakistan*), 32°41′N 69°56′E, 184
Redhakhol (*India*), 21°07′N 84°21′E, 211
Rewa (*India*), 24°32′N 81°18′E, 204
Rewah*, 141
Rewari (*India*), 28°14′N 76°38′E, 191
Rhagae (*Iran*), 35°28′N 50°48′E, 72
Rihand (*res*), (*India*), 24°09′N 83°02′E, 198, 205
Roha (*India*), 18°25′N 73°08′E, 204
Rohilkhand*, 134
Rohri (*Pakistan*), 27°39′N 68°57′E, 184
Rohtak (*India*), 28°57′N 76°38′E, 191
Rohtas (*Pakistan*), 32°59′N 73°40′E, 94
Rub al Khali (*des*), (*Saudi Arabia*), 72
Rukumkot (*Nepal*), 28°36′N 82°45′E, 217
Rupar (*India*), 30°59′N 76°36′E, 59

Sadhaura (*India*), 30°22′N 77°13′E, 80
Sadiqabad (*Pakistan*), 28°16′N 70°09′E, 184
Sad Istragh (*mt*), (*Pakistan*), 36°36′N 72°13′E, 184
Sadiya (*India*), 27°49′N 95°38′E, 199
Sadras (*India*), 12°33′N 80°10′E, 111, 134
Safavid Empire*, 111
Sagar (*isl*), (*India*), 21°44′N 88°05′E, 198
Sagar (*India*), 23°50′N 78°44′E, 204
Saharanpur (*India*), 29°58′N 77°33′E, 198
Saidapet (*India*), 13°02′N 80°15′E, 210
Saidpur (*Bangladesh*), 25°48′N 89°00′E, 220
Saidu (*Pakistan*), 34°43′N 72°24′E, 184
Saindak (*Pakistan*), 29°16′N 61°38′E, 184
Saipal (*mt*), (*Nepal*), 29°53′N 81°30′E, 217
Sakastan*, 72
Sakir (*mt*), (*Pakistan*), 31°08′N 67°54′E, 184
Salem (*India*), 11°38′N 78°08′E, 134, 210
Sallyana (*Nepal*), 28°21′N 82°11′E, 217
Salt Range (*mts*), (*Pakistan*), 184
Salween (*r*), 159
Samana (*India*), 30°09′N 76°15′E, 134
Samana*, 80
Samapa (*India*), 19°28′N 84°51′E, 70
Samarkand (Maracanda), (*Uzbekistan*), 39°40′N 66°57′E, 70, 72, 75, 94
Sambalpur (*India*), 21°28′N 84°04′E, 211
Sambhal (*India*), 28°35′N 78°34′E, 94, 111, 198
Sambhar (*l*), (*India*), 26°55′N 75°15′E, 191
Sambhar (*India*), 26°56′N 75°16′E, 191
Sanchi (*India*), 23°38′N 77°42′E, 75, 204
Sangareddi (*India*), 17°37′N 78°04′E, 210
Sangli (*India*), 16°55′N 74°37′E, 204
Sangrur (*India*), 30°16′N 75°52′E, 191
Sanjayanti (*India*), 20°27′N 82°56′E, 75
Sarai Kola (*Pakistan*), 33°50′N 72°52′E, 59
Sarangpur (*India*), 23°35′N 76°32′E, 80, 94
Sargodha (*Pakistan*), 32°01′N 72°40′E, 184
Sarkara (*Pakistan*), 28°05′N 68°58′E, 75
Sarkhej (*India*), 22°46′N 72°28′E, 134
Sarnath (*India*), 25°23′N 83°02′E, 73, 75, 198
Sarsuti*, 80
Sasaram (*India*), 24°58′N 84°01′E, 198
Satara (*India*), 17°43′N 74°05′E, 121, 204
Satavahanihara*, 72
Satna (*India*), 24°33′N 80°50′E, 204
Satpura Range (*mts*), (*India*), 12, 121, 204
Saurashtra*, 164, 175
Sauvira*, 72
Savanur (*India*), 14°58′N 75°27′E, 204
Savanur*, 121
Sawai Madhopur (*India*), 26°00′N 76°28′E, 191
Scythia*, 72
Scythica (*China*), 41°12′N 82°48′E, 72
Secunderabad (*India*), 17°27′N 78°27′E, 210
Sehwan (*Pakistan*), 26°26′N 67°52′E, 134, 184
Seoni (*India*), 22°06′N 79°36′E, 204
Serampore (*India*), 22°44′N 88°21′E, 134
Serica*, 72
Sewistan (*Pakistan*), 29°56′N 67°49′E, 94
Shahabad (*Karnataka, India*), 17°07′N 76°54′E, 204
Shahabad (*Uttar Pradesh, India*), 28°34′N 79°00′E, 198
Shahbandar (*Pakistan*), 24°08′N 67°56′E, 184
Shahdol (*India*), 23°19′N 81°26′E, 204
Shahi-Tump (*Pakistan*), 26°12′N 63°01′E, 59
Shahjahanpur (*India*), 27°53′N 79°55′E, 198
Shahpura (*India*), 25°38′N 75°01′E, 191
Shahrig (*Pakistan*), 30°11′N 67°45′E, 184
Shahr-i-Sokhta (*Afghanistan*), 30°20′N 61°18′E, 59
Shajapur (*India*), 23°27′N 76°21′E, 204
Shalunli (*mt*), (*India*), 28°58′N 96°02′E, 99
Shamgong (*Bhutan*), 27°13′N 90°40′E, 219
Shekhupura (*Pakistan*), 31°42′N 74°08′E, 184
Sherpur (*Bangladesh*), 24°40′N 89°29′E, 134
Shikarpur (*Pakistan*), 27°58′N 68°42′E, 184
Shiliguri (*India*), 26°46′N 88°30′E, 198
Shillong (*India*), 25°34′N 91°53′E, 199
Shimla (*India*), 31°02′N 77°13′E, 191
Shimoga (*India*), 13°56′N 75°31′E, 204
Shinde*, 121
Shivpuri (*India*), 25°26′N 77°39′E, 204
Sholapur (*India*), 17°43′N 75°56′E, 204
Shortughai (*Afghanistan*), 37°20′N 69°30′E, 59
Shyok (*r*), 191
Siahan Range (*mts*), (*Pakistan*), 184
Sialkot (*Pakistan*), 32°29′N 74°35′E, 80, 134, 184
Sibi (*Pakistan*), 29°31′N 67°54′E, 184
Sibsagar (*India*), 26°58′N 94°38′E, 199
Sidhi (*India*), 24°24′N 81°54′E, 205
Sigiriya (*Sri Lanka*), 7°57′N 80°46′E, 222
Sikar (*India*), 27°33′N 75°12′E, 191
Sikkim*, 158, 164, 175, 198
Sikri *see* Fatehpur Sikri
Silchar (*India*), 24°49′N 92°47′E, 198
Silgarhi (*Nepal*), 29°14′N 80°58′E, 217
Silvassa (*India*), 20°13′N 73°03′E, 204
Simhala*, 72
Simikot (*Nepal*), 29°58′N 81°49′E, 217
Sind*, 141, 164, 175, 184
Sindhu*, 72
Singareni (*India*), 17°33′N 80°19′E, 210
Sinope Phasis (*Georgia*), 41°40′N 41°45′E, 72
Sirajganj (*Bangladesh*), 24°27′N 89°42′E, 220
Sirhind (*India*), 30°39′N 76°28′E, 80
Sirohi (*India*), 25°53′N 72°58′E, 191
Sironcha (*India*), 18°52′N 80°01′E, 204
Sironj (*India*), 24°05′N 77°39′E, 111, 134
Sirpur (*India*), 19°28′N 79°36′E, 210
Sirsa (*India*), 29°32′N 75°04′E, 191
Sirsi (*India*), 14°40′N 74°51′E, 204
Sitapur (*India*), 27°33′N 80°40′E, 198
Si Thep (*Thailand*), 15°41′N 101°14′E, 75
Siwalik Range (*mts*), (*India*), 198, 217
Siwan (*India*), 26°14′N 84°21′E, 198
Siwistan*, 80
Skardu (*Pakistan*), 35°18′N 75°44′E, 185
Soda Plains (*India*), 191
Sogdiana*, 72
Solan (*India*), 30°50′N 77°08′E, 191
Somnath (*India*), 20°50′N 70°31′E, 59, 134
Son (*r*), 198, 204
Songarh (*India*), 21°17′N 73°41′E, 121
Sonipat (*India*), 29°00′N 77°01′E, 191
Sonmiani (*Pakistan*), 25°25′N 66°40′E, 184
Sopatma (*India*), 12°03′N 79°35′E, 75
Sotka Koh (*Pakistan*), 25°20′N 63°24′E, 59
Sriharikota (*isl*), (*India*), 13°40′N 81°30′E, 210
Srikakulam (*India*), 18°14′N 84°00′E, 211
Sri Kalahasti (*India*), 13°47′N 79°40′E, 210
Sriksetra (*Burma*), 18°24′N 95°17′E, 75
Srinagar (*India*), 34°08′N 74°50′E, 75, 80, 94, 134, 158, 191
Srirangapatnam (*India*), 12°25′N 76°41′E, 121, 141
Srivilliputtur (*India*), 9°31′N 77°41′E, 210
Stanley (*res*), (*India*), 12°00′N 78°00′E, 210
Sthanaka (*India*), 19°22′N 72°56′E, 75
Subansiri (*r*), 199
Sui (*Pakistan*), 28°39′N 69°21′E, 184
Sukhet (*India*), 31°22′N 76°50′E, 80
Sukhothai (*Thailand*), 17°00′N 99°51′E, 75
Sukkur (*Pakistan*), 27°42′N 68°54′E, 134, 184
Sulaiman Range (*mts*), (*Pakistan*), 12, 59, 184
Sultanpur (*India*), 26°15′N 82°04′E, 80, 198
Sumatra (*isl*), (*Indonesia*), 1°00′S 102°00′E, 13, 75
Sundarbans (*tidal forest*), (*Bangladesh*), 220
Sundargarh (*India*), 22°04′N 84°08′E, 211
Sun Kosi (*r*), 217
Suppara (*India*), 19°37′N 72°56′E, 72
Surasena*, 70
Surat (*India*), 21°10′N 72°54′E, 12, 111, 121, 134, 141, 158, 204
Surendranagar (*India*), 22°44′N 71°43′E, 204
Surkotada (*India*), 23°24′N 71°07′E, 59
Susa (*Iran*), 32°12′N 48°20′E, 75
Sutkagen Dor (*Pakistan*), 25°20′N 61°54′E, 59
Sutlej (*r*), 12, 59, 94, 134, 141, 158, 164, 175, 184, 191
Suvarnagiri (*India*), 15°08′N 77°17′E, 70
Swat (*r*), 184
Sylhet (*Bangladesh*), 24°53′N 91°51′E, 94, 220

Tagara (*India*), 17°24′N 76°42′E, 72
Takht-i-Sulaiman (*mt*), (*Pakistan*), 31°36′N 70°01′E, 184
Takkola (*Burma*), 8°34′N 98°41′E, 75
Takpa Shiri (*mt*), (*India*), 28°10′N 92°52′E, 199
Talanj*, 80
Talcher (*India*), 21°00′N 85°18′E, 211
Tamil Nadu*, 175, 210
Tamralipti (*India*), 21°13′N 87°56′E, 70, 72, 75
Tamur (*r*), 217
Tando Adam (*Pakistan*), 25°44′N 68°41′E, 184
Tando Muhammad Khan (*Pakistan*), 25°07′N 68°35′E, 184
Tangail (*Bangladesh*), 24°15′N 89°55′E, 220
Tanjore*, 121
Tapti (*r*), 12, 94, 121, 134, 141, 158, 164, 204
Tarapur (*India*), 19°47′N 72°42′E, 204
Tarbela (*res*), (*Pakistan*), 34°06′N 72°50′E, 184
Taruma (*Indonesia*), 6°07′S 106°09′E, 75
Tashigang (*Bhutan*), 27°19′N 91°33′E, 219
Tashkent (*Uzbekistan*), 41°16′N 69°13′E, 75
Taxila (*Pakistan*), 33°53′N 73°18′E, 70, 72, 75
Tehri Garwhal*, 164
Teju (*India*), 27°54′N 96°10′E, 199
Tel (*r*), 211
Tellicherry (*India*), 11°44′N 75°29′E, 111, 134, 141, 210
Tellingana*, 80
Tenali (*India*), 16°13′N 80°36′E, 210
Tenasserim (*Burma*), 12°05′N 99°00′E, 141
Tenasserim*, 141
Teratani (*r*), 184
Tezpur (*India*), 26°38′N 92°49′E, 199
Thal (*Pakistan*), 33°24′N 70°32′E, 184
Thal (*des*), (*Pakistan*), 184
Thalner (*India*), 21°17′N 75°00′E, 80
Thana (*India*), 19°14′N 73°02′E, 204
Thang (*Pakistan*), 33°45′N 72°26′E, 59
Thanjavur (*India*), 10°46′N 79°09′E, 111, 210
Thar (*des*), (*India/Pakistan*), 12, 59, 70, 72, 191
Thatta (*Pakistan*), 24°44′N 67°58′E, 75, 94, 134, 184
Thatta*, 94, 111
Thimphu (*Bhutan*), 27°32′N 89°43′E, 12, 219
Tibet*, 72, 94
Tibet, Plateau of, (*China*), 12
Tigris (*r*), 75
Tippera*, 141
Tiruchchirappalli (*India*), 10°50′N 78°43′E, 77, 210
Tirunelveli (*India*), 8°45′N 77°43′E, 210
Tirupparankunram (*India*), 9°52′N 78°17′E, 77
Tirupati (*India*), 13°39′N 79°25′E, 210
Tiruppur (*India*), 11°05′N 77°20′E, 210
Tissamaharama (*Sri Lanka*), 6°17′N 81°18′E, 222
Tista (*r*), 220
Toba and Kakar Ranges (*mts*), (*Pakistan*), 184
Tongsa (*Bhutan*), 27°33′N 90°30′E, 219
Tonk (*India*), 26°10′N 75°50′E, 191
Tosali (*India*), 20°16′N 85°30′E, 70
Tranquebar (*India*), 11°04′N 79°50′E, 111, 134
Travancore*, 141
Travancore-Cochin*, 164, 175
Trichur (*India*), 10°32′N 76°14′E, 210
Trincomalee (*Sri Lanka*), 8°34′N 81°13′E, 111, 134, 141, 222
Tripura*, 164, 175, 199
Trivandrum (*India*), 8°30′N 76°57′E, 141, 210
Trombay (*India*), 19°01′N 72°58′E, 204
Tulasi (*mt*), (*India*), 18°42′N 82°04′E, 205
Tumkur (*India*), 13°20′N 77°06′E, 204
Tump (*Pakistan*), 26°06′N 62°24′E, 184
Tunga (*pass*), (*China/India*), 29°05′N 94°15′E, 199
Tungabhadra (*r*), 121
Tungabhadra (*res*), (*India*), 15°09′N 76°00′E, 204
Tun-huang (*China*), 40°05′N 94°45′E, 72, 75
Tura (*India*), 25°32′N 90°14′E, 198
Turbat (*Pakistan*), 26°00′N 63°06′E, 184
Turfan (*China*), 42°55′N 89°06′E, 75
Tuticorin (*India*), 8°48′N 78°10′E, 111, 134, 210
Tyrus (*Lebanon*), 33°32′N 35°22′E, 74

Uch (*Pakistan*), 29°14′N 71°03′E, 80
Uch*, 80
Udagamandalam (*India*), 11°24′N 76°39′E, 210
Udaipur (*India*), 24°36′N 73°47′E, 94, 141, 191
Udayagiri (*Orissa, India*), 20°18′N 85°51′E, 77
Udayagiri (*Madhya Pradesh, India*), 23°31′N 77°47′E, 77
Udgir (*India*), 18°26′N 77°11′E, 204
Udipi (*India*), 13°23′N 74°45′E, 204
Ujjain (*India*), 23°11′N 75°50′E, 70, 72, 73, 111, 121, 204
Umarkot (*Pakistan*), 25°22′N 69°48′E, 184
United Provinces*, 158, 164
United Provinces of Agra and Oudh*, 158
Uraiyur (*India*), 10°42′N 78°20′E, 75
Uthal (*Pakistan*), 25°48′N 66°37′E, 184
U Thong (*Thailand*), 14°16′N 99°52′E, 75
Utkala*, 72
Uttarapatha*, 70
Uttar Pradesh*, 175, 198

Vadodara (Baroda), (*India*), 22°19′N 73°14′E, 12, 111, 121, 134, 141, 204
Valabhi (*India*), 21°56′N 71°46′E, 73
Valaichchenai (*Sri Lanka*), 7°54′N 81°32′E, 222
Valsad (*India*), 20°33′N 72°59′E, 204
Vanga*, 70, 72
Varanasi (Benares), (*India*), 25°20′N 83°00′E, 12, 73, 121, 134, 158, 198
Vasai (*India*), 19°21′N 72°48′E, 111, 134, 204
Vatsa*, 70
Vavuniya (*Sri Lanka*), 8°45′N 80°30′E, 222
Vellore (*India*), 12°56′N 79°09′E, 111, 121, 210
Vengurla (*India*), 15°52′N 73°38′E, 111, 134
Veraval (*India*), 20°54′N 70°22′E, 204
Vidarbha*, 72
Vijayanagara (*India*), 15°20′N 76°25′E, 80
Vijayanagara*, 80, 111
Vijayawada (*India*), 16°34′N 80°40′E, 210
Vijnot (*Pakistan*), 28°38′N 70°18′E, 75
Villupuram (*India*), 11°58′N 79°28′E, 210
Vindhya Pradesh*, 164, 175
Vindhya Range (*mts*), (*India*), 12, 121, 204
Virudunagar (*India*), 9°35′N 77°57′E, 210
Vishakhapatnam (*India*), 17°42′N 83°24′E, 111, 134, 211
Vizianagaram (*India*), 18°07′N 83°30′E, 211
Vrijji*, 70
Vuyyuru (*India*), 16°23′N 80°51′E, 210

Wad (*Pakistan*), 27°21′N 66°30′E, 184
Wah (*Pakistan*), 33°50′N 72°44′E, 184
Wana (*Pakistan*), 32°15′N 69°34′E, 184
Wan-fo-hsiu (*China*), 40°32′N 97°17′E, 75
Warangal (*India*), 18°00′N 79°35′E, 134, 210
Wardha (*India*), 20°41′N 78°40′E, 204
Washuk (*Pakistan*), 27°43′N 64°50′E, 184
West Bengal*, 164, 175, 198
Western Ghats (*mts*), (*India*), 12, 121, 204
Western India States Agency*, 158
West Pakistan*, 175
West Punjab*, 164

Xi′an (*China*), 34°11′N 108°55′E, 75

Yamuna (*r*), 12, 59, 70, 80, 94, 134, 141, 158, 164, 175, 198
Yanam (*India*), 16°45′N 82°16′E, 134, 141, 164, 211
Yarkand (*China*), 38°27′N 77°16′E, 75
Yavatmal (*India*), 20°22′N 78°11′E, 204
Yonas (*r*), 70

Zafarwal (*India*), 31°05′N 75°10′E, 134
Zaskar Mts (*India*), 191
Zhob (*r*), 184
Zhob (*Pakistan*), 31°20′N 69°33′E, 184

INDEX

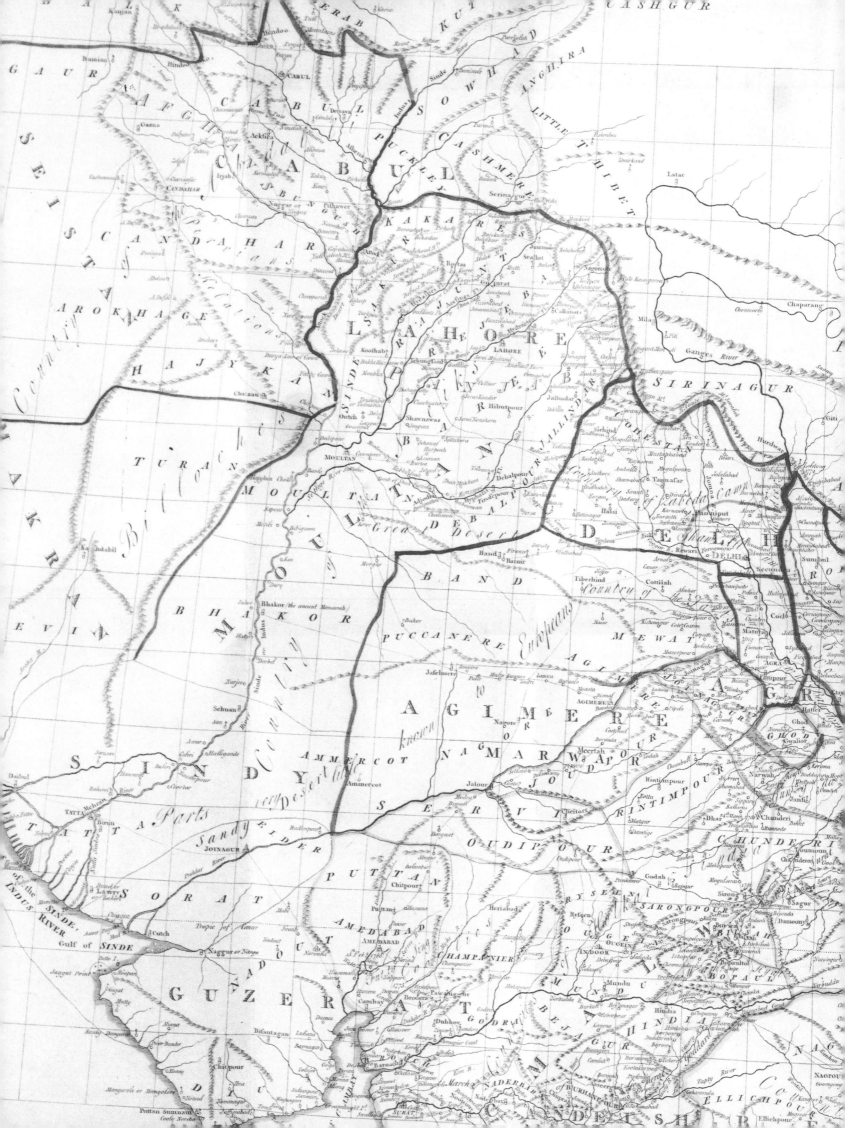